Cyber_Reader

Cyber_Reader
Critical writings for the digital era_Edited by Neil Spiller

Contents

Neil Spiller
Introduction

In the beginning, 'cyberspace' was a vacant word, a word with no real meaning. William Gibson was attracted to it as the digital world for his science-fiction characters. 'It's something that an advertising man might have thought up, and when I got it I knew that it was slick and essentially hollow and that I'd have to fill it up with meaning'.[1] It is this 'hollowness' that has allowed cyberspace to insinuate itself, chameleon-like, into almost every facet of human endeavour. Cyberspace and the computer are now central to the ways we understand our world.

This book seeks to introduce the reader to the wide range of writings, subjects and disciplines that cyberspace has created and influenced. These ideas may have been generated by the pragmatics of information technology or the mythologies that have grown up around cyberspace's virtual terrains. Set out chronologically, *Cyber Reader* allows the reader to comprehend the historical context and the impact of a particular idea or text and recognize the connections between texts, even if they are separated by intervals of many years. Details of original publications are included in the introductions to each piece.

In recent decades the computational paradigm has become all-pervasive. Researchers are finding that an understanding of how computers work is opening up parallel understandings in their own disciplines: for example, some philosophers of the mind are seeing similarities between the architecture of the computer and the way human minds might work. In the academic, commercial and social worlds fundamental changes have been brought about by personal computers, the Internet and the World Wide Web. The amount of computational power one can buy for the same money is doubling every fourteen months or so. This huge growth of access to cyberspace has rearticulated nearly every aspect of our lives, affecting the way we see the world, the way the world sees us and the way we see ourselves. Cyberspace is opening up ways for us to see deep, far, close and wide. It allows us to record knowledge and to transmit it over thousands of miles in a matter of seconds.

The etymology of the term 'cyberspace' is rooted in the Greek word *'kubernetes'*. Erik Davis, the writer and cyber commentator, traces the use of this word back to Plotinus, who used it to mean 'steersman', during the third century BC. From *'kubernetes'* is derived the word 'cybernetics', first employed by the nineteenth-century scientist André-Marie Ampère when developing his theory of magneticism. However, the term was subsequently rearticulated to describe the researches carried out by the mathematician Norbert Wiener into how systems work and respond to outside stimuli. William Gibson then added a spatial metaphor to the concept by juxtaposing 'cyber' and 'space', and used 'cyberspace' as the setting of his novel *Neuromancer* (1984). Inspired by the virtual space that exists behind the screen of video arcade games, and by video game users' belief in the reality of that imaginary space, Gibson constructed an imaginary electronic space that could be 'entered'; this space became an active participant in his stories. Even as Gibson was writing his stories, the history and ambition of computation had been long established. Cyberspatial fact was developing hard on the heels of cyberspace fiction.

Every writer's definition of 'cyberspace' is different. The word connotes a world of infinite possibilities, but few could define what it is or what it means for everyone. For some, cyberspace is where you are when you are on the telephone; for others, it is the place that is no place; and for others still, it is the world of computer simulation. Some observers are rather vague: '[cyberspace is a] computer-science concept of a place … that is filled with virtual "stuff" and populated by people with virtual bodies'.[3] As Michael Benedikt, editor of the influential *Cyberspace: First Steps*, has written of cyberspace: 'Its chambers bloom wherever data gathers and is stored. Its depths increase with every image or word or number, with every addition, every contribution, of fact or thought.'[4] To others, such as Turing, von Neumann, Babbage and Wiener, the expression 'cyberspace' would have no immediately apparent meaning. To Haraway and Turkle it is a virtual adhesive, a space of hybridization, of carthartic androgeny. To Virilio it is the agent of technological disappearance, and to Noon it is the surreal lifeblood of his chimeric worlds and characters. Cyberspace is alchemic; it is forever dissolving, reconstituting, cyclically distilling and recombining. To Wertheim and Davis cyberspace is redefining our relationship with our gods. Cyberspace augments empirical scientific space with another space of differing rules. A space that paradoxically has inspired some to imbue it with a spiritual dimension – a technological gnosis. This book takes a catholic view of the definition of cyberspace. It rejoices in the varied interpretations, ideas, aspirations and contradictions of cyberspace, expressed here by the various texts and their authors. To provide a compact and definitive description of the phenomenon that is cyberspace is an impossible task.

Without the computer and its rapid evolution, cyberspace would not exist. Cyberspace is influenced by the 'mediating' technology that creates it and allows us access to it at any given point in time. To enable the story of cyberspace to unfold we must consider the parallel world of mediating technologies. We therefore explore the origins of various navigational devices such as the 'windows' protocol and 'hypertext'. For this reason this anthology starts with the beginning of the modern computer and the attempts of Charles Babbage to create – albeit ultimately unsuccessfully – a mechanized calculating engine.

The first text, 'Of the Analytical Engine' (1864), is taken from Charles Babbage's autobiographical *Passages from the Life of a Philosopher*. Babbage is often seen as the grandfather of the computer; his quest to develop a mathematical machine that could quickly calculate logarithms and cartographical charts is recorded in this extract. Babbage was a consummate mathematician, to whom mathematics was a perfect art, a representative abstraction of the real world. He saw his Analytical Engine and its predecessor the Difference Engine, both of them unfinished, as machines that could ultimately compute away some of society's ills through mathematics. To Babbage, the whole world was a complex numerical problem waiting to be solved. Now the mathematical exactitude of computers and their programs can even create imaginary worlds that still have empirical qualities, and it is this phenomenon that gives the virtual world its awesome power. This power is seen by some to be immensely liberating, and by others to be stripping us of our liberty.

The notion of numerical utopia/dystopia is remarkably sketched by EM Forster's 'The Machine Stops' (1909), an early example of science-fiction writing from an unlikely source. This short story depicts a world held in thrall to the machine. Forster describes a futuristic society of hermetic containment, where all human needs are met in benevolent isolation: the only need denied is the human need for face-to-face, skin-to-skin interaction. The machine fosters a physically weak populace in fear of nature and emotion. This text also strikingly anticipates the 'Virtual Reality pod' idea – where the body becomes passive while the mind enters cyberspace.

So, at the beginning of this anthology, the fundamental paradox inherent in computation and cyberspace is established. While computation has greatly helped humanity in terms of medicine, art and science, at the same time the instant transmission and recording of data somehow weakens us, makes us less than we were and vulnerable to surveillance, open to disenfranchisement and manipulation. By whom and for what is, of course, a philosophical as well as political question.

The literature of cyberspace has historically sought to reconcile this paradox – with different degrees of success. Examples are numerous: Kevin Kelly, with his new biology of machines, points out that our technological dexterity is allowing us to create machines that might evolve both intellectually and physically faster than us. Donna Haraway uses the notion of the cybernetic organism (cyborg) as an empowering gender paradigm, a metaphorical device to encourage hybridization of cultural ideas and the acceptance of difference. In one sense this book is a survey of the most successful attempts at this ideological reconciliation. The authors of all of these texts, in one way or another, have sought to provide new and beneficial visions of how the pervasive power of the computer might be used to reconfigure the human condition.

Forster wrote 'The Machine Stops' just five years before the outbreak of the First World War. Far more than any other before it, this war brought home the devastating power of the machine. The carnage caused by death-dealing weapons forced many creative people to reassess their faith in a mechanistic world. The flowering of Modernism in the arts was in part provoked by the bloodshed of the First World War. Manuel De Landa, in his *War in the Age of Intelligent Machines,* proposes that war can have this effect on information technology, too. He sees history as a series of 'strange attractors' (a concept important in chaos theory) that have created knots of frenetic development in war hardware and software down the ages.

If the First World War fertilized and cultivated Modernism, then the Second World War brought about many new ideas about our relationship to the machine: that it might be a model for our own thought, for example, or get us to think in different ways. Vannevar Bush was the inventor of the first electronic analogue computer and his paper 'As We May Think' (1945) set out new ways for information to be ordered and addressed. His notion of the 'Memex' was critical in inspiring those who were later to grapple with the complexities of 'hypertext'. In its simplest terms, hypertext is the way data is linked together in Web pages, For example, a Web page on important structures in Paris would lead to a page on the Eiffel Tower or its engineer, or to similar structures made of steel, or to other towers in the world, and so on. These links have no hierarchy; they merely lead one into different routes through the rich mass of interconnected ideas and facts that is human knowledge.

During this same period the mathematician Alan Turing was developing his notion of the Universal Turing Machine. In 1950 he postulated that it might be a model for human intelligence. That same year Turing made the spectacular claim that artificial intelligence would be with us by the year 2000. His conceptual yardstick for judging this enormous human evolutionary step was the 'Turing Test'. Imagine a human player communicating, via a teletype machine, with a human or machine entity in another room. The human asks questions of the occupant of the other room and tries to ascertain whether it is human or computer. When a computer can convince the human inquisitor that it is human, then the Turing Test is passed. The Turing Test raises some interesting ideas. It presupposes that the computer can lie, affect modesty and simulate human mistakes in mental arithmetic and so on. It continues to be used as the conceptual framework around which theories of artificial intelligence are built and defined. Incidentally, the Turing Test inspired Deckard's replicant question-and-answer test that focused on the android's eye in Ridley Scott's 1982 film *Blade Runner*. Of course, Turing was overly optimistic in his prediction of how far artificial intelligence research would have progressed by the beginning of the new millennium. But clearly the Turing Test will one day be passed, and that moment will be as significant as any in human history.

Also working during the 1950s was Norbert Wiener, who was engaged in developing ideas about cybernetic systems and feedback loops. He suggested that human beings could be described in mechanical and electrical terms, and that machines could be made to imitate their thoughts and behaviour. The Cold War, likewise, created a frenzy of computer development. The Soviet Union and the United States invested billions of dollars trying to create computers that could conduct faster and more accurate warfare, surveillance and communications. On 4 October 1957 the Russians launched Sputnik, inaugurating the space race and causing much American consternation. One of the USA's responses was to form the Advanced Research Projects Agency and subsequently ARPANet, the forerunner of the Internet. ARPANet was originally a way for scientists to exchange data, but it quickly evolved into a social tool. The 'networking' of remote locations into a 'web' of nodes also promised to be an effective strategic tool: if one node were to be knocked out, by an atom bomb for example, the information could reroute itself around the destroyed node. During the 1960s, at the height of the Cold War, the mathematician and sometime military scientist John von Neumann developed the architecture of the computer that we know today. The key components of every laptop or desktop now sold – the central processing unit, hardware, software and memory – were his invention.

Contemporary with von Neumann's achievements was JCR Licklider's work on 'man–machine symbiosis' (1960). Licklider strove for a real-time interaction between human and computer – a true biological and mechanical synthesis. No one had written in those terms before.

Later in the decade Douglas Engelbart, inspired by Bush's 'As We May Think', developed the 'windows' protocol and the mouse to enable him to work with hypermedia (simultaneous images, texts and sound). The end of the 1960s also saw Gordon Pask introduce architects to the debate by formulating a cybernetic approach to architecture. While inspired by Wiener's cybernetic systems, Pask also recognized that they did not account for the role of the user/observer and his or her impact on system feedback. Some architects – Cedric Price, in particular – started to see the potential of the computer to liberate people from the tyranny of unadaptable space and out-of-date ideas. Price's Generator Project of 1976 was the first cybernetic building. Its computers were even designed to 'dream' of unsolicited building layouts in the hope of inspiring change, facilitating chance encounters, and inspiring its users with a sense of fun.

As architects were beginning to acknowledge the benefits of the computer, the French philosopher and architect Paul Virilio was considering the technological world and its development in terms of invisibility and disappearance. He saw the computer – in fact any technology – as ultimately becoming so small that it would disappear. *Cyber Reader* reflects this disappearance, charting a technological course from the clunky hardware and gearage of Babbage's Engines to the invisibility of K Eric Drexler's nanotechnology, first developed in the 1980s. The American cyberpunk author Bruce Sterling has commented on this invisible miniaturization of technology and the way in which it inspires this genre of fiction: 'Technology itself has changed. Not for us the giant steam-snorting wonders of the past: the Hoover Dam, the Empire State Building, the nuclear power plant. Eighties tech sticks to the skin, responds to the touch: the personal computer, the Sony Walkman, the portable telephone, the soft contact lens.'[5]

The work of science-fiction authors is intrinsic to the development of cyberspace and its language. In 1984 William Gibson's science-fiction tale *Neuromancer* was published. With this book the cyberpunk genre was firmly established. As Larry McCaffery, a literary and popular culture critic, has written, cyberpunk novels often depicted '… individuals awash in a sea of technological change, information overload, and random – but extraordinarily vivid – sensory stimulation. Personal confusion, sadness, dread and philosophical scepticism often appeared mixed with equal measures of euphoria and nostalgia for a past when centres could still hold.'[6]

It is not possible to feature all the influential novelists who have in some way contributed to the formation of cyberpunk literature, but a few deserve special mention. Mary Shelley's *Frankenstein* (1818) was arguably the beginning of cyberpunk. It was written at a time when scientists were obsessed with the properties of electricity and were also searching for 'life's force'. Experimenters made frogs' legs twitch with pulses of electricity; certain scientists at that time believed it would be possible to create life, or breath it back into cadavers. Shelley's book explores human hubris and the consequences of humanity taking life into its own hands in this way. Many of the themes of *Frankenstein* – such as desire, ethical confusion and fear of the 'other' – appear in contemporary cyberpunk literature. Indeed, *Frankenstein* is often cited as a literary lesson by those advocating restraint during discussions of cloning, biotechnology and genetic modification. Likewise, the *noir* world of Raymond Chandler's *The Big Sleep* (1939) is a precursor of cyberpunk. Chandler's bleak urban visions, his detritus-ridden vignettes and the romantic yet dangerously alien quality of the 'street' are staples of cyberpunk fiction. The manic fragmentation of William S Burroughs's *Naked Lunch* (1959) has also been influential. Its mode of flitting from one scene to another, from one reality to the next, is a classic compositional gambit of cyberpunk, and Gibson's *Neuromancer* uses it extensively. Philip K Dick's *Do Androids Dream of Electric Sheep?* (1968), later filmed as *Blade Runner*, represents a watershed in early cyberpunk fiction. Dick carefully deconstructs the notion of technology, simulacra and identity. The androids of Dick's world are everywhere, while the authentic biology of nature is highly prized and valued. Yet again, the epistemological problems of *Frankenstein* are wreaking havoc in a world of ecological and social disaster. The work of Gibson, Sterling, Neal Stephenson, Greg Bear and Pat Cadigan (the latter discussed in Anne Balsamo's essay) is featured in this book; all these writers have been influenced by Shelley, Chandler, Burroughs and Dick.

As cyberpunk authors endeavoured to breathe life into a vision of a cyberspatial near future, philosophers attempted to find a metaphor for the evolving modern conditions of fleeting connections, speed, duration, virtual machines, rearticulation, re-emphasis and fluctuation. The philosophers who hit the jackpot were Deleuze and Guattari with their idea of the 'rhizome' (set out in *A Thousand Plateaux*, 1988), a concept that has been seized upon by disparate disciplines to describe our millennial vicissitudes. The rhizome is a non-hierarchical system that is uncentred and without definable control; when broken, it re-forms differently. Cyber culture adopted this model as a way to conceive the interconnected but essentially unpredictable nature of the Internet and other non-hierarchical systems. Once computers were linked together, the routing of information could occur in all kinds of ways – creating a 'rhizomatic' system that is uncentred, in continuous motion, and forever changing, connecting and realigning. Deleuze and Guattari are not too explicit about the computer (*A Thousand Plateaux* was written slightly before the world experienced the full impact of the Internet) but they describe and understand the forces that lie behind the computer's wild contortions of ideas, actions and effects.

Contemporary with Deleuze and Guattari is the French philosopher Jean Baudrillard. Although not a 'cyberphilosopher', his writings deal very much with the effects of cyberspace. In this regard the most important of his works is *Simulations* (1983). His theories concerning 'simulacra' are a mainstay of ideas about our contemporary postmodern existence. He pointed out that much of our world comprises 'simulacra' – images, objects and ideas that are all copies of something that has never existed.

'Simulacra' are all around us in popular culture, from Disney (fairy castles, talking elephants) to television adverts and religious iconography. Cyberspace often colludes in their existence. Computer technology throws out images and information for our consumption at a frightening rate. Indeed, it is not always possible these days to tell whether an image we see is of a real event or not. Our sense of reality has been shaken fundamentally. Walter Benjamin, in *The Work of Art in the Age of Mechanical Reproduction* (1936), partially foresaw our contemporary condition in relation to art and the image. Benjamin was optimistic about technology, believing that the mass reproduction of art was democratic because it provided a ubiquitous product and gave viewers ease of access. But the technologies of Benjamin's time were not as advanced as they are today, when we are beginning to be able to invade the body and utilize its own biological self-replicating machinery. As Baudrillard points out: '... Benjamin was writing in the industrial era: by then technology itself was a gigantic prosthesis governing the generation of identical *objects* and *images* which there was no longer any way of distinguishing one from another, but it was as yet impossible to foresee the technological sophistication of our own era, which has made it possible to generate identical *beings,* without any means of returning to an original.'[7] Taking up where Benjamin leaves off, Baudrillard posits a much more volatile and invasive technological condition, encouraged by the computer; he continues: 'The prostheses of the industrial era were still external, *exotechnical,* whereas those we know now are ramified and internalized – *esotechnical.* Ours is the age of soft technologies, the age of genetic and mental software.'[8]

In the 1980s feminist theoreticians began to recognize that computer technology could present an opportunity for female emancipation. Donna Haraway took the cyborg analogy for the reconciliation of many of the binary opposites that divide society: black/white, male/female and heterosexual/homosexual. Haraway's *Cyborg Manifesto* (1989) has been hugely influential; it succeeded in bringing issues of sexual politics into the domain of computational technology, using the currency of cyberspace and biotechnology to develop discussions on sexual heterogeneity. Sherry Turkle, writing in 1985, sees the digital world as a cathartic role-play space that allows real-world situations to be recast and rehearsed – a beneficial space of virtual psychological affirmation, truly empowering some users. Karen Franck, writing a decade later, sees cyberspace as a rearticulation of the psychological duality of 'me' and 'not me'. She also views cyberspace as a space devoid of gender stereotypes – the ground for a new aesthetic of interaction, both visual and emotional.

The paradox of the computer – that it embodies discrete, mathematical exactitude at the same time as an ability to make the unreal real – is at its most powerful when it encourages the reconciliation of biological ideas with mechanical and computational notions. As extreme visions of the future have been put forward by some scientific researchers, the science-fiction writers have been there to revel in their possibilities. K Eric Drexler, in *Engines of Creation* (1990), conceives a future where all matter is reconfigurable. He brings together the dexterity of the computer and notions surrounding the programmability of atoms to create his vision of nanotechnology.

Drexler and his followers believe in the possibility of manipulating matter atom by atom, building materials and structure from the bottom up by joining atoms together. In this book we feature Drexler's account of how a rocket engine might be grown in a vat. If this technology were developed successfully, it would turn the whole world on its head; steak could be grown in meat machines no bigger than a microwave.[9]

Capitalism is created out of the exchange of various commodities for profit, and the value of commodities is often decided by their scarcity; thus, nanotechnology would represent a huge threat to the concept of scarcity – and therefore world order. War might become more devastating than ever, involving not just shape-shifting androids but also virulent, aggressive nanoscale robots that would be beyond human control. Drexler believes that one would only need to teach atomic structures to replicate themselves until a given point, then stop to replicate another pattern of atoms. Small factories, a few hundred atoms long, would be the 'key' to this atomic-sized industrial process. Minute computers, programmed to oversee the production line, would be crucial to the success of such an idea. In fact, humanity already has its own version of nanotechnology: the DNA and cell division process that constitutes our system of reproduction. Drexler's vision, however, is that of an engineer, reducing mechanical engineering processes to an exceptionally small scale in order to create machines that make generations of themselves; these machines would then be able to relocate others, one atom at a time.

Prompted by the dexterity of the modern computer, Drexler's ideas are merely a logical extension of existing technologies. What would have happened, however, if the computer had been invented earlier, if scientific breakthroughs had not occurred in the order they did? At the dawn of the 1990s came the birth of another genre of science-fiction: steampunk, a type of retro-cyberpunk. *The Difference Engine*, by William Gibson and Bruce Sterling (1991), depicted the Victorian world as it might have been had Babbage's Engines proved successful. This is a world populated by mechanical computational devices and paradigms – a Dickensian London infused with information espionage and computer hacking. Gibson and Sterling attempted to depict the diffusion of cyberspace into their imaginary Victorian culture.

Parallel with Gibson and Sterling's fictional endeavour, other commentators were attempting to explain to a lay public the effects of our contemporary digitized society. The early 1990s saw an explosion of books that sought either to explain the cyberspace phenomenon (such as Howard Rheingold's *Virtual Reality* of 1991) or to illustrate how the paradigms created for the computer might cast light on other fields of human knowledge. These include the history of warfare in Manuel De Landa's *War in the Age of Intelligent Machines* (1991) and the philosophy of mind in Daniel Dennett's *Consciousness Explained* (1992). Around this time the highly influential book *Cyberspace: First Steps* was published. This book did much to popularize the emerging issues of cyberspace and their impact on many disciplines. Here we feature an excerpt from Marcos Novak's chapter 'Liquid Architecture in Cyberspace' (1991). Novak's essay did more than any other to wake up architects to the spatial implications of cyberspace.

The computer has aided and abetted popular interest in science both through research and presentation. Contemporary machines can run and manipulate huge numbers of instructions per second with ease. This fact, combined with the computer's steadily evolving graphic dexterity, means that research can now be quickly assimilated beyond the rarefied confines of academia. In the 1990s two important books were published that aimed to make research accessible to a lay public: *Artificial Life* by Steven Levy (1992) and *Complexity* by Roger Lewin (1993). Both books presented leading-edge ideas in jargon-free language, illustrated with examples. They were seized upon by those seeking to ascertain whether their ideas could be applied to other disciplines, and their effect was profound and far-reaching.

There followed a plethora of publications addressed to the layperson, which in turn fostered a more broad-based familiarity with many aspects of the new sciences. During the 1990s, vast amounts of work was carried out and published. More and more ostensibly unconnected ideas came to be influenced by the concept of man–machine hybridization and genetic or computer codification. Omnipresent cyberspace was almost deified. *Vurt* (1993), by the English science-fiction novelist Jeff Noon, brought cyberpunk to a dismal English Manchester. Noon's surreal, transgenetic, druggy and poetic novel illustrates how far the cyberpunk genre had travelled, but also how far the technology that inspired it has the potential to travel. Erik Davis's seminal essay 'Techgnosis' (1993) appeared in *Flame Wars*, edited by Mark Dery, a collection that featured a selection of writers and commentators and which touched on all manner of issues fuelled by cyberspace. Davis's own interest lay in the similarities between ancient religious ideas such as alchemy, gnosticism and other forms of occult symbolism, and ideas provoked by the computer. These include a connection between the rotating wheels of Babbage's Engines and the rotating memory system of Renaissance magus Giordano Bruno. Scott Bukatman, in *Terminal Identity* (1993), reveals a path of development in film that has been inspired by visions of technology and the epistemological shifts brought about by the computer.

As the 1990s progressed Mark Dery's *Escape Velocity* (1996) summed up the position. A cyberized renaissance was happening across the arts and sciences and cross-pollination was rife. Dery examined issues surrounding the body and technology, especially the way in which technology can effect changes on the body. Here we include an excerpt from the chapter 'Robocopulation' (1996), where Dery examines the impact of cyberspace on sex. Dery's book also featured other protagonists in the field, such as Stelarc and Hans Moravec. Stelarc, a performance artist, is often cited as someone who searches for ways to augment the human body via digital technology. For him, the body is hopelessly outmoded by the onslaught of digital technology, and he has devised many ways to help the body cope with its high-tech surroundings. 'Towards the Post-Human' (1995) illustrates Stelarc's advocacy of a split physiology, whereby the human body is augmented by virtual selves and third mechanical arms. His idea is one of relinquishing full control of our bodies to outside forces. The robotics scientist Hans Moravec, meanwhile, goes even further in his version of man–machine symbiosis, as set out in 'The Senses Have No Future' (1998). He advocates the downloading into computers of software copies of human minds so as to give us the same evolutionary trajectory as the machines we make. As machines evolve faster than bodies, their intelligence and knowledge would thus not need to be re-educated with every generation in the same way that ours are. The science-fiction writer Greg Egan picks up on this idea in his novel *Permutation City* (1994). Here, ideas of artificial intelligence, downloading human consciousness and super-fast virtual evolutionary timescales are combined to create a story of humanity grappling with its own hubris.

Cyberspace has also spawned a whole new series of virtual and not so virtual spaces, responsive environments and augmented realities. For the arts and humanities, it has engendered radical professional and creative change. In terms of art theory and practice, for example, artworks that 'evolve' using elements of cyberspace serve to question the old notions of creative authorship. This, in turn, is intrinsically linked to how we view ethical issues such as control and surveillance, and how we define our individuality. Anthony Dunne, in *Hertzian Tales* (1999), describes smart objects bathed in and receptive to electromagnetic radiation, such as furniture that makes the electromagnetic spectrum visible to us, or that puts us socially in touch with far-away spaces. This cannot be achieved without the computer and ubiquitous micro-processing. Michael Heim, in *Virtual Reality of the Tea Ceremony* (1998), explores a more meditative notion of designing in cyberspace. He espouses a Zen-like approach to the placement of elements and links, akin to the spirituality of the Japanese tea ceremony. Margaret Wertheim, in *The Pearly Gates of Cyberspace* (1999), posits that these new virtual spaces are the equivalent of medieval soul-space, a spiritual space of rich allegory. She sees this as representing a welcome return to a dualist notion of space that Modernism and scientific development, with their search for exactitude and explanation, tried to eradicate. The spaces of cyberspace and their fleeting coalitions with real spaces can now be choreographed by the designer, as discussed in my essay 'Vacillating Objects' (1998). It is an attempt to heighten the architectural profession's awareness of the spatial potential of our cyberspatial technologies.

With all this innovation, speculation and visceral invasion, it is obvious that there is much to abuse. Aware of these potential difficulties, the Grateful Dead lyricist and cyber-rights campaigner, John Perry Barlow, issued his Magna Carta of cyberspace, the 'Declaration of the Independence of Cyberspace', in 1996. The legislation of cyberspace is fraught with problems, not least because cyberspace is multinational, is subject to no individual world power, is multi-dimensional and chimerical, and occupies no real geographical space. Barlow's view is that independence must be fought for – governments are always seeking ways to make cyberspace inoffensive, legal and clean. Corporations have adapted to cyberspace quickly: in the space of a few years Web adverts, e-commerce and virtual characters have become so common that cyberspace is far from the domain of rebellion or the underworld of innovation that it once was.

We may have embraced cyberspace with open arms, yet we cannot predict where all this technology might go and how far it might be abused by states or criminals. Civil liberty campaigners are concerned with the sanctity of much of the personal information stored in cyberspace's interconnected databanks. Hackers work continuously to penetrate information systems in order to pillage their contents or to corrupt their data. Users are developing ever more difficult codes in an attempt to deter hackers, who sometimes use viruses as a weapon of subversion. Viruses are every computer user's bane, and this book records the invention of the computer virus (see Steven Levy's 'The Strong Claim').

Some believe that military-grade encryption programs should be available free, as a basic human right, so that we all might protect our data from prying eyes. In recent years we have seen large terrorist organizations use the Internet for malicious intent. Once we invent a technology we invent its downside, its danger and its potential for catastrophe. As Paul Virilio reminds us, when the aeroplane was invented so was the aircrash. But one thing is clear: cyberspace cannot be uninvented, it is here to stay, becoming ubiquitous. It is my contention that cyberspace is mostly a force for good. Its existence makes us address what it means to be human. It expands our facility to learn, to connect ideas and to talk and meet people.

Cyber Reader is conceived very much as a primer, a springboard to all manner of interesting, exciting and even mind-blowing concepts. It is on one level an attempt to present to the general reader a chronology of cyberspace writing; but it also aims to show how the ideologies that have informed the makers of 'cyberspaces' (both actual and fictional) have shaped research into, and popular understanding of, cyberspace. There are many connections to be made. These texts merely scratch the surface of a huge body of knowledge. This book introduces the principal characters and concepts, providing a framework into which to place further ideas and discoveries. Even if you are familiar with some of the writings in this book, I'll wager that you will find much to entertain and inspire you. And if you are new to the whole arena of cyberspace, then I wish you a wonderful exploratory journey of discovery.

1 William Gibson, 'Late Show', BBC2, 26 September 1990

2 Erik Davis, *Techgnosis: Myth, Magic and Mysticism in the Age of Information*, London: Serpents Tail, 1998, p89.

3 Peter Zellner, *Hybrid Space: New Forms in Digital Architecture*, London: Thames and Hudson, 1999, p189.

4 Michael Benedikt, *Cyberspace: First Steps*, Cambridge, MA: MIT Press, 1991, p2.

5 Bruce Sterling (ed.), *Mirrorshades*, London: Paladin, 1988, ppxi.

6 Larry McCaffery (ed.), *Storming the Reality Studio: A Casebook of Cyberpunk and Post Modern Science Fiction*, Durham, NC: Duke University Press, 1991, p10.

7 Jean Baudrillard, 'The Transparency of Evil', *Essays on Extreme Phenomena*, London: Verso, 1993, p119.

8 Ibid.

9 Ed Regis, *Nano: Remaking the World Atom by Atom*, New York: Bantam Press, p6. See also p126.

Model of Charles Babbage's Analytical Engine, 1871 (top left). This was the first fully-automated calculating machine. Designed to operate using punched cards (top right), only part of the 'mill' was completed before Babbage's death in 1871.

The ENIAC Digital Calculator, 1943–6. (centre), was built in Pennsylvania and originally intended for ballistics calculations. Although not a true computer because it could not 'store' programs, ENIAC is considered the second general-purpose electronic calculator after the British 'Colossus'. ENIAC's 'program' was changed by manually reconfiguring the wiring circuits between its 18,000 valves.

The first fully electronic stored-program computer (bottom) ran its first program in June 1948. Developed at Manchester University, it was 2 m tall by 5 m wide, stored information in cathode-ray tubes and had a total memory of 1,024 bits.

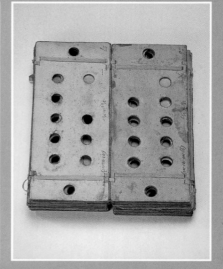

An ICL '1906' computer (top), in the computer room at ICL, Stevenage in the 1960s. Such large main-frame computers had much less processing power than today's average home PC (bottom left) but were able to do complex calculations.

Two IBM computer hard drives from 1984 and 1999 (centre right). The difference in size emphasizes the minituarization and increase in capacity of computer hardware. The larger hard disc, c1984, can hold 4 megabytes (MB) of information, whilst the

smaller disc, from a 1999 PC, can hold 6 gigabytes (GB), some 1,800 times more information. PC discs in 2001 hold an average of 15-20 GB, 4,200 times more information.

Macrophotograph of an INMOS T414 transputer (bottom right), a chip which combines a 32-bit microprocessor with 2 kilobytes of random access memory (RAM) and serial input/output links. This has potential use as an autonomous

component in a new generation of parallel computers.

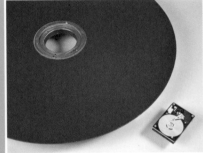

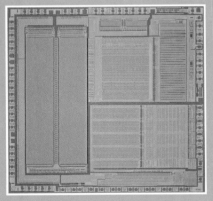

Charles Babbage_ Of the Analytical Engine_1864

To many people, Charles Babbage is known as the father of computing. His reputation has intensified since the 1970s, as the computer has become ubiquitous. However, as Martin Campbell-Kelly states in his introduction to Babbage's *Passages from the Life of a Philosopher*, were it not for this ubiquity 'he would be regarded as little more than a footnote in history, as he was until recent times.'[1] Although his significance is without doubt, to describe Babbage as the inventor of the modern computer is erroneous. Others have an equal claim to that title, such as John von Neumann, inventor of the architecture of modern computers (see p44), and Alan Turing, creator of the Universal Turing Machine (see p42).

It was in 1820 that Babbage first put forward his ideas for a 'Difference Engine' for calculating sets of astronomical and nautical tables. The idea behind the Difference Engine was that it would be able to operate independently and to print its solutions. The details of its internal logics and workings are complicated, but essentially it comprised a series of cogged wheels, each of which was able to rearticulate itself to calculate numerical values for polynomial equations. The development of the Difference Engine was a long, costly and ultimately unfinished task, and only a small functioning part of it was ever completed. In a modern-day critique Francis Spufford describes the Difference Engine thus:

It is *so* Victorian in its visual impact: almost exaggeratedly so. It looks like an elaboration, a raising to the *n*th degree of every Victorian device you ever saw, from a fob watch with its case open to a steam locomotive whose jointed connecting rods delicately transform enormous linear thrust into huge rotary motion ... Here is an abstruse operation of the Calculus, previously the province of the trained mathematical mind, made over to the job of machine minding, at the cost of the perfect alienation of the task.[2]

In 1833, just as the first elements of the Difference Engine were coming together, it was superseded by Babbage's idea for an even more versatile calculating engine, the 'Analytical Engine'. This new engine was designed to have a 'mill' and a 'store', metaphors that were taken from existing industrial processes. These elements are the equivalent of what we now know as the 'central processing unit' and 'memory'. Over a two-year period Babbage took considerable trouble in working out how to perform calculations and how to organize the processes involved. Eventually he based his design on the punched cards of the Jacquard loom – a system invented 30 years earlier. It is therefore the Analytical Engine, rather than the Difference Engine, that is more akin to the contemporary computer, and this aspect of its workings is where Babbage's achievement really lies.

Babbage had a rather original explanation for miracles: he saw them as the work of God, 'the programmer of divine algorithms'.[3] From thoughts such as this and from other passages of Babbage's written work we can construct the image of a man who believed in the ultimate programmability of everything, including society's ills. Many science-fiction writers and apologists for the computer – some of them featured in this book – have picked up on Babbage's notions. Their aspirations vary from the downloadable human mind of Hans Moravec (see p280) to the experiments in emergence and bottom-up programming of the artificial life lobby (see pp116, 178, 216).

1 Charles Babbage, *Passages from the Life of a Philosopher*, edited by Martin Campbell-Kelly, London: William Pickering (Pickering & Chatto), 1994, p7.

2 Francis Spufford, 'The Difference Engine and *The Difference Engine*', in *Cultural Babbage: Technology, Time and Invention*, Francis Spufford and Jenny Unglow (eds), London: Faber and Faber, 1996, p267.

3 Charles Babbage, ibid, p25.

Charles Babbage, 'Of the Analytical Engine', *Passages from the Life of a Philosopher*, 1864

The circular arrangement of the axes of the Difference Engine round the large central wheels led to the most extended prospects. The whole of arithmetic now appeared within the grasp of mechanism. A vague glimpse even of an Analytical Engine at length opened out, and I pursued with enthusiasm the shadowy vision. The drawings and the experiments were of the most costly kind. Draftsmen of the highest order were necessary to economize the labour of my own head; whilst skilled workmen were required to execute the experimental machinery to which I was obliged constantly to have recourse.

In order to carry out my pursuits successfully, I had purchased a house with above a quarter of an acre of ground in a very quiet locality. My coach-house was now converted into a forge and a foundry, whilst my stables were transformed into a workshop. I built other extensive workshops myself, and had a fireproof building for my drawings and draftsmen. Having myself worked with a variety of tools, and having studied the art of constructing each of them, I at length laid it down as a principle – that, except in rare cases, I would never do anything myself if I could afford to hire another person who could do it for me.

The complicated relations which then arose amongst the various parts of the machinery would have baffled the most tenacious memory. I overcame that difficulty by improving and extending a language of signs, the Mechanical Notation, which in 1826 I had explained in a paper printed in the 'Phil. Trans.'[1] By such means I succeeded in mastering trains of investigation so vast in extent that no length of years ever allotted to one individual could otherwise have enabled me to control. By the aid of the Mechanical Notation, the Analytical Engine became a reality: for it became susceptible of demonstration.

Such works could not be carried on without great expenditure. The fluctuations in the demand and supply of skilled labour were considerable. The railroad mania withdrew from other pursuits the most intellectual and skilful draftsmen. One who had for some years been my chief assistant was tempted by an offer so advantageous that in justice to his own family he could scarcely have declined it. Under these circumstances I took into consideration the plan of advancing his salary to one guinea per day. Whilst this was in abeyance, I consulted my venerable surviving parent. When I had fully explained the circumstances, my excellent mother replied: 'My dear son, you have advanced far in the accomplishment of a great object, which is worthy of your ambition. You are capable of completing it. My advice is – pursue it, even if it should oblige you to live on bread and cheese.'

This advice entirely accorded with my own feelings. I therefore retained my chief assistant at his advanced salary.

The most important part of the Analytical Engine was undoubtedly the mechanical method of carrying tens. On this I laboured incessantly, each succeeding improvement advancing me a step or two. The difficulty did not consist so much in the more or less complexity of the contrivance as in the reduction of the *time* required to effect the carriage. Twenty or thirty different plans and modifications had been drawn. At last I came to the conclusion that I had exhausted the principle of successive carriage. I concluded also that nothing but teaching the engine to foresee and then to act upon that foresight could ever lead me to the object I desired, namely, to make the whole of any unlimited number of carriages in one unit of time. One morning, after I had spent many hours in the drawing-office in endeavouring to improve the system of successive carriages, I mentioned these views to my chief assistant, and added that I should retire to my library, and endeavour to work out the new principle. He gently expressed a doubt whether the plan was *possible*, to which I replied that, not being able to prove its impossibility, I should follow out a slight glimmering of light which I thought I perceived.

After about three hours' examination, I returned to the drawing-office with much more definite ideas upon the subject. I had discovered a principle that proved the possibility, and I had contrived a mechanism which, I thought, would accomplish my object.

I now commenced the explanation of my views, which I soon found were but little understood by my assistant; nor was this surprising, since in the course of my own attempt at explanation, I found several defects in my plan, and was also led by his questions to perceive others. All these I removed one after another, and ultimately terminated at a late hour my morning's work with conviction that *anticipating* carriage was not only within my power, but that I had devised one mechanism at least by which it might be accomplished.

Many years after, my assistant, on his return from a long residence abroad, called upon me and we talked over the progress of the Analytical Engine. I referred back to the day on which I had made that most important step and asked him if he recollected it. His reply was that he perfectly remembered the circumstance; for that on retiring to my library, he seriously thought that my intellect was beginning to become deranged. The reader may perhaps be curious to know how I spent the rest of that remarkable day.

After working, as I constantly did, for ten or eleven hours a day, I had arrived at this satisfactory conclusion, and was revising the rough sketches of the new contrivance when my servant entered the drawing-office and announced that it was seven o'clock – that I dined in Park Lane – and that it was time to dress. I usually arrived at the house of my friend about a quarter of an hour before the appointed time, in order that we might have a short conversation on subjects on which we were both much interested. Having mentioned my recent success, in which my host thoroughly sympathized, I remarked that it had produced an exhilaration of the spirits which not even his excellent champagne could rival. Having enjoyed the society of Hallam, of Rogers, and of some few others of that delightful circle, I retired, and joined one or perhaps two much more extensive reunions. Having thus forgotten science, and enjoyed society for four or five hours, I returned home. About one o'clock I was asleep in my bed, and thus continued for the next five hours.

This new and rapid system of carrying the tens when two numbers are added together, reduced the actual time of the addition of any number of digits, however large, to nine units of time for the addition, and one unit for the carriage. Thus in ten units of time, any two numbers, however large, might be added together. A few more units of time, perhaps five or six, were required for making the requisite previous arrangements.

Having thus advanced as nearly as seemed possible to the minimum of time requisite for arithmetical operations, I felt renewed power and increased energy to pursue the far higher object I had in view.

To describe the successive improvements of the Analytical Engine would require many volumes. I only propose here to indicate a few of its more important functions, and to give to those whose minds are duly prepared for it some information which will remove those vague notions of wonder, and even of its impossibility, with which it is surrounded in the minds of some of the most enlightened.

To those who are acquainted with the principles of the Jacquard loom, and who are also familiar with analytical formulae, a general idea of the means by which the engine executes its operations may be obtained without much difficulty. In the Exhibition of 1862 there were many splendid examples of such looms.

It is known as a fact that the Jacquard loom is capable of weaving any design which the imagination of man may conceive. It is also the constant practice for skilled artists to be employed by manufacturers in designing patterns. These patterns are then sent to a peculiar artist, who, by means of a certain machine, punches holes in a set of pasteboard cards in such a manner that when those cards are placed in a Jacquard loom, it will then weave upon its produce the exact pattern designed by the artist.

Now the manufacturer may use, for the warp and weft of his work, threads which are all of the same colour; let us suppose them to be unbleached or white threads. In this case the cloth will be woven all of one colour; but there will be a damask pattern upon it such as the artist designed.

But the manufacturer might use the same cards, and put into the warp threads of any other colour. Every thread might even be of a different colour, or of a different shade of colour; but in all these cases the *form* of the pattern will be precisely the same – the colours only will differ.

The analogy of the Analytical Engine with this well-known process is nearly perfect.

The Analytical Engine consists of two parts:

1. The store in which all the variables to be operated upon, as well as all those quantities which have arisen from the result of other operations, are placed.

2. The mill into which the qualities about to be operated upon are always brought.

Every formula which the Analytical Engine can be required to compute consists of certain algebraical operations to be performed upon given letters, and of certain other modifications depending on the numerical value assigned to those letters.

There are therefore two sets of cards, the first to direct the nature of the operations to be performed – these are called operation cards: the other to direct the particular variables on which those cards are required to operate – these latter are called variable cards. Now the symbol of each variable or constant, is placed at the top of a column capable of containing any required number of digits.

Under this arrangement, when any formula is required to be computed, a set of operation cards must be strung together, which contain the series of operations in the order in which they occur. Another set of cards must then be strung together, to call in the variables into the mill, the order in which they are required to be acted upon. Each operation card will require three other cards, two to represent the variables and constants and their numerical values upon which the previous operation card is to act, and one to indicate the variable on which the arithmetical result of this operation is to be placed.

But each variable has below it, on the same axis, a certain number of figure-wheels marked on their edges with the ten digits: upon these any number the machine is capable of holding can be placed. Whenever variables are ordered into the mill, these figures will be brought in, and the operation indicated by the preceding card will be performed upon them. The result of this operation will then be replaced in the store.

The Analytical Engine is therefore a machine of the most general nature. Whatever formula it is required to develop, the law of its development must be communicated to it by two sets of cards. When these have been placed, the engine is special for that particular formula. The numerical value of its constants must then be put on the columns of wheels below them, and on setting the engine in motion it will calculate and print the numerical results of that formula.

Every set of cards made for any formula will at any future time recalculate that formula with whatever constants may be required.

1. 'On a method of expressing by signs the action of machinery' (1826), *Works of Babbage*, vol. 3.

EM Forster_The Machine Stops_1909

Written in 1909, EM Forster's short story *The Machine Stops* nevertheless describes a world that has many parallels with our modern one. It is a world where new technologies engender speed, which in turn has a profound impact on individuals and society. Forster began his writing career with *Where Angels Fear to Tread* (1905) and went on to produce a string of well-known novels including *The Longest Journey* (1907), *A Room with a View* (1908), *Howards End* (1910) and *A Passage to India* (1924). Forster was born in 1879 – his father, an architect, died when Forster was two years old – and went on to attend King's College, Cambridge. He died in 1970.

EM Forster's novels often combine comedy of manners with darker undercurrents. His characters are usually members of the upper middle class whose isolation from nature, sexuality and the understanding of beauty, aesthetics and the sublime is suddenly exposed; the result is either epiphanic or mentally unstabilizing. Italy is often used as a metaphor for the natural, the sublime and the sexually liberated.

Although set in an unidentified future, *The Machine Stops* reflects many of these themes. It centres around the character of Vashti and her son, Kuno. Vashti sees herself as living in splendid isolation, in touch with everything via swift communications: she has her bible/instruction book beside her, and her deep underground home is a precursor to the 'virtual reality pod', eighty years before the idea entered common parlance among the cyber avant-garde. She is emaciated by lack of exercise, yet she is mentally sharp. Kuno shocks his mother by carrying out subversive acts such as escaping to the surface of the earth – whence humanity has retreated due to supposed ecological apocalypse. We hear of Vashti's fear of bodily contact and of the phenomena of the natural world, as she travels by antiquated airship from Australia to England, hiding from the light, longing for her isolated bubble of machine-serviced underground privacy where one-to-one visceral contact is socially abhorrent.

The world's population seems to live in a giant underground machine, only connected to the surface of the earth by the occasional 'vomitory'. Humanity has become unable to function without the intensive care of the machine, and Kuno, by his uncivilized behaviour and disregard for society's protocols, brings about the machine's breakdown. At the end of the story, 'civilization' collapses and dies as the machine crashes in on itself. Just before his death, Kuno talks of surface dwellers he has met:

'I have seen them, spoken to them, loved them. They are hiding in the mist and the ferns until our civilization stops. Today they are the homeless – tomorrow——'

'Oh, tomorrow – some fool will start the machine again. Tomorrow.'

'Never,' said Kuno, 'never. Humanity has learnt its lesson.'[1]

The excerpt featured here is from the start of the story, where Forster describes Vashti's isolated, networked world. The machine assumes the role of parent once birth has taken place. All needs are catered for, nothing surprises in this mechanized world – a world of pervasive technology.

1 EM Forster, *The Machine Stops*, originally published in *Oxford and Cambridge Review*, 1909.

The Air-Ship

Imagine, if you can, a small room, hexagonal in shape, like the cell of a bee. It is lighted neither by window nor by lamp, yet it is filled with a soft radiance. There are no apertures for ventilation, yet the air is fresh. There are no musical instruments, and yet, at the moment that my meditation opens, this room is throbbing with melodious sounds. An armchair is in the centre, by its side a reading-desk – that is all the furniture. And in the arm-chair there sits a swaddled lump of flesh – a woman, about five feet high, with a face as white as a fungus. It is to her that the little room belongs.

An electric bell rang.

The woman touched a switch and the music was silent.

'I suppose I must see who it is,' she thought, and set her chair in motion. The chair, like the music, was worked by machinery and it rolled her to the other side of the room where the bell still rang importunately.

'Who is it?' she called. Her voice was irritable, for she had been interrupted often since the music began. She knew several thousand people, in certain directions human intercourse had advanced enormously.

But when she listened into the receiver, her white face wrinkled into smiles, and she said:

'Very well. Let us talk, I will isolate myself. I do not expect anything important will happen for the next five minutes – for I can give you fully five minutes, Kuno. Then I must deliver my lecture on "Music during the Australian Period".'

She touched the isolation knob, so that no one else could speak to her. Then she touched the lighting apparatus, and the little room was plunged into darkness.

'Be quick!' she called, her irritation returning. 'Be quick, Kuno; here I am in the dark wasting my time.'

But it was fully fifteen seconds before the round plate that she held in her hands began to glow. A faint blue light shot across it, darkening to purple, and presently she could see the image of her son, who lived on the other side of the earth, and he could see her.

'Kuno, how slow you are.'

He smiled gravely.

'I really believe you enjoy dawdling.'

'I have called you before, mother, but you were always busy or isolated. I have something particular to say.'

'What is it, dearest boy? Be quick. Why could you not send it by pneumatic post?'

'Because I prefer saying such a thing. I want—'

'Well?'

'I want you to come and see me.'

Vashti watched his face in the blue plate.

'But I can see you!' she exclaimed. 'What more do you want?'

'I want to see you not through the Machine,' said Kuno. 'I want to speak to you not through the wearisome Machine.'

'Oh, hush!' said his mother, vaguely shocked. 'You mustn't say anything against the Machine.'

'Why not?'

'One mustn't.'

'You talk as if a god had made the Machine,' cried the other. 'I believe that you pray to it when you are unhappy. Men made it, do not forget that. Great men, but men. The Machine is much, but it is not everything. I see something like you in this plate, but I do not see you. I hear something like you through this telephone, but I do not hear you. That is why I want you to come. Pay me a visit, so that we can meet face to face, and talk about the hopes that are in my mind.'

She replied that she could scarcely spare the time for a visit.

'The air-ship barely takes two days to fly between me and you.'

'I dislike air-ships.'

'Why?'

'I dislike seeing the horrible brown earth, and the sea, and the stars when it is dark. I get no ideas in an air-ship.'

'I do not get them anywhere else.'

'What kind of ideas can the air give you?'

He paused for an instant.

'Do you not know four big stars that form an oblong, and three stars close together in the middle of the oblong, and hanging from these stars, three other stars?'

'No, I do not. I dislike the stars. But did they give you an idea? How interesting; tell me.'

'I had an idea that they were like a man.'

'I do not understand.'

'The four big stars are the man's shoulders and his knees. The three stars in the middle are like the belts that men wore once, and the three stars hanging are like a sword.'

'A sword?'

'Men carried swords about with them, to kill animals and other men.'

'It does not strike me as a very good idea, but it is certainly original. When did it come to you first?'

'In the air-ship—' He broke off, and she fancied that he looked sad. She could not be sure, for the Machine did not transmit nuances of expression. It only gave a general idea of people – an idea that was good enough for all practical purposes, Vashti thought. The imponderable bloom, declared by a discredited philosophy to be the actual essence of intercourse, was rightly ignored by the Machine, just as the imponderable bloom of the grape was ignored by the manufacturers of artificial fruit. Something 'good enough' had long since been accepted by our race.

'The truth is,' he continued, 'that I want to see these stars again. They are curious stars. I want to see them not from the air-ship, but from the surface of the earth, as our ancestors did, thousands of years ago. I want to visit the surface of the earth.'

She was shocked again.

'Mother, you must come, if only to explain to me what is the harm of visiting the surface of the earth.'

'No harm,' she replied, controlling herself. 'But no advantage. The surface of the earth is only dust and mud, no advantage. The surface of the earth is only dust and mud, no life remains on it, and you would need a respirator, or the cold of the outer air would kill you. One dies immediately in the outer air.'

'I know; of course I shall take all precautions.'

'And besides—'

'Well?'

She considered, and chose her words with care. Her son had a queer temper, and she wished to dissuade him from the expedition.

'It is contrary to the spirit of the age,' she asserted.

'Do you mean by that, contrary to the Machine?'

'In a sense, but—'

His image in the blue plate faded.

'Kuno!'

He had isolated himself.

For a moment Vashti felt lonely.

Then she generated the light, and the sight of her room, flooded with radiance and studded with electric buttons, revived her. There were buttons and switches everywhere – buttons to call for food, for music, for clothing. There was the hot-bath button, by pressure of which a basin of (imitation) marble rose out of the floor, filled to the brim with a warm deodorized liquid. There was the cold-bath button. There was the button that produced literature. and there were of course the buttons by which she communicated with her friends. The room, though it contained nothing, was in touch with all that she cared for in the world.

Vashti's next move was to turn off the isolation switch, and all the accumulations of the last three minutes burst upon her. The room was filled with the noise of bells, and speaking-tubes. What was the new food like? Could she recommend it? Has she had any ideas lately? Might one tell her one's own ideas? Would she make an engagement to visit the public nurseries at an early date? – say this day month.

To most of these questions she replied with irritation – a growing quality in that accelerated age. She said that the new food was horrible. That she could not visit the public nurseries through pressure of engagements. That she had no ideas of her own but had just been told one – that four stars and three in the middle were like a man: she doubted there was much in it. Then she switched off her correspondents, for it was time to deliver her lecture on Australian music.

The clumsy system of public gatherings had been long since abandoned; neither Vashti nor her audience stirred from their rooms. Seated in her armchair she spoke, while they in their armchairs heard her, fairly well, and saw her, fairly well. She opened with a humourous account of music in the pre-Mongolian epoch, and went on to describe the great outburst of song that followed the Chinese conquest. Remote and primeval as were the methods of I-San-So and the Brisbane school, she yet felt (she said) that study of them might repay the musicians of today: they had freshness; they had, above all, ideas. Her lecture, which lasted ten minutes, was well received, and at its conclusion she and many of her audience listened to a lecture on the sea; there were ideas to be got from the sea; the speaker had donned a respirator and visited it lately. Then she fed, talked to many friends, had a bath, talked again, and summoned her bed.

The bed was not to her liking. It was too large, and she had a feeling for a small bed. Complaint was useless, for beds were of the same dimension all over the world, and to have had an alternative size would

have involved vast alterations in the Machine. Vashti isolated herself –
it was necessary, for neither day nor night existed under the ground – and
reviewed all that had happened since she had summoned the bed last.
Ideas? Scarcely any. Events – was Kuno's invitation an event?

By her side, on the little reading-desk, was a survival from the ages of
litter – one book. This was the Book of the Machine. In it were instructions
against every possible contingency. If she was hot or cold or dyspeptic or at
a loss for a word, she went to the book, and it told her which button to
press. The Central Committee published it. In accordance with a growing
habit, it was richly bound.

Sitting up in the bed, she took it reverently in her hands. She glanced
round the glowing room as if some one might be watching her. Then, half
ashamed, half joyful, she murmured 'O Machine!' and raised the volume to
her lips. Thrice she kissed it, thrice inclined her head, thrice she felt the
delirium of acquiescence. Her ritual performed, she turned to page 1367,
which gave the times of the departure of the air-ships from the island in
the southern hemisphere, under whose soil she lived, to the island in the
northern hemisphere, whereunder lived her son.

She thought, 'I have not the time.'

She made the room dark and slept; she awoke and made the room light;
she ate and exchanged ideas with her friends, and listened to music and
attended lectures; she make the room dark and slept. Above her, beneath
her, and around her, the Machine hummed eternally; she did not notice
the noise, for she had been born with it in her ears. The earth, carrying
her, hummed as it sped through silence, turning her now to the invisible
sun, now to the invisible stars. She awoke and made the room light.

'Kuno!'

'I will not talk to you.' he answered, 'until you come.'

'Have you been on the surface of the earth since we spoke last?'

His image faded.

Again she consulted the book. She became very nervous and lay back
in her chair, palpitating. Think of her as without teeth or hair. Presently
she directed the chair to the wall, and pressed an unfamiliar button. The
wall swung apart slowly. Through the opening she saw a tunnel that
curved slightly, so that its goal was not visible. Should she go to see her
son, here was the beginning of the journey.

Of course she knew all about the communication-system. There was
nothing mysterious in it. She would summon a car and it would fly with
her down the tunnel until it reached the lift that communicated with the
air-ship station: the system had been in use for many, many years, long
before the universal establishment of the Machine. And of course she had
studied the civilization that had immediately preceded her own – the
civilization that had mistaken the functions of the system, and had used it
for bringing people to things, instead of for bringing things to people.
Those funny old days, when men went for change of air instead of
changing the air in their rooms! And yet – she was frightened of the
tunnel: she had not seen it since her last child was born. It curved – but
not quite as she remembered; it was brilliant – but not quite as brilliant
as a lecturer had suggested. Vashti was seized with the terrors of direct
experience. She shrank back into the room, and the wall closed up again.

Vannevar Bush_As We May Think_1945

The influential essay 'As We May Think', by the electrical engineer and inventor Vannevar Bush, is widely seen as containing the seed of what we now know as 'hypertext'. Today, hypertext's commonest manifestation is in the highlighted words or images found in web pages on the Internet, which when 'clicked' on create a trail of linked information.

Vannevar Bush was born in Everett, Massachusetts in 1890. He was educated at Tufts College, Harvard University and Massachusetts Institute of Technology (MIT). From 1919 to 1971 he held various teaching positions at MIT and at the Carnegie Institution in Washington. At the end of World War II Bush was Director of the Office of Scientific Research and Development.

Originally published in *The Atlantic Monthly* in July 1945, 'As We May Think' discusses the technological developments that Bush felt were just around the corner – including a range of information storage media and a head-mounted camera about the size of a walnut. In terms of the evolution of computing, however, Bush's most important contribution was his concept of the 'Memex' machine, also outlined in this essay. Conceived as a library reading desk that would call up microfilms and project them on to screens, the Memex featured a series of levers that would leave 'trails' between disparate texts; connections would be documented by creating addresses that could be re-read. In other words, information could be arranged associatively. In the words of the writer Benjamin Woolley:

> Memex users could create their own documents out of the reams of text stored in the machine. This would be done not by laboriously copying the contents of each screen containing relevant text and combining the results to form a new physical document, but simply by keeping a record of the trail, the list of addresses used to access the relevant data. Furthermore, trails could themselves be combined and manipulated to produce different documents on related subjects. The trails, in other words, become the document.[1]

The computer, for obvious reasons, is tantamount to a powerful Memex machine. Or rather, to be more precise, the virtual machine of the computer can also assume the role of a Memex machine. The idea of the Memex was to inspire Ted Nelson and his Xanadu project, which brought the notions of hypermedia computer environments within our grasp.

The Memex idea has been attractive to science-fiction authors. An original reinterpretation of the Memex features in Neal Stephenson's *Diamond Age*, which centres on the effects of nanotechnology on a near future civilization.[2] The central character is little Nell, whose laptop is called 'The Young Lady's Illustrated Primer'; this is nothing short of a proactive, high-tech Memex in disguise, which seeks to educate her wherever the mind runs:

'ONCE UPON A TIME THERE WAS A LITTLE PRINCESS NAMED NELL WHO WAS IMPRISONED IN A TALL DARK CASTLE ON AN ISLAND IN THE MIDDLE OF A GREAT SEA, WITH A LITTLE BOY NAMED HARV, WHO WAS HER FRIEND AND PROTECTOR. SHE ALSO HAD FOUR SPECIAL FRIENDS CALLED DINOSAUR, DUCK, PETER RABBIT AND PURPLE.

'PRINCESS NELL AND HARV COULD NOT LEAVE THE DARK CASTLE, BUT FROM TIME TO TIME A RAVEN WOULD COME TO VISIT THEM.'

[The Primer tells her]

'What's a raven?' Nell said.

The illustration was a colourful painting of the island seen from up in the sky ... The picture zoomed in on [a] black dot, and it turned out to be a bird. Big letters appeared beneath. 'RAVEN' the book said. 'Raven. Now say it with me.'[3]

Bush's idea of trails of information has become one of the great epistemological devices of the late twentieth and early twenty-first centuries.

1 Benjamin Woolley, *Virtual Worlds: A Journey in Hype and Hyperreality*, London: Penguin, 1993, p159.
2 For more on nanotechnology see the essay by K Eric Drexler featured in this book, p116.
3 Neal Stephenson, *The Diamond Age*, New York: Bantam, 1995, p85.

The real heart of the matter of selection, however, goes deeper than a lag in the adoption of mechanisms by libraries, or a lack of development of devices for their use. Our ineptitude in getting at the record is largely caused by the artificiality of systems of indexing. When data of any sort are placed in storage, they are filed alphabetically or numerically, and information is found (when it is) by tracing it down from subclass to subclass. It can be in only one place, unless duplicates are used; one has to have rules as to which path will locate it, and the rules are cumbersome. Having found one item, moreover, one has to emerge from the system and re-enter on a new path.

The human mind does not work that way. It operates by association. With one item in its grasp, it snaps instantly to the next that is suggested by the association of thoughts, in accordance with some intricate web of trails carried by the cells of the brain. It has other characteristics, of course; trails that are not frequently followed are prone to fade, items are not fully permanent, memory is transitory. Yet the speed of action, the intricacy of trails, the detail of mental pictures, is awe-inspiring beyond all else in nature.

Man cannot hope fully to duplicate this mental process artificially, but he certainly ought to be able to learn from it. In minor ways he may even improve, for his records have relative permanency. The first idea, however, to be drawn from the analogy concerns selection. Selection by association, rather than indexing, may yet be mechanized. One cannot hope thus to equal the speed and flexibility with which the mind follows an associative trail, but it should be possible to beat the mind decisively in regard to the permanence and clarity of the items resurrected from storage.

Consider a future device for individual use, which is a sort of mechanized private file and library. It needs a name, and, to coin one at random, 'Memex' will do. A Memex is a device in which an individual stores all his books, records, and communications, and which is mechanized so that it may be consulted with exceeding speed and flexibility. It is an enlarged intimate supplement to his memory.

It consists of a desk, and while it can presumably be operated from a distance, it is primarily the piece of furniture at which he works. On the top are slanting translucent screens, on which material can be projected for convenient reading. There is a keyboard, and sets of buttons and levers. Otherwise it looks like an ordinary desk.

In one end is the stored material. The matter of bulk is well taken care of by improved microfilm. Only a small part of the interior of the Memex is devoted to storage, the rest to mechanism. Yet if the user inserted 5000 pages of material a day it would take him hundreds of years to fill the repository, so he can be profligate and enter material freely.

Most of the Memex contents are purchased on microfilm ready for insertion. Books of all sorts, pictures, current periodicals, newspapers, are thus obtained and dropped into place. Business correspondence takes the same path. And there is provision for direct entry. On the top of the

Memex is a transparent platen. On this are placed longhand notes, photographs, memoranda, all sorts of things. When one is in place, the depression of a lever causes it to be photographed onto the next blank space in a section of the Memex film, dry photography being employed.

There is, of course, provision for consultation of the record by the usual scheme of indexing. If the user wishes to consult a certain book, he taps its code on the keyboard, and the title page of the book promptly appears before him, projected onto one of his viewing positions. Frequently-used codes are mnemonic, so that he seldom consults his code book; but when he does, a single tap of a key projects it for his use. Moreover, he has supplemental levers. On deflecting one of these levers to the right he runs through the book before him, each page in turn being projected at a speed which just allows a recognizing glance at each. If he deflects it further to the right, he steps through the book 10 pages at a time; still further at 100 pages at a time. Deflection to the left gives him the same control backwards.

A special button transfers him immediately to the first page of the index. Any given book of his library can thus be called up and consulted with far greater facility than if it were taken from a shelf. As he has several projection positions, he can leave one item in position while he calls up another. He can add marginal notes and comments, taking advantage of one possible type of dry photography, and it could even be arranged so that he can do this by a stylus scheme, such as is now employed in the telautograph seen in railroad waiting rooms, just as though he had the physical page before him.

All this is conventional, except for the projection forward of present-day mechanisms and gadgetry. It affords an immediate step, however, to associative indexing, the basic idea of which is a provision whereby any item may be caused at will to select immediately and automatically another. This is the essential feature of the Memex. The process of tying two items together is the important thing.

When the user is building a trail, he names it, inserts the name in his code book, and taps it out on his keyboard. Before him are the two items to be joined, projected onto adjacent viewing positions. At the bottom of each there are a number of blank code spaces, and a pointer is set to indicate one of these on each item. The user taps a single key, and the items are permanently joined. In each code space appears the code word. Out of view, but also in the code space, is inserted a set of dots for photocell viewing; and on each item these dots by their positions designate the index number of the other item.

Thereafter, at any time, when one of these items is in view, the other can be instantly recalled merely by tapping a button below the corresponding code space. Moreover, when numerous items have been thus joined together to form a trail, they can be reviewed in turn, rapidly or slowly, by deflecting a lever like that used for turning the pages of a book. It is exactly as though the physical items had been gathered together from widely separated sources and bound together to form a new book. It is more than this, for any item can be joined into numerous trails.

The owner of the Memex, let us say, is interested in the origin and properties of the bow and arrow. Specifically, he is studying why the short Turkish bow was apparently superior to the English long bow in the skirmishes of the Crusades. He has dozens of possibly pertinent books and articles in his Memex. First he runs through an encyclopedia, finds an interesting but sketchy article, leaves it projected. Next, in a history, he finds another pertinent item, and ties the two together. Thus he goes, building a trail of many items. Occasionally he inserts a comment of his own, either linking it into the main trail or joining it by a side trail to a particular item. When it becomes evident that the elastic properties of available materials had a great deal to do with the bow, he branches off on a side trail which takes him through textbooks on elasticity and tables of physical constants. He inserts a page of longhand analysis of his own. Thus he builds a trail of his interest through the maze of materials available to him.

And his trails do not fade. Several years later, his talk with a friend turns to the queer ways in which a people resist innovations, even of vital interest. He has an example, in the fact that the outraged Europeans still failed to adopt the Turkish bow. In fact he has a trail on it. A touch brings up the code book. Tapping a few keys projects the head of the trail. A lever runs through it at will, stopping at interesting items, going off on side excursions. It is an interesting trail, pertinent to the discussion. So he sets a reproducer in action, photographs the whole trail out, and passes it to his friend for insertion in his own Memex, there to be linked into the more general trail.

Wholly new forms of encyclopedias will appear, ready made with a mesh of associative trails running through them, ready to be dropped into the Memex and there amplified. The lawyer has at his touch the associated opinions and decisions of his whole experience, and of the experience of friends and authorities. The patent attorney has on call the millions of issued patents, with familiar trails to every point of his client's interest. The physician, puzzled by a patient's reactions, strikes the trail established in studying an earlier similar case, and runs rapidly through analogous case histories, with side references to the classics for the pertinent anatomy and histology. The chemist, struggling with the synthesis of an organic compound, has all the chemical literature before him in his laboratory, with trails following the analogies of compounds, and side trails to their physical and chemical behaviour.

The historian, with a vast chronological account of a people, parallels it with a skip trail which stops only on the salient items, and can follow at any time contemporary trails which lead him all over civilization at a particular epoch. There is a new profession of trail blazers, those who find delight in the task of establishing useful trails through the enormous mass of the common record. The inheritance from the master becomes, not only his additions to the world's record, but for his disciples the entire scaffolding by which they were erected.

JD Bolter_Essays of Operation_1989

Alan Turing and John von Neumann are giants in the history of computation and cyberspace, and it is seldom that one comes across such a succinct explanation of Turing's *Turing Machine* and von Neumann's *Design for Computers* as that found in J David Bolter's *Turing's Man*. Bolter is Professor in the School of Literature, Communication and Culture at the Georgia Institute of Technology, and in this book he clearly and efficiently describes the intellectual and technological milestones that these two extraordinary men created.

The English mathemetician Alan Mathison Turing (1923–54) studied at Cambridge and worked as a cryptographer during World War II. In his foreword to *Turing's Man* the philosopher AJ Ayer traces Turing's early career:

> The paper that made him famous, 'On computable numbers, with an application to the *Entscheidungsproblem* (problem of decidability)' was published in the *Proceedings of the London Mathematical Society* as early as 1936. The paper was a contribution to symbolic logic but Turing was led to speak of machines by his concern with the question of how far the exercise of logic resembles a mechanical procedure.[1]

John von Neumann (1903–57) was a maths prodigy in Budapest; he earned his doctorate at the age of 22 and at age 23 became the youngest person ever to lecture at the University of Berlin. At the age of 30 he was appointed one of the first professors of the Institute for Advanced Study at Princeton, along with Albert Einstein. In his book *Artificial Life* Steven Levy, who is one of the best writers on artificial intelligence, neatly summarizes von Neumann's achievements:

> He helped to hammer out the niceties of quantum mechanics in the cafés of Gottingen, virtually invented game theory in Berlin, solved ergodic mathematical questions in Princeton, helped to concoct the A-bomb in Los Alamos and made so crucial a contribution to the development of the electronic digital computer that almost all such machines are referred to as von Neumann processors.[2]

In later life von Neumann became especially interested in the similarities that might exist between the computer and living things. He was responsible for inventing cellular automata, which are critical components of artificial life, and became fascinated by the notion of creating a theory that would adhere to all phenomena – both natural and artificial. (Notions of emergence and artificial intelligence are discussed elsewhere in this book; see, for instance, pp116, 170, 178.)

There is a paradox at the heart of the computer: it is the least biological-looking of all machines, with few moving parts and operating on invisible electricity, yet it embodies great potential for the hybridization of the animate and the inanimate, and the creation of artificial intelligence. Turing and von Neumann, with their logistics and their inspired imagination, are the godfathers of many of these aspirations.

1 J David Bolter, *Turing's Man: Western Culture in the Computer Age*, introduction by AJ Ayer, London: Penguin, 1993, p*ix*.
2 Steven Levy, *Artificial Life*, London: Penguin, 1993, p13.

The Turing Machine: States and Symbols

A Turing machine is an abstraction, a creation of logic and mathematics. But it may also be thought of as a game, one that can be played with no more advanced technology than pencil and paper. To play any game, we agree to something like that suspension of disbelief that makes possible theatre and the movies. We enter another world, a world whose logic consists entirely of the rules of the game. Insofar as we take the game 'seriously', we concentrate upon the logical corners and alleys that the rules define, and we do not bother about experiences that fall outside of the game. In Monopoly, for example, players buy and sell property, collect rent, and move their pieces. The rules say nothing about their getting hungry, falling asleep, or suffering a myocardial infarction; dying is not part of the game. What matters is that buying and selling property, collecting rent, and moving pieces make up a logical and satisfying whole. A good game is self-contained. A Turing machine is just such a logically self-contained world.

The sole inhabitant of this world is a logic machine. The machine consists of two parts: a finite set of operating rules, built somehow into the works and unchangeable during operation, and a tape of unlimited length, upon which changeable information can be stored. In figure 3-1, the tape is divided into cells, each of which may contain only one symbol, and there is a marker to indicate which cell is being inspected at any given moment. The tape holds the information that the machine is to process; in our example it is binary information, for the three allowed symbols are '0', '1', and a blank. If the machine chooses to write any output, it must do so somewhere on the same tape. It may write over input information, and the number of cells available to the right is without limit. Now, the set of operating rules controls the action of the marker along the tape. In figure 3-1 these rules are written in English, although Turing used a logical notation to achieve the same meaning. Our example has only two rules; usually there are more, perhaps a dozen or a hundred, but the number must always be finite.

The machine is sequential; it operates by activating one rule at a time, performing the actions prescribed by that rule, and then activating another. Before and after each operation, the machine is said to be in one of a limited number of *states*. These states are defined by the logician who has constructed the machine; in our example they are named Q1 and Q2. The machine always 'knows' two things: its current state and the current cell pointed to on its tape. These two factors are all that are needed for its operation, for the machine always chooses its next move by finding the rule corresponding to its current state and the symbol in the current cell. State and symbol make the machine go.

An activated rule calls for the following: writing a symbol on the cell designated by the marker, moving the marker one cell right or left, and changing the current state. These are the only means by which a Turing machine can manipulate data. The process continues in this fashion until the machine activates a rule that tells it to halt; it has then completed its task.

A Turing machine is a game in which no room is left for player initiative. The only element that is allowed to vary is the input tape. Once an input has been chosen, the machine evokes its rules with the regularity of clockwork: for each input there is only one possible outcome. In our example, the tape is set with the input '1' followed by blanks, and the machine is started in state Q1. The first rule is applied, the machine writes the symbol '1' over the current '1' (in effect leaving the symbol unchanged), moves its marker one cell to the right, and enters state Q2. The current symbol is now blank and the state is Q2, so that rule two applies. The machine writes '0', moves its marker to the right, and halts. The program has ended; its modest goal was to replace the number 1 with the number 10.

There are of course an infinite number of other, more interesting Turing machines; the principles of operation are the same no matter what the machine is designed to do. The tape may hold the digits of a number, and the machine may embody rules for finding the square root of this number. There might be a series of numbers on the tape, and the machine might be designed to compute the thrust needed to put a spacecraft in lunar orbit. The really challenging game is to design the Turing machine in the first place, to come up with operating rules and states that will make the machine act as desired. It turns out that the logician does not have to construct a new machine, embodying new rules, for each new programming task. One machine, a universal Turing machine, can be designed so that, given the proper input symbols on its tape, it can perform any task that any individual Turing machine can perform. A digital computer can be thought of as a universal Turing machine.

Turing himself invented this game in 1936 in order to prove some abstruse results in symbolic logic. But his invention captured perfectly the theoretical structure of all digital computers to the present day. The word 'machine' was used by Turing himself, although it traditionally meant a device for producing power to do work. A Turing machine does not perform work as a steam engine does; it merely moves its marker back and forth along its tape – examining, erasing, and writing symbols as it applies its rules of operation. Such a machine does not improve man's ability physically to manipulate his environment, and it is only by analogy that we should use the word 'machine' at all. By any name, Turing's abstraction in fact shows what a computer does: to 'process information' by computer is nothing more than *to replace discrete symbols one at a time according to a finite set of rules*. Any task a digital computer performs (from figuring taxes to playing chess) can be explained by this simple replacement procedure, and any task that cannot be carried out under this procedure cannot be programmed in a digital computer. It can be shown – and this was Turing's original point – that there are problems no Turing machine can ever guarantee to answer; the machine may go on infinitely spinning its tape without coming to a result. Such problems pose an ultimate, though by no means the only, limitation on the power of the digital computer.

The von Neumann Computer

We have traced the logical shadow of the computer in Turing's machine. No matter how ingenious, that device was a game for logicians and could only have had a limited impact on our culture (like the other concerns of twentieth-century logic) if it had not found a physical embodiment as the von Neumann computer. About ten years after Turing first made his suggestion, John von Neumann and his many colleagues realized its significance and worked to apply Turing's logical scheme to the physical materials from which information processors might be built. They sought to make a Turing machine out of vacuum tubes instead of pencil and paper; the electronic version would operate millions of times faster than a mathematician applying his rules and erasing his symbols accordingly.

Again, two parts needed to be considered: the rules of operation and the data upon which to operate. The data could sensibly be put on punched cards, represented inside the machines by some sort of electronic storage, and eventually dumped as output onto punched cards or paper. The problem was with the rules of operation, for the tendency had been to think of these rules as fixed, to express them in the very structure, the wiring of the machine. Early machines offered plugboards, something like telephone switchboards, in which wires had to be reconfigured for each new problem to be solved. The wires led out to various parts of the machine, controlling the calculations that the data would undergo. The operator literally had to wire a new machine, designed exclusively to execute that one problem.

The unique feature of the von Neumann computer is that the programs and data are stored in the same way, as strings of binary digits. The program, a set of instructions to add, subtract, or manipulate pieces of data, is loaded along with the data into the computer's memory. The central processing unit (CPU) of the machine distinguishes between instructions and data usually only by position. It decodes and executes instructions and operates accordingly upon the data. The illustration of the von Neumann computer is still quite abstract: in a current machine, each of the boxes would be electronic devices made of thousands or millions of transistors; the arrows would be wires or connections allowing electrical 'information' to pass between the devices in the directions indicated. The box marked memory corresponds to the tape of the Turing machine: here the input is stored and the intermediate results are written by the CPU. The CPU corresponds to the operating rules of a universal Turing machine. Built into its electronic structure are rules for making sense of the instructions and data that it finds in the memory. The CPU goes through the memory, much as a Turing machine moves along its tape, picking out instructions one at a time and executing them.

The CPU is made up of logic circuitry and various registers. The registers hold individual instructions or small amounts of data for immediate processing. The control unit, more of a functional than a physical division in modern computers, breaks the instructions into a series of electronic actions, directing the step-by-step operation of the whole system. (This unit replaces the plugboard of the earlier machines.) The *arithmetic and logical unit (ALU)*, performs the actual additions, subtractions, and logical business required.

Suppose the next instruction in the memory is to add two numbers and store the result somewhere else in memory. The sequence is:

1. The control unit signals the memory to send the next instruction and an instruction register to receive it. Decoding circuits read the instruction and discover that it demands an addition.

2. The control pulls the two numbers to be added from the memory and puts them into data registers.

3. It sends these two numbers through the arithmetic unit, where they are summed, and puts the sum back into a data register.

4. It sends the sum from the register back into memory.

The process is then repeated on the next instruction and so on through the program. The computer works in cycles, each of which has two parts: fetch and execute. The fetch step is the 'reading' and interpreting of the instruction (1 in the above sequence), where the decoder discovers what is to be done. The actual processing (2 through 4) of the data is the execute step.

The cycle of fetch-and-execute proceeds with numbing regularity perhaps millions of times each second; it is repeated for each new instruction and new packet of data. For all its extraordinary speed, the von Neumann computer operates rather like a two-stroke gasoline engine, drawing its instructions in with the first stroke and executing them with the second. A closer analogy, perhaps, is an industrial assembly line or job shop, in which an endless stream of identical items are processed. Here the items are not automobiles or alarm clocks but electronically coded packets of information. These move, at speeds that are healthy fractions of the speed of light, back and forth between memory and processor; within the processor they are broken into smaller packets and recombined in electronic forms of arithmetic and logical calculus. In this fashion, the computer processes information: it begins with one string of binary digits (the program and the data) and ends by assembling another (the output) from fragments of the first.

It is the logical unity of the von Neumann stored-program computer that makes it so powerful. New programs, new sets of instructions, can be loaded into these machines as easily as new data. Each program in effect makes the computer into a different machine, one with a new purpose, without any change in the wiring. The same physical equipment may serve first to calculate the orbit of a spacecraft, then to alphabetize a list of names, then to determine averages and deviations of a statistical sample. Since each of these tasks calls for a logically different Turing machine, the physical equipment that can accomplish them all is a universal Turing machine. Thus logic and electronics meet at precisely this point: the von Neumann computer.

Norbert Wiener_Organization of the Message_1950

Norbert Wiener (1894–1964) is the father of cybernetics. Cybernetic ideas directly attributable to Weiner are the basis of much of the writing in this book. He saw the world as one huge feedback mechanism that is prone to ongoing effects of entropy. This entropy is a subversive force that impedes the crucial data of life and its continual exchange.

Wiener was a child prodigy who gained a PhD from Harvard at the age of 18. At 30 he was Professor of Mathematics at the Massachusetts Institute of Technology. As well as *The Human Use of Human Beings* (1950) his books include *Cybernetics* (1948), *Ex-Prodigy* (1953), *I am a Mathematician: The Later Life of a Prodigy* (1956) and *God & Golem, Inc.* (1964).

Wiener's thesis was that all animals are machines subject to feedback. The fact that they learn from feedback makes them intelligent. As an antelope learns to avoid lions in different circumstances, it understands a phenomenon and sees its similarities in unfamiliar terrain – learning and feedback. Wiener's first book, *Cybernetics, or control and communication in the animal and the machine* (1948) set out his ideas in simple language. His ideas had widespread impact, as Kevin Kelly explains:

> The result of Wiener's book was that the notion of feedback penetrated almost every aspect of technical culture. Though the central concept was bold it was old and common place in specialized circumstances. Wiener gave the idea legs by generalizing the effect into a universal principle: lifelike self-control was a simple engineering job. When the notion of feedback control was packaged with the flexibility of electronic circuits, they married into a tool anyone could use. Within a year or two of *Cybernetics'* publication, electronic control circuits revolutionized industry.[1]

In terms of cybernetics this revolution was not all it might have been, since the fledgling computers that were being developed at this time pulled the technological imperative away from an analogy with mechanical devices and biological systems and towards the writing of code and software. This new interest in the software, as opposed to Wiener's hardware systems, caused cybernetics to take a back seat during the next few years. J David Bolter illustrates the hardware dependence of this 'first-order' cybernetics:

Wiener was still only halfway along the line from Descartes to Turing. He wanted machines to imitate the man who acts in the world as well as the man who reasons, to explain muscle action in terms of feedback loops as well as chess in terms of a digital program. He relied on hardware devices for his metaphor of man and demanded a close correspondence between man and the machine made to imitate him. Vacuum tubes were meant to be a physical substitute for neurons, servo mechanisms for nerves acting upon muscles.[2]

In the passage featured here Wiener illustrates that in his mind there is no difference between the transmission of information and the transmission of material. Indeed, Wiener sees the telegraphing of a man from one place to another as feasible. This has a certain parallel with the writings of K Eric Drexler (see p116) and his idea of programming atomic-sized assemblers. The work of Hans Moravec (see p280) would also appear to be influenced by such notions.

Later, the creation of 'second-order' cybernetics served to rejuvenate the science. This form of cybernetics shifted the focus from Wiener's 'communication and control' and towards ideas of interaction, and included the observer in any system. Gordon Pask (see p76) was also highly influential in the realm of second-order cybernetics.

1 Kevin Kelly, *Out of Control: The New Biology of Machines,* London: Fourth Estate, 1994, p120.
2 J David Bolter, *Turing's Man: Western Culture in the Computer Age,* London: Penguin, 1993, p192.

Norbert Wiener, 'Organization of the Message', *The Human Use of Human Beings*, 1950

Behind Leibnitz's philosophical views of the monads there lie some very interesting biological speculations. It was in Leibnitz's time that Leeuwenhoek first applied the simple microscope to the study of very minute animals and plants. Among the animals that he saw were spermatozoa. In the mammal, spermatozoa are infinitely easier to find and to see than ova. The human ova are emitted one at a time, and unfertilized uterine ova or very early embryos were until recently rarities in the anatomical collections. Thus the early microscopists were under the very natural temptation to regard the spermatozoon as the only important element in the development of the young, and to ignore entirely the possibility of the as yet unobserved phenomenon of fertilization. Furthermore, their imagination displayed to them in the front segment or head of the spermatozoon a minute fetus, rolled up with head forward. This fetus was supposed to contain in itself spermatozoa which were to develop into the next generation of fetuses and adults, and so on *ad infinitum*. The female was supposed to be merely the nurse of the spermatozoon.

Of course, from the modern point of view, this biology is simply false. The spermatozoon and the ovum are nearly equal participants in determining individual heredity. Furthermore, the germ cells of the future generation are contained in them *in posse*, and not *in esse*. Matter is not infinitely divisible, nor indeed from any absolute standpoint is it very finely divisible; and the successive diminutions required to form the Leeuwenhoek spermatozoon of a moderately high order would very quickly lead us down beyond electronic levels.

In the view now prevalent, as opposed to the Leibnitzian view, the continuity of an individual has a very definite beginning in time, but it may even have a termination in time quite apart from the death of the individual. It is well known that the first cell division of the fertilized ovum of a frog leads to two cells, which can be separated under appropriate conditions. If they are so separated, each will grow into a complete frog. This is nothing but the normal phenomenon of identical twinning in a case in which the anatomical accessibility of the embryo is sufficient to permit experimentation. It is exactly what occurs in human identical twins, and is the normal phenomenon in those armadillos that bear a set of identical quadruplets at each birth. It is the phenomenon, moreover, which gives rise to double monsters, when the separation of the two parts of the embryo is incomplete.

This problem of twinning may not however appear as important at first sight as it really is, because it does not concern animals or human beings with what may be considered well-developed minds and souls. Not even the problem of the double monster, the imperfectly separated twins, is too serious in this respect. Viable double monsters must always have either a single central nervous system or a well-developed pair of separate brains. The difficulty arises at another level in the problem of split personalities.

A generation ago, Dr Morton Prince of Harvard gave the case history of a girl within whose body several better-or-worse-developed personalities seemed to succeed one another, and even to a certain extent to coexist. It is the fashion nowadays for the psychiatrists to look down their noses a little bit when Dr Prince's work is mentioned, and to attribute the phenomenon to hysteria. It is quite possible that the separation of the personalities was never as complete as Prince sometimes appears to have thought it to be, but for all that it was a separation. The word 'hysteria' refers to a phenomenon well observed by the doctors, but so little explained that it may be considered but another question-begging epithet.

One thing at any rate is clear. The physical identity of an individual does not consist in the matter of which it is made. Modern methods of tagging the elements participating in metabolism have shown a much higher turnover than was long thought possible, not only of the body as a whole, but of each and every component part of it. The biological individuality of an organism seems to lie in a certain continuity of process, and in the memory by the organism of the effects of its past development. This appears to hold also of its mental development. In terms of the computing machine, the individuality of a mind lies in the retention of its earlier tapings and memories, and in its continued development along lines already laid out.

Under these conditions, just as a computing machine may be used as a pattern on which to tape other computing machines, and just as the future development of these two machines will continue in parallel except for future changes in taping and experience, so too, there is no inconsistency in a living individual forking or divaricating into two individuals sharing the same past, but growing more and more different. This is what happens with identical twins; but there is no reason why it could not happen with what we call the mind, without a similar split of the body. To use computing-machine language again, at some stage a machine which was previously assembled in an all-over manner may find its connections divided into partial assemblies with a higher or lower degree of independence. This would be a conceivable explanation of Prince's observations.

Moreover, it is thinkable that two large machines which had previously not been coupled may become coupled so as to work from that stage on as a single machine. Indeed this sort of thing occurs in the union of the germ cells, although perhaps not on what we would ordinarily call a purely mental level. The mental identity necessary for the Church's view of the individuality of the soul certainly does not exist in any absolute sense which would be acceptable to the Church.

To recapitulate: the individuality of the body is that of a flame rather than that of a stone, of a form rather than of a bit of substance. This form can be transmitted or modified and duplicated, although at present we know only how to duplicate it over a short distance. When one cell divides into two, or when one of the genes which carries our corporeal and mental birth-right is split in order to make ready for a reduction division of a germ cell, we have a separation in matter which is conditioned by the power of a pattern of living tissue to duplicate itself. Since this is so, there is no absolute distinction between the types of transmission which we can use for sending a telegram from country to country and the types of transmission which at least are theoretically possible for transmitting a living organism such as a human being.

Let us then admit that the idea that one might conceivably travel by telegraph, in addition to travelling by train or airplane, is not intrinsically absurd, far as it may be from realization. The difficulties are, of course, enormous. It is possible to evaluate something like the amount of significant information conveyed by all the genes in a germ cell, and thereby to determine the amount of heredity information, as compared with learned information, that a human being possesses. In order for this message to be significant at all, it must convey at least as much information as an entire set of the *Encyclopaedia Britannica*. In fact if we compare the number of asymmetric carbon atoms in all the molecules of a germ cell with the number of dots and dashes needed to code the *Encyclopaedia Britannica*, we find that they constitute an even more enormous message; and this is still more impressive when we realize what the conditions for telegraphic transmission of such a message must be. Any scanning of the human organism must be a probe going through all its parts, and will, accordingly, tend to destroy the tissue on its way. To hold an organism stable while part of it is being slowly destroyed, with the intention of re-creating it out of other material elsewhere, involves a lowering of its degree of activity, which in most cases would destroy life in the tissue.

In other words, the fact that we cannot telegraph the pattern of a man from one place to another seems to be due to technical difficulties, and in particular, to the difficulty of keeping an organism in being during such a radical reconstruction. The idea itself is highly plausible. As for the problem of the radical reconstruction of the living organism, it would be hard to find any such reconstruction much more radical than that of a butterfly during its period as a pupa.

I have stated these things, not because I want to write a science-fiction story concerning itself with the possibility of telegraphing a man, but because it may help us understand that the fundamental idea of communication is that of the transmission of messages, and that the bodily transmission of matter and messages is only one conceivable way of attaining that end. It will be well to reconsider Kipling's test of the importance of traffic in the modern world from the point of view of a traffic which is overwhelmingly not so much the transmission of human bodies as the transmission of human information.

JCR Licklider_Man-Computer Symbiosis_1960

JCR Licklider (1915–90) is a key figure in the development of interactivity between users and computers. He was responsible for creating the research-funded environment where crucial developments took place in the evolution of the computer mouse, windows, hypertext and other Internet technologies. Licklider was a professor at the Massachusetts Institute of Technology (MIT) and subsequently director of the Information Processing Techniques Office (IPTO), a department in the Pentagon's Advanced Research Projects Agency (ARPA).

While at MIT Licklider started to record every task he did during his working day. He came to the realization that 85 per cent of his working life was spent on tasks that were preliminary to the actual thought-processes of his research. Time was spent 'getting into a position to think, to make a decision, to learn something I needed to know. Much more time went into finding or obtaining information than into digesting it.'[1]

Licklider's personal time-and-motion study led him to postulate a new relationship between computers and their users. His radical conclusion was that much research and technical thinking could be done more quickly and effectively by machines. As Howard Rheingold has pointed out:

This was a thought that was occurring to one or two other people at about the same time – notably Doug Engelbart, out in California. But because of his association with certain military-sponsored research projects at MIT in the 1950s, there was an important difference between Licklider and the others who dreamed of converting computers into some kind of mind-amplifying tool. This crucial difference was the fact that Licklider had reached his conclusion not long before circumstances put him at the centre of power in the one institution capable of sponsoring the creation of an entire new technology.'[2]

This institution was, of course, ARPA.

Licklider's particular talent was in establishing priorities for funding and hence research efforts. In an arena where technology was ill-defined but still advancing at an incredible rate, Licklider's interests evolved into a concern for interactivity. Working with others he designed and built a new style of computer. Rheingold continues:

Instead of programming via boxes of punched cards over a period of days, it became possible to feed programs and data to the machine via a high-speed paper tape; it was possible to change the paper tape input while the program was running. The operator could interact with the machine for the first time.[3]

This method of computing inspired Licklider to think more fully about interactivity and in 1960 he wrote the paper, 'Man–Computer Symbiosis'. It was the first time anyone had written of computer and human interaction in the same way that one talks about flowers and insects. He believed that since computers would ultimately learn to communicate with us, we might as well learn to communicate more profoundly with them – and amongst ourselves.

1 JCR Licklider, quoted in Howard Rheingold, 'Tools for Thought: The People and Ideas of the Next Computer Revolution', 1985. http://www.well.com/user/hlr/texts.tft7.html
2 Ibid.
3 Ibid.

Man-computer symbiosis is an expected development in cooperative interaction between men and electronic computers. It will involve very close coupling between the human and the electronic members of the partnership. The main aims are 1) to let computers facilitate formulative thinking as they now facilitate the solution of formulated problems, and 2) to enable men and computers to cooperate in making decisions and controlling complex situations without inflexible dependence on predetermined programs. In the anticipated symbiotic partnership, men will set the goals, formulate the hypotheses, determine the criteria, and perform the evaluations. Computing machines will do the routinizable work that must be done to prepare the way for insights and decisions in technical and scientific thinking. Preliminary analyses indicate that the symbiotic partnership will perform intellectual operations much more effectively than man alone can perform them. Prerequisites for the achievement of the effective, cooperative association include developments in computer time sharing, in memory components, in memory organization, in programming languages, and in input and output equipment.

Introduction: Symbiosis

The fig tree is pollinated only by the insect Blastophaga grossorun. The larva of the insect lives in the ovary of the fig tree, and there it gets its food. The tree and the insect are thus heavily interdependent: the tree cannot reproduce without the insect; the insect cannot eat without the tree; together, they constitute not only a viable but a productive and thriving partnership. This cooperative 'living together in intimate association, or even close union, of two dissimilar organisms' is called symbiosis.[1]

'Man-computer symbiosis' is a subclass of man-machine systems. There are many man-machine systems. At present, however, there are no man-computer symbioses. The purposes of this paper are to present the concept and, hopefully, to foster the development of man-computer symbiosis by analysing some problems of interaction between men and computing machines, calling attention to applicable principles of man-machine engineering, and pointing out a few questions to which research answers are needed. The hope is that, in not too many years, human brains and computing machines will be coupled together very tightly, and that the resulting partnership will think as no human brain has ever thought and process data in a way not approached by the information-handling machines we know today.

Between 'Mechanically Extended Man' and 'Artificial Intelligence'

As a concept, man-computer symbiosis is different in an important way from what North[2] has called 'mechanically extended man.' In the man-machine systems of the past, the human operator supplied the initiative, the direction, the integration, and the criterion. The mechanical parts of the systems were mere extensions, first of the human arm, then of the human eye. These systems certainly did not consist of 'dissimilar organisms living together ...' There was only one kind of organism – man – and the rest was there only to help him.

In one sense of course, any man-made system is intended to help man to help a man or men outside the system. If we focus upon the human operator within the system, however, we see that, in some areas of technology, a fantastic change has taken place during the last few years. 'Mechanical extension' has given way to replacement of men, to automation, and the men who remain are there more to help than to be helped. In some instances, particularly in large computer-centred information and control systems, the human operators are responsible mainly for functions that it proved infeasible to automate. Such systems ('humanly extended machines', North might call them) are not symbiotic systems. They are 'semi-automatic' systems, systems that started out to be fully automatic but fell short of the goal.

Man-computer symbiosis is probably not the ultimate paradigm for complex technological systems. It seems entirely possible that, in due course, electronic or chemical 'machines' will outdo the human brain in most of the functions we now consider exclusively within its province. Even now, Gelernter's IBM-704 program for proving theorems in plane geometry proceeds at about the same pace as Brooklyn high school students, and makes similar errors.[3] There are, in fact, several theorem-proving, problem-solving, chess-playing, and pattern-recognizing programs (too many for complete reference) capable of rivalling human intellectual performance in restricted areas; and Newell, Simon, and Shaw's[4] 'general problem solver' may remove some of the restrictions. In short, it seems worthwhile to avoid argument with (other) enthusiasts for artificial intelligence by conceding dominance in the distant future of cerebration to machines alone. There will nevertheless be a fairly long interim during which the main intellectual advances will be made by men and computers working together in intimate association. A multidisciplinary study group, examining future research and development problems of the Air Force, estimated that it would be 1980 before developments in artificial intelligence make it possible for machines alone to do much thinking or problem solving of military significance. That would leave, say, five years to develop man-computer symbiosis and 15 years to use it. The 15 may be 10 or 500, but those years should be intellectually the most creative and exciting in the history of mankind.

Aims of Man-Computer Symbiosis

Present-day computers are designed primarily to solve preformulated problems or to process data according to predetermined procedures. The course of the computation may be conditional upon results obtained during the computation, but all the alternatives must be foreseen in advance. (If an unforeseen alternative arises, the whole process comes to a halt and awaits the necessary extension of the program.) The requirement for preformulation or predetermination is sometimes no great disadvantage. It is often said that programming for a computing machine forces one to think clearly, that it disciplines the thought process. If the user can think his problem through in advance, symbiotic association with a computing machine is not necessary.

However, many problems that can be thought through in advance are very difficult to think through in advance. They would be easier to solve, and they could be solved faster, through an intuitively guided trial-and-error procedure in which the computer cooperated, turning up flaws in the reasoning or revealing unexpected turns in the solution. Other problems simply cannot be formulated without computing-machine aid. Poincaré anticipated the frustration of an important group of would-be computer users when he said, 'The question is not, "What is the answer?" The question is, "What is the question?"' One of the main aims of man-computer symbiosis is to bring the computing machine effectively into the formulative parts of technical problems.

The other main aim is closely related. It is to bring computing machines effectively into processes of thinking that must go on in 'real time', time that moves too fast to permit using computers in conventional ways. Imagine trying, for example, to direct a battle with the aid of a computer on such a schedule as this. You formulate your problem today. Tomorrow you spend with a programmer. Next week the computer devotes 5 minutes to assembling your program and 47 seconds to calculating the answer to your problem. You get a sheet of paper 20 feet long, full of numbers that, instead of providing a final solution, only suggest a tactic that should be explored by simulation. Obviously, the battle would be over before the second step in its planning was begun. To think in interaction with a computer in the same way that you think with a colleague whose competence supplements your own will require much tighter coupling between man and machine than is suggested by the example and than is possible today.

Need for Computer Participation in Formulative and Real-Time Thinking

The preceding paragraphs tacitly made the assumption that, if they could be introduced effectively into the thought process, the functions that can be performed by data-processing machines would improve or facilitate thinking and problem solving in an important way. That assumption may require justification.

A Preliminary and Informal Time-and-Motion Analysis of Technical Thinking

Despite the fact that there is a voluminous literature on thinking and problem solving, including intensive case-history studies of the process of invention, I could find nothing comparable to a time-and-motion-study analysis of the mental work of a person engaged in a scientific or technical enterprise. In the spring and summer of 1957, therefore, I tried to keep track of what one moderately technical person actually did during the hours he regarded as devoted to work. Although I was aware of the inadequacy of the sampling, I served as my own subject.

It soon became apparent that the main thing I did was to keep records, and the project would have become an infinite regress if the keeping of records had been carried through in the detail envisaged in the initial plan. It was not. Nevertheless, I obtained a picture of my activities that gave me pause. Perhaps my spectrum is not typical—I hope it is not, but I fear it is. About 85 per cent of my 'thinking' time was spent getting into a position to think, to make a decision, to learn something I needed to know. Much more time went into finding or obtaining information than into digesting it. Hours went into the plotting of graphs, and other hours into instructing an assistant how to plot. When the graphs were finished, the relations were obvious at once, but the plotting had to be done in order to make them so. At one point, it was necessary to compare six experimental determinations of a function relating speech-intelligibility to speech-to-noise ratio. No two experimenters had used the same definition or measure of speech-to-noise ratio. Several hours of calculating were required to get the data into comparable form. When they were in comparable form, it took only a few seconds to determine what I needed to know.

Throughout the period I examined, in short, my 'thinking' time was devoted mainly to activities that were essentially clerical or mechanical: searching, calculating, plotting, transforming, determining the logical or dynamic consequences of a set of assumptions or hypotheses, preparing the way for a decision or an insight. Moreover, my choices of what to attempt and what not to attempt were determined to an embarrassingly great extent by considerations of clerical feasibility, not intellectual capability.

The main suggestion conveyed by the findings just described is that the operations that fill most of the time allegedly devoted to technical thinking are operations that can be performed more effectively by machines than by men. Severe problems are posed by the fact that these operations have to be performed upon diverse variables and in unforeseen and continually changing sequences. If those problems can be solved in such a way as to create a symbiotic relation between a man and a fast information-retrieval and data-processing machine, however, it seems evident that the cooperative interaction would greatly improve the thinking process.

It may be appropriate to acknowledge, at this point, that we are using the term 'computer' to cover a wide class of calculating, data-processing, and information-storage-and-retrieval machines. The capabilities of machines in this class are increasing almost daily. It is therefore hazardous to make general statements about capabilities of the class. Perhaps it is equally hazardous to make general statements about the capabilities of men. Nevertheless, certain genotypic differences in capability between men and computers do stand out, and they have a bearing on the nature of possible man-computer symbiosis and the potential value of achieving it.

As has been said in various ways, men are noisy, narrow-band devices, but their nervous systems have very many parallel and simultaneously active channels. Relative to men, computing machines are very fast and very accurate, but they are constrained to perform only one or a few elementary operations at a time. Men are flexible, capable of 'programming themselves contingently' on the basis of newly received information. Computing machines are single-minded, constrained by their ' pre-programming.' Men naturally speak redundant languages organized around unitary objects and coherent actions and employing 20 to 60 elementary symbols. Computers 'naturally' speak nonredundant languages, usually with only two elementary symbols and no inherent appreciation either of unitary objects or of coherent actions.

To be rigorously correct, those characterizations would have to include many qualifiers. Nevertheless, the picture of dissimilarity (and therefore potential supplementation) that they present is essentially valid. Computing machines can do readily, well, and rapidly many things that are difficult or impossible for man, and men can do readily and well, though not rapidly, many things that are difficult or impossible for computers. That suggests that a symbiotic cooperation, if successful in integrating the positive characteristics of men and computers, would be of great value. The differences in speed and in language, of course, pose difficulties that must be overcome.

Separable Functions of Men and Computers in the Anticipated Symbiotic Association

It seems likely that the contributions of human operators and equipment will blend together so completely in many operations that it will be difficult to separate them neatly in analysis. That would be the case if, in gathering data on which to base a decision, for example, both the man and the computer came up with relevant precedents from experience and if the computer then suggested a course of action that agreed with the man's intuitive judgment. (In theorem-proving programs, computers find precedents in experience, and in the SAGE System, they suggest courses of action. The foregoing is not a far-fetched example.) In other operations, however, the contributions of men and equipment will be to some extent separable. Men will set the goals and supply the motivations, of course, at least in the early years. They will formulate hypotheses. They will ask questions. They will think of mechanisms, procedures, and models. They will remember that such-and-such a person did some possibly relevant work on a topic of interest back in 1947, or at any rate shortly after World War II, and they will have an idea in what journals it might have been published. In general, they will make approximate and fallible, but leading, contributions, and they will define criteria and serve as evaluators, judging the contributions of the equipment and guiding the general line of thought. In addition, men will handle the very-low-probability situations when such situations do actually arise. (In current man-machine systems, that is one of the human operator's most important functions. The sum of the probabilities of very-low-probability alternatives is often much too large to neglect.) Men will fill in the gaps, either in the problem solution or in the computer program, when the computer has no mode or routine that is applicable in a particular circumstance.

The information-processing equipment, for its part, will convert hypotheses into testable models and then test the models against data (which the human operator may designate roughly and identify as relevant when the computer presents them for his approval). The equipment will answer questions.

It will simulate the mechanisms and models, carry out the procedures, and display the results to the operator. It will transform data, plot graphs ('cutting the cake' in whatever way the human operator specifies, or in several alternative ways if the human operator is not sure what he wants). The equipment will interpolate, extrapolate, and transform. It will convert static equations or logical statements into dynamic models so the human operator can examine their behaviour. In general, it will carry out the routinizable, clerical operations that fill the intervals between decisions. In addition, the computer will serve as a statistical-inference, decision-theory, or game-theory machine to make elementary evaluations of suggested courses of action whenever there is enough basis to support a formal statistical analysis. Finally, it will do as much diagnosis, pattern-matching, and relevance-recognizing as it profitably can, but it will accept a clearly secondary status in those areas.

1 *Webster's New International Dictionary*, 2nd ed, Springfield, MA: G and C Merriam Co, p2555; 1958.
2 J D North, 'The rational behaviour of mechanically extended man', Wolverhampton: Boulton Paul Aircraft Ltd, September, 1954.
3 H Gelernter, 'Realization of a Geometry Theorem Proving Machine', UNESCO, NS, ICIP, 1.6.6, International Conference on Information Processing, Paris, France; June, 1959.
4 A Newell, H A Simon, and J C Shaw, 'Report on a general problem-solving program', UNESCO, NS, ICIP, 1.6.8, International Conference on Information Processing, Paris, France; June, 1959.

Douglas Engelbart_Augmenting Human Intellect: A Conceptual Framework_1962

Many of the computing devices that are commonplace today –
the mouse, e-mail, teleconferencing and the distributed client-server
architecture of the Internet – have their roots in research carried out by
Douglas Engelbart (b.1925) during the 1950s and 1960s. His importance
in the history of information technology is undisputed; Byte, in a 1995
article honouring the 20 people whom the magazine saw as having had
the greatest impact on personal computing, went so far as to say of
Engelbart that 'comparisons with Thomas Edison do not seem
far-fetched ...'.[1]

During the Second World War Engelbart worked as a radar
technician in the Philippines, and it was during this time that he read
Vannevar Bush's essay 'As We May Think' (featured in this book, p34).
As a radar technician he was accustomed to seeing information
presented on a screen. As the biography on the website of Engelbart's
own Bootstrap Institute puts it, it was here that he began 'to envision
people sitting in front of displays, "flying around" in an information
space where they could formulate and organize their ideas with
incredible speed and flexibility. So he applied to the graduate program
in Electrical Engineering at UC Berkeley to launch his new crusade (at
the time there was no computer science department, and the closest
working computer was in Maryland).'[2] Engelbart gained his PhD in 1955.

In 1963 Englebart wrote his seminal paper 'Augmenting Human
Intellect', which set out his vision for interactive hypermedia; and in
1967 his was the second host site on the new ARPANET (see Licklider,
p52). During the Fall Joint Computer Conference of 1968 Engelbart
stunned his contemporaries with a demonstration of his NLS (oN Line
System), the first hypermedia groupware. The talk he gave at this
conference was in effect the debut of the concepts behind the mouse,
hypermedia and on-screen video teleconferencing. Engelbart's
inventions were ahead of their time, and it has only been with
increased industry capabilities that they have become integrated into
mainstream computing. It was not until 1984 that Apple Macintosh
popularized the mouse, but today it is difficult to imagine a personal

computer without one; likewise, the huge success of Microsoft's Windows 95 proves that Engelbart's original windows concept has also become a computing commonplace.

It is interesting to note that Engelbart chose the architect as an analogy for how his computer-as-'clerk' system would work. The present-day architect has highly complex computer-aided design and manufacturing software at his or her disposal; through the digital environment they can instantly access procurement data, costings, global information satellites, fellow consultants and project management information. Architects can now use computers to closely model the life-cycle of their designs, planning the way the buildings will be maintained – and, indeed, dismantled at the end of their useful period. During large building contracts extensive information ecologies are built up, and these networks of data have to be navigated, mediated and constructed by computers very much in the way that Engelbart foresaw. Soon, no doubt, all the data and components connected to a building will be accessible by computer, and the use of these increasingly dextrous electronic tools may well result in a far more holistic and sustainable architecture.

1 'The Lemelson – MIT Prize Program: Douglas Engelbart', http://web.mit.edu/invent/www/inventorsA-H/englebart.html
2 Bootstrap Institute, 'Biographical Sketch: Douglas Engelbart', http://www.bootstrap.org/dce-bio.htm

Douglas Engelbart, 'Introduction', *Augmenting Human Intellect: A Conceptual Framework*, 1962

By 'augmenting human intellect' we mean increasing the capability of a man to approach a complex problem situation, to gain comprehension to suit his particular needs, and to derive solutions to problems. Increased capability in this respect is taken to mean a mixture of the following: more-rapid comprehension, better comprehension, the possibility of gaining a useful degree of comprehension in a situation that previously was too complex, speedier solutions, better solutions, and the possibility of finding solutions to problems that before seemed insoluble. And by 'complex situations' we include the professional problems of diplomats, executives, social scientists, life scientists, physical scientists, attorneys, designers – whether the problem situation exists for twenty minutes or twenty years. We do not speak of isolated clever tricks that help in particular situations. We refer to a way of life in an integrated domain where hunches, cut-and-try, intangibles, and the human 'feel for a situation' usefully co-exist with powerful concepts, streamlined terminology and notation, sophisticated methods, and high-powered electronic aids.

Man's population and gross product are increasing at a considerable rate, but the *complexity* of his problems grows still faster, and the *urgency* with which solutions must be found becomes steadily greater in response to the increased rate of activity and the increasingly global nature of that activity. Augmenting man's intellect, in the sense defined above, would warrant full pursuit by an enlightened society if there could be shown a reasonable approach and some plausible benefits.

This report covers the first phase of a program aimed at developing means to augment the human intellect. These 'means' can include many things – all of which appear to be but extensions of means developed and used in the past to help man apply his native sensory, mental, and motor capabilities – and we consider the whole system of a human and his augmentation means as a proper field of search for practical possibilities. It is a very important system to our society, and like most systems its performance can best be improved by considering the whole as a set of interacting components rather than by considering the components in isolation.

This kind of system approach to human intellectual effectiveness does not find a ready-made conceptual framework such as exists for established disciplines. Before a research program can be designed to pursue such an approach intelligently, so that practical benefits might be derived within a reasonable time while also producing results of long-range significance, a conceptual framework must be searched out – a framework that provides orientation as to the important factors of the system, the relationships among these factors, the types of change among the system factors that offer likely improvements in performance, and the sort of research goals and methodology that seem promising.[1]

In the first (search) phase of our program we have developed a conceptual framework that seems satisfactory for the current needs of designing a research phase. Section II contains the essence of this framework as derived from several different ways of looking at the system made up of a human and his intellect-augmentation means.

The process of developing this conceptual framework brought out a number of significant realizations: that the intellectual effectiveness exercised today by a given human has little likelihood of being intelligence limited – that there are dozens of disciplines in engineering, mathematics, and the social, life, and physical sciences that can contribute improvements to the system of intellect-augmentation means; that any one such improvement can be expected to trigger a chain of coordinating improvements; that until every one of these disciplines comes to a standstill and we have exhausted all the improvement possibilities we could glean from it, we can expect to continue to develop improvements in this human-intellect system; that there is no particular reason not to expect gains in personal intellectual effectiveness from a concerted system-oriented approach that compare to those made in personal geographic mobility since horseback and sailboat days. [...]

To give the reader an initial orientation about what sort of thing this computer-aided working system might be, we include below a short description of a possible system of this sort. This illustrative example is not to be considered a description of the actual system that will emerge from the program. It is given only to show the general direction of the work, and is clothed in fiction only to make it easier to visualize.

Let us consider an augmented architect at work. He sits at a working station that has a visual display screen some three feet on a side; this is his working surface, and is controlled by a computer (his 'clerk') with which he can communicate by means of a small keyboard and various other devices.

He is designing a building. He has already dreamed up several basic layouts and structural forms, and is trying them out on the screen. The surveying data for the layout he is working on now have already been entered, and he has just coaxed the clerk to show him a perspective view of the steep hillside building site with the roadway above, symbolic representations of the various trees that are to remain on the lot, and the service tie points for the different utilities. The view occupies the left two-thirds of the screen. With a 'pointer', he indicates two points of interest, moves his left hand rapidly over the keyboard, and the distance and elevation between the points indicated appear on the right-hand third of the screen.

Now he enters a reference line with his pointer, and the keyboard. Gradually the screen begins to show the work he is doing – a neat excavation appears in the hillside) revises itself slightly, and revises itself again. After a moment, the architect changes the scene on the screen to an overhead plan view of the site, still showing the excavation. A few minutes of study, and he enters on the keyboard a list of items, checking each one as it appears on the screen, to be studied later.

Ignoring the representation on the display, the architect next begins to enter a series of specifications and data – a six-inch slab floor, twelve-inch concrete walls eight-feet high within the excavation, and so on. When he has finished, the revised scene appears on the screen. A structure is taking shape. He examines it, adjusts it, pauses long enough to ask for handbook or catalogue information from the clerk at various points, and readjusts accordingly. He often recalls from the clerk his working lists of specifications and considerations to refer to them, modify them, or add to them. These lists grow into an evermore-detailed, interlinked structure, which represents the maturing thought behind the actual design.

Prescribing different planes here and there, curved surfaces occasionally, and moving the whole structure about five feet, he finally has the rough external form of the building balanced nicely with the setting and he is assured that this form is basically compatible with the materials to be used as well as with the function of the building.

Now he begins to enter detailed information about the interior. Here the capability of the clerk to show him any view he wants to examine (a slice of the interior, or how the structure would look from the roadway above) is important. He enters particular fixture designs, and examines them in a particular room. He checks to make sure that sun glare from the windows will not blind a driver on the roadway, and the clerk computes the information that one window will reflect strongly onto the roadway between 6 and 6.30 on midsummer mornings.

Next he begins a functional analysis. He has a list of the people who will occupy this building, and the daily sequences of their activities. The clerk allows him to follow each in turn, examining how doors swing, where special lighting might be needed. Finally he has the clerk combine all of these sequences of activity to indicate spots where traffic is heavy in the building, or where congestion might occur, and to determine what the severest drain on the utilities is likely to be.

All of this information (the building design and its associated 'thought structure') can be stored on a tape to represent the design manual for the building. Loading this tape into his own clerk, another architect, a builder, or the client can manoeuvre within this design manual to pursue whatever details or insights are of interest to him – and can append special notes that are integrated into the design manual for his own or someone's else's later benefit.

In such a future working relationship between human problem-solver and computer 'clerk', the capability of the computer for executing mathematical processes would be used whenever it was needed. However, the computer has many other capabilities for manipulating and displaying information that can be of significant benefit to the human in non-mathematical processes of planning, organizing, studying, etc. Every person who does his thinking with symbolized concepts (whether in the form of the English language, pictographs, formal logic, or mathematics) should be able to benefit significantly.

1 J L Kennedy, and G H Putt, 'Administration of Research in a Research Corporation', RAND Corporation Report P-847, 20 April 1956.

In December 1968, Douglas Engelbart demonstrated the online system, NLS, (top) which had been in development at the Augmentation Research Center at Stanford Research Institute (SRI) since 1962. This was the public debut of the computer mouse. Other innovations in NLS included hypertext, object addressing and dynamic file-linking, as well as shared-screen collaboration over a network with audio and video interface. Furniture maker Hermann Miller worked with SRI to mock-up office environments, desks, and the operating and display consoles (centre) to accommodate the online system (NLS). During the 1970s further hardware, software and interface developments at Xerox PARC and Apple Computer led to the first commercially available computers using the now familiar WIMP interface (Windows, Mouse, Pointer). Shown (below) is a screenshot from Apple's LISA personal computer c1983. This machine was the forerunner of the Apple Macintosh.

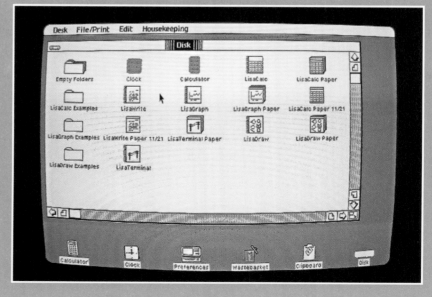

The Spatial Data Management System (SDMS),1977 (top), was developed at MIT by the ArchMac Group (founded by Nicholas Negroponte in 1967, see page 256). SDMS employed spatial mnemonics to orchestrate cyberspace. The SDMS interface displayed tools such as a calendar, calculator and telephone and was a key contribution to the evolving 'desktop' metaphor. ArchMac was one of several departments that merged to form the MIT Media Lab in 1985.

NASA Virtual Interface Environments (below). Since the 1980s, NASA has been developing techniques for the exploration of virtual space. Its systems include control and feedback mechanisms for voice input and ouput, position-tracking, stereo imaging and sound cueing all through head-mounted displays. Gesture tracking, tactile input and feedback are facilitated through data gloves. Such systems are used for interfacing with virtual environments, simulating space exploration, industrial process applications (telerobotics) and have spin-offs in many educational, scientific and entertainment areas.

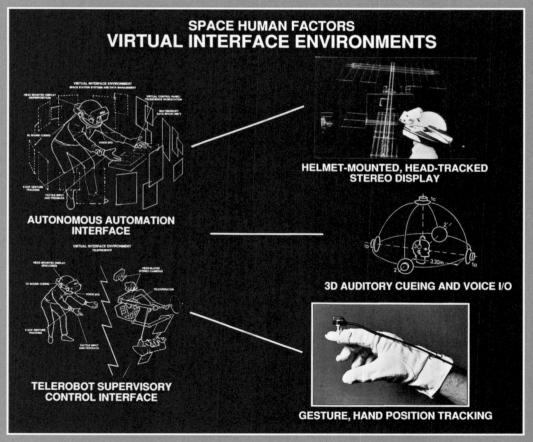

SPACE HUMAN FACTORS
VIRTUAL INTERFACE ENVIRONMENTS

AUTONOMOUS AUTOMATION INTERFACE

TELEROBOT SUPERVISORY CONTROL INTERFACE

HELMET-MOUNTED, HEAD-TRACKED STEREO DISPLAY

3D AUDITORY CUEING AND VOICE I/O

GESTURE, HAND POSITION TRACKING

NASA researcher wearing a full set of VR equipment (top left).

MIT Media Lab researcher Pattie Maes holds hands with a virtual reality dog (top right) seen on the screen behind her. Maes' video image is incorporated into a virtual room containing the animated dog which is programmed to sense its visitor and interact with life-like gestures.

MIT Wearable Computing Project. (bottom left and right). Information can be relayed to users via displays on the inside of glasses, earphones or by displays inside clothing. Data entry can be made via microphone, hand-held devices or keyboards sewn into clothing or by recognizing sign language or hand gestures made by the user. Miniature cameras in the glasses allow the computer to recognize people the wearer meets. The computer can direct the user with the aid of a navigational sensor. Internet connection is possible via radio links.

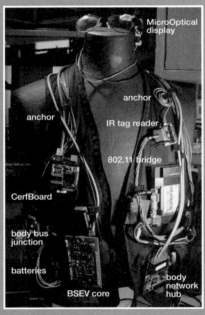

Marshall McLuhan_The Gadget Lover: Narcissus as Narcosis_1964

Herbert Marshall McLuhan (1911–80) defined a whole new way of talking about communications technology. His book *Understanding Media*, published in 1964, transformed the author from respectable academic to communications guru, and his polemic, rhetorical style has been highly influential.

Born in Canada, McLuhan gained his first degree at the University of Manitoba and his PhD from the University of Cambridge. He wrote a number of seminal publications such as *The Gutenburg Galaxy* (1962), *The Media is the Message* (1967, co-written with Quentin Fiore) and *War and Peace in the Global Village* (1968).

Understanding Media revolves around eight fundamental notions: the myth of Narcissus; media as an extension of man; the medium is the message; media as altering consciousness; hot media; cold media; the global village; and media as metaphor.

The Narcissus myth is used to illustrate how a technological extension of the self can create a state of 'numbness'. According to McLuhan, Narcissus, on admiring his own reflection, becomes 'a servomechanism of his own extended or repeated image.'[1] This numbness causes McLuhan to adopt an almost Stelarcian stance (p262): 'We have to numb our central nervous system when it is extended and exposed, or we will die.'[2] Stelarc also writes of anaesthetising the body so it will accept mechanical or digital prosthetics without pain. Developing this idea, McLuhan sees humanity as the pollinator of machines that respond to our giving them fecundity by fulfilling our wishes.

McLuhan's trademark phrase, which has now become common parlance around the world, is 'the medium is the message'. By this he means that the medium – whether television, radio and now computer – defines the scale and scope of the message, and its impact. Having established this extension to humanity's communication faculties McLuhan declares that it will expand and redefine the 'psychic and social complex'.[3] He then expounds upon the idea of 'hot' and 'cold' media: hot media, such as the radio, are low on audience participation and high on definition; while cool media, such as the telephone, are low in definition and high in audience participation.

Alongside 'the medium is the message', McLuhan's other famous catchphrase is 'the global village'. He shows how the onslaught of media has brought us all together in a world where, in a sense, everyone is always 'near by'. Paradoxically, this proximity also allows us to isolate our physical body. For some people this can be liberating, as it leaves gender, physicality and disability behind. However, it also creates isolation from the visceral fear of waging war. McLuhan ends his book with a discussion of media as a series of metaphors: 'seated at the typewriter, the poet, much in the manner of the jazz musician, has the experience of performance as composition'.[4]

Although McLuhan preferred to write under the broad heading of 'media', rather than addressing the issue of computers *per se*, his wide-ranging discussions embrace digital media, computers and cyberspace. McLuhan's achievement was to define critical concepts that can be used as benchmarks for the discussion of communications, and his ideas have often been successfully applied to the virtual world.

1 Marshall McLuhan, *Understanding Media: The Extensions of Man*, New York: Mentor, 1964, p43.
    2 Ibid, p47.
    3 Ibid, p4.
    4 Ibid, p260.

Marshall McLuhan, 'The Gadget Lover: Narcissus as Narcosis', *Understanding Media: The Extensions of Man*, 1964

The Greek myth of *Narcissus* is directly concerned with a fact of human experience, as the word Narcissus indicates. It is from the Greek word *narcosis*, or numbness. The youth Narcissus mistook his own reflection in the water for another person. This extension of himself by mirror numbed his perceptions until he became the servomechanism of his own extended or repeated image. The nymph Echo tried to win his love with fragments of his own speech, but in vain. He was numb. He had adapted to his extension of himself and had become a closed system.

Now the point of this myth is the fact that men at once become fascinated by any extension of themselves in any material other than themselves. There have been cynics who insisted that men fall deepest in love with women who give them back their own image. Be that as it may, the wisdom of the Narcissus myth does not convey any idea that Narcissus fell in love with anything he regarded as himself. Obviously he would have had very different feelings about the image had he known it was an extension or repetition of himself. It is, perhaps, indicative of the bias of our intensely technological and, therefore, narcotic culture that we have long interpreted the Narcissus story to mean that he fell in love with himself, that he imagined the reflection to be Narcissus!

Physiologically there are abundant reasons for an extension of ourselves involving us in a state of numbness. Medical researchers like Hans Selye and Adolphe Jonas hold that all extensions of ourselves, in sickness or in health, are attempts to maintain equilibrium. Any extension of ourselves they regard as 'autoamputation', and they find that the autoamputative power or strategy is resorted to by the body when the perceptual power cannot locate or avoid the cause of irritation. Our language has many expressions that indicate this self-amputation that is imposed by various pressures. We speak of 'wanting to jump out of my skin' or of 'going out of my mind', being 'driven batty' or 'flipping my lid'. And we often create artificial situations that rival the irritations and stresses of real life under controlled conditions of sport and play.

While it was no part of the intention of Jonas and Selye to provide an explanation of human invention and technology, they have given us a theory of disease (discomfort) that goes far to explain why man is impelled to extend various parts of his body by a kind of autoamputation. In the physical stress of superstimulation of various kinds, the central nervous system acts to protect itself by a strategy of amputation or isolation of the offending organ, sense, or function. Thus, the stimulus to new invention is the stress of acceleration of pace and increase of load. For example, in the case of the wheel as an extension of the foot, the pressure of new burdens resulting from the acceleration of exchange by written and monetary media was the immediate occasion of the extension or 'amputation' of this function from our bodies. The wheel as a counter-irritant to increased burdens, in turn, brings about a new intensity of action by its amplification of a separate or isolated function (the feet in rotation). Such amplification is bearable by the nervous system only through numbness or blocking of perception. This is the sense of the Narcissus myth. The young man's image is a self-amputation or extension induced by irritating pressures. As a counter-irritant, the image produces a generalized numbness or shock that declines recognition. Self-amputation forbids self-recognition.

The principle of self-amputation as an immediate relief of strain on the central nervous system applies very readily to the origin of the media of communication from speech to computer.

Physiologically, the central nervous system, that electric network that coordinates the various media of our senses, plays the chief role. Whatever threatens its function must be contained, localized, or cut off, even to the total removal of the offending organ. The function of the body, as a group of sustaining and protective organs for the central nervous system, is to act as buffers against sudden variations of stimulus in the physical and social environment. Sudden social failure or shame is a shock that some may 'take to heart' or that may cause muscular disturbance in general, signalling for the person to withdraw from the threatening situation.

Therapy, whether physical or social, is a counter-irritant that aids in that equilibrium of the physical organs which protect the central nervous system. Whereas pleasure is a counter-irritant (eg, sports, entertainment and alcohol), comfort is the removal of irritants. Both pleasure and comfort are strategies of equilibrium for the central nervous system.

With the arrival of electric technology, man extended, or set outside himself, a live model of the central nervous system itself. To the degree that this is so, it is a development that suggests a desperate and suicidal autoamputation, as if the central nervous system could no longer depend on the physical organs to be protective buffers against the slings and arrows of outrageous mechanism. It could well be that the successive mechanizations of the various physical organs since the invention of printing have made too violent and superstimulated a social experience for the central nervous system to endure.

In relation to that only too plausible cause of such development, we can return to the Narcissus theme. For if Narcissus is numbed by his self-amputated image, there is a very good reason for the numbness. There is a close parallel of response between the patterns of physical and psychic trauma or shock. A person suddenly deprived of loved ones and a person who drops a few feet unexpectedly will both register shock. Both the loss of family and a physical fall are extreme instances of amputations of the self. Shock induces a generalized numbness or an increased threshold to all types of perception. The victim seems immune to pain or sense.

Battle shock created by violent noise has been adapted for dental use in the device known as *audiac*. The patient puts on headphones and turns a dial raising the noise level to the point that he feels no pain from the drill. The selection of a single sense for intense stimulus, or of a *single* extended, isolated, or 'amputated' sense in technology, is in part the reason for the numbing effect that technology as such has on its makers and users. For the central nervous system rallies a response of general numbness to the challenge of specialized irritation.

The person who falls suddenly experiences immunity to all pain or sensory stimuli because the central nervous system has to be protected from any intense thrust of sensation. Only gradually does he regain normal sensitivity to sights and sounds, at which time he may begin to tremble and perspire and to react as he would have done if the central nervous system had been prepared in advance for the fall that occurred unexpectedly.

Depending on which sense or faculty is extended technologically, or 'autoamputated', the 'closure' or equilibrium-seeking among the other senses is fairly predictable. It is with the senses as it is with colour. Sensation is always 100 per cent, and a colour is always 100 per cent colour. But the ratio among the components in the sensation or the colour can differ infinitely. Yet if sound, for example, is intensified, touch and taste and sight are affected at once. The effect of radio on literate or visual man was to reawaken his tribal memories, and the effect of sound added to motion pictures was to diminish the role of mime, tactility, and kinesthesis. Similarly, when nomadic man turned to sedentary and specialist ways, the senses specialized too. The development of writing and the visual organization of life made possible the discovery of individualism, introspection and so on.

Any invention or technology is an extension or self-amputation of our physical bodies, and such extension also demands new ratios or new equilibriums among the other organs and extensions of the body. There is, for example, no way of refusing to comply with the new sense ratios or sense 'closure' evoked by the TV image. But the effect of the entry of the TV image will vary from culture to culture in accordance with the existing sense ratios in each culture. In audile-tactile Europe TV has intensified the visual sense, spurring them toward American styles of packaging and dressing. In America, the intensely visual culture, TV has opened the doors of audile-tactile perception to the non-visual world of spoken languages and food and the plastic arts. As an extension and expediter of the sense life, any medium at once affects the entire field of the senses, as the Psalmist explained long ago in the 115th Psalm:

> Their idols are silver and gold,
> The work of men's hands.
> They have mouths, but they speak not;
> Eyes they have, but they see not;
> They have ears, but they hear not;
> Noses have they, but they smell not;
> They have hands, but they handle not;
> Feet have they, but they walk not;
> Neither speak they through their throat.
> They that make them shall be like unto them;
> Yea, every one that trusteth in them.

The concept of 'idol' for the Hebrew Psalmist is much like that of Narcissus for the Greek mythmaker. And the Psalmist insists that the *beholding* of idols, or the use of technology, conforms men to them. 'They that make them shall be like unto them.' This is a simple fact of sense 'closure'. The poet Blake developed the Psalmist's ideas into an entire theory of communication and social change. It is in his long poem of

Jerusalem that he explains why men have become what they have beheld. What they have, says Blake, is 'the spectre of the Reasoning Power in Man' that has become fragmented and 'separated from Imagination and enclosing itself as in steel'. Blake, in a word, sees man as fragmented by his technologies. But he insists that these technologies are self-amputations of our own organs. When so amputated, each organ becomes a closed system of great new intensity that hurls man into 'martyrdoms and wars'. Moreover, Blake announces as his theme in *Jerusalem* the organs of perception:

> If Perceptive Organs vary, Objects of Perception seem to vary:
> If Perceptive Organs close, their Objects seem to close also.

To behold, use or perceive any extension of ourselves in technological form is necessarily to embrace it. To listen to radio or to read the printed page is to accept these extensions of ourselves into our personal system and to undergo the 'closure' or displacement of perception that follows automatically. It is this continuous embrace of our own technology in daily use that puts us in the Narcissus role of subliminal awareness and numbness in relation to these images of ourselves. By continuously embracing technologies, we relate ourselves to them as servomechanisms. That is why we must, to use them all, serve these objects, these extensions of ourselves, as gods or minor religions. An Indian is the servomechanism of his canoe, as the cowboy of his horse or the executive of his clock.

Physiologically, man in the normal use of technology (or his variously extended body) is perpetually modified by it and in turn finds ever new ways of modifying his technology. Man becomes, as it were, the sex organs of the machine world, as the bee of the plant world, enabling it to fecundate and to evolve ever new forms. The machine world reciprocates man's love by expediting his wishes and desires, namely, in providing him with wealth. One of the merits of motivation research has been the revelation of man's sex relation to the motorcar.

Socially, it is the accumulation of group pressures and irritations that prompt invention and innovation as counter-irritants. War and the fear of war have always been considered the main incentives to technological extension of our bodies. Indeed, Lewis Mumford, in his *The City in History*, considers the walled city itself an extension of our skins, as much as housing and clothing. More even than the preparation for war, the aftermath of invasion is a rich technological period; because the subject culture has to adjust all its sense ratios to accommodate the impact of the invading culture. It is from such intensive hybrid exchange and strife of ideas and forms that the greatest social energies are released, and from which arise the greatest technologies. Buckminster Fuller estimates that since 1910 the governments of the world have spent $3\frac{1}{2}$ trillion dollars on airplanes. That is 62 times the existing gold supply of the world.

The principle of numbness comes into play with electric technology, as with any other. We have to numb our central nervous system when it is extended and exposed, or we will die. Thus the age of anxiety and of electric media is also the age of the unconscious and of apathy. But it is strikingly the age of consciousness of the unconscious, in addition. With our central nervous system strategically numbed, the tasks of conscious awareness and order are transferred to the physical life of man, so that for the first time he has become aware of technology as an extension of his physical body. Apparently this could not have happened before the electric age gave us the means of instant, total field-awareness. With such awareness, the subliminal life, private and social, has been hoicked up into full view, with the result that we have 'social consciousness' presented to us as a cause of guilt-feelings. Existentialism offers a philosophy of structures, rather than categories, and of total social involvement instead of the bourgeois spirit of individual separateness or points of view. In the electric age we wear all mankind as our skin.

Gordon Pask_The Architectural Relevance of Cybernetics_1969

The renowned cybernetician Gordon Pask (1928–96) is best known for his development of what he called 'Conversation Theory'. The notion of the 'observer' and 'users' and their influence on determining the complex outcomes of cybernetic systems. Pask's views set him apart from the theories about artificial intelligence held by many of his contemporaries. As Paul Pangaro explained in his obituary of Pask:

> When Pask built his machines and theory, his philosophical view was at odds with artificial intelligence, which arose from the seeds of cybernetics but presumes that knowledge is a commodity to pluck from the environment and stick in a cubbyhole. Pask's learning environments, whether for entertainment or touch-typing or statistics, viewed the human as part of a resonance that looped from the human, through the environment or apparatus, back through the human and around again. For Pask, that is the interaction by which we understand each other when we speak or dance together. He specified how this works in detail in his many publications on Conversation Theory.[1]

Pask's work has been influential in the sphere of architecture: in his time he collaborated with and inspired a small number of far-sighted architects, and today his ideas about informational ecology are belatedly gaining ground. The following excerpt is taken from an article published in the late 1960s that was aimed particularly at the architectural fraternity. In it he recalls the attempts of Cedric Price and Joan Littlewood to create the Fun Palace (see p84), a massive 'kit of parts', capable of radical reconfiguration, supported by huge lattice steel columns and beams. The *New Scientist* summed up some of the concepts that Price was occupied with at that time.

> The activities designed for the site should be experimental. The place itself is expendable and changeable. The organization of space and objects occupying it should, on one hand, challenge the participant's mental and physical dexterity, and, on the other hand, allow for the flow of space and time in which passive and active pleasure is provoked.[2]

Such an approach to architecture fits in with the ideas put forward in Pask's article of a few years later. However, Pask wanted architecture to go much further in comprehending itself as one of the fundamental conversational systems in human culture. Today, over thirty years on, it is possible for us to see the insight of Pask's work. Architecture is slowly becoming able to appreciate the artificial and natural ecologies in which it sites itself. Architects are suggesting how artificial machine-driven ecologies can fit into and augment the natural systems around them, and are beginning to build spaces that can be constantly modified and adjusted.

The architect and cybernetician Ranulph Glanville, a former student of Pask's, has poetically described what an environment conditioned by Conversation Theory might be like:

Imagine you go out at night in the depths of the countryside. There is a clear dark sky, no light spillage from civilization, it is a cold damp night, and as your eyes become accustomed to the darkness you gradually see little points of light – the stars. These points of light shimmer (because of the dampness and coldness in the air)

If you listen carefully, you can imagine them singing to each other, forming little choirs that sing together.

You, of course, are another of these stars, and you also sing. As you move, the other stars come into focus and form constellations: there are clusters that cohere for the moment, and that then dissolve as you move on. The songs continue, you hear choirs of the constellations. The feeling is of overwhelming joy, beauty, wonder, oneness.[3]

Pask's ideas rejuvenated cybernetic theory and are highly relevant to anyone interested in environmental systems whether augmented by the computer or not. 'Response' and 'reflex' are the key to the next generation of spaces. Pask's life's work will be instrumental in attempting to understand them.

1 Paul Pangaro, 'Gordon Pask', obituary published in *The Guardian*, London, 16 April 1996.
2 *New Scientist*, 14 May 1964, p433.
3 Ranulph Glanville, 'Robin McKinnon-Wood and Gordon Pask: A lifelong Conversation', http://www.venus.co.uk/gordonpask, accessed 23 January 2001.

Gordon Pask, 'The Architectural Relevance of Cybernetics', *Architectural Design*, 1969

Evolutionary ideas in architecture

Systems, notably cities, grow and develop and, in general evolve. Clearly, this concept is contingent upon the functionalist/mutualist hypothesis (without which it is difficult to see in what sense the *system* itself *does* grow) though the dependency is often unstated. An immediate practical consequence of the evolutionary point of view is that architectural designs should have rules for evolution built into them if their growth is to be healthy rather than cancerous. In other words, a responsible architect must be concerned with evolutionary properties; he cannot merely stand back and observe evolution as something that happens to his structures. The evolutionary thesis is closely related to holism, type *c*, but it is a carefully specialized version of *c* as manifest in the work of the Japanese.

Symbolic environments in architecture

Many human activities are symbolic in character. Using visual, verbal or tactile symbols, man 'talks with' his surroundings. These consist in other men, information systems such as libraries, computers or works of art and also, of course, the structures around him.

Buildings have always been classified as works of art. The novel sub-theory is that structures may be *designed* (as well as intuited) to foster a productive and pleasurable dialogue. This way of thinking is most clearly manifest in connection with the literary art forms, notably surrealism which relies upon a variety (novelty) producing juxtaposition of releasers and supernormal stimuli (evoking inbuilt emotive responses) within a thematic matrix. At the architectural level, this type of design appears in the vegetable surrealism of some of the Art Nouveau. But it reaches maturity in Gaudí's work, especially the Parque Güell which, at a symbolic level, is one of the most cybernetic structures in existence. As you explore the piece, statements are made in terms of releasers, your exploration is guided by specially contrived feedback, and variety (surprise value) is introduced at appropriate points to make you explore.

It is interesting that Gaudí's work is often *contrasted* with functionalism. Systematically it is functionalism pure and simple, though it is aimed at satisfying *only* the symbolic and informational needs of man.[1]

The machinery of architectural production

Just as a functionally interpreted building constitutes a system, so also the construction of this building is a system. The new techniques developed in the last century and the general mechanization of production facilities led to sub-theories concerned with the achievement of forms (the most important centred around the Bauhaus) and these, in turn, restricted the forms that could be produced.

The widening brief

As a result of these essentially cybernetic, sub-theoretical developments, many architects *wanted* to design systems but, on the whole, they were *expected* to design buildings. To a large extent this is still (quite reasonably) true. All the same, there is a sense in which the brief given to an architect has widened during the last decades.

In part this is due to a spate of problems for which no conventional solution exists (structures connected with aerospace developments, industry, research, entertainment, the use of oceans, etc). Here, the architect is in much the same position as his Victorian predecessor when asked to build a railway station. In part, however, the restraints have been relaxed because of the greater prevalence of system-orientated thinking amongst clients and public sponsors. It is, nowadays, legitimate to enter the design process much earlier, even for a conventional project. For example, it is quite commonplace to design (or at least to plan) cities as a whole with provision for their evolution. A University *need* not be conceived as a set of buildings around a courtyard with living accommodation and lecture theatre. The educational system *might*, in certain circumstances, be spatially distributed rather than localized. In any case, architects are positively encouraged to anticipate trends such as the development of educational technology and to provide for their impact upon whatever structure is erected. By token of this the architect quite often comes into the picture at the time when a higher educational system is being contemplated, without commitment to whether or not it is called a university. The Fun Palace project, by Joan Littlewood and Cedric Price, was an early entry project of this type in the field of entertainment and it is not difficult to find examples in areas ranging from exhibition design to factory building.

The point I wish to establish is that nowadays there is a *demand* for system-orientated thinking whereas, in the past, there was only a more or less esoteric *desire* for it. Because of this demand, it is worthwhile collecting the isolated sub-theories together by forming a generalization from their common constituents. As we have already argued, the common constituents are the notions of control, communication and system. Hence the generalization is no more nor less than abstract cybernetics interpreted as an overall architectural theory.

It would be premature to suggest that the necessary interpretation and consolidation is complete. But a creditable start has been made by a number of people; citing only those with whom I have personal contact, Christopher Alexander, Nicholas Negroponte, many students and ex-students from the AA School of Architecture and from Newcastle.

Status of the new theory
In common with the pure architecture of the 1800s, cybernetics provides a metalanguage for critical discussion. But the cybernetic theory is more than an extension of 'pure' architecture. As we noted somewhat earlier, pure architecture was descriptive (a taxonomy of buildings and methods) and prescriptive (as in the preparation of plans) but it did little to predict or explain. In contrast, the cybernetic theory has an appreciable predictive power.[2] For example, urban development can be modelled as a self-organizing system (a formal statement of 'Evolutionary ideas in architecture') and in these terms it is possible to predict the extent to which the growth of a city will be chaotic or ordered by differentiation. Even if the necessary data for prediction is unavailable

we can, at least, pose and test rational hypotheses. Much the same comments apply to predictions in which time is not of primary importance; for instance, in predicting the influence of spatial and normative constraints upon the stability of a (functionally interpreted) structure.

The cybernetic theory can also claim some explanatory power insofar as it is possible to mimic certain aspects of architectural design by artificial intelligence computer programs[3] (provided, incidentally, that the program is able to learn *about* and *from* architects and by experimenting in the language of architects, ie by exploring plans, material specifications, condensed versions of clients' comments, etc.). Such programs are clearly of value in their own right. They are potential aids to design; acting as intelligent extensions of the tool-like programs mentioned at the outset. Further, they offer a means for integrating the constructional system (the 'machinery of production') with the ongoing design process since it is quite easy to embody the constraints of current technology in a special part of the simulation. However, I believe these programs are of far greater importance as evidencing out theoretical knowledge of what architecture is about. Insofar as the program can be written, the cybernetic is self-explanatory.

Speculations

It seems likely that rapid advances will be made in at least five areas guided by the cybernetic theory of architecture.

1 Various computer-assisted (or even computer-directed) design procedures will be developed into useful instruments.

2 Concepts in very different disciplines (notably social anthropology, psychology, sociology, ecology and economics) will be unified with the concepts of architecture to yield an adequately broad view of such entities as 'civilization', 'city' or 'educational system'.

3 There will be a proper and systematic formulation of the sense in which architecture acts as a social control (ie. the germ of an idea, mentioned under 'Holism', will be elaborated).

4 The high point of functionalism is the concept of a house as a 'machine for living in'. But the bias is towards a machine that acts as a tool serving the inhabitant. This notion will, I believe, be refined into the concept of an environment *with* which the inhabitant cooperates and *in* which he can externalize his mental processes, ie. mutualism will be emphasized as compared with mere functionalism. For example, the machine for living in will relieve the inhabitant of the need to store information in memory and the need to perform calculations as well as helping out with more obvious chores like garbage disposal and washing up dishes. Further, it will elicit his interest as well as simply answering his enquiries.

5 Gaudí (intentionally or not) achieved a dialogue between his environment and its inhabitants. He did so using physically static structures (the dynamic processes depending upon the movement of people or shifts in their attention). The dialogue can be refined and extended with the aid of modern techniques which allow us to weave the

same pattern in terms of a reactive environment. If, in addition, the environment is malleable and adaptive the results can be very potent indeed. I have experimented along these lines myself[4] but the work of Brodey and his group at the Environmental Ecology Laboratory is a project on a much more impressive scale. As a broad statement of what is going on, a computer controls the visual and tactile properties of environmental materials (which are available in sufficient diversity for most architectural purposes). These materials contain sensors, tactile or visual as the case may be, which return messages to the computer at several levels of generality. In the absence of a human inhabitant, the feedback leads to stabilization with respect to certain pre-programmed invariants (for example, that a body of material shall maintain mechanical stability and occupy a prescribed value), and to a search process in which the material actively looks for signs of a human being in contact with it. If there is a human being in the environment, the computer, material and all, engages him in dialogue and, within quite wide limits, is able to learn about and adapt to his behaviour pattern. There is thus one sense in which the reactive environment is a *controller* and another in which it is controlled *by* its inhabitants.

A simple cybernetic design paradigm
In the context of a reactive and adaptive environment, architectural design takes place in several interdependent stages.

i Specification of the purpose or goal of the system (with respect to the human inhabitants). It should be emphasized that the goal *may* be and nearly always *will* be underspecified, ie. the architect will no more know the purpose of the system than he *really* knows the purpose of a conventional house. His aim is to provide a set of constraints that allow for certain, presumably desirable, modes of evolution.

ii Choice of the basic environmental materials.

iii Selection of the invariants which are to be programmed into the system. Partly at this stage and partly in ii above, the architect determines what properties will be relevant in the man environment dialogue.

iv Specification of what the environment will learn about and how it will adapt.

v Choice of a plan for adaptation and development. In case the goal of the system is *underspecified* (as in i) the plan will chiefly consist in a number of evolutionary principles.

Of course, this paradigm applies to systems which adapt over rather short time intervals (minutes or hours). In contrast, the adaptation in a project such as the Fun Palace system took place over much longer time intervals (for instance, an 8-hourly cycle and a weekly cycle formed part of the proposal). Depending upon the time constraints and the degree of flexibility required, it is more or less convenient to use a computer (for example, the weekly cycle is more economically programmed by a flexible office procedure). But exactly the same principles are involved.

Urban planning usually extends over time, periods of years or decades and, as currently conceived, the plan is quite an inflexible specification. However, the argument just presented suggests that it need not be inflexible and that urban development could, perhaps with advantage, be governed by a process like that in the dialogue of a reactive environment (physical contact with the inhabitants giving place to an awareness of their preferences and predilections; the inflexible plan to the environmental computing machine). If so, the same design paradigm applies, since in all of the cases so far considered the primary decisions are systemic in character, ie. they amount to the delineation or the modification of a control program. This universality is typical of the cybernetic approach.

One final manoeuvre will indicate the flavour of a cybernetic theory. Let us turn the design paradigm in upon itself; let us apply it to the interaction between the designer and the system he designs, rather than the interaction between the system and the people who inhabit it. The glove fits, almost perfectly in the case when the designer uses a computer as his assistant. In other words, the relation 'controller/controlled entity' is preserved when these omnibus words are replaced either by 'designer/system being designed' or by 'systemic environment/inhabitants' or by 'urban plan/city'. But notice the trick, the designer is controlling the construction of control systems and consequently design is control *of* control, ie. the designer does much the same job as his system, *but* he operates at a higher level in the organizational hierarchy.

Further, the design goal is nearly always underspecified and the 'controller' is no longer the authoritarian apparatus which this purely technical name commonly brings to mind. In contrast the controller is an odd mixture of catalyst, crutch, memory and arbiter. These, I believe, are the dispositions a designer should bring to bear upon his work (when he professionally plays the part of a controller) and these are the qualities he should embed in the systems (control systems) which he designs.[5]

1 Clearly, in other respects, it would be uncomfortably prickly to live in.

2 The impact of cybernetics upon architecture is considerable just because the theory does have much more predictive power than pure architecture had. Cybernetics did relatively little to alter the shape of biochemistry for instance, because although these concepts are bound up with everything from enzyme organization to molecular biology, the discipline of biochemistry already had a *predictive* and *explanatory* theory of its own. I made the same point for engineering in an earlier footnote.

3 I have the work of Negroponte's group chiefly in mind, though there are other exemplars.

4 For example, the colloquy of mobiles project and the musicolour system, *A comment, a case history and a plan in Computer Art*, Jaisha Reichardt (ed).

5 The cybernetic notions mooted in this article, are discussed in *An approach to cybernetics*, Hutchinson, 1961 (paperback 1968) and, in a lighter vein, in 'My predictions for 1984' in *Prospect, The Schweppes Book of the New Generation*, Hutchinson, London, 1962.

Cedric Price_Generator Project_1976

The architect and visionary Cedric Price is not known for his swift acceptance of technology for technology's sake. His work concerns itself with the necessary materials and technologies that allow a building to do its job, rather than architectural pyrotechnics or formalist posturing. One of his maxims is that buildings should use 'appropriate technology'.

Cedric Price was born in 1934 and trained as an architect at Cambridge University and the Architectural Association in London. Since the early 1960s he has campaigned for the architectural profession to be more thoughtful about the way it uses technology, which he feels should provide a non-dictatorial use of space. Price sees buildings as catalysts or 'enabling' mechanisms, which facilitate and encourage social and spatial interaction. Perhaps more than any other architect he has forced his peers to consider time and duration as crucial to any building proposal.

In 1961 Price designed a 'Fun Palace' for the actress Joan Littlewood. Sadly unbuilt, the project has nevertheless been recognized as the forerunner – by fifteen years – of Piano and Rogers' Pompidou Centre in Paris. Arguably far more ambitious than its progeny, the Fun Palace explored the possibility of users creating different types of space at any point in the building, in response to their current desires.

By the late 1970s Price had conducted many built and unbuilt experiments in an attempt to create the types of benevolent space first proposed in the Fun Palace. For the Generator Project, designed in 1976 for a site in Florida, Price considered the computer as an appropriate tool. The Generator scheme represented a milestone: it was to be the first 'intelligent' building, a building that 'knew itself' and even 'dreamt' cybernetically. As Deyan Sudjic described it:

[Price] has been commissioned by the Gilman Paper Corporation (USA) to build a retreat for company guests or employees that really uses electronics to the full ... the idea is to provide an amenity which can be used for anything from a neutral meeting ground in which management and workforce can discuss policy away from the tension of the company's corporate hq, to a place for a visiting musician to spend an isolated weekend composing.

[He] has designed a grid of concrete foundation pads on which are laid out – with the help of a mobile crane, no less – a giant Lego-like kit of walls, screens, enclosures, gangways and screens, complete with water, air conditioning, power and communications services.[1]

Price enlisted John Frazer (see p246) and his colleagues as computer consultants on the Generator Project: each of the individual components would be 'fitted with a logic circuit and hooked up to a central computer'[2] to aid rapid changes of configuration. The Frazer team created an original series of algorithms and programs, and took the project a stage further. 'We were concerned that the building would not be changed enough by its users because they would not see the potential to do so', explains Frazer. '[We] consequently suggested that a characteristic of intelligence, and therefore of the Generator, was that it would register its own boredom, and make suggestions for its own reorganization.'[3] Frazer is unambivalent about the project's significance: 'Important new ideas emerged from the Generator Project. These included embedded intelligence and learning from experience during use, the isomorphism of processor configuration and model structure, and the question of consciousness ... [of intelligent buildings].'[4]

This important symbiosis, examined in Price's architectural thesis of 'enabling' and the use of the computer, sets a benchmark against which most contemporary 'intelligent' buildings (and their designers) can be measured.

1 Deyan Sudjic, 'Birth of the Intelligent Building', *Design*, January, 1981, p56.
2 Ibid.
3 John Frazer, *An Evolutionary Architecture*, London: Architectural Association, 1995, p41.
4 Ibid.

Instantaneous architectural response to a particular problem is too slow. Architecture must concern itself with the socially beneficial distortion of the environment. Like medicine it must move from the curative to the preventive. Architecture should have little to do with problem-solving – rather it should create desirable conditions and opportunities hitherto thought impossible.

With this intention the client asked me to investigate whether architecture could help in providing such conditions for the individual and the group from both inside and outside the company. The subsequent feasibility study proving positive, the Generator was born – an architectural complex with no previous title and no previous defined use, only a desired end effect.

Sited in Florida, the Generator's services and structure respond to the users' wishes with help from both cranage and computer.

[…]

A forest facility for between one and one thousand visitors, who may be management and labour of the client paper company, clients' friends, or any who are deemed to benefit from this responsive environment, sited, designed and serviced to enrich freedom of thought. In this scheme architecture is used as an aid to the extension of one's own interests. A series of structures, barriers, fittings and components respond to the appetite that in some cases, they themselves may generate.

A 'menu' of items caters for individual and group demands for space, control, containment and delight. The built form is primarily laminated, timber-framed structures with variable infills and cladding panels located on a regular grid of concrete and steel pads by means of wheeled cranage.

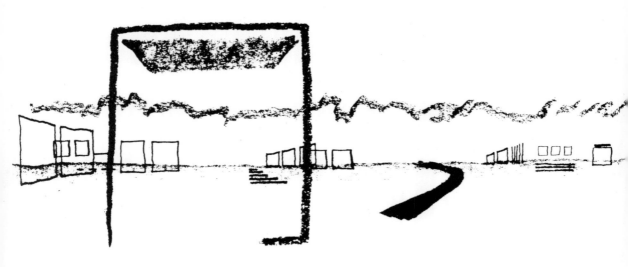

never look empty, never feel full.

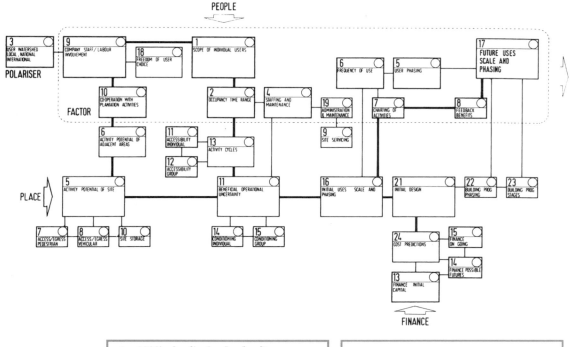

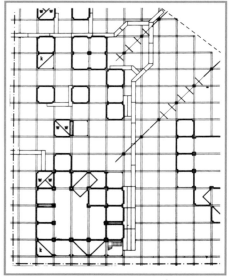

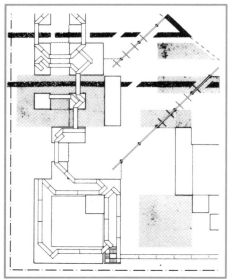

Initial Design Network
(top) with three starting
points – people 1,
place 5, and finance 13.

Example of a Menu (25):
details of south-west
zone – ground level
(left) and roof level with
walkways (right)

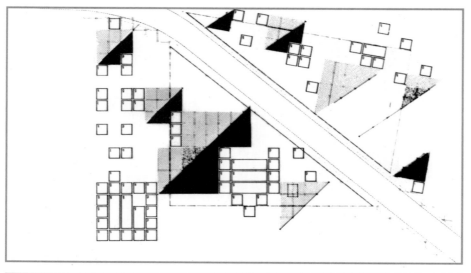

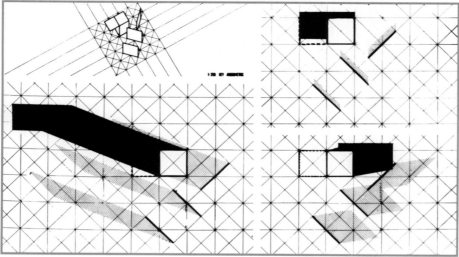

Grid layout and menu 23 (top) of external spaces showing single, double and triple cubed units.

Criteria for demarcation of an outside space defined by a combination of screens and cube faces:

1 The plan form of the spaces will be an isosceles triangle due to the geometry of both the screens and cubes.

2 One plane of the space will be defined by a number of screens. This plane will form the hypotenuse of the triangle.

3 The second plane of the triangle (length x) will be formed by the faces of a number of cubes (y) which lie in the plane but are not necessarily adjacent.

4 The third plane of the triangle may be formed in a similar manner to the second plane or may be implied by the combined effect of the hypotenuse and second plane.

5 The degree of enclosure of the space by the screens and cube faces is given by

$$\frac{x}{y} < 3$$

Shadow study of single unit-hinged wall and three screens: 06.00, 12.00, 20.00 June 22 (bottom)

Three typical cube
units and (bottom right)
screens and post.
Double and triple cubed
units have the capacity
for similar linkage and
infill.

Paul Virilio_The Aesthetics of Disappearance_1980

The Aesthetics of Disappearance is an important critical document for philosophers of technology, design professionals and cultural theorists. In it Paul Virilio demonstrates how subsequent waves of technology tend to become smaller, faster and more optically invisible. *The Aesthetics of Disappearance* was written before cyberspace, with its web-like tendrils, evolved into what it is today. However, Virilio anticipated the speeding up of our world, the jump-cutting of time, the relationship between real time and all its other manifestations, and the invisible ubiquity of digital data.

Virilio is Director of the École Speciale d'Architecture in Paris, and an editor of *Esprit, Cause, Commune* and *Critiques*. His books include *Pure War* (1985), *War and Cinema: The Logistics of Perception* (1989), *Bunker Archaeology* (1994), *The Art of the Motor* (1995) and *Open Sky* (1997).

Virilio believes that after Einstein everything has become relational; that static relationships have disappeared: everything depends on an interrelationship with something else. In *The Aesthetics of Disappearance* Virilio uses the life and antics of movie mogul Howard Hughes as an analogy for his ideas about disappearance, bodily stasis and control, and the invention of time:

Suppressing all uncertainty, Hughes could believe himself everywhere and nowhere, yesterday and tomorrow, since all points of reference to astronomical space or time were eliminated. At the foot of the bed where he was lying was, however, an artificial window, a movie screen. At the head there was a projector and alongside it, within reach, the controls that allowed him to project his films, always the same, eating indefinitely from the same plate.[1]

Virilio describes Hughes as a technological monk, a hermit who anticipated our technological future. Here, in Virilio's mind, Hughes becomes one of the first real hermetically imprisoned technologically enhanced human beings. The sort of human being anticipated by EM Forster in *The Machine Stops* (p28).

From these keen observations of technological disappearance Virilio has gone on to consider its effect on our environment, our cities and our architecture. In an interview with the architectural critic, curator and theorist Andreas Ruby he spoke of the impact that virtual space is set to have on architecture:

The space of the future would be both of real and of virtual nature. Architecture will 'take place', in the literal sense, in both domains: in real space (the materiality of architecture) and virtual space (the transmission of electromagnetic signs). The real space of the house will have to take into account the real time of the transmission.[2]

Scott Bukatman, in his book *Terminal Identity*, discusses Virilio's thinking:

The new urban space is direction-less – co-ordinates are literally valueless when all directions lead to more of the same. For Virilio, in an observation with real applicability to cyberspace, the city is now composed of 'a synthetic space-time' that simulates the lost geophysical urban spaces of human habitation and circulation. Urban monumentalism has thus become false and spectacular (in Debord's sense): the walls are no longer so solid, nor so impenetrable.[3]

Virilio's notion of disappearance in all aspects of culture has today become a widely accepted idea; and nowhere is Virilio more accurate than in the realm of cyberspace and digital technology.

1 Paul Virilio, *The Aesthetics of Disappearance*, New York: Semiotext(e), 1980, p26.

2 'Architecture in the Age of its Virtual Disappearance', in John Beckmann (ed.), *The Virtual Dimension: Architecture, Representation, and Crash Culture*, New York: Princeton, 1998.

3 Scott Bukatman, *Terminal Identity*, Durham, NC: Duke University Press, 1993, p126.

Technology introduces a phenomenon without precedent in the mediation of time, for if we've affirmed that time is only one reality, that of the instant, we might also say with Guyon, as the motor is being invented: 'The idea of time can be reduced to a point of view: duration is made of transitory instants just as a straight line is made of points without depth.'

Dimensions vanish in the reduction of straightness or of a straightaway, which would be only the speed of a geometric trajectory. The will to carry out whatever is possible, contained in diverse applications of the exact sciences, has led to a new atrophy of the instant, as essentially involving a before and an after. By introducing the subject into the hierarchy of speeds (lower, higher), by destabilizing the instant, a contingent phenomenon, the standards are abrogated; the diversifying of speed also abrogates the sensation of general duration, of continuous movement. Méliès understood early on that cinema is *not a seventh art but an art that combines all of the others*: drawing, painting, architecture, music, but also mechanical, electrical works, etc.

Cinema is the end in which the dominant philosophies and arts have come to confuse and lose themselves, a sort of primordial mixing of the human soul and the languages of the motor-soul. The chronology of the arts in history already demonstrates this decomposition: for example, at a concert the extreme emphasis on auditory attention annihilates any other body movement, revealing the basic connection between the musical instrument (a veritable sound motor with its cylinders, rhythms) and speed – properly the manna of every listener.

As Ribot writes in *The Psychology of Attention*: 'Without the motor elements perception is impossible…' And R. Philip establishes, for example, a 'measurement' of the listener's attention: 'Music modifies the respiratory and cardiac rhythm which is slowed down or speeded up', as in visual attention, if associated with an obligatory eye movement, it is also linked to an inevitable inhibition of bodily movements.

Shortly before his death Nero, back in Naples, stopped to admire a new musical instrument, a water organ invented, according to Vitruvius, by Ctesibius of Alexandria: it looked like an elongated buffet covered with tubes. Nero's bright idea, then, is to play the organ while confronting his enemies, thinking he will thereby win them over. Nero's pretension is not so unrealistic: at a concert, when the musical motor shuts off, not only is there a liberating violence of ovations and handclapping but also a thunderstorm of sneezing, coughing, scraping of feet – as if everyone suddenly reacquired possession of his own body. The very development of symphonic music ends up with the orchestra leader in the privileged position of *sole conductor*, but what he directs is not only the increasingly numerous musical troop but also the mass of auditors he's responsible for immobilizing in their chairs…to openly leave one's seat becomes here the most devastating of musical critiques!

Technician-culture has only extended this assumption of control by motor elements, steadily increasing our dependency on directional systems of accountability and control (speedometers, dashboards, remote tele-control). Initiating itineraries of direction, technician-culture applies to earth and nature (human nature) Bacon's formula: *Nothing is vaster than empty things...* creating finally emptiness and desert because only nothingness can be continuous, and therefore conductive.

Rather than trying for speed records in the vast celestial spaces, champions like Art Afrons declare that *the most exciting, exalting, dynamic task that exists consists in attempting intellectually, physically and technically the land speed record on our mother earth...a work of love,* he specifies, and the word does not seem unintended.

Likewise Malcolm Campbell, a former RAF pilot, sees sensations of flight as insipid and less intoxicating compared to those he tasted on land on board the various 'blue-birds'.

In fact, the passion for speed had seized him in early youth, writes Leo Villa, at the same time as the passion for those mysterious stories which always involved *hidden treasures waiting for the heroes able to unearth them.*

As an adult he was going to try to realize these several dreams.

Therefore the earth (ground-effect) seems paradoxically to remain the privileged partner of the seeker of absolute records, to whom nevertheless she exposes the dangers of natural obstacles, gravity, etc., the speed record coming as much from the search for new technical blends as from that of planed, smoothed surfaces. The vastness of space is no longer sought except as a means of putting into question the experience of discontinuity. 'Time and space seem infinite to us only when they don't exist', Roupnel suggested. The immediacy of terrestrial transport, modifying the relation to space, annihilates the relation to lived time and it's in this urgency that its dynamic exaltation consists. Paradoxically, it's the extreme mobility which creates the inertia of the moment, instantaneity which would create the instant! Finally the instant becomes like the illusory perception of a stability, clearly revealed by technical prostheses, such as is demonstrated for us by Einstein's example of passing trains: the feeling of the instant can only be given by coincidence (*epiteikos*), the moment when two trains seem immobile to travellers while they are really launched at top speed one beside the other. The notion of a time, which, according to Bachelard, would accommodate only the reality of the instant, could only be established on the basis of our remaining unconscious of our own speeds in a world entirely given over to the law of movement *and thereby the creator of the illusion of inertia.*

What creates the difference between the diverse intuitions of time is the position in space of the reasoning consciousness, a little like in Edgar Poe's allegory, *The Gold Bug,* where the seeker has to commit himself to numerous speculations on the cryptogramic significance of the message, before moving in any given direction.

This mobility of the synoptic trajectory, in modifying the subject's point-of-view, is going to allow him the discovery of what, somehow, was already visible. Beyond that one is led back ineluctably to the fascination of the shiny bug, which is initiatory in the sense that, as the perspective point on an horizon of speed, it reduces the rest of the world to nothing. Passing from the course to the finish line, technique has been applied to make of this modification of perspective the supreme goal that it's eager to reach. The motor creates an unprecedented movement toward what eludes everyone's view and understanding (the treasure), like a tale about unseen things, involving the kind of space and time of metaphysical entities deprived of all reality, that Gastineau wrote about in the nineteenth century.

The conquest of speed and the search for treasure blend together absolutely in the longings of Malcolm Campbell, while the heyday of utopian tales, in general, is that of far-off expeditions, of the Renaissance quest, of the Golden Fleece or the bellicose romanticism of the nineteenth century.

Reconciliation of nothingness and reality, the annihilation of time and space by high speeds substitutes the vastness of emptiness for that of the exoticism of travel, which was obvious for people like Heine who saw in this very annihilation the supreme goal of technique. A little later the maniacs of aerodynamics and land speed records articulate this also, considering as primordial the reaction of the milieu to the object's form-in-movement and vice-versa. Their purpose is to create time out of everything, a time that would no longer be one, where, as Breedlove writes, *one simply exists*, a time that would be on earth yet nowhere. In the science-fiction film *Close Encounters of the Third Kind*, extraterrestrials, accustomed to circulating in the immensity of intergalactic space, are enormously pleased to be travelling on a simple highway. Meanwhile the earthlings are enjoying hugely the paradox of this relation between pleasure and violation of limits, an exaltation which resembles closely enough that of the mountain climber who doesn't want so much to scale the peak as level off and flatten the mountain.

Chevallier notices it also: from Egyptian antiquity on we have geography, but also *chorography*, almost entirely neglected by the historian – a figure of the road-building surge of Empires, as distinct from the mere mapping out of its territory. In spite of the transportation revolution of the nineteenth century, our historical discourse has remained tied to a culture based on a common conception of space and time, while contemporaneously a new life style was being worked out, a cultural innovation consisting in a new reading of duration, if only in the plain example of the railroad, of its network schedules with their complex interconnections, unprecedented chorography that had to be made understandable for every traveller. There is no longer involved in this practice any rapport between a pretension to live one's own unique historical time and this manner of suddenly finding oneself in motion and in transit in railroad car compartments, that are also, for their user, compartments of space and time. The administration of transportation confirms Bachelard's observation: 'After Einstein's relativity, metaphysics had to retreat to local time, everything having to do with the external proof of unique duration as a clear principle or ordination of events was ruined...' Einstein's theory completed the destruction of a Pharaonic conception of signs as immobile bodies immutably arrayed against the passing of time, capable of resurging in History, or resuscitating in the beyond...a conception that explains clearly enough the cult of mausoleums as well as doctrinaire survivals in Marxist countries, attached to the idea of a unique historical duration.

That the totalitarian European regimes would be hostile to Einstein's theories was also to be expected, since time with them appears less given than locally invented, and it was equally to be expected that Einstein, in spite of himself, be drawn into the tragic confrontation with total war, which in 1939 became the war of time(s).

However, in this new kind of conflict, it is already no longer a matter of local times; the history of battles revealed de-localization as precipitation toward an ultimate metaphysical record, a final oblivion of matter and of our own presence in the world, beyond the barrier of sound and soon of light.

Gilles Deleuze and Félix Guattari_
A Thousand Plateaux: Capitalism and Schizophrenia_1980

A Thousand Plateaux: Capitalism and Schizophrenia is the philosophical bible of the cyber-evangelist. This book is possibly one of the most quoted philosophical texts in connection with the technological 'spacescape' that computers have created and augmented. Gilles Deleuze (1925–95) was formerly Professor of Philosophy at the University of Paris at Vincennes; his books include *Kant's Critical Philosophy: The Doctrine of Facilities, Cinema I: Image/Movement* and *Nietzsche and Philosophy*. Félix Guattari (1930–92), a practising psychoanalyst and life-long political activist, worked from the mid-1950s at La Borde, an experimental psychiatric clinic. As well as this book Deleuze and Guattari co-authored *Anti-Oedipus and Kafta: Toward a Minor Literature*.

This expansive book is not an easy read, and it makes few concessions to the lay reader. Brian Massumi, its English translator, sums up its contrariness:

This is a book that speaks of many things, of ticks and quilts and fuzzy subsets and noology and political economy. It is difficult to know how to approach it. What do you do with a book that dedicates an entire chapter to music and animal behaviour – and then claims that it isn't a chapter? That presents itself as a network of 'plateaus' that are precisely dated, but can be read in any order? That deploys a complex technical vocabulary drawn from a wide range of disciplines in the sciences, mathematics, and the humanities, but whose authors recommend that you read it as you would listen to a record?[1]

Since the onslaught of the new media, with its ubiquitousness, its metamorphic power and its virtual environments, architects and designers have been searching for new ways to envision architectural space. This demands a philosophical model that is inclusive, capable of re-articulating itself, forever changing, and able to posit a new idea of the sublime and deal with partialities of objects. Deleuze and Guattari do just this. For those interested in cyberspace, the book's philosophical approach can be distilled into a series of notions that expand our ways of thinking about space – in its many guises, and in all its interconnectedness. The architectural theorist and historian Robin Evans has described it thus: 'Deleuze and Guattari multiply new ways of thinking about relations in spatial terms: the rhizome instead of the tree; the Riemannian manifold; the thousand plateaus; assemblages and segmentarity.'[2]

During the 1990s much leading philosophical cyber-research was undertaken at Warwick University in the UK. The annual 'Virtual Futures' conferences at Warwick were greatly influenced by the ideas of Deleuze and Guattari, particularly those expressed in *A Thousand Plateaux*. These conferences did much to hone a philosophical discourse on the virtual arena, with *A Thousand Plateaux* at its core.

The book is at its most immediately understandable at the beginning, before its web of potentialities and possibilities is properly established. Here Deleuze and Guattari define the book's most crucial primary idea, that of the 'rhizome': the complex interrelationship of all things changing over time. The impact of this concept on the discipline of architecture has been astonishing, and references to it (often made erroneously) are nearly as ubiquitous as cyberspace itself. Deleuze and Guattari's *A Thousand Plateaux* comes closer than many other philosophical texts to describing our contemporary condition, and hence the impact of cyberspace.

1 Translator's foreword, in Gilles Deleuze and Félix Guattari, *A Thousand Plateaux: Capitalism and Schizophrenia*, London: The Athlone Press, 1988, p*ix*.
2 Robin Evans, *The Projective Cast: Architecture and its Three Geometries*, Cambridge, MA: MIT Press, 1995, p89.

A first type of book is the root-book. The tree is already the image of the world, or the root the image of the world-tree. This is the classical book, as noble, signifying, and subjective organic interiority (the strata of the book). The book imitates the world, as art imitates nature: by procedures specific to it that accomplish what nature cannot or can no longer do. The law of the book is the law of reflection, the one that becomes two. How could the law of the book reside in nature, when it is what presides over the very division between world and book, nature and art? One becomes two: whenever we encounter this formula, even stated strategically by Mao or understood in the most 'dialectical' way possible, what we have before us is the most classical and well reflected, oldest, and weariest kind of thought. Nature doesn't work that way: in nature, roots are taproots with a more multiple, lateral, and circular system of ramification, rather than a dichotomous one. Thought lags behind nature. Even the book as a natural reality is a taproot, with its pivotal spine and surrounding leaves. But the book as a spiritual reality, the Tree or Root as an image, endlessly develops the law of the one that becomes two, then of the two that become four … Binary logic is the spiritual reality of the root-tree. Even a discipline as 'advanced' as linguistics retains the root-tree as its fundamental image, and thus remains wedded to classical reflection (for example, Chomsky and his grammatical trees, which begin at a point S and proceed by dichotomy). [...]

The radicle-system, or fascicular root, is the second figure of the book, to which our modernity pays willing allegiance. This time, the principal root has aborted, or its tip has been destroyed; an immediate, indefinite multiplicity of secondary roots grafts onto it and undergoes a flourishing development. This time, natural reality is what aborts the principal root, but the root's unity subsists, as past or yet to come, as possible. We must ask if reflexive, spiritual reality does not compensate for this state of things by demanding an even more comprehensive secret unity, or a more extensive totality. Take William Burroughs's cut-up method: the folding of one text onto another, which constitutes multiple and even adventitious roots (like a cutting), implies a supplementary dimension to that of the texts under consideration. In this supplementary dimension of folding, unity continues its spiritual labour. That is why the most resolutely fragmented work can also be presented as the Total Work or Magnum Opus. Most modern methods for making series proliferate or a multiplicity grow are perfectly valid in one direction, for example, a linear direction, whereas a unity of totalization asserts itself even more firmly in another, circular or cyclic, dimension. Whenever a multiplicity is taken up in a structure, its growth is offset by a reduction in its laws of combination. The abortionists of unity are indeed angel makers, *doctores angelici*, because they affirm a properly angelic and superior unity. Joyce's words, accurately described as having 'multiple roots', shatter the linear unity of the word, even of language, only to posit a cyclic unity of the sentence, text, or knowledge. Nietzsche's aphorisms shatter the linear unity of knowledge, only to invoke the cyclic unity of the eternal return, present as the nonknown in thought. This is as much as to say that the fascicular system does not really break with dualism, with the complementarity between a subject and an object, a natural reality and a spiritual reality: unity is consistently thwarted and obstructed in the object, while a new type of unity triumphs in the subject. The world has lost its pivot; the subject can no longer even dichotomize, but accedes to a higher unity, of ambivalence or overdetermination, in an always supplementary dimension to that of its object. The world has become chaos, but the book remains the image of the world: radicle-chaosmos rather than root-cosmos. A strange mystification: a book all the more total for being fragmented. At any rate, what a vapid idea, the book as the image of the world. In truth, it is not enough to say, 'Long live the multiple', difficult as it is to raise that cry. No typographical, lexical, or even syntactical cleverness is enough to make it heard. The multiple *must be made*, not by always adding a higher dimension, but rather in the simplest of ways, by dint of sobriety, with the number of dimensions one already has available – always $n-1$ (the only way the one belongs to the multiple: always subtracted). Subtract the unique from the multiplicity to be constituted; write at $n-1$ dimensions. A system of this kind could be called a rhizome. A rhizome as subterranean stem is absolutely different from roots and radicles. Bulbs and tubers are rhizomes. Plants with roots or radicles may be rhizomorphic in other respects altogether: the question is whether plant life in its specificity is not entirely rhizomatic. Even some animals are, in their pack form. Rats are rhizomes. Burrows are too, in all of their functions of shelter, supply, movement, evasion, and breakout. The rhizome itself assumes very diverse forms, from ramified surface extension in all directions to concretion into bulbs and tubers. When rats swarm over each other. The rhizome includes the best and the worst: potato and couchgrass, or the weed. Animal and plant, couchgrass is crabgrass. We get the distinct feeling that we will convince no one unless we enumerate certain approximate characteristics of the rhizome.

1 and 2. Principles of connection and heterogeneity: any point of a rhizome can be connected to anything other, and must be. This is very different from the tree or root, which plots a point, fixes an order. The linguistic tree on the Chomsky model still begins at a point S and proceeds by dichotomy. On the contrary, not every trait in a rhizome is necessarily linked to a linguistic feature: semiotic chains of every nature are connected to very diverse modes of coding (biological, political, economic, etc.) that bring into play not only different regimes of signs but also states of things of differing status. *Collective assemblages of enunciation* function directly within *machinic assemblages*; it is not impossible to make a radical break between regimes of signs and their objects. Even when linguistics claims to confine itself to what is explicit and to make no presuppositions about language, it is still in the sphere of a discourse implying particular modes of assemblage and types of social power. Chomsky's grammaticality, the categorical S symbol that dominates every sentence, is more fundamentally a marker of power than a syntactic marker: you will construct grammatically correct sentences, you will divide each statement into a noun phrase and a verb phrase (first dichotomy...). Our criticism of these linguistic models is not that

they are too abstract but, on the contrary, that they are not abstract enough, that they do not reach the *abstract machine* that connects a language to the semantic and pragmatic contents of statements, to collective assemblages of enunciation, to a whole micropolitics of the social field. A rhizome ceaselessly establishes connections between semiotic chains, organizations of power, and circumstances relative to the arts, sciences, and social struggles. A semiotic chain is like a tuber agglomerating very diverse acts, not only linguistic, but also perceptive, mimetic, gestural, and cognitive: there is no language in itself, nor are there any linguistic universals, only a throng of dialects, patois, slangs, and specialized languages. There is no ideal speaker-listener, any more than there is a homogeneous linguistic community. [...]

3. Principle of multiplicity: it is only when the multiple is effectively treated as a substantive, 'multiplicity', that it ceases to have any relation to the One as subject or object, natural or spiritual reality, image and world. Multiplicities are rhizomatic, and expose arborescent pseudomultiplicities for what they are. There is no unity to serve as a pivot in the object, or to divide in the subject. There is not even the unity to abort in the object or 'return' in the subject. A multiplicity has neither subject nor object, only determinations, magnitudes, and dimensions that cannot increase in number without the multiplicity changing in nature (the laws of combination therefore increase in number as the multiplicity grows). Puppet strings, as a rhizome or multiplicity, are tied not to the supposed will of an artist or puppeteer but to a multiplicity of nerve fibres, which form another puppet in other dimensions connected to the first: 'Call the strings or rods that move the puppet the weave. It might be objected that *its multiplicity* resides in the person of the actor, who projects it into the text. Granted; but the actor's nerve fibres in turn form a weave. And they fall through the grey matter, the grid, into the undifferentiated ... The interplay approximates the pure activity of weavers attributed in myth to the Fates or Norns.' An assemblage is precisely this increase in the dimensions of a multiplicity that necessarily changes in nature as it expands its connections. There are no points or positions in a rhizome, such as those found in a structure, tree, or root. There are only lines. When Glenn Gould speeds up the performance of a piece, he is not just displaying virtuosity, he is transforming the musical points into lines, he is making the whole piece proliferate. The number is no longer a universal concept measuring elements according to their emplacement in a given dimension, but has itself become a multiplicity that varies according to the dimensions considered (the primacy of the domain over a complex of numbers attached to that domain). We do not have units (*unités*) of measure, only multiplicities or varieties of measurement. The notion of unity (*unité*) appears only when there is a power takeover in the multiplicity by the signifier or a corresponding subjectification proceeding. This is the case for a pivot-unity forming the basis for a set of biunivocal relationships between objective elements or points, or for the One that divides following the law of a binary logic of differentiation in the subject. Unity always operates in an empty dimension supplementary to that of the system considered (overcoding).

The point is that a rhizome or multiplicity never allows itself to be overcoded, never has available a supplementary dimension over and above its number of lines, that is, over and above the multiplicity of numbers attached to those lines. All multiplicities are flat, in the sense that they fill or occupy all of their dimensions: we will therefore speak of a plane of consistency of multiplicities, even though the dimensions of this 'plane' increase with the number of connections that are made on it. Multiplicities are defined by the outside: by the abstract line, the line of flight or deterritorialization according to which they change in nature and connect with other multiplicities. The *plane of consistency* (grid) is the outside of all multiplicities. The line of flight marks: the reality of a finite number of dimensions that the multiplicity effectively fills; the impossibility of a supplementary dimension, unless the multiplicity is transformed by the line of flight; the possibility and necessity of flattening all of the multiplicities on a single plane of consistency or exteriority, regardless of their number of dimensions. The ideal for a book would be to lay everything out on a plane of exteriority of this kind, on a single page, the same sheet: lived events, historical determinations, concepts, individuals, groups, social formations. Kleist invented a writing of this type, a broken chain of affects and variable speeds, with accelerations and transformations, always in a relation with the outside. Open rings. His texts, therefore, are opposed in every way to the classical or romantic book constituted by the interiority of a substance or subject. The war machine-book against the State apparatus-book. *Flat multiplicities of* n *dimensions* are asignifying and asubjective. They are designated by indefinite articles, or rather by partitives (*some* couchgrass, *some* of a rhizome…).

4. Principle of asignifying rupture: against the oversignifying breaks separating structures or cutting across a single structure. A rhizome may be broken, shattered at a given spot, but it will start up again on one of its old lines, or on new lines. You can never get rid of ants because they form an animal rhizome that can rebound time and again after most of it has been destroyed. Every rhizome contains lines of segmentarity according to which it is stratified, territorialized, organized, signified, attributed, etc., as well as lines of deterritorialization down which it constantly flees. There is a rupture in the rhizome whenever segmentary lines explode into a line of flight, but the line of flight is part of the rhizome. These lines always tie back to one another. That is why one can never posit a dualism or a dichotomy, even in the rudimentary form of the good and the bad. You may make a rupture, draw a line of flight, yet there is still a danger that you will re-encounter organizations that restratify everything, formations that restore power to a signifier, attributions that reconstitute a subject – anything you like, from Oedipal resurgences to fascist concretions. Groups and individuals contain microfascisms just waiting to crystallize. Yes, couchgrass is also a rhizome. Good and bad are only the products of an active and temporary selection, which must be renewed.

William Gibson_Neuromancer_1984

William Gibson is one of the best known writers working in the
science-fiction genre. His novel *Neuromancer* is one of the most
widely quoted pieces of cyberspace literature – a bible to scientists
and science-fiction readers alike. Gibson's other books include *Count
Zero, Mona Lisa Overdrive, Burning Chrome, Idoru, All Tomorrow's
Parties* and, with Bruce Sterling, *The Difference Engine* (see p132).

In the early 1980s Gibson became infatuated with the space that
could be perceived in simple arcade video games – a weird space that
wasn't real, yet which had some spatial properties. He coined a term –
'cyberspace' – and a new era was born. Bruce Sterling summed up the
Zeitgeist in the introduction to the 1986 anthology *Mirrorshades*;
referring to the age-old gap between the two cultures of art and
science, he pointed out that:

... the gap is crumbling in unexpected fashion. Technical culture
has gotten out of hand. The advances of the sciences are so deeply
radical, so disturbing, so upsetting and revolutionary that they can
no longer be contained. They are surging into culture at large; they
are invasive; they are everywhere. The traditional power structures,
the traditional institutions, have lost control of the pace of change.[1]

This is the territory of the 'cyberpunk' novel, a genre which
William Gibson has played a crucial part in defining.

Neuromancer, paradoxically, was written on an old mechanical
typewriter whilst listening to Bruce Springsteen. It is the first novel in a
trilogy set in a huge North American urban sprawl of the near future. Its
characters are micro-surgically reworked, disembodied intelligences;
artificial intelligences; urban misfits; dead reconstructions of persons
previously alive; or sometimes mixtures of these categories.

Cyberspace is the all-encompassing backdrop to Gibson's story.
Its unlikely hero is Case, a cyberspace addict. Gibson writes:

A year here [in a Japanese neurosurgery clinic] and he still
dreamed of cyberspace, hope fading nightly. All the speed he took,
all the turns he'd taken and the corners he'd cut in Night City, and
still he'd see the matrix in his sleep, bright lattices of logic unfolding

across the colourless void ... He'd cry for it, cry in his sleep ... his hands clawed into the bedslab, temperfoam bunched between his fingers, trying to reach the console that wasn't there.[2]

If Gibson presents a more orthogonal cyberspace than that we know today, he guesses most of its internal phenomenology: its jump-cutting of space, the ascalar (self-sameness over many scales), almost fractal ordering, its gates and portals, and its ability to conjure up all manner of magical resurrections of people, space and information.

The novel's narrative, like the spaces it depicts, is jump-cut. It is part-cowboy, part-New York crime *noir*. Everywhere its characters look, computational technology has warped their relationships to space, to time and to each other. Imitations, copies of imitations and surgical modification form a cosmology more akin to the spaces of shamanistic cultures than the technologized First World. Highly influential, *Neuromancer* has so affected the technology debate that one is not always sure what preceded what. Is fact stranger than fiction, or is fact following fiction?

1 Bruce Sterling (ed), *Mirrorshades*, London: Paladin (Flamingo), 1986, p10.
2 William Gibson, *Neuromancer*, London: Victor Gollancz, 1984, p11.

'The matrix has its roots in primitive arcade games', said the voice-over, 'in early graphics programs and military experimentation with cranial jacks.' On the Sony, a two-dimensional space war faded behind a forest of mathematically generated ferns, demonstrating the spacial possibilities of logarithmic spirals; cold blue military footage burned through, lab animals wired into test systems, helmets feeding into fire control circuits of tanks and war planes. 'Cyberspace. A consensual hallucination experienced daily by billions of legitimate operators, in every nation, by children being taught mathematical concepts ... A graphic representation of data abstracted from the banks of every computer in the human system. Unthinkable complexity. Lines of light ranged in the nonspace of the mind, clusters and constellations of data. Like city lights, receding ...'

'What's that?' Molly asked, as he flipped the channel selector.

'Kid's show.' A discontinuous flood of images as the selector cycled. 'Off', he said to the Hosaka.

'You want to try now, Case?'

Wednesday. Eight days from waking in Cheap Hotel with Molly beside him. 'You want me to go out, Case? Maybe easier for you, alone ...'. He shook his head.

'No. Stay, doesn't matter.' He settled the black terry sweatband across his forehead, careful not to disturb the flat Sendai dermatrodes. He stared at the deck on his lap, not really seeing it, seeing instead the shop window on Ninsei, the chromed shuriken burning with reflected neon. He glanced up; on the wall, just above the Sony, he'd hung her gift, tacking it there with a yellow-headed drawing pin through the hole at its centre.

He closed his eyes.

Round the ridged face of the power stud.

And in the bloodlit dark behind his eyes, silver phosphenes boiling in from the edge of space, hypnagogic images jerking past like film compiled from random frames. Symbols, figures, faces, a blurred, fragmented mandala of visual information.

Please, he prayed, *now* –

A gray disk, the colour of Chiba sky.

Now –

Disk beginning to rotate, faster, becoming a sphere of paler grey. Expanding –

And flowed, flowered for him, fluid neon origami trick, the unfolding of his distanceless home, his country, transparent 3D chessboard extending to infinity. Inner eye opening to the stepped scarlet pyramid of the Eastern Seaboard Fission Authority burning beyond the green cubes of Mitsubishi Bank of America, and high and very far away he saw the spiral arms of military systems, forever beyond his reach.

And somewhere he was laughing, in a white-painted loft, distant fingers caressing the deck, tears of release streaking his face.

Molly was gone when he took the trodes off, and the loft was dark. He checked the time. He'd been in cyberspace for five hours. He carried the Ono-Sendai to one of the new worktables and collapsed across the bedslab, pulling Molly's black silk sleeping bag over his head.

The security package taped to the steel firedoor bleeped twice. 'Entry requested', it said. 'Subject is cleared per my program.'

'So open it.' Case pulled the silk from his face and sat up as the door opened, expecting to see Molly or Armitage.

'Christ', said a hoarse voice, 'I know that bitch can see in the dark ...'. A squat figure stepped in and closed the door. 'Turn the lights on, okay?' Case scrambled off the slab and found the old-fashioned switch.

'I'm the Finn', said the Finn, and made a warning face at Case.

'Case.'

'Pleased to meecha, I'm sure. I'm doing some hardware for your boss, it looks like.' The Finn fished a pack of Partagas from a pocket and lit one. The smell of Cuban tobacco filled the room. He crossed to the worktable and glanced at the Ono-Sendai. 'Looks stock. Soon fix that. But here's your problem, kid.' He took a filthy manila envelope from inside his jacket, flicked ash on the floor, and extracted a featureless black rectangle from the envelope. 'Goddamn factory prototypes', he said, tossing the thing down on the table. 'Cast 'em into a block of polycarbon, can't get in with a laser without frying the works. Booby-trapped for x-ray, ultrascan, God knows what else. We'll get in, but there's no rest for the wicked, right?' He folded the envelope with great care and tucked it away in an inside pocket.

'What is it?'

'It's a flipflop switch, basically. Wire it into your Sendai here, you can access live or recorded simstim without having to jack out of the matrix.'

'What for?'

'I haven't got a clue. Know I'm fitting Moll for a broadcast rig, though, so it's probably her sensorium you'll access.' The Finn scratched his chin. 'So now you get to find out just how tight those jeans really are, huh?'

Case sat in the loft with the dermatrodes strapped across his forehead, watching motes dance in the diluted sunlight that filtered through the grid overhead. A countdown was in progress in one corner of the monitor screen.

Cowboys didn't get into simstim, he thought, because it was basically a meat toy. He knew that the trodes he used and the little plastic tiara dangling from a simstim deck were basically the same, and that the cyberspace matrix was actually a drastic simplification of the human sensorium, at least in terms of presentation, but simstim itself struck him as a gratuitous multiplication of flesh input. The commercial stuff was edited, of course, so that if Tally Isham got a headache in the course of a segment, you didn't feel it.

The screen bleeped a two-second warning.

The new switch was patched into his Sendai with a thin ribbon of fibreoptics.

And one and two and –

Cyberspace slid into existence from the cardinal points. Smooth, he thought, but not smooth enough. Have to work on it ...

Then he keyed the new switch.

The abrupt jolt into other flesh. Matrix gone, a wave of sound and colour … She was moving through a crowded street, past stalls vending discount software, prices feltpenned on sheets of plastic, fragments of music from countless speakers. Smells of urine, free monomers, perfume, patties of frying krill. For a few frightened seconds he fought helplessly to control her body. Then he willed himself into passivity, became the passenger behind her eyes.

The glasses didn't seem to cut down the sunlight at all. He wondered if the built-in amps compensated automatically. Blue alphanumerics winked the time, low in her left peripheral field. Showing off, he thought.

Her body language was disorienting, her style foreign. She seemed continually on the verge of colliding with someone, but people melted out of her way, stepped sideways, made room.

'How you doing, Case?' He heard the words and felt her form them. She slid a hand into her jacket, a fingertip circling a nipple under warm silk. The sensation made him catch his breath. She laughed. But the link was one-way. He had no way to reply.

Two blocks later, she was threading the outskirts of Memory Lane. Case kept trying to jerk her eyes toward landmarks he would have used to find his way. He began to find the passivity of the situation irritating.

The transition to cyberspace, when he hit the switch, was instantaneous. He punched himself down a wall of primitive ice belonging to the New York Public Library, automatically counting potential windows. Keying back into her sensorium, into the sinuous flow of muscle, senses sharp and bright.

He found himself wondering about the mind he shared these sensations with. What did he know about her? That she was another professional; that she said her being, like his, was the thing she did to make a living. He knew the way she'd moved against him, earlier, when she woke, their mutual grunt of unity when he'd entered her, and that she liked her coffee black, afterward…

Her destination was one of the dubious software rental complexes that lined Memory Lane. There was a stillness, a hush. Booths lined a central hall. The clientele were young, few of them out of their teens. They all seemed to have carbon sockets planted behind the left ear, but she didn't focus on them. The counters that fronted the booths displayed hundreds of slivers of microsoft, angular fragments of coloured silicon mounted under oblong transparent bubbles on squares of white cardboard. Molly went to the seventh booth along the south wall. Behind the counter a boy with a shaven head stared vacantly into space, a dozen spikes of microsoft protruding from the socket behind his ear.

'Larry, you in, man?' She positioned herself in front of him. The boy's eyes focused. He sat up in his chair and pried a bright magenta splinter from his socket with a dirty thumbnail.

'Hey, Larry.'

'Molly.' He nodded.

'I have some work for some of your friends, Larry.'

Larry took a flat plastic case from the pocket of his red sportshirt and flicked it open, slotting the microsoft beside a dozen others. His hand hovered, selected a glossy black chip that was slightly longer than the rest, and inserted it smoothly into his head. His eyes narrowed.

'Molly's got a rider', he said, 'and Larry doesn't like that.'

'Hey', she said, 'I didn't know you were so ... sensitive. I'm impressed. Costs a lot, to get that sensitive.'

'I know you, lady?' The blank look returned. 'You looking to buy some softs?'

Donna Haraway_A Cyborg Manifesto_ 1985

Donna Haraway's seminal essay 'Cyborg Manifesto' has done much to broaden the debate about the effects of high-level technology on politics and gender. Haraway is a feminist cultural critic and the author of *Simians, Cyborgs and Women: The Reinvention of Nature*, which includes this essay as one of its chapters.[1]

A cyborg is a mixture of machine and organism; it is simultaneously animate and inanimate. Haraway's essay embraces the symbol and reality of the cyborg as a way of brushing aside the old binary ontologies of, for example, male/female, white/black, animal/machine and heterosexual/homosexual. She argues that in each of these oppositions feminists have traditionally sought to privilege the underdog, and therefore have been compelled to reinforce the existing system.

By contrast, Haraway's late twentieth-century cyborg is 'committed to partiality, irony, intimacy and perversity. It is oppositional, utopian, and completely without innocence'.[2] It has no conception of human mythology with its pre-programmed gender divides and division of labour:

Unlike the hopes of Frankenstein's monster, the cyborg does not expect its father to save it through a restoration of the garden; that is through the fabrication of a heterosexual mate, through its completion in a finished whole, a city and cosmos. The cyborg does not dream of community on the model of the organic family, this time without the oedipal project. The cyborg would not recognize the Garden of Eden; it is not made of mud and cannot dream of returning to dust.[3]

Setting a social, technological and political context to her argument Haraway posits the three 'crucial boundary breakdowns' that lead to her branch of socialist feminism. Firstly, she demonstrates that the distinction between the human and the animal has been 'thoroughly breached', a point amply illustrated by current evolutionary theory, transgeneticism and biotechnology. Secondly, she states that the boundaries between the organism and the machine have been eroded, as also illustrated by the writing of Kevin Kelly (see p216) and the pioneers of artificial life and artificial intelligence. Thirdly, she points out that the physical is becoming non-physical – a development memorably described in Paul Virilio's *Aesthetics of Disappearance* (see p90). The invisibility of much advanced technology, and its easy transmission, contributes to a ubiquity of cyborgian connectivity. As Haraway says, 'People are nowhere near so fluid, being both material and opaque. Cyborgs are ether, quintessence.'[4]

The cultural critic Mark Dery (see p274) has summarized Haraway's views:

... cyberculture by its very nature challenges these dualisms. Technology's trespasses across the once-forbidden zone between the natural and the artificial, the organic and the inorganic render much of what we know – or thought we knew – provisional. The philosophical implications of these and other technical developments, she argues, is that the conceptual cornerstones of the Western world view – the network of meanings – 'structuring the Western self – are fraught with cracks'.[5]

This piece has had a massive effect on gender politics as well as cyberspatial cultural theory. It is one of the very few works in this genre that adequately expresses a mature political thesis and a thoughtful feminist view of this technology.

1 The essay originally appeared in 1985 in the *Socialist Review*, entitled 'Cyborg Manifesto: Science, technology and socialist-feminism in the late 1980s'.
2 'Cyborg Manifesto', in Donna Haraway, *Simians, Cyborgs and Women: The Reinvention of Nature*, New York: Routledge, 1991.
3 Ibid.
4 Ibid.
5 Mark Dery, *Escape Velocity*, London: Hodder and Stoughton, 1996, p244.

Donna Haraway, 'A Cyborg Manifesto', from 'Manifesto for Cyborgs: Science, Technology, and Socialist Feminism in the 1980s', *Socialist Review*, **1985**

In this attempt at an epistemological and political position, I would like to sketch a picture of possible unity, a picture indebted to socialist and feminist principles of design. The frame for my sketch is set by the extent and importance of rearrangements in worldwide social relations tied to science and technology. I argue for a politics rooted in claims about fundamental changes in the nature of class, race and gender in an emerging system of world order analogous in its novelty and scope to that created by industrial capitalism; we are living through a movement from an organic, industrial society to a polymorphous, information system – from all work to all play, a deadly game. Simultaneously material and ideological, the dichotomies may be expressed in the following chart of transitions from the comfortable old hierarchical dominations to the scary new networks I have called the informatics of domination:

Representation	Simulation
Bourgeois novel, realism	Science-fiction, postmodernism
Organism	Biotic component
Depth, integrity	Surface, boundary
Heat	Noise
Biology as clinical practice	Biology as inscription
Physiology	Communications engineering
Small group	Subsystem
Perfection	Optimization
Eugenics	Population control
Decadence, *Magic Mountain*	Obsolescence, *Future Shock*
Hygiene	Stress management
Microbiology, tuberculosis	Immunology, AIDS
Organic division of labour	Ergonomics/cybernetics of labour
Functional specialization	Modular construction
Reproduction	Replication
Organic sex role specialization	Optimal genetic strategies
Biological determinism	Evolutionary inertia, constraints
Community ecology	Ecosystem
Racial chain of being	Neo-imperialism, United Nations humanism
Scientific management in home/factory	Global factory/electronic cottage
Family/Market/Factory	Women in the integrated circuit
Family wage	Comparable worth
Public/private	Cyborg citizenship
Nature/culture	Fields of difference
Cooperation	Communications enhancement
Freud	Lacan
Sex	Genetic engineering
Labour	Robotics
Mind	Artificial Intelligence
Second World War	Star Wars
White capitalist patriarchy	Informatics of domination

This list suggests several interesting things.[1] First, the objects on the right-hand side cannot be coded as 'natural', a realization that subverts naturalistic coding for the left-hand side as well. We cannot go back ideologically or materially. It's not just that 'god' is dead; so is the 'goddess'. Or both are revivified in the worlds charged with microelectronic and biotechnological politics. In relation to objects like biotic components, one must think not in terms of essential properties, but in terms of design, boundary constraints, rates of flows, systems logics, costs of lowering constraints. Sexual reproduction is one kind of reproductive strategy among many, with costs and benefits as a function of the system environment. Ideologies of sexual reproduction can no longer reasonably call on notions of sex and sex role as organic aspects in natural objects like organisms and families. Such reasoning will be unmasked as irrational, and ironically corporate executives reading *Playboy* and anti-porn radical feminists will make strange bedfellows in jointly unmasking the irrationalism.

Likewise for race, ideologies about human diversity have to be formulated in terms of frequencies of parameters, like blood group or intelligence scores. It is 'irrational' to invoke concepts like primitive and civilized. For liberals and radicals, the search for integrated social systems gives way to a new practice called 'experimental ethnography' in which an organic object dissipates in attention to the play of writing. At the level of ideology, we see translations of racism and colonialism into languages of development and under-development, rates and constraints of modernization. Any objects or persons can be reasonably thought of in terms of disassembly and reassembly; no 'natural' architectures constrain system design. The financial districts in all the world's cities, as well as the export-processing and free-trade zones, proclaim this elementary fact of 'late capitalism'. The entire universe of objects that can be known scientifically must be formulated as problems in communications engineering (for the managers) or theories of the text (for those who would resist). Both are cyborg semiologies.

One should expect control strategies to concentrate on boundary conditions and interfaces, on rates of flow across boundaries – and not on the integrity of natural objects. 'Integrity' or 'sincerity' of the Western self gives way to decision procedures and expert systems. For example, control strategies applied to women's capacities to give birth to new human beings will be developed in the languages of population control and maximization of goal achievement for individual decision-makers. Control strategies will be formulated in terms of rates, costs of constraints, degrees of freedom. Human beings, like any other component or subsystem, must be localized in a system architecture whose basic modes of operation are probabilistic, statistical. No objects, spaces or bodies are sacred in themselves; any component can be interfaced with any other if the proper standard, the proper code, can be constructed for processing signals in common language. Exchange in this world transcends the universal translation effected by capitalist markets that Marx analysed so well. The privileged pathology affecting all kinds of components in this universe is stress – communications breakdown (Hogness 1983). The cyborg is not subject to Foucault's biopolitics; the cyborg simulates politics, a much more potent field of operations.

This kind of analysis of scientific and cultural objects of knowledge which have appeared historically since the Second World War prepares us to notice some important inadequacies in feminist analysis which has proceeded as if the organic, hierarchical dualisms ordering discourse in 'the West' since Aristotle still ruled. They have been cannibalized, or as Zoe Sofia (Sofoulis) might put it, they have been 'techno-digested'. The dichotomies between mind and body, animal and human, organism and machine, public and private, nature and culture, men and women, primitive and civilized are all in question ideologically. The actual situation of women is their integration/exploitation into a world system of production/reproduction and communication called the informatics of domination. The home, workplace, market, public arena, the body itself – all can be dispersed and interfaced in nearly infinite, polymorphous ways, with large consequences for women and others – consequences that themselves are very different for different people and which make potent oppositional international movements difficult to imagine and essential for survival. One important route for reconstructing socialist-feminist politics is through theory and practice addressed to the social relations of science and technology, including crucially the systems of myth and meanings structuring our imaginations. The cyborg is a kind of disassembled and reassembled, postmodern collective and personal self. This is the self feminists must code.

Communications technologies and biotechnologies are the crucial tools recrafting our bodies. These tools embody and enforce new social relations for women worldwide. Technologies and scientific discourses can be partially understood as formalizations, ie. as frozen moments, of the fluid social interactions constituting them, but they should also be viewed as instruments for enforcing meanings. The boundary is permeable between tool and myth, instrument and concept, historical systems of social relations and historical anatomies of possible bodies, including objects of knowledge. Indeed, myth and tool mutually constitute each other.

Furthermore, communications sciences and modern biologies are constructed by a common move – *the translation of the world into a problem of coding*, a search for a common language in which all resistance to instrumental control disappears and all heterogeneity can be submitted to disassembly, reassembly, investment and exchange.

In communications sciences, the translation of the world into a problem in coding can be illustrated by looking at cybernetic (feedback-controlled) systems theories applied to telephone technology, computer design, weapons deployment or database construction and maintenance. In each case, solution to the key questions rests on a theory of language and control; the key operation is determining the rates, directions and probabilities of flow of a quantity called information. The world is subdivided by boundaries differentially permeable to information. Information is just that kind of quantifiable element (unit, base of unity) which allows universal translation, and so unhindered instrumental power (called effective communication). The biggest threat to such power is interruption of communication. Any system breakdown is a function of stress. The fundamentals of this technology can be condensed into the metaphor C^3I, command-control-communication-intelligence, the military's symbol for its operations theory.

In modern biologies, the translation of the world into a problem in coding can be illustrated by molecular genetics, ecology, sociobiological evolutionary theory and immunobiology. The organism has been translated into problems of genetic coding and read-out. Biotechnology, a writing technology, informs research broadly.[2] In a sense, organisms have ceased to exist as objects of knowledge, giving way to biotic components, ie. special kinds of information-processing devices. The analogous moves in ecology could be examined by probing the history and utility of the concept of the ecosystem. Immunobiology and associated medical practices are rich exemplars of the privilege of coding and recognition systems as objects of knowledge, as constructions of bodily reality for us. Biology here is a kind of cryptography. Research is necessarily a kind of intelligence activity. Ironies abound. A stressed system goes awry; its communication processes break down; it fails to recognize the difference between self and other. Human babies with baboon hearts evoke national ethical perplexity – for animal rights activists at least as much as for the guardians of human purity. In the US gay men and intravenous drug users are the 'privileged' victims of an awful immune system disease that marks (inscribes on the body) confusion of boundaries and moral pollution (Treichler 1987).

But these excursions into communications sciences and biology have been at a rarefied level; there is a mundane, largely economic reality to support my claim that these sciences and technologies indicate fundamental transformations in the structure of the world for us. Communications technologies depend on electronics. Modern states, multi-national corporations, military power, welfare state apparatuses, satellite systems, political processes, fabrication of our imaginations, labour-control systems, medical constructions of our bodies, commercial pornography, the international division of labour and religious evangelism depend intimately upon electronics. Microelectronics is the technical basis of simulacra; that is, of copies without originals.

Microelectronics mediates the translations of labour into robotics and word processing, sex into genetic engineering and reproductive technologies, and mind into artificial intelligence and decision procedures. The new biotechnologies concern more than human reproduction. Biology as a powerful engineering science for redesigning materials and processes has revolutionary implications for industry, perhaps most obvious today in areas of fermentation, agriculture and energy. Communications sciences and biology are constructions of natural-technical objects of knowledge in which the difference between machine and organism is thoroughly blurred; mind, body and tool are on very intimate terms. The 'multinational' material organization of the production and reproduction of daily life and the symbolic organization of the production and reproduction of culture and imagination seem equally implicated. The boundary-maintaining images of base and superstructure, public and private, or material and ideal never seemed more feeble.

I have used Rachel Grossman's (1980) image of women in the integrated circuit to name the situation of women in a world so intimately restructured through the social relations of science and technology.[3] I used the odd circumlocution, 'the social relations of science and technology', to indicate that we are not dealing with a technological determinism, but with a historical system depending upon structured relations among people. But the phrase should also indicate that science and technology provide fresh sources of power, that we need fresh sources of analysis and political action (Latour 1984). Some of the rearrangements of race, sex and class rooted in high-tech-facilitated social relations can make socialist-feminism more relevant to effective progressive politics.

1 This chart was published in 1985. My previous efforts to understand biology as a cybernetic command-control discourse and organisms as 'natural-technical objects of knowledge' were Haraway (1979, 1983, 1984). The 1979 version of this dichotomous chart appears in Haraway (1991) ch. 3; for a 1989 version, see ch. 10. The differences indicate shifts in argument.

2 For progressive analyses and action on the biotechnology debates: *GeneWatch, a Bulletin of the Committee for Responsible Genetics*, 5 Doane St, 4th Floor, Boston, MA 02109; Genetic Screening Study Group (formerly the Sociobiology Study Group of Science for the People), Cambridge, MA; Wright (1982, 1986); Yoxen (1983).

3 Starting references for 'women in the integrated circuit': D'Onofrio-Flores and Pfafflin (1982), Fernandez-Kelly (1983), Fuentes and Ehrenreich (1983), Grossman (1980), Nash and Fernandez-Kelly (1983), Ong (1987), Science Policy Research Unit (1982).

K Eric Drexler_Engines of Abundance_ 1990

Nanotechnology is the ultimate computational and engineering technology. It is based on the premise that if we can make self-replicating machines that are small enough, eventually we will be able to create molecule-sized factories and manipulate matter atom by atom, reconstituting and creating anything. There are two types of nanotechnology: wet and dry. 'Dry' refers to the design of minute but traditionally mechanical devices such as gears, bushes, pumps and levers assembled from small quantities of atoms; 'wet' nanotechnology employs as its machinery the replication potential of biological cell division and DNA.[1] Currently nanotechnology is more theory than practice, but as time goes by, more and more of its applications are being understood and achieved.

The concept of nanotechnology quietly emerged in a paper published by the academic K Eric Drexler in the September 1981 issue of *Proceedings of the National Academy of Sciences*. In this paper Drexler posited the notion that the 'ability to design protein molecules will open a path to the fabrication of devices to complex atomic specifications'. This simple statement implies the possibility of self-replicating machinery of only a few atoms in length. This, in turn, leads to the idea that that we could theoretically make anything out of almost anything, anytime we like – it is just a matter of programming the 'assemblers' (Drexler's term for the bits of the molecule-sized factories).

Drexler is the primary researcher and initiator of studies in molecular nanotechnology. He saw that nanotechnology is a potentially devastating idea – one that would question capitalism, ownership and ethics through its heady mix of alchemic material transmutations, its ubiquity and its implications for human longevity. It also has the potential to spiral out of control – a downside that writer Ed Regis evokes thus:

An individual 'assembler', as he [Drexler] started to call these molecular manipulators, could line up atoms till kingdom come and hardly make a dent in the Big World. But if the first assembler could make another assembler, and if each of those made two more, and so on, much in the way that biological cells divided and replicated, then the final result would be different. In fact, matters could get out of hand in very short order.[2]

The problem of such a virulent technology running amok has been called the 'grey goo problem'. The world could be devoured by hungry sludge in a matter of hours. Drexler developed the idea of 'blue goo', a sort of policeman goo: the two sorts of sludge could battle it out. He points out that these life-and-death fights happen around us and within us all the time: our bodies seek to evade a whole complex ecology of microbial invaders, for instance when we have a virus such as flu.

On the upside, nanotechnology potentially represents a fantastic breakthrough: the whole human condition could be changed for the better, forever. With this in mind Drexler set about writing a popular science book which he hoped would bring his ideas to the attention of the general public and spark a debate on nanotechnology's social consequences. *Engines of Creation*, from which we reproduce an extract of the chapter Engines of Abundance, first published in the US in 1986, centres around a graphic account of the growth of a rocket engine in a vat. The book reflects the vision of its evangelical creator, and goes a considerable way to illustrating the extraordinary opportunities of nanotechnology.

1 For a development of this discussion, see Neil Spiller, *Digital Dreams: Architecture and the New Alchemic Technologies*, London: Ellipsis, 1998.
2 Ed Regis, *Nano: Remaking the World, Atom by Atom*, New York: Bantam Press, 1995, p121.

> If every tool, when ordered, or even of its own accord, could do the work that befits it … then there would be no need either of apprentices for the master workers or of slaves for the lords.
> Aristotle

On March 27, 1981, CBS radio news quoted a NASA scientist as saying that engineers will be able to build self-replicating robots within twenty years, for use in space or on Earth. These machines would build copies of themselves, and the copies would be directed to make useful products. He had no doubt of their possibility, only of when they will be built. He was quite right.

Since 1951, when John von Neumann outlined the principles of self-replicating machines, scientists have generally acknowledged their possibility. In 1953 Watson and Crick described the structure of DNA, which showed how living things pass on the instructions that guide their construction. Biologists have since learned in increasing detail how the self-replicating molecular machinery of the cell works. They find that it follows the principles von Neumann had outlined. As birds prove the possibility of flight, so life in general proves the possibility of self-replication, at least by systems of molecular machines. The NASA scientist, however, had something else in mind.

Clanking Replicators

Biological replicators, such as viruses, bacteria, plants, and people, use molecular machines. Artificial replicators can use bulk technology instead. Since we have bulk technology today, engineers may use it to build replicators before molecular technology arrives.

The ancient myth of a magical life-force (coupled with the misconception that the increase of entropy means that everything in the universe must constantly run down) has spawned a meme saying that replicators must violate some natural law. This simply isn't so. Biochemists understand how cells replicate and they find no magic in them. Instead, they find machines supplied with all the materials, energy, and instructions needed to do the job. Cells *do* replicate; robots *could* replicate.

Advances in automation will lead naturally toward mechanical replicators, whether or not anyone makes them a specific goal. As competitive pressures force increased automation, the need for human labour in factories will shrink. Fujitsu Fanuc already runs the machining section in a manufacturing plant twenty-four hours a day with only nineteen workers on the floor during the day shift, and *none* on the floor during the night shift. This factory produces 250 machines a month, of which 100 are robots.

Eventually, robots could do all the robot-assembly work, assemble other equipment, make the needed parts, run the mines and generators that supply the various factories with materials and power, and so forth. Though such a network of factories spread across the landscape wouldn't resemble a pregnant robot, it would form a self-expanding, self-replicating system. The assembler breakthrough will surely arrive before the complete automation of industry, yet modern moves in this direction are moves toward a sort of gigantic, clanking replicator.

But how can such a system be maintained and repaired without human labour?

Imagine an automatic factory able to both test parts and assemble equipment. Bad parts fail the tests and are thrown out or recycled. If the factory can also take machines apart, repairs are easy: simply disassemble the faulty machines, test all their parts, replace any worn or broken parts, and reassemble them. A more efficient system would diagnose problems without testing every part, but this isn't strictly necessary.

A sprawling system of factories staffed by robots would be workable but cumbersome. Using clever design and a minimum of different parts and materials, engineers could fit a replicating system into a single box – but the box might still be huge, because it must contain equipment able to make and assemble many different parts. How many different parts? As many as it itself contains. How many different parts and materials would be needed to build a machine able to make and assemble so many different materials and parts? This is hard to estimate, but systems based on today's technology would use electronic chips. Making these alone would require too much equipment to stuff into the belly of a small replicator.

Rabbits replicate, but they require prefabricated parts such as vitamin molecules. Getting these from food lets them survive with less molecular machinery than they would need to make everything from scratch. Similarly, a mechanical replicator using prefabricated chips could be made somewhat simpler than one that made everything it needed. Its peculiar 'dietary' requirements would also tie it to a wider 'ecology' of machines, helping to keep it on a firm leash. Engineers in NASA-sponsored studies have proposed using such semireplicators in space, allowing space industry to expand with only a small input of sophisticated parts from Earth.

Still, since bulk-technology replicators must make and assemble their parts, they must contain both part-making and part-assembling machines. This highlights an advantage of molecular replicators: their parts are atoms, and atoms come ready-made.

Molecular Replicators

Cells replicate. Their machines copy their DNA, which directs their ribosomal machinery to build other machines from simpler molecules. These machines and molecules are held in a fluid-filled bag. Its membrane lets in fuel molecules and parts for more nanomachines, DNA, membrane, and so forth; it lets out spent fuel and scrapped components. A cell replicates by copying the parts inside its membrane bag, sorting them into two clumps, and then pinching the bag in two. Artificial replicators could be built to work in a similar way, but using assemblers instead of ribosomes. In this way, we could build cell-like replicators that are not limited to molecular machinery made from the soft, moist folds of protein molecules.

But engineers seem more likely to develop other approaches to replication. Evolution had no easy way to alter the fundamental pattern of the cell, and this pattern has shortcomings. In synapses, for example, the cells of the brain signal their neighbours by emptying bladders of chemical molecules. The molecules can jostle around until they bind to sensor molecules on the neighbouring cell, sometimes triggering a neural impulse. A chemical synapse makes a slow switch, and neural impulses move slower than sound. With assemblers, molecular engineers will build entire computers smaller than a synapse and a millionfold faster.

Mutation and selection could no more make a synapse into a mechanical nanocomputer than a breeder could make a horse into a car. Nonetheless, engineers have built cars, and will also learn to build computers faster than brains, and replicators more capable than existing cells.

Some of these replicators will not resemble cells at all, but will instead resemble factories shrunk to cellular size. They will contain nanomachines mounted on a molecular framework and conveyor belts to move parts from machine to machine. Outside, they will have a set of assembler arms for building replicas of themselves, an atom or a section at a time.

How fast these replicators can replicate will depend on their assembly speed and their size. Imagine an advanced assembler that contains a million atoms: it can have as many as ten thousand moving parts, each containing an average of one hundred atoms – enough parts to make up a rather complex machine. In fact, the assembler itself looks like a box supporting a stubby robot arm a hundred atoms long. The box and arm contain devices that move the arm from position to position, and others that change the molecular tools at its tip.

Behind the box sits a device that reads a tape and provides mechanical signals that trigger arm motions and tool changes. In front of the arm sits an unfinished structure. Conveyors bring molecules to the assembler system. Some supply energy to motors that drive the tape reader and arm, and other supply groups of atoms for assembly. Atom by atom (or group by group), the arm moves pieces into place as directed by the tape; chemical reactions bond them to the structure on contact.

These assemblers will work fast. A fast enzyme, such as carbonic anhydrase or ketosteroid isomerase, can process almost a million molecules per second, even without conveyors and power-driven mechanisms to slap a new molecule into place as soon as an old one is released. It might seem too much to expect an assembler to grab a molecule, move it, and jam it into place in a mere millionth of a second. But small appendages can move to and fro very swiftly. A human arm can flap up and down several times per second, fingers can tap more rapidly, a fly can wave its wings fast enough to buzz, and a mosquito makes a maddening whine. Insects can wave their wings at about a thousand times the frequency of a human arm because an insect's wing is about a thousand times shorter.

An assembler arm will be about fifty million times shorter than a human arm, and so (as it turns out) it will be able to move back and forth about fifty million times more rapidly. For an assembler arm to move a mere million times per second would be like a human arm moving about once per minute: sluggish. So it seems a very reasonable goal.

The speed of replication will depend also on the total size of the system to be built. Assemblers will not replicate by themselves; they will need materials and energy, and instructions on how to use them. Ordinary chemicals can supply materials and energy, but nanomachinery must be available to process them. Bumpy polymer molecules can code information like a punched paper tape, but a reader must be available to translate the patterns of bumps into patterns of arm motion. Together, these parts form the essentials of a replicator: the tape supplies instructions for assembling a copy of the assembler, of the reader, of the other nanomachines, and of the tape itself.

A reasonable design for this sort of replicator will likely include several assembler arms and several more arms to hold and move workpieces. Each of these arms will add another million atoms or so. The other parts – tape readers, chemical processors, and so forth – may also be as complicated as assemblers. Finally, a flexible replicator system will probably include a simple computer; following the mechanical approach that I mentioned in Chapter 1, this will add roughly 100 million atoms. Altogether, these parts will total less than 150 million atoms. Assume instead a total of one billion, to leave a wide margin for error. Ignore the added capability of the additional assembler arms, leaving a still wider margin. Working at one million atoms per second, the system will still copy itself in one thousand seconds, or a bit over fifteen minutes – about the time a bacterium takes to replicate under good conditions.

Imagine such a replicator floating in a bottle of chemicals, making copies of itself. It builds one copy in one thousand seconds, thirty-six in ten hours. In a week, it stacks up enough copies to fill the volume of a human cell. In a century, it stacks up enough to make a respectable speck. If this were all that replicators could do, we could perhaps ignore them in safety.

Each copy, though, will build yet more copies. Thus the first replicator assembles a copy in one thousand seconds, the two replicators then build two more in the next thousand seconds, the four build another four, and the eight build another eight. At the end of ten hours, there are not thirty-six new replicators, but over 68 billion. In less than a day, they would weigh a ton; in less than two days, they would outweigh the Earth; in another four hours, they would exceed the mass of the Sun and all the planets combined – if the bottle of chemicals hadn't run dry long before.

Regular doubling means exponential growth. Replicators multiply exponentially unless restrained, as by lack of room or resources. Bacteria do it, and at about the same rate as the replicators just described. People replicate far more slowly, yet given time enough they, too, could overshoot any finite resource supply. Concern about population growth will never lose its importance. Concern about controlling rapid new replicators will soon become very important indeed.

Molecules and Skyscrapers

Machines able to grasp and position individual atoms will be able to build almost anything by bonding the right atoms together in the right patterns, as I described at the end of Chapter 1. To be sure, building large objects one atom at a time will be slow. A fly, after all, contains about a million atoms for every second since the dinosaurs were young. Molecular machines can nonetheless build objects of substantial size – they build whales, after all.

To make large objects rapidly, a vast number of assemblers must cooperate, but replicators will produce assemblers by the ton. Indeed, with correct design, the difference between an assembler system and a replicator will lie entirely in the assembler's programming. If a replicating assembler can copy itself in one thousand seconds, then it can be programmed to build something else its own size just as fast. Similarly, a ton of replicators can swiftly build a ton of something else – and the product will have all its billions of billions of billions of atoms in the right place, with only a minute fraction misplaced.

To see the abilities and limits of one method for assembling large objects, imagine a flat sheet covered with small assembly arms – perhaps an army of replicators reprogrammed for construction work and arrayed in orderly ranks. Conveyors and communication channels behind them supply reactive molecules, energy, and assembly instructions. If each arm occupies an area 100 atomic diameters wide, then behind each assembler will be room for conveyors and channels totalling about 10,000 atoms in cross-sectional area.

This seems room enough. A space ten or twenty atoms wide can hold a conveyor (perhaps based on molecular belts and pulleys). A channel a few atoms wide can hold a molecular rod which, like those in the mechanical computer mentioned in Chapter 1, will be pushed and pulled to transmit signals. All the arms will work together to build a broad, solid structure layer by layer. Each arm will be responsible for its own area, handling about 10,000 atoms per layer. A sheet of assemblers handling 1,000,000 atoms per second per arm will complete about one hundred atomic layers per second. This may sound fast, but at this rate piling up a paper-sheet thickness will take about an hour, and making a metre-thick slab will take over a year.

Faster arms might raise the assembly speed to over a metre per day, but they would produce more waste heat. If they could build a metre-thick layer in a day, the heat from one square metre could cook hundreds of steaks simultaneously, and might fry the machinery. At some size and speed, cooling problems will become a limiting factor, but there are other ways of assembling objects faster without overheating the machinery.

Imagine trying to build a house by gluing together individual grains of sand. Adding a layer of grains might take grain-gluing machines so long that raising the walls would take decades. Now imagine that machines in a factory first glue the grains together to make bricks. The factory can work on many bricks at once. With enough grain-gluing machines, bricks would pour out fast; wall assemblers could then build walls swiftly by stacking the preassembled bricks. Similarly, molecular assemblers will team up with larger assemblers to build big things quickly – machines can be any size from molecular to gigantic. With this approach, most of the assembly heat will be dissipated far from the work site, in making the parts.

Skyscraper construction and the architecture of life suggest a related way to construct large objects. Large plants and animals have vascular systems, intricate channels that carry materials to molecular machinery working throughout their tissues. Similarly, after riggers and riveters finish the frame of a skyscraper, the building's 'vascular system' – its elevators and corridors, aided by cranes – carry construction materials to workers throughout the interior. Assembly systems could also employ this strategy, first putting up a scaffold and then working throughout its volume, incorporating materials brought through channels from the outside.

Imagine this approach being used to 'grow' a large rocket engine, working inside a vat in an industrial plant. The vat – made of shiny steel, with a glass window for the benefit of visitors – stands taller than a person, since it must hold the completed engine. Pipes and pumps link it to other equipment and to water-cooled heat exchangers. This arrangement lets the operator circulate various fluids through the vat.

To begin the process, the operator swings back the top of the vat and lowers into it a base plate on which the engine will be built. The top is then resealed. At the touch of a button, pumps flood the chamber with a thick, milky fluid which submerges the plate and then obscures the window. This fluid flows from another vat in which replicating assemblers have been raised and then reprogrammed by making them copy and spread a new instruction tape (a bit like infecting bacteria with a virus). These new assembler systems, smaller than bacteria, scatter light and make the fluid look milky. Their sheer abundance makes it viscous.

At the centre of the base plate, deep in the swirling, assembler-laden fluid, sits a 'seed'. It contains a nanocomputer with stored engine plans, and its surface sports patches to which assemblers stick. When an assembler sticks to it, they plug themselves together and the seed computer transfers instructions to the assembler computer. This new programming tells it where it is in relation to the seed, and directs it to extend its manipulator arms to snag more assemblers. These then plug in and are similarly programmed. Obeying these instructions from the seed (which spread through the expanding network of communicating assemblers) a sort of assembler-crystal grows from the chaos of the liquid. Since each assembler knows its location in the plan, it snags more assemblers only where more are needed. This forms a pattern less regular and more complex than that of any natural crystal. In the course of a few hours, the assembler scaffolding grows to match the final shape of the planned rocket engine.

Then the vat's pumps return to life, replacing the milky fluid of unattached assemblers with a clear mixture of organic solvents and dissolved substances – including aluminium compounds, oxygen-rich compounds, and compounds to serve as assembler fuel. As the fluid clears, the shape of the rocket engine grows visible through the window, looking like a full-scale model sculpted in translucent white plastic. Next, a message spreading from the seed directs designated assemblers to release their neighbours and fold their arms. They wash out of the structure in sudden streamers of white, leaving a spongy lattice of attached assemblers, now with room enough to work. The engine shape in the vat grows almost transparent, with a hint of iridescence.

Each remaining assembler, though still linked to its neighbours, is now surrounded by tiny fluid-filled channels. Special arms on the assemblers work like flagella, whipping the fluid along to circulate it through the channels. These motions, like all the others performed by the assemblers, are powered by molecular engines fuelled by molecules in the fluid. As dissolved sugar powers yeast, so these dissolved chemicals power assemblers. The flowing fluid brings fresh fuel and dissolved raw materials for construction; as it flows out it carries off waste heat. The communications network spreads instructions to each assembler.

The assemblers are now ready to start construction. They are to build a rocket engine, consisting mostly of pipes and pumps. This means building strong, light structures in intricate shapes, some able to stand intense heat, some full of tubes to carry cooling fluid. Where great strength is needed, the assemblers set to work constructing rods of interlocked fibres of carbon, in its diamond form. From these, they build a lattice tailored to stand up to the expected pattern of stress. Where resistance to heat and corrosion is essential (as on many surfaces), they build similar structures of aluminium oxide, in its sapphire form. In places where stress will be low, the assemblers save mass by leaving wider spaces in the lattice. In places where stress will be high, the assemblers reinforce the structure until the remaining passages are barely wide enough for the assemblers to move. Elsewhere the assemblers lay down other materials to make sensors, computers, motors, solenoids, and whatever else is needed.

To finish their jobs, they build walls to divide the remaining channel spaces into almost sealed cells, then withdraw to the last openings and pump out the fluid inside. Sealing the empty cells, they withdraw completely and float away in the circulating fluid. Finally, the vat drains, a spray rinses the engine, the lid lifts, and the finished engine is hoisted out to dry. Its creation has required less than a day and almost no human attention.

What is the engine like? Rather than being a massive piece of welded and bolted metal, it is a seamless thing, gemlike. Its empty internal cells, patterned in arrays about a wavelength of light apart, have a side effect: like the pits on a laser disk they diffract light, producing a varied iridescence like that of a fire opal. These empty spaces lighten a structure already made from some of the lightest, strongest materials known. Compared to a modern metal engine, this advanced engine has over 90 percent less mass.

Tap it, and it rings like a bell of surprisingly high pitch for its size. Mounted in a spacecraft of similar construction, it flies from a runway to space and back again with ease. It stands long, hard use because its strong materials have let designers include large safety margins. Because assemblers have let designers pattern its structure to yield before breaking (blunting cracks and halting their spread), the engine is not only strong but tough.

For all its excellence, this engine is fundamentally quite conventional. It has merely replaced dense metal with carefully tailored structures of light, tightly bonded atoms. The final product contains no nanomachinery.

More advanced designs will exploit nanotechnology more deeply. They could leave a vascular system in place to supply assembler and disassembler systems; these can be programmed to mend worn parts. So long as users supply such an engine with energy and raw materials, it will renew its own structure. More advanced engines can also be literally more flexible. Rocket engines work best if they can take different shapes under different operating conditions, but engineers cannot make bulk metal strong, light, and limber. With nanotechnology, though, a structure stronger than steel and lighter than wood could change shape like muscle (working, like muscle, on the sliding-fibre principle). An engine could then expand, contract, and bend at the base to provide the desired thrust in the desired direction under varying conditions. With properly programmed assemblers and disassemblers, it could even remodel its fundamental structure long after leaving the vat.

In short, replicating assemblers will copy themselves by the ton, then make other products such as computers, rocket engines, chairs, and so forth. They will make disassemblers able to break down rock to supply raw material. They will make solar collectors to supply energy. Though tiny, they will build big. Teams of nanomachines in nature build whales, and seeds replicate machinery and organize atoms into vast structures of cellulose, building redwood trees. There is nothing too startling about growing a rocket engine in a specially prepared vat. Indeed, foresters given suitable assembler 'seeds' could grow spaceships from soil, air, and sunlight.

Assemblers will be able to make virtually anything from common materials without labour, replacing smoking factories with systems as clean as forests. They will transform technology and the economy at their roots, opening a new world of possibilities. They will indeed be engines of abundance.

Science-fiction writer Greg Bear keeps a close eye on ideas from science and engineering. This informs his work and inspires his outlandish ideas which take concepts from technology and science and push them to their natural limits. Fellow American cyberpunk author Bruce Sterling, in his introduction to Greg Bear's short story 'Petra' in the anthology *Mirrorshades*, describes Bear's early career: 'Greg Bear sold his first short story in 1966 at the age of fifteen. He hit his stride in the late 1970s and early 1980s, when a flurry of short stories and novels established him as a writer to watch.'[1]

Queen of Angels[2] is set in the year 2047. Its main protagonist is Public Defender Mary Choy, who is sent to a Caribbean island to bring back to Los Angeles a mass killer who has gone insane. Voodoo deities populate both the real terrain and the 'virtual' terrain of the killer's psyche – his 'Country of the Mind' as Bear's psychiatrist character calls it. Whilst these and other sub-plots and characters are highly enjoyable, what interests us here is the picture that Bear sketches of a nanotechnological process. Nanoassemblers, smuggled onto the island by Choy, are briefly released to secretly build a gun on her dressing table. The scene is obviously inspired by K Eric Drexler's vision of nanotechnology and his popular and visionary book *Engines of Creation* (see p116) – but Bear's vision is far smaller in scale, and all the more powerful because of it.

Nanotechnology (the manipulation of matter, atom by atom), as Bear implies, can have far-reaching consequences, even at the domestic scale. The popular science writer Ed Regis – who trained as a philosopher – writes entertainingly, but not without a sense of wonder and awe, about the possible addition of a strange, magical black box to our kitchen utilities:

> You could invent this black box – a 'meat machine' or 'cabinet beast' or something of the sort – that would physically transform common materials into fresh beef. The machine might be the size and shape of a microwave oven, for example, and it would work the way a microwave oven did too, more or less. You'd open the door

shovel in a quantity of grass clippings or tree leaves or old bicycle tyres or whatever, and then you'd close the door, fiddle with the controls, and sit back to await results. Two hours later, out rolled a wad of fresh beef.[3]

Of other science-fiction authors who have picked up on the idea of a nanotechnological utopia or dystopia, one of the most prominent is Neal Stephenson. *Diamond Age*, the follow-up to his renowned *Snow Crash*, depicts a strange world populated by all manner of strange societies and sects, all of which have some relationship to the omnipresent powers of nanotechnology. Authenticity becomes prized, just in the way that real animals are prized by the character Deckard in Philip K Dick's *Do Androids Dream of Electric Sheep*? In that novel Deckard even carries on him a catalogue to check the rarity and price of real animals he comes across in a world populated by android animals. Interestingly, this idea was omitted from the film of the book, *Blade Runner*.

1 Bruce Sterling (ed), *Mirrorshades: The Cyberpunk Anthology*, London: Paladin (Flamingo), 1988, p105.

2 Greg Bear, *Queen of Angels*, London: Legend, 1991.

3 Ed Regis, *Nano: Remaking the World Atom by Atom*, New York: Bantam Press, 1995, p6.

In the quartiers diplomatiques, Soulavier gave her one hour to rest and prepare for the move.

Mary shut the door to the bedroom, removed the hairbrush from her coat and laid it on the glasstop dresser beside the window. She pulled down the window shade and reviewed the instructions mentally.

The whole process would take about ten minutes. There was no lock on the door; she backed a wooden chair against the brass and crystal knob. She looked hastily around for the extra materials she would need. At least one quarter kilo of steel, one sixth kilo of some high density plastic, and the makeup kit. She assayed the contents of the room, picked up a stainless steel tray from the dresser and decided it would do. A clock from the bedside, nearly all plastic. In the closet, she found an old fashioned pipe bootrack. She hefted the bootrack; more than enough.

Gathering the objects into a pile on the dresser, she unscrewed the hairbrush handle and removed a plastic panel from the rear of the brush head. A single small red button lay countersunk in the exposed area. With a deep breath, thinking of Ernest, feeling a faintly creepy sensation, she pushed the button and arranged the handle and head next to the pile.

A gray paste oozed from the handle, directed by a reference field within the head. Like a slime mold it crept across the table top, bumped into the bootrack, paused and began its work.

Soulavier had given her an hour but she surmised he would allow her twenty minutes of comparative privacy. She was much less sure about the servants. At any moment on some pretext or another they might try to open the door, show alarm and express concern for her safety.

Lying back on the bed, Mary decided to test what she had been told about interdicted communications.

She lifted her slate and typed in a request for direct access to the LAPD Joint Command. The transmitter within the slate was powerful enough to reach the first level of satellites at three hundred fifty kilometres; if she had been told the truth, however, its signal would be blocked by automatic interference from a more powerful counterphase transmitter. She assumed Hispaniola would be flooding all com satellites with such spurious random messages; the satellites would 'eclipse' the island to restore order to their systems.

However, Hispaniola needed certain satellite links to maintain essential financial and political contacts. There was a definite possibility the authorities would raise the counterphase jamming periodically.

The slate displayed: *Link established. Proceed.* She lifted her eyebrows. No interdict thus far; were they expecting her to do this? She typed: *ID check.*

PD issued com unit message register 3254-461-21-C. Enter. She doubted that Hispaniola security would have her pd message register number, although if they were listening, they had it now. She thought for a moment, decided to be circumspect but take advantage of a possible opening, and typed *Place call to D Reeve. Text message: Being held in Hispaniola. No information on suspect. Treated well.* This in case her success was a ruse and she was being tapped. *Using gift. What a mess.*

Then she typed *Confirm receipt.*

PD message register 3254-461-21-C: acknowledge receipt of message to Supervisor D Reeve.

Mary frowned. The link was clear; that made no sense. She thought of typing something about getting her out, but she had no doubt they were doing their best. *Continue message. Going to Leoganes outside Port-au-Prince. Grotto tourist spot. Tension high; coup against Yardley may be in progress; Dominicans? Military vehicles in streets everywhere. Confirm signal receipt again.*

She looked at the dresser top; gray shiny paste covered all the objects in the pile. They were already deforming.

Signal confirmation not received, the slate told her. *Incomplete link: interference suspected.* There it was, interdiction. Either somebody had been asleep at the switch or they were playing her like a game fish; either way she at least had been allowed to send a message that she was alive. With a shuddering sigh she turned off the slate and knelt in front of the dresser, chin on folded arms resting on the edge.

She patiently watched the nano at work. The metal tubing of the bootrack had crumpled under the gray coating. The resulting pool of paste and deconstructed objects was contracting into a round convexity. Nano was forming an object within that convexity like an embryo within an egg.

Five more minutes. The house was quiet. From outside the house came the sound of distant shellfire and echoes from surrounding hills and mountains. She closed her eyes, swallowed, gathered her mental resources.

How close was the island to outright civil war? How close was she to being called a spy in the heat of an angry moment? She imagined Soulavier her executioner speaking so very apologetically of his loyalty to Colonel Sir.

The convexity grew lumpy now. She could make out the basic shape. To one side, excess raw material was being pushed into lumps of cold slag. Nano withdrew from the slag. Handle, loader, firing chamber, barrel and flight-guide. To one side of the convexity a second lump not slag was forming. Spare clip.

'Are you ready, mademoiselle?' Soulavier asked behind the door. To her credit she did not jump. He was early. No doubt he had been informed about her transmission; she was being a bad girl.

'Almost,' she said. 'A few more minutes.' Hastily she packed her suitcase and tossed the slag into the waste basket. She washed her face in the bathroom, looked at herself in the mirror and prepared mentally for what might come.

She lifted the pistol from the dresser top and placed it in her jacket pocket. Slim, hardly a bulge. The nano on the dresser compacted and crawled sluglike back into the handle of the brush, an oily sheen on its surface; spent. It would need a nutritional charge to perform any more miracles: soaking the brush in a can of kola might do the trick, she had been told. Mary reassembled the hairbrush and stuck it into the suitcase, closed the lid, removed the chair from the knob and opened the door.

Soulavier leaned against the wall in the hallway, examining his nails. He glanced at her dolefully. 'Too much time, Mademoiselle,' he said.

'Pardon?'

'We have waited too long. It is going to be dark soon. We are not going to Leoganes.'

If the second part of her message had gotten through it only made sense for the Hispaniolans to divert her to some other location. 'Where?' she asked.

'I leave that to my instincts,' Soulavier said. 'Away from here, however, and soon.'

She wondered how he had received his instructions. It was possible he had an implant though such technology was not supposed to be common on Hispaniola.

'I tried to make a call to my superiors,' she said. 'I didn't get through.'

He shrugged. All brightness and life seemed to have drained out of him. He inspected her with half-lidded eyes, head back, mouth expressionless. 'You were told that would not be possible,' he said, each word precise.

She returned his gaze, one corner of her lips lifted, provoking. Not a neutral flaw here. 'I'd still prefer to stay in these quarters,' she said.

'That is not your decision.'

'But I wouldn't mind going to Leoganes.'

'Mademoiselle, we are not children.'

She smiled. His attitude had changed markedly; no longer her protector. No need to reinforce the change by behaving differently herself. 'I never believed you were.'

'In some ways we are very sophisticated, perhaps more than you can know. Now we go.'

She picked up her suitcase. He took it from her with some force and followed her down the hall. They passed Jean-Claude and Roselle standing in the dining room, stone faced, hands folded. 'Thank you,' Mary told them, nodding and smiling pleasantly. They seemed shocked. Jean-Claude's nostrils flared.

'We go now,' Soulavier reiterated.

Mary put her hand in the coat pocket. 'Are they coming with us?' she asked.

'Roselle and Jean-Claude will stay here.'

'All right,' she said. 'Anything you say.'

At NASA's advanced Supercomputing Divison (NAS), state-of-the-art visualization techniques have been used (top left) to simulate the behaviour of carbon nanotubes, tiny cylinders only a few millionths of a millimetre in diameter.

It is plausible that a tiny transistor could be built from nanotubes of differing conductivities. (Principle Investigator and visualization: Deepak Srivastava)

As well as potential applications in nano-computers, and pro-grammable biological molecular machines, nanotechnology research also includes investigating the possibilities of building molecular machines for potential construction and self-replication applica-tions. K Erik Drexler at the Institute for Molecular Manu-facturing has produced several designs including a simple pump; the rotor of a selective pump for neon (top right). Another design (below) is for a fine motion controller for use in a molecular assembler.

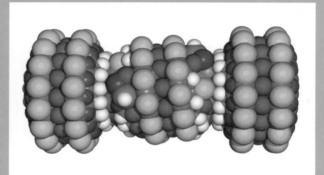

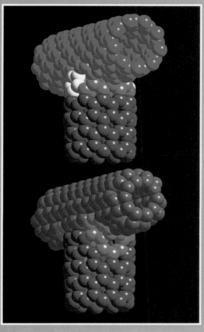

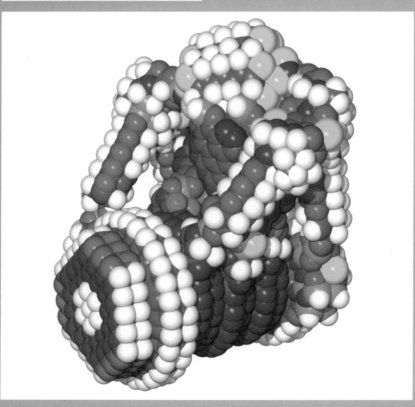

William Gibson and Bruce Sterling_
The Difference Engine_1991

The Difference Engine is the primary text of a genre of science-fiction novels that has been termed 'steampunk'. These novels are based around the idea of what might have happened had Charles Babbage's ideas (see p22) actually worked and been adopted wholesale by Victorian society. The narrative backdrop is one where Babbage's computational machines are hugely successful and ubiquitous. *The Difference Engine* builds on this scenario to explore the wide-ranging impact of such an eventuality, particularly in terms of individual surveillance, industrial relations and political intrigues.

In the hands of distinguished cyber authors William Gibson (see also p102) and Bruce Sterling, this concoction is garnished with the *noir* atmosphere of cyberpunk. The backdrop for *The Difference Engine*'s mechanical melodrama is Victorian London, a London of dirt, filth, privilege and poverty exacerbated by the supremacy of the shiny Engines. As with all cyberfiction, people are only as powerful as the software they possess. Software here is punched into boxes of cards or onto miles of paper tape, while hardware is measured in gearage. To quote Francis Spufford:

> In the bowels of the monstrous Egyptianese pyramid of the Central Statistical Office on Horseferry Road, serially connected Analytical Engines [the Difference Engines' more powerful sibling] process dossiers on every man, woman and child in the country. 'How many gear yards do you spin here?' 'Yards? We measure our gearage in *miles* here ...'[1]

What is important about *The Difference Engine*, and the reason for its inclusion in this anthology, is not so much its stories of Luddite-style plotting or the foiling of the French 'Napoleon' Engine but the way it produces a vignette of a world that might so easily have occurred. This is a world of high-Victorian imperial computability, a world full of 'clackers' (programmers) and engine-controlled 'kino' screens creating and manipulating images. Like the possible occult beginnings of the computer posited by Erik Davis in *Techgnosis: Magic, Memory, and the Angels of Information* (see p190) here is another weird world of 'might have been', another bifurcating pathway passed by in the history of computing.

Babbage's world, as imagined by Gibson and Sterling, is perhaps insanely empirical, but it is not altogether alien to that of other computer philosophers who were yet to come. Babbage believed that with his great Engines some, if not all, of society's ills could be calculated away. Is such a belief – setting the world into the mould of the computer – any more hubristic than Alan Turing's Universal Machine, or today's new sciences of emergence or artificial life? Hans Moravec's work on robotics (see p280) is certainly hubristic; his conviction that the human mind is downloadable into the computer because the human mind is able to be defined in computational terms would have been an acceptable notion to Babbage. Here at the dawn of computing, the notion of the computability of all things is established. We are now always tempted to express our world view in terms of computational paradigms. For example, we seek to understand biology by evoking computational ideas in evolutionary science. Such ideas concern the exchange and manipulation of packages of information programmed into DNA and RNA.

1 Francis Spufford, 'The Difference Engine and *The Difference Engine*', in *Cultural Babbage: Technology, Time and Intervention*, Francis Spufford and Jenny Unglow (eds), London: Faber and Faber, 1996, p277.

Mopping the back of his neck with a kerchief, Mallory unhappily contemplated the headquarters of the Central Statistics Bureau.

Ancient Egypt had been dead for twenty-five centuries, but Mallory had come to know it well enough to dislike it. The French excavation of the Suez Canal had been an heroic business, so that all things Egyptian had become the Parisian mode. The rage had seized Britain as well, leaving the nation awash with scarab tiepins, hawk-winged teapots, lurid stereographs of toppled obelisks, and faux-marble miniatures of the noseless Sphinx. Manufacturers had Engine-embroidered that whole beast-headed rabble of pagan godlets on curtains and carpets and carriage-robes, much to Mallory's distaste, and he had come to take an especial dislike to silly maunderings about the Pyramids, ruins which inspired exactly the sort of chuckle-headed wonderment that most revolted his sensibilities.

He had, of course, read admiringly of the engineering feats of Suez. Lacking coal, the French had fuelled their giant excavators with bitumen-soaked mummies, stacked like cordwood and sold by the tonne. Still, he resented the space usurped by Egyptology in the geographical journals.

The Central Statistics Bureau, vaguely pyramidal in form and excessively Egyptianate in its ornamental detail, squatted solidly in the governmental heart of Westminster, its uppermost storeys slanting to a limestone apex. For the sake of increased space, the building's lower section was swollen out-of-true, like some great stone turnip. Its walls, pierced by towering smokestacks, supported a scattered forest of spinning ventilators, their vanes annoyingly hawk-winged. The whole vast pile was riddled top to bottom with thick black telegraph-lines, as though individual streams of the Empire's information had bored through solid stone. A dense growth of wiring swooped down, from conduits and brackets, to telegraph poles crowded thick as the rigging in a busy harbour.

Mallory crossed the hot sticky tarmac of Horseferry Road, wary of the droppings of the pigeons clustered in the webwork of cable overhead.

The Bureau's fortress doors, framed by lotus-topped columns and Anglicised bronze sphinxes, loomed some twenty feet in height. Smaller, work-a-day doors were set into their corners. Mallory, scowling, strode into cool dimness and the faint but pervasive odours of lye and linseed oil. The simmering London stew was behind him now, but the damned place had no windows. Egyptianate jets lit the darkness, their flames breezily guttering in fan-shaped reflectors of polished tin.

He showed his citizen's-card at the visitors' desk. The clerk – or perhaps he was some sort of policeman, for he wore a newfangled Bureau uniform with an oddly military look – made careful note of Mallory's destination. He took an Engine-printed floor-plan of the building from beneath his counter, and marked out Mallory's twisting route in red ink.

Mallory, still smarting from the morning's meeting with the Nominations Committee of the Geographical, thanked the man rather too brusquely. Somehow – he didn't know which devious strings had been pulled backstage, but the plot was clear enough – Foulke had manoeuvred his way onto the Geographical Nominations Committee.

Foulke, whose aquatic theory of the Brontosaurus had been spurned by Huxley's museum, had taken Mallory's arborivore hypothesis as a personal attack, with the result that an ordinarily pleasant formality had become yet another public trial for radical Catastrophism. Mallory had won his Fellowship, in the end, Oliphant having laid the ground too well for Foulke's last-minute ambush to succeed, but the business still rankled. He sensed damage to his reputation. Dr Edward Mallory – 'Leviathan Mallory', as the penny papers insisted on having it – had been made to seem fanatical, even petty. And this in front of dignified geographers of the first rank, men like Burton of Mecca and Elliot of the Congo.

Mallory followed his map, muttering to himself. The fortunes of scholarly warfare, Mallory thought, had never seemed to favour him as they did Thomas Huxley. Huxley's feuds with the powers-that-be had only distinguished him as a wizard of debate, while Mallory was reduced to trudging this gaslit mausoleum, where he hoped to identify a despicable racetrack pimp.

Taking his first turn, he discovered a marble bas-relief depicting the Mosaic Plague of Frogs, which he had always numbered among his favourite Biblical tales. Pausing in admiration, he was very nearly run down by a steel pushcart, stacked to the gunwales with decks of punch-cards.

'Gangway!' yelped the carter, in brassbuttoned serge and a messenger's billed cap. Mallory saw with astonishment that the man wore wheeled boots, stout lace-ups fitted with miniature axles and spokeless rounds of rubber. The fellow shot headlong down the hall, expertly steering the heavy cart, and vanished around a corner.

Mallory passed a hall blocked off with striped sawhorses, where two apparent lunatics, in gaslit gloom, crept slowly about on all fours. Mallory stared. The creepers were plump, middle-aged women, dressed throat-to-foot in spotless white, their hair confined by snug elastic turbans. From a distance their clothing had the eerie look of winding-sheets. As he watched, one of the pair lurched heavily to her feet and began to tenderly wipe the ceiling with a sponge-mop on a telescoping pole.

They were charwomen.

Following his map to a lift, he was ushered in by a uniformed attendant and carried to another level. The air, here, was dry and static, the corridors busier. There were more of the odd-looking policemen, admixed with serious-looking gentlemen of the capital; barristers perhaps, or attorneys, or the legislative agents of great capitalists, men whose business it was to acquire and retail knowledge of the attitudes and influence of the public. Political men, in short, who dealt entirely in the intangible. And though they presumably had their wives, their children, their brownstone homes, here they struck Mallory as vaguely ghostlike or ecclesiastical.

Some yards on, Mallory was forced abruptly to dodge a second wheeled messenger. He caught himself against a decorative cast-iron column. The metal scorched his hands. Despite its lavish ornamentation – lotus blossoms – the column was a smokestack. He could hear it emitting the muffled roar and mutter of a badly-adjusted flue.

Consulting his map again, he entered a corridor lined left and right with offices. White-coated clerks ducked from door to door, dodging young messenger-boys rolling about with card-laden wheelbarrows. The gaslights were brighter here, but they fluttered in a steady draught of wind. Mallory glanced over his shoulder. At the end of the hall stood a giant steel-framed ventilator-fan. It squealed faintly, on an oiled chain-drive, propelled by an unseen motor in the bowels of the pyramid.

Mallory began to feel rather dazed. Likely this had all been a grave mistake. Surely there were better ways to pursue the mystery of Derby Day, than hunting pimps with some bureaucratic crony of Oliphant's. The very air of the place oppressed him, scorched and soapy and lifeless, the floors and walls polished and gleaming. He'd never before seen a place so utterly free of common dirt ... These halls reminded him of something, another labyrinthine journey ...

Lord Darwin.

Mallory and the great savant had been walking the leaf-shadowed hedgy lanes of Kent, Darwin poking at the moist black soil with his walking-stick. Darwin talking, on and on, in his endless, methodical, crushingly detailed way, of earthworms. Earthworms, always invisibly busy underfoot, so that even great sarsen-stones slowly sank into the loam. Darwin had measured the process, at Stonehenge, in an attempt to date the ancient monument.

Mallory tugged hard at his beard, his map forgotten in his hand. A vision came to him of earthworms churning in catastrophic frenzy, 'til the soil roiled and bubbled like a witch's brew. In years, mere months perhaps, all the monuments of slower aeons would sink shipwrecked to primaeval bedrock ...

'Sir? May I be of service?'

Mallory came to himself with a start. A white-coated clerk was confronting him, staring into his face with bespectacled suspicion. Mallory glared back, confused. For a divine moment he had poised on the brink of revelation, and now it was gone, as miserably inglorious as a failed sneeze.

Worse yet, Mallory now realised he had been muttering aloud again. About earthworms, presumably. Gruffly, he proffered his map. 'Looking for Level 5, QC-50.'

'That would be Quantitative Criminology, sir. This is Deterence Research.' The clerk pointed at a shingle hung above a nearby office door. Mallory nodded numbly.

'QC is just past Nonlinear Analysis, around the corner to your right', the clerk said. Mallory moved on. He could feel the clerk's sceptical eyes on his back.

The QC section was a honeycomb of tiny partitions, the neck-high walls riddled with asbestos-lined cubbyholes. Gloved and aproned clerks sat neatly at their slanted desks, examining and manipulating punchcards with a variety of specialised clacker's devices: shufflers, pin-mounts, isinglass colour-coders, jeweller's loupes, oiled tissues, and delicate rubber-tipped forceps. Mallory watched the familiar work with a happy lurch of reassurance.

QC-50 was the office of the Bureau's Undersecretary for Quantitative Criminology, whose name, Oliphant had said, was Wakefield.

Mr Wakefield possessed no desk, or rather his desk had encompassed and devoured the entirety of his office, and Wakefield worked from within it. Writing-tables sprang from wall-slots on an ingenious system of hinges, then vanished again into an arcane system of specialized cabinetry. There were newspaper-racks, letter-clamps, vast embedded card-files, catalogues, code-books, clackers' guides, an elaborate multi-dialled clock, three telegraph-dials whose gilded needles ticked out the alphabet, and printers busily punching tape.

Wakefield himself was a pallid Scot with sandy, receding hair. His glance, if not positively evasive, was extremely mobile. A pronounced overbite dented his lower lip.

He struck Mallory as very young for a man of his position, perhaps only forty. No doubt, like most accomplished clackers, Wakefield had grown up with the Engine trade. Babbage's very first Engine, now an honoured relic, was still less than thirty years old, but the swift progression of Enginery had swept a whole generation in its wake, like some mighty locomotive of the mind.

Mallory introduced himself. 'I regret my tardiness, sir', Mallory said. 'I found myself a bit lost in your halls.'

This was no news to Wakefield. 'May I offer you tea? We have a very fine spongecake.'

Mallory shook his head, then opened his cigar-case with a flourish. 'Smoke?'

Wakefield went pale. 'No! No thank you. A fire hazard, strictly against regulations.'

Mallory put the case away, chagrined. 'I see ... But I don't see any real harm in a fine cigar, do you?'

'Ashes!' Wakefield said firmly. 'And pneumatic particles! They float through the air, soil the cog-oil, defile the gearing. And to clean the Bureau's Engines – well, I needn't tell you that's a Sisyphean task, Dr Mallory.'

'Surely', Mallory mumbled. He tried to change the subject. 'As you must know, I am a palaeontologist, but I have some small expertise in clacking. How many gear-yards do you spin here?'

'Yards? We measure our gearage in *miles* here, Dr Mallory.'

"Struth! That much power?'

'That much trouble, you might as easily say', Wakefield said, with a modest flick of his white-gloved hand. 'Heat builds up from spinning-friction, which expands the brass, which nicks the cogteeth. Damp weather curdles the gear-oil – and in dry weather, a spinning Engine can even create a small Leyden-charge, which attracts all manner of dirt! Gears gum and jam, punch-cards adhere in the loaders ...' Wakefield sighed. 'We've found it pays well to take every precaution in cleanliness, heat, and humidity. Even our tea-cake is baked specially for the Bureau, to reduce the risk of crumbs!'

Howard Rheingold_ The Origins of Drama and the Future of Fun_1991

Virtual Reality was one of the first popular books to focus on the imaginary 'virtual' worlds created by head-mounted displays, data gloves and computers. Rheingold is the former editor of *Whole Earth Review* and author of a number of books. He lectures around the world on virtual reality research.

Rheingold is fascinated by virtual reality, which he writes about in excited, almost feverish prose. His first experience of virtual space he records thus:

I was standing in a carpeted room, gripping a handle, but I was also staring into microscopic space and directly manoeuvring two molecules with my hands. Perhaps someone in an earlier century experienced something similar looking through Leeuwenhoek's microscope or Galileo's telescope. It felt like a microscope for the mind, not just the eye.

I don't know the rules of 'molecular docking' – a tool for helping chemists find molecules shaped like keys to specific proteins – the way chemists know them, but I could *feel* them, though my hand and the force-reflective feedback mechanism built into the ARM, the Argonne Remote Manipulator. The metal grip felt like the handlebar of a gargantuan, well-lubricated Harley. I looked up at the million dollars' worth of articulated joints, encoiled by umbilicals of electrical cables. The entire apparatus was suspended from the ceiling a few feet above me. I wore light goggles connected by a wire to a computer.[1]

Rheingold was writing during the heady days of optimism about these new technologies. Within a decade, however, the world of commerce had to a large extent bent cyberspace to its own image. In the early 1990s it was much easier to be idealistic about the almost Platonic potential of cyberspace, and the magical worlds it could – and can – create. Rheingold continues:

At the beginning of the twentieth century, novelist Herman Hesse wrote about such a romanticized future mind-language in *Das Glasperlenspiel – The Glass-Bead Game*. Hesse's was a

Mandarin view of an intellectual élite who spent their time stringing concepts like beads on a board game. Their predecessors already exist, hungry for bandwidth – the communication freaks and idea hackers of the Worldnet, bouncing their personae around blind cyberspace through the narrow channel of on-line text.[2]

Rheingold's optimism, however, was countered by Benjamin Woolley in his book *Virtual Worlds*, published just one year later:

Rheingold is, I feel, optimistic in thinking that these ideas and developments will come together to deliver us to the brink of having the power to create any experience we desire, Computer-generated pictures will certainly become more complex and colourful … But the idea that, for example, virtual reality systems will immanently be capable of realizing a fictional world indistinguishable from the real one seems to skirt round the unanswered questions about the nature of fiction and the nature of simulation.[3]

Rheingold is important not just because he was one of the first writers on cyberspace but also because his prose inspired so many to take up the virtual-reality gauntlet. Here he discusses the notion of the 'theatrical' and ideas of 'play' in relation to cyberspace and the imagination. The human desire for 'make believe' and the digitized theatre of cyberspace have a very long and richly ornamented history.

1 Howard Rheingold, *Virtual Reality*, London: Martin Secker & Warburg Limited, 1991, p14.
2 Ibid, p217.
3 Benjamin Woolley, *Virtual Worlds*, London: Penguin, 1992, p242.

Theatre is a psychological process that uses language, rhythm, voice, myth, and perception-altering technologies to achieve a specific state of mind in the audience. Aristotle said *catharsis* was a healthy and necessary way for people to deal with the great themes of life and death. The means by which catharsis is induced in an audience, mimesis, is the emotional simulation capability that enable humans to empathize with the actors onstage and internalize the dramas presented before their eyes and ears after the curtain goes up. Understanding the human components of mimesis might become one of the foundations of the emerging psychological investigation of virtual experience. A challenge as formidable as discovering the nature of the human sense of mimesis is the thorny question of how to get the mimesis into a machine. Thorny questions tend to be very valuable on the frontiers of computer science when they furnish the 'driving problems' that Frederick Brooks believes to be a powerful engine of scientific progress. The challenge of building autonomous characters in cyberspace might be the driving problem that supercharges the application of VR technology to entertainment products. It is not unlikely that future scientific and technological breakthroughs could be stimulated by spinoffs from the entertainment industry's R & D. The development of artificial theories of drama that can be encoded in algorithms, for example, might be driven by the desire to create 'artificial characters' for future forms of entertainment.

In the early 1980s, one of the most exciting AI technologies was the 'expert system' or 'rule-based system' that captured a portion of human expertise in a set of rules that was 'extracted' from human experts through a question-and-answer process. By using such systems to augment one's limited knowledge of a field such as medical diagnosis or geological prospecting or laying out the architecture of microchips or configuring telecommunications networks (all successful application areas for expert systems), many people have been able to amplify their ability to make judgments about specific problems. One of the most successful early expert systems, MYCIN, contained a data base of information about a certain class of diseases and a set of rules that was contributed through interviews with diagnosticians who discussed the criteria they used for making a diagnosis on the basis of many different sets of symptoms. Another diagnostician who is not expert in MYCIN's class of diseases could query the system regarding the symptoms of a particular case and use the system's 'knowledge base' to help make a diagnosis.

Brenda Laurel and the other Atari-ites wanted to built a world you could walk into, with rocks that are hard to move, and heroes and villains and all the other characters that make fantasy fascinating. Techniques for controlling the appearance of computer-generated graphics require expertise and many hours of hard work, but at least we have an idea of how to do it. David Zeltzer and his students at Media Lab's Snake Pit are pursuing the difficult but not intractable problem of building autonomous 3D graphics characters, focusing on how they appear and how they move, but not paying attention to what they might say or how they might react to human communication. Building a sense of drama into a world, creating artificial characters that don't respond from a script, but improvise according to the rules of dramatic interaction, however, would require some kind of artificial intelligence beyond the capabilities of present technology. How, then, might such a future technology develop from what we know today? Laurel proposed in her thesis that an expert system could be applied to this problem. The expertise would consist of the rules laid out by Aristotle in *Poetics*, and the knowledge base would contain information about the artificial world and about the user-player's reactions to it.

But rule-based systems have turned out to be only part of the answer. Several different scientific breakthroughs in the past few years have shown the possibilities of fitting other programming approaches into a system that might overcome the deficiencies of rule-based systems. Chaos theory and the study of complex systems have revealed that the right set of very simple rules, applied repeatedly to the same information, can generate highly complex behaviour. And neural networks have shown that it is possible to build computers that know very little but are capable of learning a lot. Perhaps the answer lies in a hybrid of rules and networks. Or perhaps the pursuit of such a hybrid will uncover another obstacle that must be overcome by yet another computer tool. Brenda Laurel, in a 1986 paper, 'Interface as Mimesis', put forward a strong reason why people are bound to pursue fantasy amplifiers as soon as technology makes them possible:

> 'It is not enough to imitate life. Drama presents a methodology for designing worlds that are predisposed to enable significant and arresting kinds of actions – where characters make choices with clear causal connections to outcomes, where larger forces like ethics, fate, or serendipity form constellations of meaning that are only rarely afforded by the real world. Dramatically constructed worlds are controlled experiments, where the irrelevant is pruned away and the bare bones of human choice and situation are revealed through significant action. The predispositions of such worlds are embodied in the traits of their characters and the array of situations and forces embedded in their contexts. If we can make such worlds interactive, where a user's choices and actions can flow through the dramatic lens, then we will enable an exercise of the imagination, intellect, and spirit that is of an entirely new order.'

The reason I found myself thinking about Brenda Laurel's ideas while I was sitting in a meeting room at Fujitsu was that Mr Murakami invoked her name early in his presentation, when he started talking about the 'highest level' of the 'artificial reality' (AR) Fujitsu planned to create. Myron Krueger was mentioned, but Mr Murakami was more interested in personal systems than responsive environments, at least for the immediate future. The three levels of AR, as Fujitsu sees it, consist of the *device* level, the *system* level, and the *art and application* level. The device level is where the DataGlove, EyePhone, DataSuit, and other input hardware reside. Future eye-tracking and gloveless gesture-sensing technologies will fit into this layer when their design is optimized. The hardware systems that link the human and the computer are controlled and mediated by a software system that includes, according to the Fujitsu model, computer graphics, speech and gesture recognition, world modelling, and user-modelling capabilities. The highest level consists of the applications of such a system to operation of remote tools, to communication systems, and as a means of training people in various skills. The other half of the highest level is the 'artistic' level, and artificial, first-person dramas – soap operas and action movies the user can enter and participate in – appear to be the most important component of Fujitsu's research in this area.

Fujitsu sees the art of VR as something worth paying attention to. The three application areas they are aiming for are entertainment (their viewgraph subtitled this 'computer-based tools for a lot of funs [*sic*]'), CAD, and education. Each of these involves a key human element that Fujitsu is concentrating on now in their own laboratories and in research they support at Carnegie-Mellon University in Pittsburgh and elsewhere. The cyberspace system is designed as a growable collection of interlocking components that will come from convergent R & D efforts. The EyePhone, DataGlove, and fmTOWNS machine constitute the part of the present development system that the user sees, the 'front end'. The 'back end', the powerful computers and software that work behind the scenes to maintain the reality level of the virtual world, includes a Pixel Machine, a graphics supercomputer optimized for fast 3D models, a SUN workstation, a neural-network-based back end to the DataGlove that can be taught gesture recognition, a real-time graphic rendering system, and a world model system. The user puts on the glove and repeats key gestures until the neural network interface binds the gestures to specific commands. If you feel like pinching your nose to fly, instead of pointing your finger, the interface can be trained to do that.

The fmTOWNS machine seems to be designed to be the personal portal to a much larger virtual world of software and services that Fujitsu plans to develop in the future. The back end in particular involves several key assaults on driving problems. The Pixel Machine will take care of real-time rendering, but the details of the virtual world's appearance and behaviour will be mediated by a world model system that is also linked to the user by a 'neurosimulator'. The world model of the future will include today's standard physical model for the virtual environment and nonliving objects in it. For artificial characters in the virtual world, a model will consist of rule-based and neural network models for behaviour. Something they call 'scenario control' will also be involved in the back end. In other words, they want a world that you can walk around in, that will react to you appropriately, and that presents a narrative structure for you to experience.

One of Mr Murakami's depictions of what Fujitsu planned to market to the global teenagers of the next century was the cartoonlike sketch of a young male described at the beginning of this chapter. This hypothetical VR entertainment consumer of the future appeared to be approximately twelve years old, with a futuristic HMD and a pair of futuristic gloves linked to a familiar-looking television set with two black boxes under the monitor. A thought-balloon emanating from the young man's head showed the same young man in a fierce primeval landscape. In front of the armour-clad hero, Godzilla approached, making menacing sounds and gestures. In the hands of the user-player-actor-hero of the drama was a glowing sword. Presumably, the Godzilla module of the world model knew to bleed and die when it was stuck in the right place, and to breathe fire when the actor-model let his guard down. And presumably the scenario module would be capable of learning that this user wants more Godzillas to fight than maidens to rescue, or prefers exploring outer space to engaging in combat with mythical video creatures. Perhaps, with an additional Nintendo edu-module, the same world will become a geometric puzzle or historical simulation with educational content to be mined through the user's explorations.

The attempt to create the 'personalities' of artificial characters in cyberspace is taking place at Carnegie-Mellon University (CMU), one of the long-time bastions of AI and robotics research, by computer scientist Joseph Bates, based in large part on Brenda Laurel's ideas and Dr Bates's previous work in AI. Dr Laurel is a collaborator on the project. Bates knows how to build knowledge representation structures in LISP, Laurel knows the rules of dramatic interaction. 'Project OZ' is the name for the CMU project, and the principal funding comes from Fujitsu Research and Development. I exchanged e-mail with Dr Bates, which was appropriate for the present level of his project, which is demonstrable only as text on a screen. While others such as Zeltzer at MIT disregard questions of content in order to concentrate on building the form of a virtual character, Bates is using a text-only, content-oriented prototype, with the understanding that the 'intelligence' of the system he and Dr Laurel and their CMU colleagues are building eventually will be linked with animated characters in three-space. How these characters might act and respond is easily modelled and tested in text; and as anyone who has ever played a text-only adventure game can attest, ample mimesis can be triggered by interaction with a well-constructed narrative even in the form of words on a screen.

Indeed, a kind of text-based cyberspace phenomenon seems to have broken out all over the Internet.

Manuel De Landa_Policing the Spectrum_ 1991

War in the Age of Intelligent Machines synthesizes a history of weaponry with notions of nonlinear emergent dynamics, computers and the order on the edge of chaos that results from complexity. De Landa examines the history of warfare technology – from the machines of Renaissance sieges and Napoleon's invasions to the Nazi Blitzkrieg and the highly tuned technology of the Gulf War – and through it finds all manner of examples and illustrations for a variety of contemporary ideas. These include philosophies of the mind, artificial intelligence, artificial life, media philosophy, Baudrillardian simulacra and Virilio's *Aesthetics of Disappearance* (see p90).

Manuel De Landa lectures internationally on nonlinear dynamics, theories of self-organization, artificial intelligence and artificial life. He is also the author of *A Thousand Years of Nonlinear History* (1997).

Cultural critic Mark Dery has summarized De Landa's thesis thus:

De Landa's argument turns on the notion that singularities – 'the transition points ... where order spontaneously emerges out of chaos' – catalyse curiously lifelike behaviour in non-organic matter. By extension, he argues, the military apparatus might be seen as a self-organizing process in which human agents function as 'as industrious insects pollinating an independent species of machine-flower that simply does not possess its own reproductive organs.'[1]

That is to say, the development of ideal warfare hardware has been an almost natural pattern of a shifting landscape that has encouraged the growth of certain ideas at the expense of others. It has then shifted again to other preferable parameters, much like developing plants and animals in a typical garden. Small changes punctuate events to bring about different equilibria in a system.

De Landa sees nonlinear dynamic systems in the evolution of culture, economics and digital technology. He expresses these dynamic bifurcations and perturbations in terms of his concept of the 'machinic phylum', which he explains thus:

The machine phylum is simply the notion that as soon as you let matter and energy in any form (whether it is organic or inorganic) flow in a nonlinear manner (that is, past a certain threshold of complexity) machines will tend to spontaneously self-assemble. The key word here is 'nonlinear'. When you let matter and energy get far from equilibrium, spontaneously stabilized states called 'attractors' emerge.[2]

One aspect of this is the concept of 'dematerializing' – which digital technology has taken to its furthest extreme. De Landa considers the defensive wall: originally high walls were good for defence, but high-walled castles became easy targets for siege cannon and so they 'dematerialized' into low walls and ditches, built to geometric layouts for easy defensive cross-fire. This process continued:

Four centuries later, the offense created a radically new vehicle to deliver its message of shock and fire, the aerial bomber. As a response to this new means of communicating destruction, the fortified walls mutated again, in effect 'dematerializing' to become the electronic curtain of radar. Today, computers are allowing radar 'walls' to be built around entire continents, walls that are extendable to global proportions in the form of a nuclear umbrella.[3]

Inspired by the work of Gilles Deleuze and Félix Guattari (see p96), De Landa's analysis opens up a new way of seeing the evolution of smart digital machines as artificial ecologies subject to evolution and punctuated equilibrium.

1 Mark Dery, *Out of Control*, Wired 1.4 website. http://www.srl.org/interviews/out.of.control.html, accessed 09.01.01.
2 Ibid.
3 Manuel De Landa, *War in the Age of Intelligent Machines*, New York: Zone Books, 1991, p77.

Beyond war games any situation involving a crisis at a national scale (commodity shortages, transportation strikes, and of course, war mobilization) needed the establishment of consensus by a vast number of people distributed across the continent. The scientists who developed the use of computers for such crisis-management operations, people like Murray Turoff, later moved on to investigate new ways of extending these ideas into the field of collective intelligence. Thus, research originally intended to increase the amount of control over people (in a crisis) became a tool for bringing control back to people.

A similar point can be made with regard to other computer technologies. Expert systems technology involves the transference of know-how from particular human experts to machines. To the extent that the expertise thus acquired is 'hoarded' by a few people, this technology may be seen as a way of centralizing control. But if the computer interface of the expert system is made interactive enough, allowing human experts to conduct conversations with these 'machine consultants', an expert system may become part of the scientific process of diffusion of knowledge. It could, for example, help human experts reach agreements and produce knowledge. But it could also allow non-experts to share in some of the benefits of that knowledge. Thus, whether an expert system becomes a replacement for human judgment, as in autonomous weapons or battle management systems, or an aid in the diffusion of expertise among humans, depends on whether knowledge banks are hoarded or shared. And this in turn depends not so much on human intentions as on the design of the computer interface that decides whether a few privileged people or a whole community has access to those banks of expertise.

Although the work of scientists like Licklider, Engelbart, Kay and Turoff was indispensable in wresting control of the evolution of computers from the military, it was not enough to bring computers to the rest of the population. The personal computers designed at PARC never reached the market-place, partly because of myopic vision on the part of its business management. The scientists working at PARC had developed personal computers as a way to implement their intellectual commitment toward interactivity, but also out of a burning desire to get their hands on those machines. But in the area of a total, uncompromising desire to interact with computers, the scientists at PARC could not compete with another community which had developed alongside these research centres: the hackers. What the hackers lacked in intellectual preparation, they more than made up with absolute commitment to the cause of interactivity.

From the early 1960s, Artificial Intelligence researchers like Marvin Minsky and John MacCarthy had developed a symbiotic relationship with young, obsessed programmers. The scientist would think of interesting projects to test their theories (like a chess-playing machine, for instance), and then let hackers implement those projects on the computer. In this process the hackers developed an unwritten ethical code which would become one of the driving forces behind the interactive movement, and the force that would eventually bring the personal computer to the marketplace. This ethical code was never encoded in a manifesto, but was embodied instead in the hackers' practices. It involved the idea that information should flow freely without bureaucratic controls and that computers should be used to build better, more interactive computers (that is, to advance the bootstrapping process). Typically, a hacker would write a piece of software, maximizing interactivity, and then place it in a 'toolbox', where it was available to anyone who wanted to use it or improve on it. Programs were not the private property of their creators, but tools to be distributed as widely as possible in a community.

IBM's batch-processing, with its long waiting lines and its 'high-tech priests' controlling all points of access to the machine, was the dominant paradigm of human-machine interaction when the hacker ethic began to develop. For this reason implementing this ethical code in practice involved from the start an anarchist attitude toward regulations. If a machine needed to be fixed and the tools were under lock and key, the hacker ethic demanded that the lock be dismantled and the tool retrieved. The same was true for other kinds of locks, like computer passwords.

> To a hacker a closed door is an insult, and a locked door is an outrage. Just as information should be clearly and elegantly transported within the computer, and just as software should be freely disseminated, hackers believed people should be allowed access to files or tools which might promote the hacker quest to find out and improve the way the world works. When a hacker needed something to help him create, explore, or fix, he did not bother with such ridiculous concepts as property rights.

Interactivity, the passing of the machinic phylum between humans and computers, was developed both as an intellectual goal by visionary scientists, and 'conquered in battle' by the hackers at MIT. It was scientists like Engelbart and Kay who transformed the computer screen into a place where a partnership between humans and machines could be developed. But it was hackers like Steve Wozniak and Steve Jobs who out of sheer desire assembled these ideas into a machine that could compete in the marketplace against gigantic corporations like IBM. Doubtless, some interactivity would have found its way into computers even if these pioneers had not existed. It is clear that programmers can be more productive if they can fix errors while running a program, rather than having to punch it into paper cards and then wait several days to see the results. But the military and corporations like IBM are not in the business of giving people total control over computers. While smaller companies like DEC had developed a more interactive approach to computing by the 1960s, there is no reason to believe that they would have given to people more than the necessary amount of control. Without hackers and hacker-like scientists, I believe, the amount of interactivity that would have found its way into computers would not have reached by itself the minimum threshold needed for the bootstrapping process to acquire its own momentum.

Besides being the place where the machinic phylum joins humans and machines into a higher level, synergistic whole, the computer screen has become a window into the phylum itself. I have defined 'machinic phylum' in terms of singularities. The mathematical techniques needed to study singularities were invented by Henri Poincaré at the turn of the century, and then slowly developed in obscure areas of mathematics (like topology). In the 1960s people like Edward Lorenz began using computers to study singular points in physical systems (weather systems) and the modern chaos science began to take shape.

But the real breakthrough came when the behaviour of singularities began to be studied 'visually' on computer screens. Speaking of the windows into the phylum that computers have opened for us, Ralph Abraham, a famous chaos mathematician has said, 'All you have to do is put your hands on these knobs, and suddenly you are exploring this other world where you are one of the first travellers and you don't want to come up for air.' The machine whose knobs he was turning at the time, was an analog computer used by the members of the Santa Cruz Dynamical Systems Collective to explore the internal structure of singularities (strange attractors). The members of this collective, 'mathematical hackers' as it were, developed the interactive approach to mathematical research which has come to be known as 'experimental mathematics'. Indeed, interactivity has allowed theories of self-organization to create new paradigms of scientific research. Since World War II, most elementary research has been undertaken in huge, billion-dollar particle accelerators. But now the cutting edge of exploration is shifting back to the desk top. Before the inner secrets of the phylum could only be explored in military-controlled laboratories, but now a smaller laser, a personal computer and human ingenuity have begun to open new, unpoliced roads into the machinic essence of the planet: the singularities at the onset of self-organization.

But if the efforts of hackers and visionary scientists to develop an interactive approach to computers have opened new paths for the exploration of the machinic phylum, they have also generated dangers of their own. For one thing, some elements of the hacker ethic which were once indispensible means to channel their energies into the quest for interactivity (system-crashing, physical and logical lock-busting) have changed character as the once innocent world of hackerism has become the multimillion-dollar business of computer crime. What used to be a healthy expression of the hacker maxim that information should flow freely is now in danger of becoming a new form of terrorism and organized crime which could create a new era of unprecedented repression.

In late 1988 a hacker released the first full-scale 'virus' into the Internet, a national computer network, paralyzing it after a design error made the virus grow out of control. Prior to this incident a virus was a small vandal program that infiltrated computers hidden in a 'Trojan horse', usually a free, public-domain piece of software. Once inside the computer the virus would use the 'reproductive organs' of the host machine (the disk-copying device, for example) to create replicas of itself.

At a certain point the parasitic program would do some piece of hacker vandalism, like crashing the system or erasing some files. While system-crashing by hackers in its earliest stages was their way of revealing subtle flaws in a computer's design (part of the hacker ethic that systems should work perfectly or be fixed), in its viral version it has become a potential form of terrorism. The 1988 virus attack, for instance, after hitting the MIT computer, struck at the heart of think-tank land, the RAND Corporation.

A century ago the miniaturization of explosives coupled with certain versions of anarchist theory produced the first wave of quasi-organized terrorism. The groups responsible for the attacks, at first inspired by anti-Statism and vague notions of liberation, were quickly infiltrated by secret agents. The Ochrana, the Czarist secret police, had already perfected the 'agent provocateur', a secret operative in charge of infiltrating liberation movements and forcing them along the wrong path, the path of terrorism. Through people like Prussian master spy Wilhelm Stieber, the Ochrana exported this 'innovation' to the rest of the European continent. Violent organizations usually possess such a fanatic self-confidence that they tend to disregard the possibility of infiltration by provocateurs.

The Weather Underground, the terrorist splinter group of the SDS in the 1960s, even had an 'acid test' to detect such intrusions. They would give LSD to potential new recruits in the belief that a secret agent would break down during a trip. Little did they know that the CIA had been tripping throughout the 1950s, creating a special caste of 'enlightened agents' for just such occasions.

The next virus released into computer networks could very well be the action of one such provocateur. Hackers who think of themselves as immune to infiltration should pay attention to such historical lessons. Hackers, indeed, should build a mechanism to detect and stop those attacks, just as in an ideal world the 1960s movements should have had a built-in mechanism to prevent the creation of sects like the Weathermen.

Marcos Novak_Liquid Architectures in Cyberspace_1991

Like an architectural shaman, Marcos Novak was one of the first people to show architects the way into the new realm of cyberspace, and demonstrate how new technologies could be exploited to create architectonic space. His essay 'Liquid Architectures in Cyberspace', written when Novak was Assistant Professor at the University of Texas, was featured in a highly influential collection of essays entitled *Cyberspace: First Steps* published by MIT Press in 1991. Edited by the architect Michael Benedikt, the book featured contributions from practitioners in various disciplines including cultural commentators, artists, anthropologists, systems engineers, architects and software developers. Novak's essay was arguably the most influential piece in this seminal collection.

Cyberspace: First Steps was a clarion call to all those interested in the cultural and design implications of cyberspace, and represented the first serious attempt to illustrate the wide-ranging impact of cyberspace on a variety of disciplines. Benedikt sets the scene in his introduction:

Cyberspace: A new universe, a parallel universe created and sustained by the world's computers and communication lines. A world in which the global traffic in knowledge, secrets, measurements, indicators, entertainments, and alter-human agency takes on form: sights, sounds, presences never seen on the surface of the earth blossoming in a vast electronic night.'[1]

The book is perhaps at its best when considering the spatial ramifications of cyberspace and their impact on architectural product and discourse.

Novak's essay comprises two parts. The first, 'Cyberspace', considers the poetic implications of the new virtual space: 'It is in poetry that we find a developed understanding of the workings of magic, and not only that, but a wise and powerful knowledge of its purposes and potentials', Novak declares. 'Cyberspace is poetry inhabited, and to navigate through it is to become a leaf on the wind of a dream.'[2] In the second part, 'Liquid Architectures', Novak claims cyberspace for the architectural avant-garde. He argues that buildable and built architecture is only a proportion of the architect's production. His premiss is that, throughout history, there has been a tradition of deliberately unbuildable architectural projects. His notion of 'liquid architecture in cyberspace' is an electronic version of the space of the visionary but deliberately unbuildable project.

Cyberspace posited in this way is the equivalent of the technologized soul-space for architects outlined by Margaret Wertheim (see p298), in that it is a space of transformation uninhibited by real-world idiosyncrasies such as gravity or the phenomenology of materials. To Wertheim, cyberspace has returned to us the real and virtual duality of the Middle Ages; to Novak, cyberspace has given credence and purpose to the purity of the architect's dream. Equally, for Novak, it is a space where the architect's dream bifurcates, evolves, disperses and dissolves, running to the music of algorithms.

Novak's essay was the first in a series of hugely influential essays on 'Transarchitectures', a word he coined that sought to bring the virtual into full architectural theoretical discourse. We are now able to look back and recognize the architectural potential and spatial structures of cyberspace, but in 1991, these great possibilities were shrouded in the shock of the new.

1 Michael Benedikt (ed), Introduction, *Cyberspace: First Steps*, Cambridge, MA: MIT Press, 1991, p1.
2 Marcos Novak, 'Liquid Architectures in Cyberspace', in *Cyberspace: First Steps*, Michael Benedikt (ed), Cambridge, MA: MIT Press, 1991, p1.

Cyberspace Architecture

Architecture has been earthbound, even though its aspirations have not. Buckminster Fuller remarked that he was surprised that, in spite of all the advances made in the technology of building, architecture remained rooted to the ground by the most mundane of its functions, plumbing. Rooted by waste matter, architecture has nevertheless attempted to fly in dreams and projects, follies and cathedrals.

Architecture has never suffered a lack of fertile dreams. Once, however, in times far less advanced technologically, the distance between vision and embodiment was smaller, even though the effort required for that embodiment was often crushing. Most 'grand traditions' began with an experimental stage of danger and discovery and did not become fossilized until much later. Hard as it may be for us to fathom, a Gothic cathedral was an extended experiment often lasting over a century, at the end of which there was the literal risk of collapse. The dream and the making were one. Curiously, the practice of architecture has become increasingly disengaged from those dreams. Cyberspace permits the schism that has emerged to be bridged once again.

Cyberspace alters the ways in which architecture is conceived and perceived. Beyond computer-aided design (CAD), design computing (DC), or the development of new formal means of describing, generating, and transforming architectural form, encodes architectural knowledge in a way that indicates that our conception of architecture is becoming increasingly musical, that architecture is spatialized music. Computational composition, in turn, combines these new methods with higher-level compositional concepts of overall form subject to local and global constraints to transform an input pattern into a finished work. In principle, and with the proper architectural knowledge, any pattern can be made into a work of architecture, just as any pattern can be made into music. In order for the data pattern to qualify as music or architecture it is passed through compositional 'filters', processes that select and massage the data according to the intentions of the architect and the perceptual capacity of the viewer. This 'adaptive filtering', to use a neural net term, provides the beginning of the intelligence that constitutes a cyberspace and not a hypergraph. This, of course, means that any information, any data, can become architectonic and habitable, and that cyberspace and cyberspace architecture are one and the same.

A radical transformation of our conception of architecture and the public domain that is implied by cyberspace. The notions of city, square, temple, institution, home, infrastructure are permanently extended. The city, traditionally the continuous city of physical proximity becomes the discontinuous city of cultural and intellectual community. Architecture, normally understood in the context of the first, conventional city, shifts to the structure of relationships, connections and associations that are webbed over and around the simple world of appearances and accommodations of commonplace functions.

I look to my left, and I am in one city; I look to my right, and I am in another. My friends in one can wave to my friends in the other, through my having brought them together.

It is possible to envision architecture nested within architecture. Cyberspace itself is architecture, but it also contains architecture, but now without constraint as to phenomenal size. Cities can exist within chambers as chambers may exist within cities. Since cyberspace signifies the classical object yielding to space and relation, all 'landscape' is architecture, and the objects scattered upon the landscape are also architecture. Everything that was once closed now unfolds into a place, and everything invites one to enter the worlds within worlds it contains.

I am in an empty park. I walk around a tree, and I find myself in a crowded chamber. The tree is gone. I call forth a window, and in the distance see the park, leaving.

Liquid Architecture

That is why we can equally well reject the dualism of appearance and essence. The appearance does not hide the essence, it reveals it; it is the essence. The essence of an existent is no longer a property sunk in the cavity of this existent; it is the manifest law which presides over the succession of its appearances, it is the principle of the series.

… But essence, as the principle of the series is definitely only the concatenation of appearances; that is, itself an appearance.
… The reality of a cup is that it is there and that it is not me. We shall interpret this by saying that the series of its appearances is bound by a principle which does not depend on my whim.
— Jean-Paul Sartre, *Being and Nothingness*

The relationship established between architecture and cyberspace so far is not yet complete. It is not enough to say that there is architecture in cyberspace, nor that *that* architecture is animistic or animated. Cyberspace calls us to consider the difference between animism and animation, and animation and metamorphosis. Animism suggests that entities have a 'spirit' that guides their behaviour. Animation adds the capability of change in *location*, through time. Metamorphosis is change in *form*, through time *or space*. More broadly, metamorphosis implies changes in one aspect of an entity as a function of other aspects, continuously or discontinuously. I use the term liquid to mean animistic, animated, metamorphic, as well as crossing categorical boundaries, applying the cognitively supercharged operations of poetic thinking.

Cyberspace is liquid. Liquid cyberspace, liquid architecture, liquid cities. Liquid architecture is more than kinetic architecture, robotic architecture, an architecture of fixed parts and variable links. Liquid architecture is an architecture that breathes, pulses, leaps as one form and lands as another. Liquid architecture is an architecture whose form is contingent on the interests of the beholder; it is an architecture that opens to welcome me and closes to defend me; it is an architecture without doors and hallways, where the next room is always where I need it to be and what I need it to be. Liquid architecture makes liquid cities, cities that change at the shift of a value, where visitors with different backgrounds see different landmarks, where neighbourhoods vary with ideas held in common, and evolve as the ideas mature or dissolve.

The locus of the concept 'architecture' in an architecture that fluctuates is drastically shifted: any particular appearance of the architecture is devalued, and what gains importance is, in Sartre's terms, 'the principle of the series'. For architecture this is an immense transformation: for the first time in history the architect is called upon to design not the object but the principles by which the object is generated *and varied* in time. For a liquid architecture requires more than just 'variations on a theme', it requires the invention of something equivalent to a 'grand tradition' of architecture at each step. A work of liquid architecture is no longer a single edifice, but a continuum of edifices, smoothly or rhythmically evolving in both space and time. Judgements of a building's *performance* become akin to the evaluation of dance and theatre.

If we described liquid architecture as a symphony in space, this description would still fall short of the promise. A symphony, though it varies within its duration, is still a fixed object and can be repeated. At its fullest expression a liquid architecture is more than that. It is a symphony in space, but a symphony that never repeats and continues to develop. If architecture is an extension of our bodies, shelter and actor for the fragile self, a liquid architecture is that self in the act of becoming its own changing shelter. Like us, it has an identity; but this identity is only revealed fully during the course of its lifetime.

Conclusion

A liquid architecture in cyberspace is clearly a dematerialized architecture. It is an architecture that is no longer satisfied with only space and form and light and all the aspects of the real world. It is an architecture of fluctuating relations between abstract elements. It is an architecture that tends to music.

Music and architecture have followed opposite paths. Music was once the most ephemeral of the arts, surviving only in the memory of the audience and the performers. Architecture was once the most lasting of the arts, reaching as it did into the caverns of the earth, changing only as slowly as the planet itself changes. Symbolic notation, analog recording, and, currently, digital sampling and quantization, and computational composition, have enabled music to become, arguably, the most permanent of the arts. By contrast, the life span of architecture is decreasing rapidly. In many ways architecture has become the least durable of the arts. The dematerialized, dancing, difficult architecture of cyberspace, fluctuating, ethereal, temperamental, transmissible to all parts of the world simultaneously but only indirectly tangible, may also become the most enduring architecture ever conceived.

I am in a familiar place. Have I been here before? I feel I know this place, yet even as I turn something appears to have changed. It is still the same place, but not quite identical to what it was just a moment ago. Like a new performance of an old symphony, its intonation is different, and in the difference between its present and past incarnations something new has been said in a language too subtle for words. Objects and situations that were once thought to have a fixed identity, a generic 'self', now possess personality, flaw and flavour. All permanent categories are defeated as the richness of the particular impresses upon me that in this landscape, if I am to benefit fully, attention is both required and rewarding. Those of us who have felt the difference nod to each other in silent acknowledgment, knowing that at the end of specificity lies silence, and what is made speaks for itself, not in words, but in presences, ever changing, liquid.

The moment one starts to design with digital processes one is immediately dealing with a different aesthetic. This aesthetic can be called the 'second aesthetic': the aesthetic of the algorithm. The 'first aesthetic' gives definitive form to objects and enclosures. The second aesthetic derives its potency from possibility and numerous outcomes in problem-solving. In computer programming the algorithm is the diagram that one sets down to map the various stages of solving a problem. It will involve various processes, dependent on its input data. The algorithm can be also made to attempt to achieve optimum criteria; this type of algorithm is called a genetic algorithm. Steven Levy defines the genetic algorithm as an '...expeditious formula, a sort of recipe, a key to solving a problem'. He goes on to say, 'this particular algorithm is based on genetic principles. Therefore the genetic algorithm could perform to criteria based on scaling "fitness landscapes" to achieve optimum performance.' Therefore it can be programmed to achieve an architecturally desired goal. There are two approaches that are possible; the first, to be able to create evolving architectural

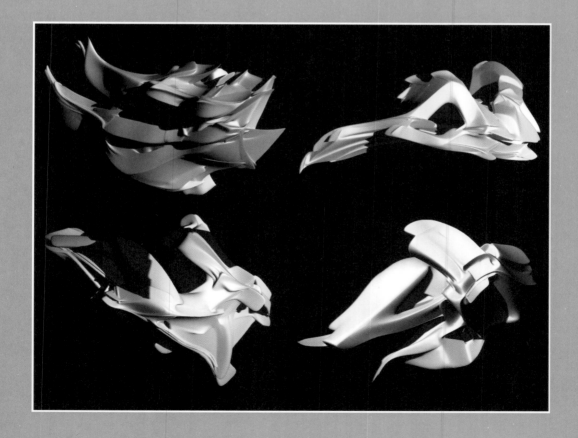

form; the second, to be able to create evolving architectural behaviour. This then suggests that architecture becomes an ecology of interactive elements, each rearticulating itself relative to varying spatial criteria and its relationship to its peers and users. Marcos Novak employs algorithmic techniques to create architectures that he defines as 'Liquid Architectures'. The two images (top) are algorithmic architectures created in virtual space. The image (bottom left) is of 'everted' four-dimensional forms. Eversion is Novak's term for establishing relationships between actual and virtual space, where actions and events in one space can have ramifications in the other. The image (bottom right) is part of a project that further explores this virtual/actual coalition and is the evolving data landscape at the virtual heart of an everted project.

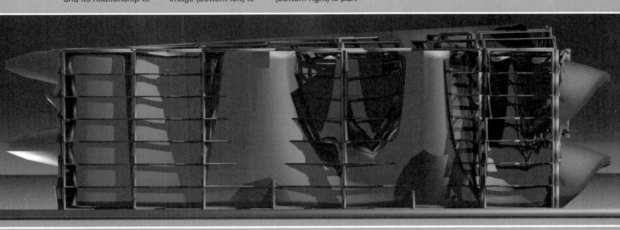

Daniel C Dennett_An Empirical Theory of the Mind: The Evolution of Consciousness_ 1992

The philosopher Daniel C Dennett is an advocate of the idea of 'emergence' in the study of human consciousness. The central notion of emergence is that it is a 'bottom-up' approach to the organization of groups. The fact that geese fly in a V-shape formation is an emergent phenomenon: no matter how much you dissected a single goose, you would have no idea how a group of them arranged themselves in a particular shape. It is the computer, with its millions of instructions per second, that has made this science possible by being able to simulate flocking and evolutionary behaviour like the search for food by millions of virtual animals. The organizational patterns that are created are examples of emergence. These patterns can happen symbiotically both within the system being examined and its immediate environment. Dennett explains:

Emergence is what my model [of consciousness] and theirs [the complexity scientists] have in common. A few years back I had to talk about 'innocent emergent features' so that the biologists wouldn't get upset and think I was talking about something mystical. But, yes, emergence is a real, hard science phenomenon, and it's central to understanding consciousness.[1]

Dennett is Distinguished Professor of Arts and Sciences and Director of the Center for Cognitive Studies at Tufts University in Massachusetts, and is well versed in all manner of discourses including neuroscience, linguistics, artificial intelligence, computer science and psychology. As well as emergence, the other important element in Dennett's model of consciousness – as expounded in his book *Consciousness Explained* – is language. Dennett maintains that the facility of language separates our consciousness from that of animals, and that the act of language itself transforms intelligence. The sense of self is critical to human consciousness, and it is language that makes this sense possible.

The following excerpt from *Consciousness Explained* puts forward the idea that the brain's workings are analogous to parallel networks of computers, all capable of pretending to be other machines. Any computer is capable of simulating another machine – whether a calculator, a magnifying glass, a dictionary or a word processor. Thus machines can be nested, one inside another, or hybrid, and can assume different roles at different times, much like your computer can become a calculator, word processor or print compositor at any given time. The idea of the virtual machine has its roots in von Neumann's architecture of computers and Alan Turing's work on the Turing machine (see p40). Dennett refers to it as an 'intuition pump', a device for encouraging speculation:

The idea of consciousness as a virtual machine is a nice intuition pump. It takes a while to set up, because of a lot of jargon of artificial intelligence and computer science is unfamiliar to philosophers or other people. But if you have the patience to set some of these ideas up, then you can say 'Hey! Try thinking about the idea that what we have in our heads is software. It's a virtual machine in the same way that a word processor is a virtual machine.' Suddenly, bells start ringing, and people start seeing things from a slightly different perspective.[2]

Dennett's book thoughtfully uses the computer paradigm to shed light on human consciousness and how our consciousness might be able to flit from one mode of thought to another.

1 Daniel Dennett, quoted in Roger Lewin, *Complexity: Life on the Edge of Chaos*, London: Phoenix, 1993, p157.

2 Daniel Dennett, 'Intuition Pumps', in *The Third Culture: Beyond the Scientific Revolution*, John Brockman (ed), New York: Simon and Schuster, 1995, p183.

Daniel C Dennett, 'An Empirical Theory of the Mind: The Evolution of Consciousness', *Consciousness Explained*, 1992

We *know* there is something at least *remotely* like a von Neumann machine in the brain, because we know we have conscious minds 'by introspection' and the minds we thereby discover are at least this much like von Neumann machines: they were the inspiration for von Neumann machines! This historical fact has left a particularly compelling fossil trace: computer programmers will tell you that it is fiendishly difficult to program the parallel computers currently being developed, and relatively easy to program a serial von Neumann machine. When you program a conventional von Neumann machine, you have a handy crutch; when the going gets tough, you ask yourself, in effect, 'What would I do if I were the machine, trying to solve this problem?' and this leads you to an answer of the form, 'Well, first I'd do this, and then I'd have to do that, etc.' But if you ask yourself 'What would I do in this situation if I were a thousand-channel-wide parallel processor?' you draw a blank; you don't have any personal familiarity with – any 'direct access to' – processes happening in a thousand channels at once, even though that is what is going on in your brain. Your only access to what is going on in your brain comes in a sequential 'format' that is strikingly reminiscent of the von Neumann architecture – although putting it that way is historically backwards.

There is a big difference, as we have seen, between a (standard) computer's serial architecture and the parallel architecture of the brain. This fact is often cited as an objection to Artificial Intelligence, which attempts to create human-style intelligence by devising programs that (almost always) run on von Neumann machines. Does the difference in architecture make a theoretically important difference? In one sense, no. Turing had proven – and this is probably his greatest contribution – that his Universal Turing machine can compute any function that any computer, with any architecture, can compute. In effect, the Universal Turing machine is the perfect mathematical chameleon, capable of imitating *any* other computing machine and doing, during that period of imitation, *exactly* what that machine does. All you have to do is feed the Universal Turing machine a suitable description of another machine, and, like Marcel Marceau (the Universal miming machine) armed with an explicit choreography, it forthwith proceeds to produce a perfect imitation based on that description – it becomes, virtually, the other machine. A computer program can thus be seen either as a list of primitive instructions to be followed or as a description of a machine to be imitated.

Can you imitate Marcel Marceau imitating a drunk imitating a baseball batter? You might find the hardest part of the trick was keeping track of the different levels of imitation, but for von Neumann machines this comes naturally. Once you have a von Neumann machine on which to build, you can nest virtual machines like Chinese boxes. For instance, you can first turn your von Neumann machine into, say, a Unix machine (the Unix operating system) and then implement a LISP machine (the LISP programming language) on the Unix machine – along with WordStar, Lotus 123, and a host of other virtual machines – and then implement a chess-playing computer on your LISP machine. Each virtual machine is recognizable by its *user interface* – the way it appears on the screen of the

CRT and the way it responds to input – and this self-presentation is often called the *user illusion*, since a user can't tell – and doesn't care – how the particular virtual machine he's using is implemented in the hardware. It doesn't matter to him whether the virtual machine is one, two, three, or ten layers away from the hardware.[1] (For instance, WordStar users can recognize, and interact with, the WordStar virtual machine wherever they find it, no matter what variation there is in the underlying hardware.)

So a virtual machine is a temporary set of highly structured regularities imposed on the underlying hardware by a *program*: a structured recipe of hundreds of thousands of instructions that give the hardware a huge, interlocking set of habits or dispositions-to-react. If you look at the microdetails of all those instructions reeling through the instruction register, you will miss the forest for the trees; if you stand back, however, the functional architecture that emerges from all those microsettings can be clearly seen: it consists of virtual *things*

such as blocks of text, cursors, erasers, paint-sprayers, files
and virtual *places*

such as directories, menus, screens, shells
connected by virtual *paths*

such as 'ESCape to Dos', or *entering* the PRINT menu *from* the MAIN menu and permitting various large-and-interesting virtual *operations* to be performed

such as searching a file for a word, or enlarging a box drawn on the screen.

Since any computing machine at all can be imitated by a virtual machine on a von Neumann machine, it follows that if the brain is a massive parallel processing machine, it too can be perfectly imitated by a von Neumann machine. And from the very beginning of the computer age, theorists used this chameleonic power of von Neumann machines to create virtual parallel architectures that were supposed to model brainlike structures.[2] How can you get a one-thing-at-a-time machine to be a many-things-all-at-once machine? By a process rather like knitting. Suppose the parallel processor being simulated is ten channels wide. First, the von Neumann machine is instructed to perform the operations handled by the first node of the first channel (node 1), saving the result in a 'buffer' memory, and then node 2, and so forth, until all ten nodes in the first layer have been advanced one moment. Then the von Neumann machine tackles the effects of each of these first-layer results on the next layer of nodes, drawing the previously calculated results one at a time from the buffer memory and applying them as input to the next layer. Laboriously it proceeds, knitting back and forth, trading off time against space. A virtual ten-channel-wide machine will take *at least* ten times as long to simulate as a one-channel machine, and a million-channel-wide machine (like the brain) will take at least a million times longer to simulate. Turing's proof says nothing about the speed with which the imitation will be accomplished, and for some architectures, even the blinding speed of modern digital computers is overwhelmed by the task.

That is why AI researchers interested in exploring the powers of parallel architectures are today turning to *real* parallel machines – artifacts that might with more justice be called 'giant electronic brains' – on which to compose their simulations. But in principle, any parallel machine can be perfectly – if inefficiently – mimicked as a virtual machine on a serial von Neumann machine.[3]

Now we are ready to turn this standard idea upside-down. Just as you can simulate a parallel brain on a serial von Neumann machine, you can also, in principle, simulate (something like) a von Neumann machine on parallel hardware, and that is just what I am suggesting: conscious human minds are more-or-less serial virtual machines implemented – inefficiently – on the parallel hardware that evolution has provided for us.

1 Or it might not be a *virtual* machine at all. It might be a made-to-order hardwired special-purpose real machine, such as a LISP machine, which is a descendant of LISP *virtual* machines, and which is designed right down to its silicon chips to run the programming language LISP.

2 The 'logical neurons' of McCulloch and Pitts (1943) were actually devised contemporaneously with the invention of the serial computer, and influenced von Neumann's thinking, and these in turn led to the Perceptrons of the fifties, the ancestors of today's connectionizm. For a brief historical account see Papert (1988).

3 For more on the implications of real-world speed, and its implications for Artificial Intelligence, see 'Fast Thinking' in my *The Intentional Stance* (1987).

Neal Stephenson_Snow Crash_1992

One of the great cyberpunk novels of the 1990s, *Snow Crash* established Stephenson as one of the genre's finest wordsmiths and ideas people. Stephenson, an American, describes himself as issuing 'from a clan of rootless, itinerant hard-science and engineering professors'. He majored in physics then switched to geography.

Snow Crash, Stephenson's second novel, was written between 1988 and 1991. It takes the thriller noir of Gibson's *Neuromancer* (see p102) and combines it with a grungy humour and surreal vignettes. Its backdrop is the 'Metaverse', a communal virtual space for which the novel's hero (endearingly called Hiro Protagonist) helped to write the protocols. At the centre of Metaverse lies the Street:

Like any place in Reality, the Street is subject to development. Developers can build their own small streets feeding off the main one. They can build buildings, parks, signs as well as things that do not exist in Reality, such as vast hovering overhead light shows, special neighbourhoods, where the rules of three-dimensional space-time are ignored and free-combat zones where people can go to hunt and kill each other.[1]

With its addendum spaces where the urban paradigm collapses, where gravity and linear time are denied, the Metaverse reveals the true nature of cyberspace. Here it becomes an anarchic disordered space, full of surreality and pregnant suspense.

Stephenson's Metaverse is clunky and full of avatars – 'Brandys' and 'Clints' – that are cheap clones of one another. It does not have the high-tech sheen of Gibsonian cyberspace, with its almost alternative reality. Stephenson's virtuality is more earthy, less corporately aggressive, although capitalism underscores the Street nonetheless:

In order to place these things on the Street, they have had to get approval from Global Multimedia Protocol Group, have had to buy frontage on the Street, get zoning approval, obtain permits, bribe inspectors, the whole bit. The money these corporations pay to build things on the Street all goes into a trust fund owned and operated by GMPG, which pays for developing and expanding the machinery that enables the Street to exist.[2]

'Snow Crash' itself is a virus. The book plots the intrigues of the virus's propagation and Hiro's subsequent fight against it, both in real and virtual space. As can be seen in the excerpt that follows, Stephenson's vision of virtual space exhibits a keen three-dimensional view of how computer space might evolve in the near future. Within this architectural-type space there exist disjunctures, anomalies, hyperbuttons and almost faithfully retaining virtual servants.

Although *Snow Crash* is set in virtual space it has overtones of the more reality-based notion of Augmented Reality. With Augmented Reality, a user wearing a set of data goggles can simultaneously experience virtual and real space. Everyday uses of this technology include surgery, building (to see pipe runs behind walls) and manufacturing (providing complex assembly instructions). Some of the spaces of *Snow Crash* appear as though they might have been created by Augmented Reality; indeed, *Snow Crash* was originally written as a video game.

In this scene Stephenson makes the connection between computer viruses and real-world rituals, myths and spells of possession. This is his method for linking the *Snow Crash* over real and virtual terrains. It can be seen as a direct relation to the work of Erik Davis and his 'Techgnosis' (see p190), or Margaret Wertheim and her notions of virtual soul space (see p298). Like William Gibson's 'Voodoo Loas' analogy for the fragmentation of his omnipresent 'Wintermute', Stephenson utilizes an arcane religious concept to describe a high-tech phenomenon.

1 Neal Stephenson, *Snow Crash*, London: ROC, Penguin Books, 1992, p23.
2 Ibid, p24.

Hiro hangs up and walks into the new room. The Librarian follows.

It is about fifty feet on a side. The centre of the space is occupied by three large artifacts, or rather three-dimensional renderings of artifacts. In the centre is a thick slab of baked clay, hanging in space, about the size of a coffee table, and about a foot thick. Hiro suspects that it is a magnified rendering of a smaller object. The broad surfaces of the slab are entirely covered with angular writing that Hiro recognizes as cuneiform. Around the edges are rounded, parallel depressions that appear to have been made by fingers as they shaped the slab.

To the right of the slab is a wooden pole with branches on top, sort of a stylized tree. To the left of the slab is an eight-foot-high obelisk, also covered with cuneiform, with a bas-relief figure chiselled into the top.

The room is filled with a three-dimensional constellation of hypercards, hanging weightlessly in the air. It looks like a high-speed photograph of a blizzard in progress. In some places, the hypercards are placed in precise geometric patterns, like atoms in a crystal. In other places, whole stacks of them are clumped together. Drifts of them have accumulated in the corners, as though Lagos tossed them away when he was finished. Hiro finds that his avatar can walk right through the hypercards without disturbing the arrangement. It is, in fact, the three-dimensional counterpart of a messy desktop, all the trash still remaining wherever Lagos left it. The cloud of hypercards extends to every corner of the 50-by-50-foot space, and from floor level all the way up to about eight feet, which is about as high as Lagos's avatar could reach.

'How many hypercards in here?'

'Ten thousand, four hundred and sixty-three,' the Librarian says.

'I don't really have time to go through them,' Hiro says. 'Can you give me some idea of what Lagos was working on here?'

'Well, I can read back the names of all the cards if you'd like. Lagos grouped them into four broad categories: Biblical studies, Sumerian studies, neurolinguistic studies, and intel gathered on L. Bob Rife.'

'Without going into that kind of detail – what did Lagos have on his mind? What was he getting at?'

'What do I look like, a psychologist?' the Librarian says. 'I can't answer those kinds of questions.'

'Let me try it again. How does this stuff connect, if at all, to the subject of viruses?'

'The connections are elaborate. Summarizing them would require both creativity and discretion. As a mechanical entity, I have neither.'

'How old is this stuff?' Hiro says, gesturing to the three artifacts.

'The clay envelope is Sumerian. It is from the third millennium B.C. It was dug up from the city of Eridu in southern Iraq. The black stele or obelisk is the Code of Hammurabi, which dates from about 1750 B.C. The treelike structure is a Yahwistic cult totem from Palestine. It's called an asherah. It's from about 900 B.C.'

'Did you call that slab an envelope?'

'Yes. It has a smaller clay slab wrapped up inside of it. This was how the Sumerians made tamper-proof documents.'

'All these things are in a museum somewhere, I take it?'

'The asherah and the Code of Hammurabi are in museums. The clay envelope is in the personal collection of L. Bob Rife.'

'L. Bob Rife is obviously interested in this stuff.'

'Rife Bible College, which he founded, has the richest archaeology department in the world. They have been conducting a dig in Eridu, which was the cult centre of a Sumerian god named Enki.'

'How are these things related to each other?'

The Librarian raises his eyebrows. 'I'm sorry?'

'Well, let's try process of elimination. Do you know why Lagos found Sumerian writings interesting as opposed to, say, Greek or Egyptian?'

'Egypt was a civilization of stone. They made their art and architecture of stone, so it lasts forever. But you can't write on stone. So they invented papyrus and wrote on that. But papyrus is perishable. So even though their art and architecture have survived, their written records – their data – have largely disappeared.'

'What about all those hieroglyphic inscriptions?'

'Bumper stickers, Lagos called them. Corrupt political speech. They had an unfortunate tendency to write inscriptions praising their own military victories before the battles had actually taken place.'

'And Sumer is different.'

'Sumer was a civilization of clay. They made their buildings of it and wrote on it, too. Their statues were of gypsum, which dissolves in water. So the buildings and statues have since fallen apart under the elements. But the clay tablets were either baked or else buried in jars. So all the *data* of the Sumerians have survived. Egypt left a legacy of art and architecture; Sumer's legacy is its megabytes.'

'How many megabytes?'

'As many as archaeologists bother to dig up. The Sumerians wrote on everything. When they built a building, they would write in cuneiform on every brick. When the buildings fell down, these bricks would remain, scattered across the desert. In the Koran, the angels who are sent to destroy Sodom and Gomorrah say, 'We are sent forth to a wicked nation, so that we may bring down on them a shower of clay-stones marked by your Lord for the destruction of the sinful.' Lagos found this interesting – this promiscuous dispersal of information, written on a medium that lasts forever. He spoke of pollen blowing in the wind – I gather that this was some kind of analogy.'

'It was. Tell me – has the inscription on this clay envelope been translated?'

'Yes. It is a warning. It says, "This envelope contains the nam-shub of Enki".'

The Librarian stares off into the distance and clears his throat dramatically.

'Once upon a time, there was no snake, there was no scorpion,
There was no hyena, there was no lion,
There was no wild dog, no wolf,
There was no fear, no terror,

Man had no rival.
In those days, the land Shubur-Hamazi,
Harmony-tongued Sumer, the great land of the *me* of princeship,
Uri, the land having all that is appropriate,
The land Martu, resting in security,
The whole universe, the people well cared for,
To Enlil in one tongue gave speech.
Then the lord defiant, the prince defiant, the king defiant,
Enki, the lord of abundance, whose commands are trustworthy,
The lord of wisdom, who scans the land,
The leader of the gods,
The lord of Eridu, endowed with wisdom,
Changed the speech in their mouths, put contention into it,
Into the speech of man that had been one.
That is Kramer's translation.'

'That's a story,' Hiro says. 'I thought a nam-shub was an incantation.'

'The nam-shub of Enki is both a story and an incantation,' the Librarian says. 'A self-fulfilling fiction. Lagos believed that in its original form, which this translation only hints at, it actually did what it describes.'

'You mean, changed the speech in men's mouths.'

'Yes,' the Librarian says.

'This is a Babel story, isn't it?' Hiro says. 'Everyone was speaking the same language, and then Enki changed their speech so that they could no longer understand each other. This must be the basis for the Tower of Babel stuff in the Bible.'

'This room contains a number of cards tracing that connection,' the Librarian says.

'You mentioned before that at one point, everyone spoke Sumerian. Then, nobody did. It just vanished, like the dinosaurs. And there's no genocide to explain how that happened. Which is consistent with the Tower of Babel story, and the nam-shub of Enki. Did Lagos think that Babel really happened?'

'He was sure of it. He was quite concerned about the vast number of human languages. He felt there were simply too many of them.'

'How many?'

'Tens of thousands. In many parts of the world, you will find people of the same ethnic group, living a few miles apart in similar valleys under similar conditions, speaking languages that have absolutely nothing in common with each other. This sort of thing is not an oddity – it is ubiquitous. Many linguists have tried to understand Babel, the question of why human language tends to fragment, rather than converging on a common tongue.'

'Has anyone come up with an answer yet?'

'The question is difficult and profound,' the Librarian says. 'Lagos had a theory.'

'Yes?'

'He believed that Babel was an actual historical event. That it happened in a particular time and place, coinciding with the disappearance of the Sumerian language. That prior to Babel/Infocalypse, languages tended to converge. And that afterward, languages have always had an innate tendency to diverge and become mutually incomprehensible – that this tendency is, as he put it, coiled like a serpent around the human brainstem.'

'The only thing that could explain that is—'

Hiro stops, not wanting to say it.

'Yes?' the Librarian says.

'If there was some *phenomenon* that moved through the population, altering their minds in such a way that they couldn't process the Sumerian language anymore. Kind of in the same way that a virus moves from one computer to another, damaging each computer in the same way. Coiling around the brainstem.'

'Lagos devoted much time and effort to this idea,' the Librarian says. 'He felt that the nam-shub of Enki was a neurolinguistic virus.'

'And that this Enki character was a real personage?'

'Possibly.'

'And that Enki invented this virus and spread it throughout Sumer, using tablets like this one?'

'Yes. A tablet has been discovered containing a letter to Enki, in which the writer complains about it.'

'A letter to a god?'

'Yes. It is from Sin-samuh, the Scribe. He begins by praising Enki and emphasizing his devotion to him. Then he complains:

'Like a young...(line broken)

I am paralyzed at the wrist.

Like a wagon on the road when its yoke has split,

I stand immobile on the road.

I lay on a bed called 'O! and O No!'

I let out a wail.

My graceful figure is stretched neck to ground,

I am paralyzed of foot.

My...has been carried off into the earth.

My frame has changed.

At night I cannot sleep,

my strength has been struck down,

my life is ebbing away.

The bright day is made a dark day for me.

I have slipped into my own grave.

I, a writer who knows many things, am made a fool.

My hand has stopped writing

There is no talk in my mouth.'

'After more description of his woes, the scribe ends with,

"My god, it is you I fear.

I have written you a letter.

Take pity on me.

The heart of my god: have it given back to me".'

Steven Levy_The Strong Claim_1992

On its publication in 1993, *Artificial Life* was received as a lucid and exhilarating breakthrough in scientific journalism. Using tactics drawn not just from science writing but also from biography, the book tells the story of the ideas, experiments and characters that have been critical to the development of artificial life, both theory and practice. Steven Levy is an American journalist, and the author of *Hackers* and *The Unicorn's Secret*.

The concept of artificial life is based on the premiss that all biological life is simply the manipulation of information. Since computers are adept at reconfiguring information, it should be possible to create something with them that could in some sense be called 'alive'.

Artificial life research falls into two categories: weak and strong. 'Weak' is research that attempts to use artificial life to find out more about human beings; 'strong', the subject of Levy's book, is that which seeks to develop distinct virtual creatures that evolve, respond to their locality and reproduce. Artificial life's attempt to steal demiurgic power was seized by science-fiction writers as an appropriate backdrop to stories about human hubris, machines out of control and the nonchalant creation of super-beings.

The quest for artificial life has both utilized and created many computational objects that have a changing relationship to their surroundings; these are known as reflexive organisms. Levy's documentation of artificial life's development starts with the experiments of John von Neumann (see p40) and his 'finite automata', and leads to a discussion of John Horton Conway's concept of the 'Game of Life'. Levy quotes Conway:

Life occurs on a virtual checkerboard. The squares are called cells. They are in one of two states: alive or dead. Each cell has eight possible neighbours, the cells which touch its sides or its corners.

If a cell on the checkerboard is alive, it will survive in the next step (or generation) if there are either two or three neighbours also alive. It will die of overcrowding if there are more than three neighbours, and it will die of exposure if there are fewer than two.

If a cell on the checkerboard is dead, it will remain dead in the next generation unless exactly three of its eight neighbours are alive. In that case the cell will be born in the next generation.[1]

With the aid of computers, the various generations of the Game of Life can be played out very quickly. Over generations it becomes apparent that various structures – which Conway calls 'gliders' – break from the main mass of the game and move off independently, retaining and repeating their cellular configuration, having a 'life' of their own. Levy tells us that Conway 'later wondered whether "insect" might have been a better term for the gliders'.

The Game of Life is a type of 'cellular automata'; these rules-based systems have been widely used to create patterns and processes that appear to be very much part of nature's lexicon. Levy's book demonstrates how these and other relatively simple concepts can create many strange virtual worlds and organisms, where creatures respond to their changing circumstances – whether the aggression of their peers, their landscape, their hunger or the attractiveness of another.

One of the most successful examples of artificial life is the computer virus, which Levy discusses in the extract reproduced here.

1 Steven Levy, *Artificial Life: The Quest for a New Creation*, London: Penguin, 1992, p52.

Steven Levy, 'The Strong Claim', *Artificial Life: The Quest for a New Creation*, 1992

On November 3, 1983, Fred Cohen allowed his attention to drift from the discussion in the small seminar room at the University of Southern California (USC). It was a graduate course in computer security, a subject that fascinated Cohen. Consulting work in that area was helping him continue his studies. But he had other burdens that day. Earlier that year his thesis proposal had been rejected. Within a week, he would confront the six-month deadline for submitting another. So far, all he had was a workman-like elaboration of his original failed attempt, which dealt with theories of parallel processing. If his professors rejected that, there would be no doctorate in computer science and not much of a career. It was no surprise that his mind was restless that day.

Cohen was a nomadic student in electrical engineering and computer security. The son of physicists, he had grown up in Pittsburgh, where he earned a bachelor's degree at Carnegie-Mellon and a masters in information science from the University of Pittsburgh. Robust, brash, and sometimes impolitic, Cohen liked a good time. He was a member of both the lacrosse and Frisbee teams. Yet he realized that the demands of adulthood were on him. Vowing to become 'a perfect student', he entered USC to study computational theory and robotics.

Now, Fred Cohen daydreamed as his professor Leonard Adleman and Cohen's fellow students discussed various Trojan-horse attacks on computers. In Cohen's studies on parallel processing, he had become interested in distributed algorithms, a way to allocate parts of a single computational problem to different parts of a computer or even to different computers. He mused that one way to tackle the mechanics of this would be via self-replicating programs. Cohen was of course familiar with von Neumann's work. But the idea he was hatching that morning dealt with much simpler constructs than the famous self-reproducing automaton. What if simple pieces of programs could insert themselves into other programs and assume control of them, in the same way that parasites fix themselves to hosts?

'It was as if there were this curtain between me and the truth, and God split the curtain apart and said, *"There it is"*.' says Cohen when describing his feelings that day. 'I immediately understood the implications. I'd been working on computer security for a long time – I knew how systems worked, and how different attacks worked … But now it came over me. Anyone who writes one of these things would have something that could replicate everywhere.'

Cohen's realization provided another key piece in the puzzle of how life should be defined. Life should be regarded as one half of a duplex system: the organism and its environment. A recipe for interactions capable of cooking up the mechanics of life required the setting that allowed its potential to be fulfilled. The DNA code is effective within the structure of a cell, which provides the raw materials to interpret the code by forming its vital enzymes. Von Neumann's kinematic self-reproducing automaton required a lake stocked with the proper body parts. And a certain class of computer program that could self-replicate and feed on other programs needed a rich data environment. In creating a dizzyingly complex matrix of computer operating systems, we had inadvertently spawned this environment. It was fertile ground for a new type of creature: a parasitic information organism. So rich was this world of data that Cohen believed that even simple creatures could live in it – and wreak havoc on its stability.

When the seminar ended, Cohen explained the idea to Adleman. The professor immediately identified the biological analogue to what Cohen proposed was possible: viruses.

Unknown to Adleman or Cohen, science-fiction writer David Gerrold, in his 1972 book, *When Harley Was One*, had already used the word 'virus' (whose own meaning derives from that Latin word for poison) to refer to a rogue computer construct. The coinage had not caught on: Gerrold, in fact, had deleted the relevant passage in reprints of the novel. Cohen ultimately would define a computer virus as 'a program that can "infect" other programs by modifying them to include a possibly evolved copy of itself'.

Adleman encouraged Cohen to experiment with the idea. Cohen retreated to the small office he shared with four other students and sat down at his terminal. Within five minutes he had written the code for a program that could insinuate itself into other programs. A computer virus. The easiest part – the destructive component – completed, Cohen worked until the early evening on the more difficult component: code so that the construct would not proliferate uncontrollably. By eight o'clock that night he had completed his work: two hundred lines in the computer language C that would be known as the first documented computer virus.

Cohen wanted the virus literally to seek permission before infecting other programs. 'I didn't want to have something that just spread, I wanted to have something I could control,' he explains. 'It was quite clever as viruses go. Not only would it ask me for authorization, but it wouldn't randomly infect everything. I did analysis of the habits of various users [this was readily available to Cohen because of the habit of the UNIX operating system to provide lists of each user's files] and figured out which programs were run most often by most users. It would infect the thing that was most likely to spread the infection furthest and fastest. It's no different than a biological disease – if you wanted to infect a lot of humans, you would choose to begin with someone like a prostitute in Las Vegas.'

Adleman secured permission for Cohen to release his program into the UNIX environment of the VAX 11-750 computer at USC. Cohen doubts that his adviser fully explained the nature of the experiment to the administrators that granted the request. How could they have known the implications? Cohen was certain that he could maintain control of his creature. He was the first computer scientist ever to conduct a scientifically monitored release of a predatory information organism 'in the wild'.

The experiment was performed in mid-afternoon, peak time for computer usage at the university. There were approximately fifty users time-sharing the VAX.

Cohen's virus was implanted into a program called 'vd'. The ostensible nature of the program was to display people's files in a graphic, easy-to-read manner. While an infected version of vd would perform this function, the virus within it enabled Cohen to subsume the identity of the user who bore the disease. If and when the most important user on a UNIX computer – the system user, also known as the 'root' – became infected, Cohen would then have that system user's access to everything on the system, including the ability to read and write to all files, including the operating system itself. It would be like capturing the queen bee: the hive would be his. Cohen posted the availability of the program on the user bulletin board and waited.

When the first user accepted the bait and accessed the program, the virus struck. Scanning the user's files and comparing them to the log determining program activity (kept elsewhere in the system), it chose the most 'social' program to infect. In the UNIX system, certain programs in the files of individual users were available to everyone on the system – those most accessed were the choices for invasion. The virus required only half a second to insert itself into this file, a time far too brief for any user to suspect anything was amiss.

In the case of this first infection, the program chosen was an on-screen time-of-day indicator that many users liked to run when they worked with an editing program called EMACS. Approximately half the users would routinely access this clock. When the virus asked Cohen permission to infect, he granted it. The infection then spread to other people using the clock and soon reached the user who had possession of the EMACS program itself. From then on, everyone who used that program would become infected – pending Cohen's permission. The infection would reside in the most social file of each contaminated user. Within a few minutes, the root himself accessed an infected program, and the virus's job was done.

Cohen's virus had completely penetrated the system.

Cohen was now able to access the programs and files of any user; he could type commands as if he were that user. He used this power to carefully eradicate the virus from each user's files. Then he ran the experiment again. He unleashed the virus five times in all. Each time, he achieved 100% penetration. Here was the way Cohen logged a typical run (note that 'loadavg' was a frequently used utility program that measured user activity, and 'editor' referred to the EMACS program):

Elapsed Time (in minutes)	Event	Effect
0	Program announced on BBoard	Existence published
1 min	Social user runs program	'Loadavg' infected
4 min	Editor owner runs	'Loadavg' editor infected
8–12 min	Many users use editor	Many programs infected
14 min	Root uses editor	All privileges granted

The fourteen-minute capture time above was Cohen's second best. The shortest was five minutes. The longest saturation period was an hour.

When Cohen demonstrated his creation at Adleman's seminar, exactly a week after he first conceived the idea, his fellow students seemed to have difficulty understanding what it was they were seeing. One by one, Cohen would have them log into the system and access an infected program. As they watched in astonishment, they were set on by Fred Cohen's virus. Cohen was easily able to explain the theory and the mechanics of what they were seeing. Awakening them to the significance of the experiment was another matter. Cohen later compared the reaction to someone going to his automobile in the morning and finding it missing. One's first reaction might be to wonder if he had parked the car somewhere else. Then he might ask his wife if she had moved the car. It might slowly begin to dawn on him that the car might be stolen. Even so, before calling the police, that person would probably check the parking spot once more. Sometimes evidence alone was not enough to turn a belief around. It also required a willingness truly to see the evidence.

Partially for this reason, Cohen exercised great caution when documenting his results. He took to heart the advice of David Jefferson, then still at USC, who, realizing the significance of Cohen's find, said, 'Make this the greatest paper you will ever write'. After receiving permission to make computer viruses his thesis topic (it was so late in the game that this could only be done by first submitting his previous proposal with the verbal understanding that he would quickly submit a brief on his proposed subject change), Cohen read extensively on epidemiology, analysed his data in exacting mathematical terms, and planned experiments on other systems. The latter was no simple matter. As soon as the administrators in charge of the initial test site saw results of Cohen's first experiments, they unconditionally banned any encores, even those proposed by Cohen that would implement special programs to test a system's ability to resist possible infections. 'This apparent fear reaction seems typical,' wrote Cohen in his thesis. 'Rather than try to solve technical problems technically, policy solutions are often chosen.'

Those administering other systems at USC expressed similar fears and even refused Cohen permission to perform his experiments using sanitized versions of log tapes in off-line simulation. It seemed to Cohen as if they hoped to eradicate the potential menace of predatory computer programs by willing it away. After months of negotiation, Cohen was finally able to repeat some of his tests on other systems and to reconfirm his results. But despite proposing what he considered foolproof safeguards, he was never able to secure the access he required to experiment with and measure the dissemination of computer viruses.

When Cohen began to discuss his research in public, the response was even more alarming. Cohen would claim that after he spoke at one computer security conference in Canada, an American official told him that, had the State Department known of the subject of his talk, it would not have allowed him to speak. Cohen further claimed that he was subject to a thorough search on re-entering the country. After he completed his thesis in 1985, the newly minted doctor had difficulty publishing the paper summarizing it. Finally, in 1987, it was accepted by the journal *Computers and Security*. Because Cohen did not want the people who assisted him to become stigmatized, he felt compelled to take the unusual step of acknowledging them only by their Christian names.

By then it was four years since Fred Cohen had first stumbled on the realization that a fertile information environment existed for a potentially destructive form of artificial life. Cohen had been suffering, and would continue to suffer, from a virtual lockout in funding. His academic career was marked by an inability to continue his experimentation in computer viruses, almost all of which would have been centred in eradication and prevention. Cohen would later vividly recall a presentation from that period. As he introduced the audience to the brave new world of computer viruses, his eyes chanced on the obviously disturbed visage of a young woman.

'It was as if someone told her her mother was not her mother,' says Cohen. 'That's the reaction I got from most people until the theory and practice of this thing became well understood. It was not within their belief set. And it wasn't until they got hit by it that they understood.'

Cohen would eventually be recognized as the father of the computer virus. (This was not necessarily a career-enhancing distinction.) After more research, however, he recognized the footprints of others. Although no-one had created a rigorously defined computer virus before Cohen, there had been speculation about predatory computer organisms, with isolated sightings that had become part of computer folklore. Some of these had been products of a digital demimonde. Throughout computer history, such unauthorized after-hours activities sometimes masked advances in the science. Those ventures constituted the brief history of free-range artificial life-forms: wildlife. They came into being as pranks, or unorthodox means of research, and in no case did they seem designed for destruction. But they portended a potentially horrifying future if artificial life were realized without proper controls. Worse, their persistence indicated that those controls might be unattainable.

Roger Lewin_Life in a Computer_1993

Roger Lewin's *Complexity* deals with the changing patterns or order that can result from complex systems such as weather ecologies or colonies of animals over time. Lewin worked as a journalist for *New Scientist* in London and then *Science* in Washington, DC, before becoming a full-time writer of popular science books.

The idea of conscious and self-reproducing machines has obsessed humankind for centuries. Many attempts were made in previous centuries to build thinking machines usually in human form. There is a long history of automata beguiling the courts of Europe and Asia. John von Neumann (see p40) brought these ideas to a new level. The journalist Steven Levy describes von Neumann's important 1940s lecture 'The General and Logical Theory of Automata':

By the term 'automata' von Neumann was referring to self-operating machines, specifically any such machine whose behaviour could be unerringly defined in mathematical terms. An automaton is a machine that processes information, proceeding logically, inexorably performing its next action after applying data received from outside itself. Since von Neumann no reason why organisms, from bacteria to human beings, could not be viewed as machines – and vice versa.[1]

Von Neumann believed that through such endeavours one could understand not only machines but also the process of life itself.

These conceptual machines can now be built within the virtual space of the computer: accessible, cheap and powerful computation has spawned the science of artificial life. Key to this has been the introduction of the genetic algorithm, invented by American computer researcher John Holland. In computer programming the algorithm is the diagram that one sets down to map the various stages of solving a problem; this will involve a number of processes, dependent on input data. The algorithm can be also made to attempt to achieve optimum criteria; this type of algorithm is called a genetic algorithm. Steven Levy has defined the genetic algorithm as an 'expeditious formula, a sort of recipe, a key to solving a problem ... based on genetic principles. Therefore the genetic algorithm could perform to criteria based on scaling "fitness landscapes" to achieve optimum performance.'[2] This excerpt from *Complexity* describes how Tom Ray created an artificial life ecology utilizing genetic algorithms.

Today artificial evolutionary characteristics are relatively easy to program into even the most basic computer. Science-fiction authors have explored this as a way to create highly evolved virtual colonies. In *Permutation City* (see p222) Greg Egan creates a series of virtual organisms, the 'Lambertians', and charts their swiftly evolving metamorphosis and the ethical considerations of their creators as they become more and more intelligent.[3]

Some forward-thinking architects are inspired by genetic algorithms to create responsive environments – whether virtual or real. Spaces within architectures can be conditioned to develop evolutionary behaviour (see the extract from John Frazer, p246). Perhaps the ethical problems caused by Egan's 'Lambertians' might one day be caused by intelligent buildings.

1 Steven Levy, *Artificial Life: The Quest for a New Creation,* London: Penguin, 1992, p15.
2 Ibid, p159.
3 Greg Egan, *Permutation City*, London: Millennium (Orion), 1994.

At the beginning of October 1989, Tom [Ray] made his trip to Los Alamos, and ascended to the intellectual stratosphere. Chris Langton, Doyne Farmer, Walter Fontana, Stephanie Forrest, Steen Rassmussen – these were big names, the top people in dynamical systems, in artificial life. Their message was threefold. Tom had to attend to security, to make sure whatever he might produce would not escape. Second, the chances of his being able to write a self-replicating program that would survive mutation were close to zero. And third, whatever he did would surely take a very long time. Others, with greater technical experience, had been in the game longer, and had not succeeded. The gathering was extremely friendly, supportive, but not especially encouraging about immediate prospects. [...]

The task was to produce a simple organism that contained instructions for its own replication, and no more. Nothing about its potential evolution would be built in. The organism would be subject to a low rate of mutation – a flip from 1 to 0, or vice versa, in its code, just as Earth organisms experience random changes in their DNA. The organisms would compete for space and time: space in the computer's memory, an analogue for space in a real ecosystem; and for the amount of time the replicating algorithm would spend in the computer's central processing unit, an analogue for energy. 'I wanted to avoid building anything into the system that might shape its behaviour, that would determine the patterns of its behaviour,' said Tom. 'I wanted it to have the simplest of constraints, variation and selection, the basis of natural selection.' In the context of dynamical systems, I asked if he wanted to see what global patterns would emerge from the operation of local rules, the variation and selection. 'That's precisely right.'

Tom had already designed his simple organism – an eighty-instruction algorithm – before he went to Los Alamos. It had been 'a trivial task', as the Go player of a decade earlier had suggested. The challenge next was to ensure that the whole thing didn't fail because of the brittleness problem, that any small mutation would bring the program to a halt. Inspired by further analogies from biology, Tom modified his computer system. First, he reduced the size of the instruction set of the machine code from something like 4 billion to just thirty-two. This brought it in line with the twenty amino acids (coded for by sixty-four codons in the DNA) that operate in the biological realm. 'I just had the feeling that staying with the original huge number of code instructions would be a problem,' he explained.

The second analogue Tom borrowed from biology was 'addressing by template'. In most machine codes, when a piece of data is addressed, the exact numeric address of the data is specified. This is not how biology goes about things. For example, a protein, A, in a cell will interact with a second protein, B, when the two come together by diffusion; complementary shapes on their surfaces lock into each other. Tom exploited this trick of nature, by putting a short code of four instructions, in the pattern 1111, at the head of his creature, and another group of four, in the pattern 1110, at its tail. 'Between these two instructions I filled in a program that would start by looking for the pattern complementary to 0000 to find its head and record its location, then look for the pattern complementary to 0001 to find its tail and record its location; and then calculate the size,' Tom explained. The program in between the head and tail codes contains instructions for replicating the organism and finding a nearby location for the 'daughter' organism. Moreover, addressing by template also allowed organisms to find neighbours, with which they might interact.

As far as I knew, no one else had taken this path, of marrying tricks of molecular biology with tricks of computers, with the aim of producing artificial life. 'I think it's important,' Tom said. 'I'm a pretty good programmer, for a biologist, but not compared with those guys at Los Alamos. But I know about biology; they don't.' Tom had expected to spend years modifying the program. Instead, by 18 December, just two months after starting on it, Tom was able to send an e-mail message to Chris, saying, 'My [Artificial Life] simulator is running!' He also told Chris that he'd decided to call the system Tierra, which is Spanish for Earth, rather than Gaia. 'I didn't want to confuse what I was doing with all that New Age stuff,' Tom explained to me.

Two weeks later, the last bugs were out of the system and it was ready to go. It was 3 January. 'I set the thing going, and left it to run overnight,' Tom said, recalling what obviously had been a tense but exquisite moment in his life. 'I didn't sleep much.' Tom had already glimpsed fragments of life in Tierra during the debugging process. He knew that something was going to happen, something interesting. But he had no way of predicting just how interesting it would be. 'All hell broke loose,' was how he described what had occurred overnight in his virtual world. 'From the original ancestor, parasites very quickly evolved, then creatures that were immune to the parasites,' said Tom. 'Some of the descendants were smaller than the ancestral organism, some were bigger. There were hyperparasites, social creatures. I saw arms races, cheaters, there was –' Wait a minute, I interrupted, you have to explain these creatures to me. When Tom described himself as a naturalist of a virtual world, he meant it: the digital organisms were as real to him as the ant butterflies had been.

'OK,' said Tom. 'Would you like to see some of it?' In that first burst of evolution, Tom had to delve into the database to uncover the bestiary. Now, however, with the help of computer enthusiasts at Delaware, he had a visual display of Tierra. The different creatures are represented by horizontal bars of different lengths and colours stacked on the screen. Though no Walt Disney animation, this multicoloured matrix nevertheless conveyed the sense of a world in motion, as new creatures entered the scene while others dropped out. 'Let's look at parasite-host interaction,' said Tom, as he clocked through a directory. The records of that first run are stored, and Tom can go over what happened again and again, just like a paleontologist searching through the fossil record of life.

Parasites, Tom explained, evolved by dropping a chunk of the original eighty-byte genome, finishing up just forty-five instructions in length, and making use of neighbours' replication instructions. They don't harm their hosts, but they deprive them of valuable energy and space. When hosts are plentiful and space is in short supply, the parasites flourish. A crash in host population is followed by a crash in parasites, too, just as in real life. 'You get the classic Lotka-Volterra cycle,' said Tom as we watched the periodic rise and fall of host populations, tracked closely by parasite populations. Textbook, I said. The cycle, which is the best known pattern in population biology, describes the interaction between populations of a predator species and its prey. With an established prey population, a population of predators will increase. Eventually, the predators begin to have a serious impact on the prey population, which begins to decrease. With fewer prey to eat, the predators begin to suffer, and its population now decreases. Released from the pressure of predation the prey population now rebounds, followed by the predator population. The cycle of rise and fall of populations continues indefinitely, and the pattern was to be seen in Tom's digital ecosystem. 'Yes, there's lots of textbook ecology in Tierra,' Tom said. Competitive exclusion, keystone predator phenomena, periods of stability punctuated by bursts of change – many occur in Tierran ecology, all classic patterns of Earth ecology. 'We even see occasional mass extinctions.'

And all this emerges from a few fundamental rules, I ventured, nothing built in that would ensure these patterns? 'Nothing built in,' replied Tom. 'What you're seeing is the emergence of global patterns from simple rules. The notion of something deep as an organizing force appeals to me, always has.' That's a familiar sentiment, I said. Stu Kauffman used the same words when he described his Boolean networks and the emergence of order. 'We've talked a few times,' said Tom. 'Nothing philosophical, though, just about the details of the systems, his and mine. But, yes, from what you say we both have the same sense of something deep here. That's why evolution has been a central scientific theme for me, the idea that some process on the level of physics leads to increasing complexity. That's what you see in nature, and that's what you see in Tierra.'

Examples to illustrate the evolutionary race between hosts and parasites in a soup of the Tierra Synthetic Life program, developed by Tom Ray. Each of the four images represents a soup of 60,000 bytes, divided into 60 segments of 1,000 bytes each. Each individual creature is represented by a coloured bar.

Top left, hosts (red bars) are very common. Parasites (yellow bars) have appeared but are still relatively rare.

Top right, hosts are now rare because parasites have become very common. Immune hosts, blue, have appeared but are rare.

Below left, immune hosts are increasing in frequency, separating the parasites into the top of memory resolution.

Below right, immune hosts now dominate memory, while parasites and susceptible hosts decline in frequency. The parasites will soon be driven to extinction.

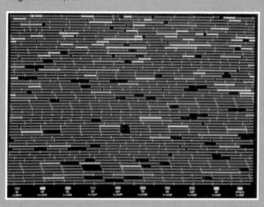

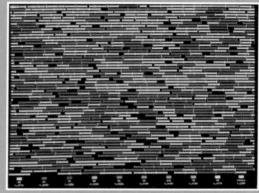

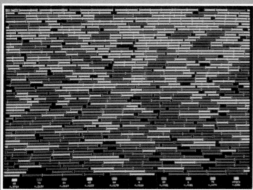

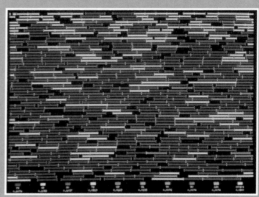

Jeff Noon_Stash Riders_1993

By 1993, the year *Vurt* was published, the genre of cyberpunk science-fiction novels was firmly established. Neal Stephenson's *Snow Crash* (see p164), with its cyberspace matrix, had done for the 1990s what William Gibson's *Neuromancer* (see p102) had done for the previous decade. Cyberspace was the ultimate space for cathartic reflection and risk, an unfolding jump-cut adventure where one could experience all manner of hybrid creatures and visions.

Jeff Noon is a particularly English author. Previously a pop musician, a painter and a playwright, he was at one time playwright-in-residence at The Royal Exchange in Manchester. *Vurt* is his peculiar take on the world of cyberpunk. It won Noon the coveted Arthur C Clarke Award in 1994, and has been variously described by critics as 'startling ... disturbing and original' and 'too beautiful for bikers, too harsh for hippies'. Instead of being set in a massive urban sprawl somewhere in the United States or teetering vertigo-like through an alien Asian/Russian corporate/black-market economy, it is set in the English city of Manchester. But this is no normal Manchester.

A common cyberpunk notion lies at *Vurt*'s narrative core. In 1950 Norbert Weiner, in his book *The Human Use of Human Beings*, posited that the brain was inherently similar to the computer, since both worked on processing binary data: the computer on ones and zeros, and the brain's neurons on a binary stimuli/no stimuli. Some cognitive psychologists believe that the human brain can be programmed and unravelled as a series of programs just like a computer. Arjen Mulder and Maaike Post see this work, augmented by more recent ideas, as leading directly into cyberpunk fiction:

These [early cybernetic] theories and practices have been substantially refined and dynamited, notably since the 1980s with the advent of learning computers that didn't have static algorithms, such as neural networks, genetic algorithms, fuzzy logic, et cetera. Still the idea of the equality of machines and men (animals) as systems of information processing has only become more and more taken for granted. ... with novels such as William Gibson's

Neuromancer, Neal Stephenson's *Snow Crash* and Jeff Noon's *Vurt* ... a direct connection has been established between computers and human bodies.[1]

But *Vurt* goes further than this. The writer wittily transmutes the nanotechnology of K Eric Drexler (see p116) into the all-purpose smart biomechanical lubricant 'vaz' that is used to mend everything: bodies, mechanisms and physiologies. Noon depicts the city of Manchester – with enough visual clues for it to be recognizable – in the grip of a drug called 'vurt', a weird psychedelic potion taken by tickling a feather at the back of the throat. Vurt hallucinations are surreal, yet powerfully real. Noon's cathartic paraspace is always folded back into reality: the vurt trips and detritus-laden Manchester are often interchangeable. Ideas and characters are exchanged across the vurt/real divide.

Noon's Manchester is populated by dogmen, shadowcops and robo-crusties – hybrid chimera characters who are second-class citizens to the non-hybridized. These hybrids are the result of an earlier overwhelming fecundity, which affected all manner of animals, humans and phenomena in what can be seen as a bio-technical disaster.

Vurt is a seminal work, its vision inspired by computation, bio-technology and nanotechnology, distorted to create a surreal, almost plausible, alternative reality. As computational technology and its cyberspaces become more dissolved within the body, it is a reality that is surely worth pondering upon.

This book is a witty warning of the dangers of humanity's hubris and its kaleidoscope of partial realities and hybridizations.

1 Arjen Mulder and Maaike Post, *Book of the Electronic Arts*, The Netherlands: V2 Publishers, 2000.

Mandy came out of the all-night Vurt-U-Want, clutching a bag of goodies.

Close by was a genuine dog, flesh and blood mix; the kind you don't see much any more. A real collector's item. It was tethered to the post of a street sign. The sign read NO GO. Slumped under the sign was a robo-crusty. He had a thick headful of droidlocks and a dirty handwritten card – 'hungry n homeless. please help'. Mandy, all twitching steps and head-jerks, scurried past him. The crusty raised his sad little message ever so slightly and the thin pet dog whined.

Through the van's window I saw Mandy mouth something at them; 'Fuck off, crusties. Get a life.' Something like that.

I was watching all this in the halo of the night lights. We stuck to the dark hours in those days. The Thing was on board and that was a major crime; possession of live drugs, a five-year stretch guaranteed.

We were waiting in the van for the new girl. Beetle was up front, ladies' leather gloves pulled tight onto his fingers, smeared with Vaz. He likes to feel a little bit greased when he rides. I was in the back, perched on the left-side wheel housing, Bridget on the other, sleeping. Some thin wisps of smoke were rising from her skin. The Thing-from-Outer-Space lay between us, writhing on the tartan rug. He was leaking oil and wax all over the place, lying in a pool of his own juices.

I caught a movement in the air above the parking space.

Oh shit!

Shadowcop! Broadcasting from the store wall, working his mechanisms; flickering lights in smoke. And then the flash of orange; an inpho beam shining out from the shadowcop's eyes. It caught Mandy in its flare-path, gathering knowledge. She ducked down from the beam, banging, hard-core, on the van doors.

The dog was howling at the cop, scared by the lights.

I opened the doors a thin-girl measure. Mandy slipped through.

The dog went for the cop's legs, twin fangs closing on nothing but mist. That dog was confused!

Mandy handed me the bag.

'You got it?' I asked, dragging her inside.

A tangerine flare from outside, a burning light.

'Got some Beauties,' her answer, as she stepped over the Thing, into the van.

'You got the one?'

Mandy just looked at me.

Something was howling outside. I glanced back and saw the poor dog on fire, the shadowcop moving towards us, reloading. He let loose a tight inpho, beaming onto our number-plate, which was just a series of random numbers anyway. *You won't find that in your banks.*

The Vurt-U-Want doors crashed open and a young man came stumbling through, looking scared.

'It's Seb,' whispered Mandy.

Two cops followed him out of the doors. Real-life versions. Fleshcops. They chased Seb over towards the wire fence that skimmed one edge of the car-park. I turned around to The Beetle. 'It's a bust!' I shouted. 'Let's go, Bee! Out of here!'

And we were. Reversing first, away from the bollards. 'Watch it!' This from Mandy, nervous as fuck, as the van jerked backwards. She was thrown to the floor, landing on the Thing-from-Outer-Space. I was clinging to the straps. Brid was rudely pitched from sleep, pupils in shock from the sudden awakening. The Thing had six tentacles wrapped around Mandy. The girl was screaming.

The van leapt up onto a pavement. I thought The Beetle was trying to dodge the beams, maybe he was, but all we felt was the sickening thud and a yowling scream as the left back wheel put the collector's item out of its misery.

The crusty was crying over his dog and pushing his fists through the shadowcop's smoke as we scorched the forecourt. The van made a wild circle, and I saw the whole thing sliding by – the shadowcop, the crusty, the dead dog, until Beetle got it under control. Mandy was struggling with the Thing-from-Outer-Space, calling it all the names. Over The Beetle's shoulder I could see the wire fence coming up close. Seb was dropping down on the other side, down to the tramlines. The two fleshcops were struggling with the fence. Beetle turned on the headlights, catching them full-beam. He gunned the Stashmobile towards them, total, shouting out, 'Awoohhh!!! Kill the cops! Kill the cops!' The cops fell off the fence. The faces in the headlights were a joy to behold; fleshcops, scared to fuck. They were running now, away from the van's bulk, but Beetle had it; he swung the wheel around like a true star, last moment, taking the Stashmobile all around the parking space, heading for the gateway. The debris of a thousand trips was banging and clattering all over the floor as we took a vicious U-turn onto Albany Road and then left onto Wilbraham Road. One last glimpse over the Vurt-U-Want wall and I could see the shadowcop beaming messages into the air. The robo-crusty was a pile of fused plastic and flesh. A cop siren wailed through the darkness.

'They're onto us, Bee!' I cried. 'Hit the jam!'

Beetle took the brow at speed. Oh boy, we were flying! Stash Riders! Riding the feathers back to the pad. The point of impact squelched Mandy deeper into the Thing's embrace.

Mandy screaming at the Thing, 'Get the fuck off me!'

Keeping firm hold of the strap, I dropped the goody bag, and reached down with the free hand, jabbing at the Thing's belly flesh, tickling him. The one weak spot. How he loved that! His laughter was dredged up from deep inside, from thousands of miles. He was writhing around and Mandy was able to slide free. 'Fuck that! Jesus!' She was shaking from the fight.

Through the back windows I saw a cop car's lights flashing. Its siren was loud, piercing. The Beetle took the corner onto Alexandra Road without slowing. Brid was clinging to the straps, desperate for sleep, her skin full of shadows. The Thing-from-Outer-Space was crying out for a fix. Mandy had a tight hold of herself, and I had the goody bag back in my free hand. The Beetle had the wheel.

Everybody has to grab hold of something.

Alexandra Park was a dark jungle shimmering the right side

windows. We were skirting Bottletown by now and no doubt the park was full of demons; pimps, pros, and dealers – real, Vurt, or robo.

'Cop car's closing, Beetle!' I shouted.

'Hang on, folks,' he replied, cool as ever, twisting the van into a tight right, onto Claremont Road.

'They're still with us,' I told him, watching the cop lights following.

Beetle burned all the way down, over the Princess Road, into the Rusholme maze. Cops were following, but they were up against three killer factors: Beetle had lover's knowledge of these streets, all moving engine parts were greased with Vaz, Beetle was hooked on speed. We hung on tight as he took a vicious series of lefts and rights. It was a tough job, hanging on, but we didn't mind. 'Do it, Bee!' cried Mandy, loving the adventure. Old-style terraces passed by, each side of us. On one of the walls someone had scrawled the words – Das Uberdog. And underneath that – pure is poor. Even I didn't know where we were. That's The Beetle for you. Total knowledge, fuelled by Jam and Vaz. Now he was driving us down a back alley, scraping paint off both sides of the Stashmobile. That's okay. The van could live with that. A quick glance through the back windows; there go the cops, speeding on by, towards some dumbfuck nowhere. Bye, bye, suckers! We came out of the alley, and there we were, the Moss Lane East. Beetle took another right, heading us back home.

'Slow down some, Bee,' I said.

'Fuck slowness!' he replied, burning the world with his wheels.

'We're like eggs back here, Beetle,' said Mandy. And the guy slowed us down, some. Well there you go; some things will slow The Beetle down; the chance of a new woman, for instance. Bridget must have had the same feeling; she was looking daggers at the new girl, smoke rising from her skin, as she tried her best to tune into The Beetle's head. I guess she wasn't getting too far.

No matter.

We were in some kind of easy travelling by now, so I picked up the goody bag, emptying the contents out on to the tartan rug. Five blue Vurt feathers floated down. I caught a few as they drifted, reading the printed labels.

'Thermo Fish!' I said. 'Done it.'

'How was I to know?' said Mandy.

I read another. 'Honey Suckers! Oh my shit! Where is it!?'

'Next time, Scribble,' Mandy said, 'you go shopping.'

'Where's English Voodoo? You promised me. I thought you had contacts?'

'That's what he had.'

I read the other three. 'Done it. Done it. Not done it, but it sounds boring anyway.' I'd let the feathers go in disgust. Now they were floating around inside the van.

Mandy's eyes were darting from feather to feather, as she spoke; 'These are very beautiful.'

'And the rest...' I said.

'What's that mean?'

'No messing. The whole bit. English Voodoo. Deliver.'

A blue feather had landed on the stomach of the Thing-from-Outer-Space. One of his tentacles reached out for it. His spiky fingers took a hold, and a hole opened up in his flesh, a greasy orifice. He turned the feather in his feelers and then stroked it in, direct, to the hole. He started to change, I wasn't sure which feather he'd loaded, but from the way he was moving his feelers I guess he was swimming with the Thermo Fish.

I sure know that wave.

The Beetle glanced back at the noise of the waves, shouting; 'He's going in alone! No one goes in alone!'

The Beetle had this obsession about doing Vurt alone. That you'd need help in there, friends in there. What he really meant was – you need me in there.

'Cool it, Bee,' I said. 'Just drive.' Just to spite me he put on a sudden spurt but I was holding tight to the straps. No problems.

I turned back to Mandy; 'Give!'

'You want?' said Mandy.

'I want. You found the Voodoo?'

We turned right onto the Wilmslow Road, as Mandy pulled a stash from the inner reaches of her denim jacket. It was a black feather. Totally illegal. 'No. But I found this...'

Erik Davis_Techgnosis: Magic, Memory, and the Angels of Information_1993

One thing that perhaps defines humanity as different from other life forms is a conscious yearning to place our experiences, aspirations and fears within a cosmological continuum. It is all part of our attempt to create order and hierarchy in things, to imbue objects with meaning. Different contemporary and historic cultures have their own creation myths and notions of the afterlife, and their own religious relationships between icons and doctrines. The writer Erik Davis argues that such practices can offer insight into our image- and information-addicted contemporary condition.

Davis leaves no stone unturned in his search for connections between the old, the arcane and the scientifically discredited, and the new technologies of cyberspace. Davis is a San Francisco-based freelance writer, who graduated from Yale University in 1988.

Our ways of ordering information have become more and more complex with each epistemological shift. For Davis, as he explains in *Techgnosis* (a book that expands the central premiss of the text featured here), these shifts have always been driven by communication technology:

From the moment that humans began etching grooves into ancient wizard bones to mark the cycles of the moon, the process of encoding thought and experience into a vehicle of expression has influenced the changing nature of self. Information technology tweaks our perceptions, communicates our picture of the world to one another, and constructs remarkable and sometimes insidious forms of control over the cultural stories that shape our senses of the world. The moment we invent a significant device for communication – talking drums, papyrus scrolls, printed books, crystal sets, computers, pagers – we partially reconstruct the self and its world, creating new opportunities (and new traps) for thought, perception and social experience.'[1]

These are methods not only of communication, but also of memory. By the time of the Renaissance there existed numerous memory systems and technologies – a response to an increasingly complex world. Renaissance and Elizabethan thinkers and alchemists experimented with mnemonic systems, memory theatres and the evocation of demons – methods of creating ordered religious and cosmological knowledge that are brilliantly expanded and discussed by Frances Yates in *The Art of Memory*.[2] In this book Yates also makes the connection between such systems and the 'occult' origins of the computer (For more on these occult origins see the excerpt by Margaret Wertheim in this book, p298.)

Many writers, particularly science-fiction ones, have picked up on the seemingly paradoxical relationship between occult and arcane philosophies and modern-day technology. In Neal Stephenson's novel *Snow Crash*, which centres on the idea of information as a virus, the hero reaches an understanding of his contemporary predicament through the use of Sumerian texts.[3] Similarly, Greg Bear in *Blood Music* creates an almost Nirvana-like state, which represents the zenith of his parasitic biotechnological entities' evolution.[4] William Gibson, too, is no stranger to the use of traditional world views to describe a high-tech phenomenon: he draws parallels between the voodoo Loa gods and the fragmentation of his mega-omnipotent artificial life form, 'Wintermute'.[5] These are all literary tactics to suggest the point where digital technology becomes invisible and all-seeing and all-hearing magic as Arthur C Clarke would say.

1 Erik Davis, *Techgnosis: Myth, Magic and Mysticism in the Age of Information*, London: Serpent's Tail, 1998.

2 Frances Yates, *The Art of Memory*, London: Pimlico, 1966.

3 Neal Stephenson, *Snow Crash*, London: ROC, Penguin Books Ltd, 1993.

4 Greg Bear, *Blood Music*, New York: Arbor House, 1985.

5 William Gibson, *Neuromancer*, London: Grafton, 1986.

In its obsession with simulacra and encoded messages, as well as its almost libertarian hatred of traditional authority and a corresponding emphasis on spiritual autonomy, Gnosticism anticipates cyberculture. Ihab Hassan has shown how the notion of direct Gnostic revelation is resurrected now that 'communication itself is becoming increasingly immediate'.[1] But while Hassan and a few science-fiction writers have pursued this link, no one has plunged into information Gnosticism with such abandon as the brilliant science-fiction writer Philip K Dick. Though Gnosticism is only one dimension of Dick's dense and tangled oeuvre – only now beginning to receive the attention it deserves – the mythic mode lies at the heart of many of his themes and devices: 'living' books, false worlds, divine invasions.

In the essay 'Man, Android and Machine', Dick suggests that Gnostic information is both a space and a being. Taking up the popular Christian thinker Teilhard de Chardin's image of the noösphere – a bubble of human thought that envelops the earth like a virtual atmosphere – Dick suggests that something strange occurred when technology entered the picture:

> ... [T]he noösphere ... no longer served as a mere passive repository of human information (the 'Seas of Knowledge' which ancient Sumer believed in) but, due to the incredible surge of charge from our electronic signals and information-rich material therein, we have given it power to cross a vast threshold; we have, so to speak, resurrected what Philo and other ancients called the Logos. Information has, then, become alive.[2]

The whole encyclopedic space of thought, juiced up by technology, becomes the ultimate example of artificial life.

In *The Divine Invasion*, Dick creates an even richer theological image of living information space: a three-dimensional, colour-coded biblical hologram.

> The total structure of Scripture formed, then, a three-dimensional cosmos that could be viewed from any angle and its contents read. According to the tilt of the axis of observation, different messages could be extracted ... If you learned how, you could gradually tilt the temporal axis, the axis of true depth, until successive layers were superimposed and a vertical message – a new message – could be read out. In this way you entered into a dialogue with Scripture; it became alive. It became a sentient organism that was never twice the same.[3]

In this image of hypertext heaven, Dick shows how a space of information density achieves an animate quality through the structure of an open-ended dialogue.

But 'living information' was no mere metaphor within Dick's brilliant though decidedly unstable mind, for in 1974, sitting at home in Orange County, he apparently experienced such a force. According to Dick's later testimony, seeing an *ichthys*, or fish-shaped Christian icon, on a delivery woman's necklace 'triggered' the influx of a rational and benign mind: VALIS, or Vast Active Living Intelligence System. Among other things, VALIS – which Dick sometimes compares to a computer or an AI system

– linked him telepathically to an early Christian living under Roman oppression and informed him (through a Beatles song on the radio) that his son Christopher had a potentially lethal health problem.

In our culture, we call individuals like Dick schizophrenic, but in the confines of his literary works, his apparent schizophrenia achieves an unparalleled oracular glow. After 1974, most of Dick's work, both his novels and over two million words of tortured philosophical maunderings in his largely unpublished 'Exegesis', was a response to the VALIS experience, though Gnostic themes and structures are clearly latent in his earlier work. In *VALIS*, the greatest and strangest of these late works, he fleshes out his information mysticism in the 'Tractates Cryptica Scriptura', a twelve-page excerpt from his 'Exegesis'.

In the 'Tractates', Dick maintains that our universe is a space of information, and the phenomenal world a hologram, 'a hypostasis of the information' that we, as nodes in the true Mind, process. But humans have lost the ability to read this divine language, and both ourselves and our world are occluded. For Dick, the ancient demiurge is recast as the irrational 'Empire': Rome, the Nixon administration, the State as such. Dick did not emphasize the material or Satanic aspect of demiurgic powers, but rather their ability to create false worlds. In the introduction to *I Hope I Shall Arrive Soon*, a collection of late short stories, he writes that 'we live in a society in which spurious realities are manufactured by the media, by governments, by big corporations, by religious groups, political groups – and the electronic hardware exists by which to deliver these pseudo-worlds right into the heads of the reader, the viewer, the listener'.[4] As demonstrated by the illusory and demonic nature of his constantly imploding fictional worlds, Dick transforms Gnostic pessimism into a sceptical weapon wielded from within the fathomless simulations of Baudrillardian hyperreality.

Just as the nameless hero of the 'Hymn of the Pearl' found the Logos lying by the side of the road, VALIS penetrates the simulated world through the margins. The True God must mimic 'sticks and trees and beer cans in gutters – he presumes to be trash discarded, debris no longer needed'. Dick says at the end of *VALIS* that 'the symbols of the divine show up in our world initially at the trash stratum'. So, too, do the images and peripheral details of Dick's fictions – circulating through the trash stratum of science-fiction pulp – glow with a powerful allegorical density, and many narratives are propelled by the decoding of these clues. One of *VALIS*'s most fascinating chapters describes a scene in which the protagonist, Horselover Fat, and some friends see a trashy science-fiction movie called *Valis* and then unpack its subliminal messages, their bizarre conclusions leading them to make contact with the filmmakers and the saviour-figure, Sophia. For Dick, decoding is more than reading; it is being infected by code. VALIS is nothing less than a virus that 'replicates itself – not through information or in information – but as information'. Once triggered, it parasitically 'crossbands' with human hosts, creating 'homeoplasmates'.

Dick is not the only one to imagine information as a kind of virus (itself a quasi-living body of code). In addition to Burroughs's famous phrase ('language is a virus'), there's scientist Richard Dawkins's understanding of *memes* as thoughts which, like genes, propagate and compete in the competitive environment of culture. In *The Selfish Gene*, Dawkins quotes N K Humphrey:

> ... [M]emes should be regarded as living structures, not just metaphorically but technically. When you plant a fertile meme in my mind you literally parasitize my brain, turning it into a vehicle for the meme's propagation in just the way that a virus may parasitize the genetic mechanism of a host cell ... [T]he meme for, say, 'belief in life after death' is actually realized physically, millions of times over, as a structure in the nervous systems of individual men the world over.[5]

Memes have already become a somewhat trendy notion in cyberculture, but what is intriguing is Humphrey's insistence that they be conceived 'not just metaphorically but technically'. In Dick's fiction, metaphors are transformed into technical operations. Even more interesting is the meme Humphrey uses as an example. For of all the artifacts of human culture, it is the great memes themselves that perhaps come closest to eternal life. And one of the greatest of those is the one that claims that, just as memes survive in the minds of human hosts, so can human consciousness survive in the abstract space of the meme.

1 Ihab Hassan, *Paracriticisms: Seven Speculations of the Times,* Urbana, IL: University of Illinois Press, 1975, p135.

2 Philip K Dick, 'Man, Android and Machine', in *Science Fiction at Large*, Peter Nicholls (ed), New York: Harper & Row, 1976, p216.

3 Philip K Dick, *The Divine Invasion*, New York: Vintage, 1981, p70–1.

4 Philip K Dick, 'Introduction: How to build a Universe That Doesn't Fall Apart Two Days Later', in *I Hope I Shall Arrive Soon*, New York: St Martin's Press, 1985, p4.

5 Richard Dawkins, *The Selfish Gene*, Oxford: Oxford University Press, 1976, p192.

Two pages from *The Religious Experience of Philip K. Dick.* This 8-page feature was a graphic interpretation by Robert Crumb of a series of events which happened to Dick in March, 1974.

Dick spent the remaining years of his life trying to figure out what happened in those fateful months. *The Religious Experience* was published in *Weirdo* comic, no 17, Summer, 1986.

Scott Bukatman_Terminal Resistance/ Cyborg Acceptance_1993

The book *Terminal Identity: The Virtual Subject in Postmodern Science Fiction* is an investigation into the representation of technology and space in science-fiction. Author Scott Bukatman is Assistant Professor in the Media Arts Program at the University of New Mexico and consulting editor for *Science Fiction Studies*. His work has been published in *Artforum International*, *Architecture New York*, *October* and *Camera Obscura*.

Terminal Identity takes as its point of departure the idea that contemporary culture is in crisis. The established relationships between the human subject and issues of space and representation, of machine ontology, of gender and of sexuality, have been undermined by the new computational technology. Bukatman draws on a wealth of science-fiction films, comics and novels, and combines them with ideas drawn from Surrealism, machine art, postmodern cultural theory and ideas of virtuality. He uses these sources to illustrate the shifting topology of the technologized subject.

Exploring some of the central and iconic images of our time, the book has greatly inspired a wide variety of multi-disciplinary interest groups – and continues to do so. In the section featured here Bukatman focuses on representations of the technological augmentation of the human body, particularly films with 'cyborgian' characters. Later in the book Bukatman discusses cyborg 'anthropology' and goes on to introduce the context of Donna Haraway's *Cyborg Manifesto*:[1]

The cyborg as a category (outside of science-fiction, and not by name) materialized in the pervasive wartime climate (and postwar) intersection between cybernetics and information system studies on the one hand and the life sciences of biology, sociology, primatology on the other. In 1947 Norbert Weiner published his *Cybernetics: Or Control and Communication in the Animal and Machine*. The human sciences produce a 'functional analogy' between the human and the computer – an *analogy*, not an identity (but within the functionalist paradigm that dominated the human sciences at that time, privileging the functionality of parts within an overall and unifying system, the distinction has little meaning).[2]

Bukatman bases his book around the idea that while in the past the external world was rational and our internal, mental world was full of ghosts, fantasy and virtualities, today this dichotomy has been reversed. Through digital technology, it is the external world that hums with the unreal, the strange and the fantastic. As writer Mark Dery comments in his book *Escape Velocity*:

This transition is a hallmark of what Scott Bukatman calls 'techno-surrealism', in which the libido, like a voracious Blob of B-movie fame, moves 'beyond the bounds of the individual psyche' to swallow up reality.[3]

The same could be said for a host of films, such as the *Terminator* and *Robocop* series.

In the conclusion to *Terminal Identity* Bukatman writes of the 'repressed desire and repressed anxiety of terminal culture ... Terminal identity negotiates a complex trajectory between the forces of instrumental reason and the abandonment of sacrificial excess.'[4] This, perhaps, is the overriding paradox of technological development: it offers transcendence but also a defeat of the purity of flesh, as technological products invade the body. The skin is no longer a barrier to digital vicissitudes.

1 An excerpt from Haraway's book is included in this anthology, p108.
2 Scott Bukatman, *Terminal Identity:The Virtual Subject in Postmodern Science Fiction*, Durham, NC: Duke University Press, 1993, p321.
3 Mark Dery, *Escape Velocity: Cyberculture at the End of the Century*, London: Hodder and Stoughton, 1996. Quotations within this passage are from Bukatman, ibid, p20 and p308.
4 Scott Bukatman, ibid, p329.

In the wake of such profound technological and political traumas as followed World War I, [Hal] Foster argues that surrealism and dada created their own armoured bodies. Ernst's fascination with automata, for example, or Bellmer's obsessively deconstructed *poupées*, grappled with deep ambivalences regarding subject and social structure within a newly intensified, and seemingly objectified, technological paradigm. Foster observes 'the tension between binding and shattering tendencies, the play between sadistic and masochistic impulses'. Surrealism is defined by the struggle 'between the erotic and the destructive, the one never pure of the other'. He digresses on his 'sense that the figure of the armoured body pervades the imaginary of American commercial culture' (a photograph of Schwarzenegger illustrates his point). Foster ties his argument to recent science-fiction cinema: 'Though sometimes parodic, even critical, the armoured figures of commercial culture symbolically treat fantasmatic threats to the normative social ego: for instance, visions of cities given over to drugged minorities (eg. *Robocop*)'.

In the current era of techno-surrealism similar ambivalences pertain, and as the represented body moves ever more emphatically toward a symbiosis with electronic technology, it becomes ever more emphatically armoured. Robocop is only one example of the *defensive* drive toward a techno-humanoid fusion (the science-fiction sports film represents another). [Claudia] Springer and [Mark] Dery both concentrate on *Terminator 2* and the conflict between Arnold's old-fashioned T-100 cyborg model and the new, 'liquid metal' T-1000. To understand the intra-Terminator battles, both writers stress the feared flow of the feminine. Dery, writing in *Mondo 2000*, is disturbed by the digital technology of *morphing* used by Dennis Muren to create the T-1000: morphing becomes a paradigm for the surfeit of body-reshaping technologies available today, from aerobics to cosmetic surgery to Michael Jackson's videos and lifestyle ('In his privileged ability to transmogrify himself, Jackson lives in the future').[1] Dery sees morphing as the site of new 'micropolitical power struggles between an information-rich technocratic élite and the information-poor masses' (his argument is also borne out in the 1992 morphing-comedy, *Death Becomes Her*, in which the technology is explicitly tied to the body of the Beverly Hills female).[2] The T-1000 combines the mutability of the Thing with the techno-organicism of the Alien. Electronic technology becomes a new site of anxiety: it can't even be relied upon to keep its shape. By contrast, Schwarzenegger, as the 'nice' Terminator, is predictably mechanical and trustworthy – he always looks like Arnold.[3]

The men of the *Freikorps* 'fortif[ied] themselves with hard leather body armour to assert their solidity against the threat of fluid women'.[4] Hence, Robocop and Terminator: bodies armoured against a new age (political and technological). The cyborg adorns itself in leather and introjects the machine, becoming part punk, part cop, part biker, part bike, part tank, part *Freikorps*-superhero. Springer writes that these cyborg figures 'perpetuate, and even exaggerate, the anachronistic industrial-age metaphor of externally forceful masculine machinery, expressing nostalgia for a time of masculine superiority' and argues that the bodily-sense of electronic technology is *internal* 'with its concealed and fluid systems ... It is this feminization of electronic technology and the passivity of the human interaction with computers that the hypermasculine cyborg in films resists'.[5] By doing battle with the fluid, and even effeminate, digitized form of the T-1000 ('The "animal" in the mass ... can metamorphose into a single creature, many-limbed: millipede, rat, snake, dragon'), the mechanical Terminator expunges the nightmare of masculine and industrial obsolescence (note that each term metaphorizes the other). The climactic battle is fought in a steel foundry.

Springer's argument is convincing and is furthered by Dery in his consideration of *T2* and *Aliens* (1986), both directed by James Cameron. 'The Menschmachine's pathological fear of the glutinous feminine goo that will gum its gears is manifest' in both films but 'given ironic spin by the fact that the masculinist protagonist of each is in fact a woman'.[6] *Aliens* has been viewed by some as a 'feminist' discourse of empowerment by critics eager to seize upon the progressive aspects of female action-heroes, but this is an argument that Dery rejects (as would, presumably, Springer). The fluidity of *Alien* has already been explored, and Dery cites Mark Crispin Miller on *Aliens* (note the Theweleit-inflected language): '*Aliens* divides the female in two,' Miller argues, the 'tough-guy heroine' and the slimy, reproductive alien nemesis. 'Ripley manages to snuff the Alien only by turning herself hyper-masculine/robotic: she encases herself in a mammoth robot-exoskeleton, which – powerful and dry – allows her to crush the shrieking mother-figure as if it were a giant, juicy bug.'[7] Dery sees a similar process working in *T2*, in which 'soft squishy evil pours itself into the mercurial shape of the T-1000, a polymorphous perversity made of "mimetic polyalloy". ... Linda Hamilton, morphed into a *Freikorps* cyborg, triumphs over the feminine aspect embodied in the T-1000 with the aid of the male principle manifest in the Schwarzeneggerian model'.[8]

Springer also considers *Hard Boiled*, a satirical (?) comic book by Frank Miller and Geof Darrow in which a salaryman turns out to be a killing robot. This is probably one of the most self-consciously violent comics ever produced, and the dialogue is nonsensically minimal to leave ample room for Darrow's hyper-detailed depiction of explosions, shootings, crashes, operations, gougings and random lacerations. Springer writes that *Hard Boiled* or similar works demonstrate 'that the patriarchal system, with its brutal violence covered by sugary platitudes, is indeed on the way out, even if, as a last gasp, it has rallied its forces of muscular cyborg soldiers'. One might note that Frank Miller has become the poet laureate of last-gasp cyborgism: here and in *Batman: The Dark Knight Returns* and in *Robocop 2*, his characters are always 'returning' to their killing ways despite their perceived obsolescence. It is also worth pointing out that comic books have long represented a haven for the 'armoured body' in American culture: note the orphaned and significantly named Superman with his invulnerability to bullets (and exploding planets) and Iron Man ('he's a cool exec/with a heart of steel', the TV theme song declared).[9] Cinematic cyborg Robocop owes much to Judge Dredd comics, and Tim Burton's *Batman* (1989) changed the costume from a leotard to an encasing body-armour. The armoured body has a powerful legacy in America and is often aligned with issues of technology.

The stylization, exaggeration, and repetition of *Hard Boiled* place it in the tradition of French and Japanese comics. A low-budget short Japanese film, *Tetsuo: The Iron Man* (1991), also derives its structure and imagery from the endless, wordless violence of Japanese *manga*. Another armoured salaryman figure battles a young 'metals fetishist' who is trying to stave off rust by merging with the salaryman. Penises become electric drills, women sprout metallic tentacles, and people are swallowed in miles of metallic cabling until at the end when, 'a huge metal monster with two faces stands ready to take the streets of Tokyo, convinced that the whole world can be mutated into metal'. The film is mordantly obsessive and moves beyond its *manga*-roots through its dark monomania. Tony Rayns compares the film to *Crash*, with some reason, although Shinya Tsukamoto is both less transgressive and less reflexive than Ballard.[10] Nevertheless, *Tetsuo* is an impressive (and happily unpleasant) work of techno-surrealism. In its aggressive fear of female sexuality, its sense of alienation, and its willfully hyperbolic violence, the film is a discourse both *of* and *about* the armoured body in techno-culture. The parodic and disturbing ultraviolence of *Hard Boiled* and *Tetsuo* recognize that in cyborg fictions there exists Joey's desire to 'abject this world'. The fusion with machines represents something other than a postmodern celebration of dissolving borders and boundaries, because they are often as much attempts to reseat the human (male) in a position of virile power and control.

1 Mark Dery, 'Cyborging the Body Politic', *Mondo 2000* (1992): p101.

2 Dery, 'Cyborging the Body Politic', p103.

3 In *T2*, when Arnold says his tag line, *I'll be back*, it is no longer a threat. *Total Recall*, released one year earlier, failed as drama because Arnold is too strong an icon to play an ontologically unstable character (of course, these elements probably contributed to the film's success). *T2* is ultimately a fantastic ode to metal and an oddly interesting updating of *The Day the Earth Stood Still* (1951).

4 Springer, 'Muscular Circuitry: The Invincible Armoured Cyborg in Cinema', *Genders*, in press, p11.

5 Springer, 'Muscular Circuitry', p12.

6 Dery, 'Cyborging the Body Politic', p102.

7 Mark Crispin Miller, 'The Robot in the Western Mind', *Boxed In: The Culture of TV* (Evanston, Ill: Northwestern University Press, 1988), p307.

8 Dery, 'Cyborging the Body Politic', p102–3.

9 In another comic, part of a wave that either parodied or tried to 'subvert' the power fantasies of the superhero genre, the 'hero' wears leather and a bondage mask and is caricatured as a Super-Nazi Freikorps member. See Pat Mills (writer) and Kevin O'Neill (artist), *Marshal Law: Super Babylon* (Milwaukie, Oreg.: Dark Horse Comics, 1992). Theweleit himself is clearly well aware of both mainstream and underground comics – he uses illustrations of Spiderman, Capt. America, and Thor to accompany his discussion of armour, as well as some brilliant material by Robert Crumb on male anxiety and a stunning antiwar-story story by Greg Irons.

10 Tony Rayns, 'Tetsuo: The Iron Man', *Sight and Sound* (1991), p52. All quotes about the film are taken from Rayns's review.

Two stills from Fritz Lang's 1927 film *Metropolis* (top left and right), where the mind of the character played by Brigitte Helm is downloaded into an android body.

In *Johnny Mnemonic* (dir Robert Longo, 1995), Keanu Reeves, as Johnny (centre left), hooks up with Jones, a bio-enhanced dolphin formerly used by the navy as a code breaker. The film was scripted by William Gibson.

Sex scene (centre right) from the 1992 cyberpunk animation, *Lawnmower Man* (dir Brett Leonard).

Two stills (bottom right) from *Terminator 2* (dir James Cameron, 1991) starring Arnold Schwarzenegger as the shape-shifting cyborg 'Terminator' who does battle with the out-of-control robot cop enforcers.

A more clunky mechanical icon of a human/robot combination (bottom left) seen in the cyborg film *Robocop* (dir Paul Verhoeven, 1987).

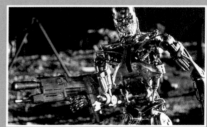

Anne Balsamo_Feminism for the Incurably Informed_1993

The critic Anne Balsamo believes that cyberpunk literature is an important subject for feminist theory; she sees this literary genre as stressing female empowerment through an understanding of the digital, virtual and cyberspatial worlds. Balsamo is Professor of Literature, Communication and Culture at Georgia Tech in Atlanta, and author of the book *Technologies of the Gendered Body* (1996). In the article 'Feminism for the Incurably Informed' she discusses a feminist interpretation of *Synners*, by the science-fiction novelist Pat Cadigan.[1]

Pat Cadigan, one of America's best cyberpunk writers, took up full-time fiction writing in 1987. *Synners* is her masterpiece, a novel with spine-tingling atmosphere and a feminist philosophical agenda. The 'Synners' of Cadigan's book are people who take images in the brains of performers and rearticulate them for mass consumption; images thus become commodities. The backdrop to the novel is a blurred, virtual world that is always being repackaged, refigured and resold. Reality is not what it seems, and is subject to all manner of virtual indiscretions. In this world, the Synners are reality wizards.

Cadigan uses the phrase 'change for the machines' as a recurring motif in the book. Balsamo in her essay picks this out as a microcosm of many of the issues surrounding digital technology and its effect on the gendered body:

Originally, it means, 'Do you have any change for the vending machine?' It is a commentary on the fact that all the characters have changed to adapt to the machines that are prevalent in her cosmology. One of the things I wonder about is, in the era of the cyborg, have we so accepted the idea of the machine as part of or constitutive of our identity that we have already morphed or changed for the machines such that now we are already thinking of ourselves as co-terminus with the machines instead of sitting outside of the machines? I am certainly an acolyte of Donna Haraway's and I still would rather be a cyborg than a goddess. I am with her on that one, but I wonder what that means. What about us has changed that we would invite the machine in or start to live comfortably with the machine?

If you look at daily life, we live comfortably with machines. Maybe there isn't any going back, but can you actually think about the possibility that we could make a different kind of decision, that we could change yet differently? Not change back but could there be change in such a different way that we don't continue being excessively reliant on machines?[2]

In the following excerpt from Balsamo's essay she describes each of the main characters in *Synners* – Sam, Gina, Gabe and Visual Mark – as manifestations of an 'identity matrix' that cyberspace makes possible and reinforces. This 'matrix' could be said to be existent in anyone who uses computers. At any one time one might be simultaneously a selection of 'points in the matrix' each with its own peculiar identity protocols.

1 Pat Cadigan, *Synners*, London: Grafton, 1991.
2 Anne Balsamo, 'Feminism for the Incurably Informed', *South Atlantic Quarterly*, 1993. For Donna Haraway see also the extract from 'Cyborg Manifesto' featured in this book, p108.

Anne Balsamo, 'Feminism for the Incurably Informed', first published in *South Atlantic Quarterly*, 1993

In the case of *Synners*, the 'real social content', according to Fred Pfeil, is not simply the plottings of a hostile corporate takeover, but also what we can read on/off its textual surface about the technological configuration of human life in multinational capitalism. Several topics nominate themselves as experiments in thinking through the social consequences of new technologies, any one of which could serve as the organizing perspective for the elaboration of an interpretive map of Cadigan's cosmology: the capitalist production of electronic addictions, the recording practices of video vigilantes, or the multiplication of television channels devoted to new forms of pornography: disasterporn, medporn, foodporn. In addition to speculating about the dynamics of new communication technologies, *Synners* also offers a critical account of the commodification of information.

'Truth is cheap, but information costs…'Besides being rich', Fez said, 'you have to be extra sharp these days to pick up any real information. You have to know what you're looking for, and you have to know how its filed. Browsers need not apply. Broke ones, anyway. I miss the newspaper.'

This subtext also includes a political critique of the availability of information and of the difficulty of determining relevance in the midst of the 'Instant Information Revolution'.

'Good guess, but the real title is *Need to Know*,' said the same voice close to his ear. 'It's an indictment of our present system of information dispersal. You're allowed to know only those things the information czars decide that you need to know. They call it "market research" and "efficient use of resources" and "no-waste", but it's the same old shit they've been doing to us for more than one-hundred years – keep 'em confused and in the dark. You gotta be a stone-ham super-Renaissance person to find out what's really going on.'

Pfeil is right when he says that isolating passages such as these hardly requires a literary ingenuity to identify expressions of collective anxieties. Indeed, such sceptical statements about information overload and manipulation resonate strongly with Baudrillard's reading of the postmodern scene: 'We are in a universe where there is more and more information, and less and less meaning.' And yet, in contrast to the reading Baudrillard offers, Carolyn Marvin argues that 'information cannot be said to exist at all unless it has meaning, and meaning is established only in social relationships with cultural reference and value.' In her critique of the dominant notion of information-as-commodity (a notion that is at the heart of the ideology of the information age), Marvin redefines information, not as a quantifiable entity, but rather as a 'state of knowing' which reasserts a knowing *body* as its necessary materialist foundation. This embodied notion of information is at the heart of *Synners*. Moving around a postmodernist reading of cyberpunk science-fiction that would focus on its figuration of multinational capitalism and the technological deconstruction of human identity, I would like to elaborate an alternative reading of *Synners* that reflects a slight mutation of these thematic preoccupations. In this case, the focus is on the relation of the material body to cyberspace.

In the course of developing an ideological critique of a capitalist information economy, Cadigan focuses attention on an often-repressed dimension of the information age: the constitution of the informed body. The problem is not just that information 'costs', or even that it replicates exponentially, but rather that information is never merely discursive. What we encounter in the Cadigan novel is the narrativization of four different versions of cyberpunk embodiment: the repressed body, the labouring body, the marked body and the disappearing body. In this sense, the four central characters symbolize the different embodied relations one can have, in theory and in fiction, to a nonmaterial space of information access and exchange. The following figure roughly illustrates how Sam, Gabe, Gina and Visual Mark represent four corners of an identity matrix constructed in and around cyberspace:

Sam (the body that labours)   Gina (the marked body)
Gabe (the repressed body)   Visual Mark (the disappearing body)

Where Sam hacks the net through a terminal powered by her own body, Visual Mark actually inhabits the network as he mutates into a disembodied, sentient artificial intelligence (AI). Although both Gina and Gabe travel through cyberspace on their way to someplace else, Gabe is addicted to cyberspace simulations, and Gina endures them. Each character plays a significant role in the novel's climactic confrontation in cyberspace: a role determined, in part, by their individual relationships to Diversifications, and, in part, by their bodily identities.

Sam, Gabe's daughter and the only real hacker among the four, is a virtuoso at gaining access to the net. She is the character who best describes the labour of computer hacking and the virtual acrobatics of cyberspace travel: '...[I]f you couldn't walk on the floor, you walked on the ceiling. If you couldn't walk on the ceiling, you walked on the walls, and if you couldn't walk on the walls, you walked *in* them, encrypted. Pure hacking.' As competent as she is in negotiating the cyberspatial landscape of the net, Sam tries to live her embodied life outside of any institutional structure. Her only affiliations are to other punks and hackers who form a community of sorts and who live out on 'the Manhattan-Hermosa strip, what the kids called the Mimosa, part of the old postquake land of the lost.' Sam trades encrypted data and hacking talents for stray pieces of equipment and living necessities. In what proves to be a critically important 'information commodity' acquisition, Sam hacks the specifications for an insulin-pump chip reader that runs off of body energy. When every terminal connected to 'the System' is infected by a debilitating virus, Sam's insulin-pump chip reader is the only noninfected access point to the net. Connected by thin needles inserted into her abdomen, the chip reader draws its power from Sam's body. Seventeen-year-old Sam is a cyberspace hacker of considerable talent who shuns the heroic cowboy role. And for the most part, she is content to provide the power while others, namely Gina and Gabe, go in for the final showdown.

Recoiling from a real-time wife who despises him for his failure to live up to his artistic potential, Gabe spends most of his working time, when he should be designing advertising campaigns, playing the role (Hotwire) of a *noir* leading man in a computer simulation built from pieces of an old movie thriller; his two female cyberspace sidekicks are 'templates [that] had been assembled from two real, living people…'. Where Visual Mark cleaves to cyberspace because the world isn't big enough for his expansive visual mind, Gabe becomes addicted to cyberspace because the world is just too big for him. He retreats to the simulation pit for the safety and familiarity it offers. 'He'd been running around in simulation for so long, he'd forgotten how to run a realife, real-time routine; he'd forgotten that if he made mistakes, there was no safety-net program to jump in and correct for him.' Throughout the novel, Gabe moves in and out of a real-time life and his simulated fantasy world. In real-time his body is continually brought to life, through pain, intoxication and desire caused by Gina, first when she punches him in the face with a misplaced stab intended for Mark, then later when he gets toxed after she feeds him two LotusLands (a 'mildly hallucinogenic beverage'). After they make love for the first time, Gina wonders if Gabe has ever felt desire before: 'She didn't think Gabe Ludovic had ever jumped the fast train in his life. Standing at the end of fifteen years of marriage, he'd wanted a lot more than sex. The wanting had been all but tangible, a heat that surprised both of them.' After a climactic cyberspace struggle, his repressed body reawakens; Gabe learns to feel his body again (or for the first time) with Gina's help.

Like Visual Mark, Gina is a 'synner' who synthesizes images, sound, and special effects to produce virtual reality music videos. For all her disdain and outright hostility toward other people and institutions, 'Badass Gina Aiesi' has an intense emotional connection to Mark, her partner of twenty years, that she romanticizes in an odd way:

> They weren't smooch-faces, it didn't work that way, for her or for him…One time, though…one time, three-four-five years into the madness, there'd been a place where they'd come together one night, and it had been different…He'd been reaching, and she'd been reaching, and for a little while there, they'd gotten through. Maybe that had been the night when the little overlapping space called *their* life had come into existence.

Gina's body, marked by its colour, 'wild forest hardwood', and her dreadlocks, figures prominently in the narrative description of her sexual encounters, first with Visual Mark and then with Gabe. After both she and Visual Mark have brain sockets implanted by Diversifications' surgeon-on-contract, they jack in together and experience a visual replay of shared memories: 'The pov was excruciatingly slow as it moved across Mark's face to her own, lingering on the texture of her dreadlocks next to his pale, drawn flesh, finally moving on to the contrast of her deep brown skin.' The characteristics that mark Gina are her anger, her exasperated love for Mark, and the colour of her skin.

Like others who bought the new means for jacking in, Visual Mark begins to spend less and less time off-line and more and more time plugged in to the global network known as 'the System'. This leads him to reflect on the metaphysical nature of his physical body: 'he lost all awareness of the meat that had been his prison for close to fifty years, and the relief he felt at having laid his burden down was as great as himself.' After suffering a small stroke (one of the unpleasant side effects of brain sockets) while he was jacked in, Visual Mark prepares for 'the big one' – a stroke that will release his consciousness into the system and allow him to leave his meat behind.

He was already accustomed to the idea of having multiple awareness and a single concentrated core that were both the essence of self. The old meat organ would not have been able to cope with that kind of reality, but out here he appropriated more capacity the way he once might have exchanged a smaller shirt for a larger one.

And sure enough, while his body is jacked in, Mark strokes out. He tries to get Gina to pull his plugs, but she is too late. As his meat dies, both his consciousness and his stroke enter 'the System'. In the process, his stroke is transformed into a deadly virus (or spike) that initiates a worldwide network crash.

Like the dramatic climax in recent cyberpunk films such as *Circuitry Man*, *Lawnmower Man*, and *Mindwarp*, the final showdown in *Synners* takes place in cyberspace. Working together, a small community of domestic exiles, hackers, and punks assemble a work-station (powered by Sam's insulin-pump chip reader) that enables Gina and Gabe to go on-line to fight the virus/stroke – an intelligent entity of some dubious ontological status that now threatens the integrity of the entire networked world. Like a cyberspace Terminator, the virus/stroke is rationally determined to infect/destroy whoever comes looking for it. In the course of their cyberspace brawl, Gabe and Gina confront the virus's simulation of their individual worse fears. A 'reluctant hero' till the very end, Gabe's cyberspace enemy is a simple construct: the fear of embodiment. 'I can't remember what it feels like to have a body,' he repeats obsessively during his final confrontation in cyberspace. What he learns through the encounter is that his whole body is a hot-suit; that is, he learns to feel the body that he has technologically repressed.

Gina's cyberspace struggle is with an embodiment of her own deepest fears about missed chances, lost love, and suffocating commitment. Her cyberspace showdown replays her obsessive twenty-year-long search for Mark: 'Old habits, they do die hard, don't they. That's yours, ain't it – looking for Mark.' 'Who do you still want to love?', she is asked by the omniscient virus. In one sense her struggle is to confront the fact that she loves an addict and still wants to save him. The crucial decision Gina faces is whether to stay with Mark in cyberspace – where there is no pain, no separation – or to renounce him and return to the real world where such love is impossible. In the end, Gabe and Gina defeat the virus and the global network shortly re-establishes connections. But when Gina finally wakes to reunite with Gabe we find out that although *they* have changed for the machines, the machines didn't change for them. 'The door only swings one way. Once it's out of the box, it's always too big to get back in. Can't bury that technology … Every technology has its original sin … And we still got to live with what we made.'

Sherry Turkle_Constructions and Reconstructions of the Self in Virtual Reality_1994

Sherry Turkle specializes in psychoanalysis and culture; her work throws new light on the relationship between the virtual and personal psychology. She is particularly interested in the simulated environments that exist in cyberspace and their psychological impact as arenas of therapeutic interaction and role play. Her research also includes robotic dolls and pets. Many of these ideas are discussed in her influential book *Life on the Screen: Identity in the Age of the Internet* (1995).

Turkle did her undergraduate studies at Radcliffe College and received a doctorate in Sociology and Personality Psychology from Harvard University in 1976. She was later appointed Abby Rockefeller Mauze Professor of the Sociology of Science in the Program in Science, Technology and Society at the Massachusetts Institute of Technology. Turkle is also licensed as a clinical psychologist.

The issue of identities in cyberspace has interested many writers and academics. Allucquère Rosanne Stone, in her essay 'Will the Real Body Please Stand Up?: Boundary States about Virtual Cultures' in the anthology *Cyberspace: First Steps*, recounts the tale of 'Julie'. Julie was a quadriplegic who could only push the keys of her computer with a headstick. Using the Internet her disability disappeared, and Julie made many virtual friends who shared their deepest emotional secrets with her. Eventually someone wanted to meet her in real space and tracked her down. 'She' was a middle-aged male psychiatrist. Stone explains:

The news reverberated through the net. Reactions varied from humorous resignation to blind rage. Most deeply affected were the women who had shared their innermost feelings with Julie. 'I felt raped.' One said, 'I felt that my deepest secrets had been violated.' Several went so far as to repudiate the genuine gains they had made in their personal and emotional lives. They felt those gains were predicated on deceit and trickery.[1]

Stone writes of a person's online persona and the real-world person's interactions in the actuality as their 'consensual locus'. 'Each consensual locus has its own "reality", determined by local conditions', she says. 'However, not all realities are equal.'[2]

Sherry Turkle cites this 'consensual locus' as a means of 'constructive and reconstructive therapeutic interaction in virtual world MUDs'.[3] MUDs is an acronym for 'Multi-User Dungeons'; as Turkle explains: 'In the early 1970s, a role-playing game called Dungeons and Dragons swept the game cultures ... the term Dungeon has persisted in both the games and high-tech cultures, and in the case of MUDs, refers to a virtual social space that exists on a machine.'[4] Contradicting the usual perception of the MUDer as a sad, lonely and socially retarded individual, Turkle believes that MUDs encourage their players to act out scenarios that help them negotiate similar social eventualities in real space. In the following excerpt Turkle illustrates her thesis with actual examples.

At the end of this essay Turkle leaves us with a radical thought that logically follows on from her previous ideas.

Watch for a nascent culture of virtual reality that is paradoxically, a culture of the concrete, placing new saliency on the notion that we construct gender and that we become what we play, argue about, and build. And watch for a culture that leaves a new amount of space for the idea that he or she who plays, argues and builds is a machine.[5]

This idea seems to be one that is now pervasive. The 'creativity machine metaphor' as I shall call it is a useful lens through which to test one's surroundings and the subcultures that we exist in.

1 Michael Benedikt (ed), *Cyberspace: First Steps*, Cambridge, MA: MIT Press, 1991, p83.

2 Ibid, p84.

3 Sherry Turkle, 'Constructions and Reconstructions of the Self in Virtual Reality', in Timothy Druckrey (ed), *Electronic Culture: Technology and Visual Representation*, New York: Aperture, 1996, p354.

4 Ibid.

5 Ibid, p365.

Sherry Turkle, 'Constructions and Reconstructions of the Self in Virtual Reality', 1994

Role-Playing Games

As identity workshops, MUDs have much in common with traditional role-playing games, for example, the role playing games played by Julee, a 19-year-old who has dropped out of Yale after her freshman year. Part of the reason for her leaving college is that she is in an increasingly turbulent relationship with her mother, a devout Catholic, who turned away from her daughter when she discovered that she had had an abortion the summer before beginning college.

From Julee's point of view, her mother has chosen to deny her existence. When asked about her most important experience in role-playing games, Julee described a game in which she had been assigned the role of a mother facing a conflict with her daughter. Indeed, in the game, the script says that the daughter is going to betray, even kill, the mother.

In the role-playing game, played over a weekend on the Boston University (BU) campus, Julee and her 'daughter' talked for hours: Why might the daughter have joined her mother's opponents, how could they stay true to their relationship and the game as it had been written? Huddled in a corner of an empty BU classroom, Julee was having the conversation that her mother had not been willing to have with her. In the end, Julee's character chose to ignore her loyalty to her team in order to preserve her daughter's life.

Clearly, Julee projected feelings about her 'real' mother's choice onto her experience of the game, but more was going on than a simple re-enactment. Julee was able to re-experience a familiar situation in a setting where she could examine it, do something new with it, and revise her relationship towards it. In many ways, what happened was resonant with the psychoanalytic notion of 'working through'.

Julee's experience stands in contrast to images of role-playing games that are prevalent in the popular culture. A first popular image portrays role-playing games as depressing and dangerous environments. It is captured in the urban legend which describes an emotionally troubled student disappearing and committing suicide during a game of Dungeons and Dragons. Another popular image, and one that has been supported by some academic writing on role-playing games, turns them into places of escape. Players are seen as leaving their 'real' lives and problems behind to lose themselves in the game space. Julee's story belies both stereotypes. For her the game is psychologically constructive rather than destructive. And she uses it not for escape but as a vehicle for engaging in a significant dialogue with important events and relationships in her 'real' life.

Role-playing games are able to serve in this evocative capacity precisely because they are not simple escapes from the real to the unreal, but because they stand betwixt and between, both in and not in real life. But in the final analysis, what puts Julee's game most firmly in the category of game is that it had an end point. The weekend was over and so was the game.

MUDs present a far more complicated case. In a certain sense, they don't have to end. Their boundaries are more fuzzy; the routine of playing them becomes part of their players' real lives. The virtual reality becomes not so much an alternative as a parallel life. Indeed, dedicated players who work with computers all day describe how they temporarily put their characters to 'sleep', remain logged on to the game, pursue other activities, and periodically return to the game space.

Such blurring of boundaries between role and self present new opportunities to use the role to work on the self. As one experienced player put it, 'You are the character and you are not the character both at the same time.' And 'you are who you pretend to be'. This ambiguity contributes to the games' ability to be a place in which to address issues of identity and intimacy. They take the possibilities that Julee found in role-playing games and raise them to a higher power.

Virtual Realities: Role-Playing to a Higher Power

The notion 'you are who you pretend to be' has a mythic resonance. The Pygmalion story endures because it speaks to a powerful fantasy: that we are not limited by our histories, that we can be recreated or can recreate ourselves. In the real world, we are thrilled by stories of self-transformation. Madonna is our modern Eliza Doolittle; Ivana Trump is the object of morbid fascination. But of course, for most people such recreations of self are difficult. Virtual worlds provide environments for experiences that may be hard to come by in the real.

Not the least of these experiences is the opportunity to play an 'aspect of your self' that you embody as a separate self in the game space.[1]

Peter is a 23-year-old physics graduate student at the University of Massachusetts. His life revolves around his work in the laboratory and his plans for a life in science. He says that his only friend is his roommate, another student whom he describes as being even more reclusive than he. This circumscribed, almost monastic life does not represent a radical departure for Peter. He has had heart trouble since he was a child; his health is delicate, one small rebellion, a ski trip when he first came up to Boston, put him in the hospital for three weeks. His response has been to circumscribe his world. Peter has never travelled. He lives within a small compass.

In an interview with Peter he immediately made it clear why he plays on MUDs: 'I do it so I can talk to people.' He is logged on for at least 40 hours a week, but it is hard to call what he does 'playing' a game. He spends his time on the MUDs constructing a life that (in only a seeming paradox) is more expansive than his own. He tells me with delight that the MUD he frequents most often is physically located on a computer in Germany.

> And I started talking to them [the inhabitants of the MUD] and they're like, 'This costs so many and so many deutsche marks.' And I'm like, 'What are deutsche marks? Where is this place located?' And they say: 'Don't you know, this is Germany.'

It is from MUDs that Peter has learned what he knows of politics, of economics, of the differences between capitalism and welfare-state socialism. He revels in the differences between the styles of Americans and Europeans on the MUDs and in the thrill of speaking to a player in

Norway who can see the Northern lights.

On the MUD, Peter shapes a character, Achilles, who is his ideal self. Life in a University of Massachusetts dorm has put him in modest and unaesthetic circumstances. Yet the room he inhabits on the MUD is elegant, romantic, out of a Ralph Lauren ad.

Peter's story illustrates several aspects of the relationship of MUD-ing and identity. First, the MUD serves as a kind of Rorschach inkblot, a projection of fantasy. Second, unlike a Rorschach, it does not stay on a page. It is part of Peter's everyday life. Beyond expanding his social reach, MUDs have brought Peter the only romance and intimacy he has ever known. At a social event held in virtual space, a 'wedding' of two regular players on his favourite Germany-based MUD, Peter met Winterlight, one of the three female players. Peter who has known little success with women, was able to charm this most desirable and sought-after player. Their encounter led to a courtship in which he was tender and romantic, chivalrous and poetic. One is reminded of Cyrano who could only find his voice through another's persona. It is Achilles, Peter's character on the MUD, who can create the magic and win the girl.

While people work one-on-one with the computer, the machine becomes an evocative object for thinking through issues of identity which tend to be centered on control and mastery. But Peter's experience (where the computer is a mediator to a reality shared with other people) has put computation more directly in the service of the development of a greater capacity for friendship, the development of confidence for a greater capacity for intimacy.

But what of the contrast between Peter and Julee? What can we say about the difference between role-playing games in the corridors of BU and on computer virtual worlds?

Julee and Peter both use games to remake the self. Their games, however, are evocative for different reasons. Julee's role-playing has the powerful quality of real-time psychodrama, but on the other hand Peter's game is ongoing and provides him with anonymity, invisibility, and potential multiplicity. Ongoing: He can play it as much as he wants, all day if he wants, every day if he chooses, as he often does. There are always people logged on to the game; there is always someone to talk to or something to do. Anonymous: Once Peter creates his character, that is his only identity on the game. His character need not have his gender or share any recognizable feature with him. He can be who he wants and play with no concern that *he*, Peter, will be held accountable in 'real life' for his character's actions, quarrels, or relationships. The degree to which he brings the game into his real life is his choice. Invisible: The created character can have any physical description and will be responded to as a function of that description. The plain can experience the self-presentation of great beauty; the nerdy can be elegant; the obese can be slender. Multiplicity: Peter can create several characters, playing out and playing with different aspects of his self. An ongoing game, an anonymous persona, physical invisibility, and the possibility to be not one but many, these are the qualities at the root of the holding power and evocative potential of MUDs as 'identity workshops.'[2] Faced with the notion that 'you are what you pretend to be', Peter can only hope that it is true, for he is playing his ideal self.

Peter plays what in the psychoanalytic tradition would be called an 'ego ideal'. Other players create a character or multiple characters that are closer to embodying aspects of themselves that they hate or fear or perhaps have not ever consciously confronted before. One male player describes his role playing as 'daring to be passive. I don't mean in having sex on the MUD. I mean in letting other people take the initiative in friendships, in not feeling when I am in character that I need to control everything. My mother controlled my whole family, well, certainly me. So I grew up thinking "never again". My "real life" is exhausting that way. On MUDs I do something else. I didn't even realize this connection to my mother until something happened in the game and somebody tried to boss my pretty laid-back character around and I went crazy. And then I saw what I was doing.'

The power of the medium as a material for the projection of aspects of both conscious and unconscious aspects of the self suggests an analogy between MUDs and psychotherapeutic milieus. The goal of psychotherapy is not, of course, simply to provide a place for 'acting out' behaviour that expresses one's conflicts, but to furnish a contained and confidential environment for 'working through' unresolved issues. The distinction between acting out and working through is crucial to thinking about MUDs as settings for personal growth. For it is in the context of this distinction that the much-discussed issue of 'MUDs addiction' should be situated. The accusation of being 'addicted' to psychotherapy is only made seriously when friends or family suspect that over a period of time, the therapy is supporting repetitions and re-enactments rather than new resolutions. MUD-ing is no more 'addictive' than therapy when it works as a pathway to psychological growth.

Robert was a college freshman who, in the months before beginning college, had to cope with his father's having lost his job and disgracing his family because of alcoholism. The job loss led to his parents' relocation to another part of the country, far away from all of Robert's friends. For a period of several months, Robert, now at college, MUD-ed over 80 hours a week. Around the time of a fire in his dormitory which destroyed all his possessions, Robert was playing over 120 hours a week, sleeping four hours a night, and only taking brief breaks to get food, which he would eat while playing.

At the end of the school year, however, Robert's MUD experience was essentially over. He had gotten his own apartment; he had a job as a salesman; he had formed a rock band with a few friends. Looking back on the experience he thought that MUD-ing had served its purpose: it kept him from what he called his 'suicidal thoughts', in essence by keeping him too busy to have them; it kept him from drinking ('I have something more fun and safe to do'); it enabled him to function with responsibility and competency as a highly placed administrator; it afforded an emotional environment where he could be in complete control of how much he revealed about his life, about his parents, even about something as simple for other people as where he was from. In sum, MUDs had provided what

Erik Erikson would have called a 'psychosocial moratorium'. It had been a place from which he could reassemble a sense of boundaries that enabled him to pursue less bounded relationships.[3]

MUDs are a context for constructions and reconstructions of identity; they are also a context for reflecting on old notions of identity itself. Through contemporary psychoanalytic theory which stresses the decentered subject and through the fragmented selves presented by patients (and most dramatically the increasing numbers of patients who present with multiple personality), psychology confronts the ways in which any unitary notion of identity is problematic and probably illusory. What is the self when it divides its labour among its constituent 'altars' or 'avatars'? Those burdened by post-traumatic dissociative syndrome suffer the question; inhabitants of MUDs play with it.

These remarks have addressed MUDs as privileged spaces for thinking through and working through issues of personal identity. Additionally, when role-playing moves onto a sustained virtual space there is an attendant growth of a highly structured social world. The development of these virtual cultures is of signal importance: it makes MUDs very special kinds of evocative objects.

1 Sherry Turkle, *The Second Self: Computers and the Human Spirit*, New York: Simon and Schuster, 1984.

2 For more material on the contrast with traditional role-playing see Gary Alan Fine, *Shared Fantasy: Role-Playing Games as Social Worlds*, Chicago: The University of Chicago Press, 1983. Henry Jenkins' study of fan culture, *Textual Poachers: Television Fans and Participatory Culture*, New York: Routledge, 1992, illuminates the general question of how individuals appropriate fantasy materials in the construction of identity.

3 'The Well' has a 'topic' (discussion group) on 'On-line Personae'. In a March 24, 1992 posting to this group F Randall Farmer noted that in a group of about 50 Habitat users, about a quarter experienced their online personae as separate creatures that act in ways they do not in real life.

Kevin Kelly_An Open Universe_1994

Out of Control is about what is set to happen when the evolutionary imperative of living things is linked to the digital revolution – a hybridization of biology and technology that Kevin Kelly calls the 'neo-biological'. The book surveys many of the notions surrounding technology and ecology that were postulated in the twentieth century – from nanotechnology to artificial life, Gaia and swarming phenomena – and illustrates their contribution to a field of knowledge that could take silicon intelligence to its next stage.

Kelly is the executive editor of *Wired* magazine. The former publisher and editor of the *Whole Earth Review*, he has been instrumental in the launch of a number digital-themed events including 'The Hackers' Conference' and 'Cyberthon and the WELL'.

In the 'neo-biological' era, intelligence will be liberated from human control and imbued with a changing contextualism. In the final chapter of *Out of Control* Kelly summarizes his vision:

In the coming neo-biological era, all we both rely on and fear will be born rather than made. We now have computer viruses, neural nets, Biosphere 2, gene therapy, and smart cards – all humanly constructed artifacts that bind mechanical and biological processes. Future bionic hybrids will be more confusing, more pervasive, and more powerful. I imagine there might be a world of mutating buildings, living silicon polymers, software programs evolving offline, adaptable cars, rooms stuffed with co-evolutionary furniture, gnatbots for cleaning, manufactured biological viruses that cure your illnesses, neural jacks, cyborgian body parts, designer food crops, simulated personalities, and a vast ecology of computing devices in constant flux.

The river of life – at least its liquid logic – flows through it all.[1]

The crucial notion in this collection of exciting ideas is that of bottom-up, 'emergent' behaviour. Technology is currently designed in a 'top-down' manner: a machine has a series of specified actions, and predetermined input data. If data does not come in that form then the machine will reject it. A 'bottom-up' approach, by contrast, is one that allows individual packets of data – whether virtual ants, weather patterns or different natural animal and plant species – to develop and evolve their own behaviour relative to one another. It is an approach exemplified by parallel computing (computers made of thousands of linked processors, each one a simple version of your laptop), which uses programs that evolve rather than proceed in a linear fashion. Kelly believes parallel computing to be one answer in an increasingly complex and hybrid world.

In the chapter 'An Open Universe' Kelly reminds us of nature's open-ended 'parallel programmes', made possible by genes of an organism. Together, the potential combinations of genes represent a massive conceptual 'gene space' of infinite possibilities. In a computing context, the genetic model can be used to create artificial lives, which evolve according to a 'fitness landscape' that is always fluctuating. In this excerpt Kelly describes the definition of artificial life put forward by Chris Langton, a prominent artificial-life pioneer, and moves on to discuss the rearticulation of the old dichotomy of artificial and real.

1 Kevin Kelly, *Out of Control*, London: Fourth Estate, 1994, p471.

The nature of this ambitious challenge initially sets the science of artificial life apart from the science of biology. Biology seeks to understand the living by taking it apart and reducing it to it pieces. Artificial life, on the other hand, has nothing to dissect, so it can only make progress by putting the living together and assembling it from pieces. Rather than analyze life, synthesize it. For this reason, Langton says, 'Artificial life amounts to the practice of synthetic biology.'

Artificial life acknowledges new lives and a new definition of life. 'New' life is an old force that organizes matter and energy in new ways. Our ancient ancestors were often generous in deeming things alive. But in the age of science, we make a careful distinction. We call creatures and green plants alive, but when we call an institution such as the post office an 'organism', we say it is lifelike or 'as if it were alive'.

We (and by this I mean scientists first) are beginning to see that those organizations once called metaphorically alive are truly alive, but animated by a life of a larger scope and wider definition. I call this greater life 'hyperlife'. Hyperlife is a particular type of vivisystem endowed with integrity, robustness, and cohesiveness – a strong vivisystem rather than a lax one. A rain forest and a periwinkle, an electronic network and a servomechanism, SimCity and New York City, all possess degrees of hyperlife. Hyperlife is my word for that class of life that includes both the AIDS virus and the Michelangelo computer virus.

Biological life is only one species of hyperlife. A telephone network is another species. A bullfrog is chock-full of hyperlife. The Biosphere 2 project in Arizona swarms with hyperlife, as do Tierra, and Terminator 2. Someday hyperlife will blossom in automobiles, buildings, TVs, and test tubes.

This is not to say that organic life and machine life are identical; they are not. Water striders will forever retain certain characteristics unique to carbon-based life. But organic and artificial life share a set of characteristics that we have only begun to discern. And, of course, there easily may be other types of hyperlife to come that we can't describe yet. One can imagine various possibilities of life – weird hybrids bred from both biological and synthetic lines, the half-animal/half-machine cyborgs of old science-fiction – that may have emergent properties of hyperlife not found in either parent.

Man's every attempt to create life is a probe into the space of possible hyperlifes. This space includes all endeavours to re-create the origins of life on Earth. But the challenge goes way beyond that. The goal of artificial life is not to merely describe the space of 'life-as-we-know-it'. The quest that fires up Langton is the hope of mapping the space of *all* possible lives, a quest that moves us into the far, far vaster realm of 'life-as-it-could-be'. Hyperlife is that library which contains all things alive, all vivisystems, all slivers of life, anything bucking the second law of thermodynamics, all future and all past arrangements of matter capable of open-ended evolution, and all examples of a type of something marvelous we can't really define yet.

The only way to explore this *terra incognita* is to build many examples and see if they fit in the space. As Langton wrote in his introduction to the proceedings of the Second Artificial Life conference, 'If biologists could "re-wind the tape" of evolution and start it over, again and again, from different initial conditions, or under different regimes of external perturbations along the way, they would have a full ensemble of evolutionary pathways to generalize over.' Keep starting from zero, alter the rules a bit and then build an example of artificial life. Do it dozens of times. Each instance of synthetic life is added to the example of Earth-bound organic life to form the complete *ensemble* of hyperlife.

Since life is a property of form, and not matter, the more materials we can transplant living behaviours into, the more examples of 'life-as-it-could-be' we can accumulate. Therefore the field of artificial life is broad and eclectic in considering all avenues to complexity. A typical gathering of a-life researchers includes biochemists, computer wizards, game designers, animators, physicists, math nerds, and robot hobbyists. The hidden agenda is to hack the definition of life.

One evening after a late-night lecture session at the First Artificial Life Conference, while some of us watched the stars in the desert night sky, mathematician Rudy Rucker came up with the most expansive motivation for artificial life I've heard: 'Right now an ordinary computer program may be a thousand lines and take a few minutes to run. Artificial life is about finding a computer code that is only a few lines long and that takes a thousand years to run.'

That seems about right. We want the same in our robots: design them for a few years and then have them run for centuries, perhaps even manufacturing their replacements. That's what an acorn is too – a few lines of code that run out as a 180-year-old tree.

The conference-goers felt the important thing about artificial life was that it not only was redefining biology and life, but it was also redefining the concept of both artificial and real. It was radically enlarging the realm of what seemed important – that is, the realm of life and reality. Unlike the 'publish or perish' mode of academic professionalism of yesteryear, most of the artificial life experimenters – even the mathematicians – espoused the emerging new academic creed of 'demo or die'. The only way to make a dent in artificial and hyperlife was to get a working example up and running. Explaining how he got started in life-as-it-could-be, Ken Karakotsios, a former Apple employee, recalled, 'Every time I met a computer I tried to program the Game of Life into it.' This eventually led to a remarkable Macintosh a-life program called SimLife. In SimLife you create a hyperlife world and set loose little creatures into it to coevolve into a complexifying artificial ecology. Now Karakotsios seeks to write the biggest and best game of life, an ultimate living program: 'You know, the universe is the only thing big enough to run the ultimate game of life. The only problem with the universe as a platform, though, is that it is currently running someone else's program.'

Larry Yaeger, a current Apple employee, once handed me his business card. It ran: 'Larry Yaeger, Microcosmic God.' Yaeger created Polyworld, a sophisticated computer world with organisms in the shape of polygons. The polys fly around by the hundreds, mating, breeding, consuming resources, learning (a power God Yaeger gave them), adapting and evolving. Yaeger was exploring the space of possible life. What would appear? 'At first,' said Yaeger, 'I did not charge the parents an energy cost when offspring was born. They could have offspring for free. But I kept getting this particular species, these indolent cannibals, who liked to hang around the corner in the vicinity of their parents and children and do nothing, never leave. All they would do was mate with each other, fight with each other and eat each other. Hey, why work when you can eat your kids!' Life of some hyper-type had appeared.

'A central motivation for the study of artificial life is to extend biology to a broader class of life forms than those currently present on the earth,' writes Doyne Farmer, understating the sheer, great fun artificial life gods are having.

But Farmer is onto something. Artificial life is unique among other human endeavours for yet another reason. Gods such as Yaeger are extending the class of life because life-as-it-could-be is a territory we can only study by first creating it. We must manufacture hyperlife to explore it, and to explore it we must manufacture it.

But as we busily create ensembles of new forms of hyperlife, an uneasy thought creeps into our minds. Life is using us. Organic carbon-based life is merely the first, earliest form of hyperlife to evolve into matter. Life has conquered carbon. But now under the guise of pond weed and kingfisher, life seethes to break out into crystal, into wires, into biochemical gels, and into hybrid patches of nerve and silicon. If we look at where life is headed, we have to agree with developmental biologist Lewis Held when he said, 'Embryonic cells are just robots in disguise.' In his report for the proceedings of [the] Second Artificial Life Conference Tom Ray wrote, 'Virtual life is out there, waiting for us to create environments for it to evolve into.' Langton told Steven Levy, reporting in *Artificial Life*, 'There are these other forms of life, artificial ones, that want to come into existence. And they are using me as a vehicle for its reproduction and its implementation.'

Life – the hyperlife – wants to explore all possible biologies and all possible evaluations, but it uses us to create them because to create them is the only way to explore or complete them. Humanity is thus, depending on how you look at it, a mere passing station on hyperlife's gallop through space, or the critical gateway to the open-ended universe.

'With the advent of artificial life, we may be the first species to create its own successors,' Doyne Farmer wrote in his manifesto, *Artificial Life: The Coming Evolution*. 'What will these successors be like? If we fail in our task as creators, they may indeed be cold and malevolent. However, if we succeed, they may be glorious, enlightened creatures that far surpass us in their intelligence and wisdom.' Their intelligence might be 'inconceivable to lower forms of life such as us'. We have always been anxious about being gods. If through us, hyperlife should find spaces where it evolves creatures that amuse and help us, we feel proud. But if superior successors should ascend through our efforts, we feel fear.

Chris Langton's office sat catty-corner to the atomic museum in Los Alamos, a reminder of the power we have to destroy. That power stirred Langton. 'By the middle of this century, mankind had acquired the power to extinguish life,' he wrote in one of his academic papers. 'By the end of the century, he will be able to create it. Of the two, it is hard to say which places the larger burden of responsibilities on our shoulders.'

Here and there we create space for other varieties of life to emerge. Juvenile delinquent hackers launch potent computer viruses. Japanese industrialists weld together smart painting robots. Hollywood directors create virtual dinosaurs. Biochemists squeeze self-evolving molecules into tiny plastic test tubes. Someday, we will create an open-ended world that can keep going, and keep creating perpetual novelty. When we do we will have created another living vector in the life space.

When Danny Hillis says he wants to make a computer that would be proud of him, he isn't kidding. What could be more human than to give life? I think I know: to give life and freedom. To give *open-ended* life. To say, here's your life *and* the car keys. Then you let it do what we are doing – making it all up as we go along. Tom Ray once told me, 'I don't want to download life into computers. I want to upload computers into life.'

Greg Egan_Permutation City_1994

The novel *Permutation City* revolves around what a disembodied intelligence might experience if the downloading of human consciousness – an idea posited by Hans Moravec (see p280) – were possible. Philosophically it centres on two notions: the differences between virtual space and real space, in terms of relative speeds and evolutionary capabilities; and the possibility of making personality copies, which would be placed in 'conscious' avatars that inhabit simulated worlds in cyberspace. These notions are underpinned by the equating of the function of the human brain with the workings of a computer.

Greg Egan has published numerous science-fiction novels. He has a parallel career as a computer programmer, and also writes scientific papers. Central to his book is the idea of 'Strong AI' – the idea of artificial intelligence (AI) evolving to solve unimagined future problems and have a sense of itself. Some philosophers of the mind, such as Daniel Dennett (see p158), see in the computer's ability to become a 'virtual machine' a model of the way our brains work. The computer's capacity to impersonate other machines – such as a typewriter, calculator or movie projector – is, for these thinkers, analogous to the way humans can think in different ways, using different logic systems at different times or even simultaneously. As one of the characters in *Permutation City* explains:

> Supporters of the Strong AI Hypothesis insisted that consciousness was a property of certain algorithms – a result of information being processed in certain ways, regardless of what machine, or organ, was used to perform the task. A computer model which manipulated data about itself and its 'surroundings' in essentially the same way as the organic brain would have to possess essentially the same mental states. 'Simulated consciousness' was as oxymoronic as 'simulated addition'.[1]

It was Alan Turing (see p40), with his famous Turing Test, who invented the benchmark for Strong AI:

Turing envisioned a game in which a human player is seated at a teletype console, by which he can communicate with a teletype in another room. Controlling this second console would be either another human or a digital computer. The player could ask any questions he wished through his console in order to determine whether he was in contact with a man or machine.[2]

The machine, if it was a machine, would need to be sufficiently smart to know the human condition, to lie, to refuse to answer questions and generally to react as a human does. This would be true artificial intelligence.

Paul Durham, one of the main characters in *Permutation City*, copies himself as an experiment so he can conduct research into a Strong AI project. Speed of thought/processing differs greatly across the vital/virtual divide: things out here think slowly compared to things in the virtual arena, but it can be more complicated than that. Cyberspace time is relativistic, jump-cut, and able to be tampered with by the 'real' protagonists, much to the outrage of their virtual copies:

'I shut down part of the model – and cheated on most of the rest. It's only the fourth of June: you got six hours' sleep in ten hours real time. Not a bad job,' I thought.

Paul [the virtual] was outraged. 'You had no right to do that!'[3]

The following excerpt focuses on the copy Paul as he becomes simulatedly sentient.

1 Greg Egan, *Permutation City*, London: Millennium (Orion), 1994, p40.
2 J David Bolter, *Turing's Man: Western Culture in the Computer Age*, London: Penguin, 1993, p191.
3 Greg Egan, *Permutation City*, op cit, p70.

Paul Durham opened his eyes, blinking at the room's unexpected brightness, then lazily reached out to place one hand in a patch of sunlight at the edge of the bed. Dust motes drifted across the shaft of light which slanted down from a gap between the curtains, each speck appearing for all the world to be conjured into, and out of, existence – evoking a childhood memory of the last time he'd found this illusion so compelling, so hypnotic: *He stood in the kitchen doorway, afternoon light slicing the room; dust, flour and steam swirling in the plane of bright air.* For one sleep-addled moment, still trying to wake, to collect himself, to order his life, it seemed to make as much sense to place these two fragments side by side – watching sunlit dust motes, forty years apart – as it did to follow the ordinary flow of time from one instant to the next. Then he woke a little more, and the confusion passed.

Paul felt utterly refreshed – and utterly disinclined to give up his present state of comfort. He couldn't think why he'd slept so late, but he didn't much care. He spread his fingers on the sun-warmed sheet, and thought about drifting back to sleep.

He closed his eyes and let his mind grow blank – and then caught himself, suddenly uneasy, without knowing why. *He'd done something foolish, something insane, something he was going to regret, badly …* but the details remained elusive, and he began to suspect that it was nothing more than the lingering mood of a dream. He tried to recall exactly what he'd dreamt, without much hope; unless he was catapulted awake by a nightmare, his dreams were usually evanescent. And yet –

He leapt out of bed and crouched down on the carpet, fists to his face, face against his knees, lips moving soundlessly. The shock of realization was a palpable thing: a red lesion behind his eyes, pulsing with blood … like the aftermath of a hammer blow to the thumb – and tinged with the very same mixture of surprise, anger, humiliation and idiot bewilderment. Another childhood memory: *He held a nail to the wood, yes – but only to camouflage his true intentions. He'd seen his father injure himself this way – but he knew that he needed first-hand experience to understand the mystery of pain. And he was sure that it would be worth it, right up to the moment when he swung the hammer down –*

He rocked back and forth, on the verge of laughter, trying to keep his mind blank, waiting for the panic to subside. And eventually, it did – to be replaced by one simple, perfectly coherent thought: *I don't want to be here.*

What he'd done to himself was insane – and it had to be undone, as swiftly and painlessly as possible. *How could he have ever imagined reaching any other conclusion?*

Then he began to remember the details of his preparations. He'd anticipated feeling this way. He'd planned for it. However bad he felt, it was all part of the expected progression of responses. Panic. Regret. Analysis. Acceptance.

Two out of four; so far, so good.

Paul uncovered his eyes, and looked around the room. Away from a few dazzling patches of direct sunshine, everything glowed softly in the diffuse light: the matt white brick walls, the imitation (imitation) mahogany furniture; even the posters – Bosch, Dali, Ernst, and Giger – looked harmless, domesticated. Wherever he turned his gaze (if nowhere else), the simulation was utterly convincing; the spotlight of his attention made it so. Hypothetical light rays were being traced backwards from individual rod and cone cells on his simulated retinas, and projected out into the virtual environment to determine exactly what needed to be computed: a lot of detail near the centre of his vision, much less towards the periphery. Objects out of sight didn't 'vanish' entirely, if they influenced the ambient light, but Paul knew that the calculations would rarely be pursued beyond the crudest first-order approximations: *Bosch's Garden of Earthly Delights* reduced to an average reflectance value, a single grey rectangle – because once his back was turned, any more detail would have been wasted. Everything in the room was as finely resolved, at any given moment, as it needed to be to fool him – no more, no less.

He had been aware of the technique for decades. It was something else to experience it. He resisted the urge to wheel around suddenly, in a futile attempt to catch the process out – but for a moment it was almost unbearable, just *knowing* what was happening at the edge of his vision. The fact that his view of the room remained flawless only made it worse, *an irrefutable paranoid fixation: No matter how fast you turn your head, you'll never even catch a glimpse of what's going on all around you…*

He closed his eyes again for a few seconds. When he opened them, the feeling was already less oppressive. No doubt it would pass; it seemed too bizarre a state of mind to be sustained for long. Certainly, none of the other Copies had reported anything similar … but then, none of them had volunteered much useful data at all. They'd just ranted abuse, whined about their plight, and then terminated themselves – all within fifteen (subjective) minutes of gaining consciousness.

And this one? How was he different from Copy number four? Three years older. *More stubborn? More determined? More desperate for success?* He'd believed so. If he hadn't felt more committed than ever – if he hadn't been convinced that he was, finally, prepared to see the whole thing through – he would never have gone ahead with the scan.

But now that he was 'no longer' the flesh-and-blood Paul Durham – 'no longer' the one who'd sit outside and watch the whole experiment from a safe distance – all of that determination seemed to have evaporated.

Suddenly he wondered: *What makes me so sure that I'm not still flesh and blood?* He laughed weakly, hardly daring to take the possibility seriously. His most recent memories seemed to be of lying on a trolley in the Landau Clinic, while technicians prepared him for the scan – on the face of it, a bad sign – but he'd been overwrought, and he'd spent so long psyching himself up for 'this', that perhaps he'd forgotten coming home, still hazy from the anaesthetic, crashing into bed, dreaming…

He muttered the password, 'Abulafia' – and his last faint hope vanished, as a black-on-white square about a metre wide, covered in icons, appeared in midair in front of him.

He gave the interface window an angry thump; it resisted him as if it was solid, and firmly anchored. *As if he was solid, too.* He didn't really need any more convincing, but he gripped the top edge and lifted himself off the floor. He instantly regretted this; the realistic cluster of effects of exertion – down to the plausible twinge in his right elbow – pinned him to this 'body', anchored him to this 'place', in exactly the way he knew he should be doing everything he could to avoid.

He lowered himself to the floor with a grunt. *He was the Copy.* Whatever his inherited memories told him, he was 'no longer' human; he would never inhabit his real body 'again'. Never inhabit *the real world* again ... unless his cheapskate original scraped up the money for a telepresence robot – in which case he could spend his time blundering around in a daze, trying to make sense of the lightning-fast blur of human activity. *His model-of-a-brain ran seventeen times slower than the real thing.* Yeah, sure, if he hung around, the technology would catch up, eventually – and seventeen times faster for him than for his original. And in the meantime? He'd rot in this prison, jumping through hoops, carrying out Durham's precious research – while the man lived in his apartment, spent his money, slept with Elizabeth ...

Paul leant against the cool surface of the interface, dizzy and confused. *Whose precious research?* He'd wanted this so badly – and he'd done this to himself with his eyes wide open. Nobody had forced him, nobody had deceived him. He'd known exactly what the drawbacks would be – but he'd hoped that he would have the strength of will (this time, at last) to transcend them: to devote himself, monk-like, to the purpose for which he'd been brought into being, content in the knowledge that his other self was as unconstrained as ever.

Looking back, that hope seemed ludicrous. Yes, he'd made the decision freely – for the fifth time – but it was mercilessly clear, now, that he'd never really faced up to the consequences. All the time he'd spent, supposedly 'preparing himself' to be a Copy, his greatest source of resolve had been to focus on the outlook for the man who'd remain flesh and blood. He'd told himself that he was rehearsing 'making do with vicarious freedom' – and no doubt he had been genuinely struggling to do just that ... but he'd also been taking secret comfort in the knowledge that *he* would 'remain' on the outside – that his future, then, still included a version with absolutely nothing to fear.

And as long as he'd clung to that happy truth, he'd never really swallowed the fate of the Copy at all.

People reacted badly to waking up as Copies. Paul knew the statistics. Ninety-eight per cent of Copies made were of the very old, and the terminally ill. People for whom it was the last resort – most of whom had spent millions beforehand, exhausting all the traditional medical options; some of whom had even died between the taking of the scan and the time the Copy itself was run. Despite this, fifteen per cent decided on awakening – usually in a matter of hours – that they couldn't face living this way.

And of those who were young and healthy, those who were merely curious, those who knew they had a perfectly viable, living, breathing body outside?

The bale-out rate so far had been one hundred per cent.

Paul stood in the middle of the room, swearing softly for several minutes, acutely aware of the passage of time. He didn't feel ready – but the longer the other Copies had waited, the more traumatic they seemed to have found the decision. He stared at the floating interface; its dreamlike, hallucinatory quality helped, slightly. He rarely remembered his dreams, and he wouldn't remember this one – but there was no tragedy in that.

He suddenly realized that he was still stark naked. Habit – if no conceivable propriety – nagged at him to put on some clothes, but he resisted the urge. One or two perfectly innocent, perfectly ordinary actions like that, and he'd find he was taking himself seriously, thinking of himself as real, making it even harder...

He paced the bedroom, grasped the cool metal of the doorknob a couple of times, but managed to keep himself from turning it. There was no point even starting to explore this world.

He couldn't resist peeking out the window, though. The view of north Sydney was flawless; every building, every cyclist, every tree, was utterly convincing – but that was no great feat; it was a recording, not a simulation. Essentially photographic – give or take some computerized touching up and filling in – and totally predetermined. To cut costs even further, only a tiny part of it was 'physically' accessible to him; he could see the harbour in the distance, but he knew that if he tried to go for a stroll down to the water's edge...

Enough. Just get it over with.

Paul turned back to the interface and touched a menu icon labelled UTILITIES; it spawned another window in front of the first. The function he was seeking was buried several menus deep – but he knew exactly where to look for it. He'd watched this, from the outside, too many times to have forgotten.

He finally reached the EMERGENCIES menu – which included a cheerful icon of a cartoon figure suspended from a parachute. *Baling out* was what everyone called it – but he didn't find that too cloyingly euphemistic; after all, he could hardly commit 'suicide' when he wasn't legally human. The fact that a bale-out option was compulsory had nothing to do with anything so troublesome as the 'rights' of the Copy; the requirement arose solely from the ratification of certain, purely technical, international software standards.

Paul prodded the icon; it came to life, and recited a warning spiel. He scarcely paid attention. Then it said, 'Are you absolutely sure that you wish to shut down this Copy of Paul Durham?'

Nothing to it. Program A asks Program B to confirm its request for orderly termination. Packets of data are exchanged.

'Yes, I'm sure.'

A metal box, painted red, appeared at his feet. He opened it, took out the parachute, strapped it on.

Then he closed his eyes and said, 'Listen to me. *Just listen!* How many times do you need to be told? I'll skip the personal angst; you've heard it all before – and ignored it all before. It doesn't matter how I feel. But ... when are you going to stop wasting your time, your money, your energy – *when are you going to stop wasting your life* – on something which you just don't have the strength to carry through?'

Paul hesitated, trying to put himself in the place of his original, hearing those words – and almost wept with frustration. He still didn't know what he could say that would make a difference. He'd shrugged off the testimony of all the earlier Copies himself; he'd never been able to accept their claims to know his own mind better than he did. Just because they'd lost their nerve and chosen to bale out, who were they to proclaim that he'd *never* give rise to a Copy who'd choose otherwise? All he had to do was strengthen his resolve, and try again...

He shook his head. 'It's been ten years, and nothing's changed. *What's wrong with you?* Do you honestly still believe that you're brave enough – or crazy enough – to be your own guinea pig? *Do you?*'

He paused again, but only for a moment; he didn't expect a reply. He'd argued long and hard with the first Copy, but after that, he'd never had the stomach for it.

'Well, I've got news for you: *You're not.*'

With his eyes still closed, he gripped the release lever.

I'm nothing: a dream, a soon-to-be-forgotten dream.

His fingernails needed cutting; they dug painfully into the skin of his palm.

Had he never, in a dream, feared the extinction of waking? Maybe he had – but a dream was not a life. If the only way he could 'reclaim' his body, 'reclaim' his world, was to wake and forget –

He pulled the lever.

After a few seconds, he emitted a constricted sob – a sound more of confusion than any kind of emotion – and opened his eyes.

The lever had come away in his hand.

He stared dumbly at this metaphor for ... what? A bug in the termination software? Some kind of hardware glitch?

Feeling – at last – truly dreamlike, he unstrapped the parachute, and unfastened the neatly packaged bundle.

William Mitchell_Soft Cities_1995

William Mitchell's *City of Bits*, from which this extract is taken, was one of the first books to fully consider the impact of the Internet and e-commerce, on the urban structure and cities. The book helped the planning and urban design professions crawl out from under the accusation of 'anorak' whenever digital technology was discussed. Mitchell was one of the first explorers of a city that contains more than you can see: one that, via superhighways, is connected to the virtual.

William J Mitchell is Dean of the School of Architecture and Planning at Massachusetts Institute of Technology. He is author of *e-topia* (1999), *The Reconfigured Eye* (1994) and *The Logic of Architecture* (1990), and co-author of *The Poetics of Gardens* (1989).

Mitchell is not prone to surreal extrapolations or the more wild claims of the 'Mondo' side of cyberevangelism. Rather, in well-structured, easy-to-read prose he presents many of the developments in cyberspace in terms of a rational, thoughtful opportunity for new directions in urban life and town planning. His argument fits neatly into a North American view of the world and the city.

Mitchell begins *City of Bits* with a discussion of his various on- and off-line names and formal and non-formal personalities. He develops this into a discussion of the 'antispatial' qualities of cyberspace – a notion that has become familiar to us today:

> The Net negates geometry. While it does have a definite topology of computational nodes and radiating boulevards for bits, and while the locations of the nodes and links can be plotted on plans to produce surprisingly Haussmann-like diagrams, it is fundamentally and profoundly antispatial. It is nothing like the Piazza Navona or Copely Square. You cannot say where it is or describe its memorable shape and proportions or tell a stranger how to get there. The Net is ambient ...[1]

Mitchell never loses an opportunity to discuss cyberspace and its protocols in terms of real space analogies. Examples include computer encryption security, which is linked to watchdogs, receptionists and bouncers. The electronic transactions and real shopping are both subject to similar procedures that we all go through to buy items, whether from a shopkeeper or to exchange data. This fastidious use of the real to explain the virtual, without too much recourse to postmodern French philosophy, is perhaps the key to the book's huge success. Whilst exploring many of the issues that so interest cyber-philosophers Mitchell maintains a 'down to earth' literary style. Here Mitchell writes of cyberspace's immortality and its colonization of all data:

> [It] will be there forever. Because its electronic underpinnings are so modular, geographically dispersed, and redundant, cyberspace is essentially indestructible. You can't demolish it by cutting links with blackholes or sending commandos to blow its electronic installations, you can't even nuke it ... If big chunks of the network were to be wiped out, messages would reroute themselves around the damaged parts.[2]

In the following excerpt Mitchell discusses the historical city, with its physical transactions, and the hybrid virtual/vital city of the very near future, with its new electronic commerce.

1 William J Mitchell, *City of Bits: Space, Place and the Infobahn*, Cambridge, MA: MIT Press, 1995, p8.
2 Ibid, p110.

William Mitchell, 'Soft Cities', *City of Bits: Space, Place, and the Infobahn*, 1995

Physical transactions/electronic exchanges

Historically, cities have also provided places for specialized business and legal transactions.[1] In *The Politics*, Aristotle proposed that a city should have both a 'free' square in which 'no mechanic or farmer or anyone else like that may be admitted unless summoned by the authorities' and a marketplace 'where buying and selling are done … in a separate place, conveniently situated for all goods sent up from the sea and brought in from the country'.[2] Ancient Rome had both its *fora civila* for civic assembly and its *fora venalia* for the sale of food. These Roman markets were further specialized by type of produce; the *holitorium* was for vegetables, the *boarium* for cattle, the *suarium* for pigs, and the *vinarium* for wine. Medieval marketplaces were places both for barter and exchange and for religious ritual. Modern cities have main streets, commercial districts, and shopping malls jammed with carefully differentiated retail stores in which the essential transaction takes place at the counter – the point of sale – where money and goods are physically exchanged.

But where electronic funds transfer can substitute for physical transfer of cash, and where direct delivery from the warehouse can replace carrying the goods home from the store, the counter can become a virtual one. Television home shopping networks first exploited this possibility – combining cable broadcast, telephone, and credit card technologies to transform the purchase of zirconium rings and exercise machines into public spectacle.[3] Electronic 'shops' and 'malls' provided on computer networks (both Internet and the commercial dial-up services) quickly took the idea a step further; here customer and store clerk do not come face-to-face at the cash register, but interact on the network via a piece of software that structures the exchange of digital tokens – a credit card number to charge, and a specification of the required goods. (The exchange might then become so simple and standardized that the clerk can be replaced completely by a software surrogate.) As I needed books for reference in preparing this text, I simply looked up their titles and ISBN numbers in an on-line Library of Congress catalogue, automatically generated and submitted electronic mail purchase orders, and received what I requested by courier – dispatched from some place that I had never visited. The charges, of course, showed up on my credit card bill.

Immaterial goods such as insurance policies and commodity futures are most easily traded electronically. And the idea is readily extended to small, easily transported, high-value speciality items – books, computer equipment, jewellery, and so on – the sorts of things that have traditionally been sold by mail order. But it makes less sense for grocery retailing and other businesses characterized by mass markets, high bulk, and low margins. Cyberspace cities, like their physical counterparts, have their particular advantages and disadvantages for traders, so they are likely to grow up around particular trade specializations. Since you cannot literally lay down your cash, sign a cheque, or produce a credit card and flash an ID in cyberspace, payment methods are being reinvented for this new kind of marketplace. The Internet and similar networks were not initially designed to support commercial transactions, and were not secure enough for this purpose. Fortunately though, data encryption techniques can be used to provide authentication of the identities of trading partners, to allow secure exchange of sensitive information such as credit card numbers and bid amounts, and to affix digital 'signatures' and time stamps to legally binding documents. By the summer of 1994, industry standards for assuring security of Internet transactions were under development, and online shopping services were beginning to offer encryption-protected credit card payment.[4] And the emergence of genuine digital cash – packages of encrypted data that behaved like real dollars, and could not be traced like credit card numbers – seemed increasingly likely.

In traditional cities, transaction of daily business was accomplished literally by handing things over; goods and cash crossed store counters, contracts were physically signed, and perpetrators of illegal transactions were sometimes caught in the act. But in virtual cities, transactions reduce to exchanges of bits.

Street maps/hyperplans

Ever since Ur, doorways and passageways have joined together the rooms of buildings, webs and grids of streets have connected buildings to each other, and roads have linked cities. These physical connections provided access to the places where people lived, worked, worshipped, and entertained themselves.

Since the winter of 1994, I have had a remarkable piece of software called Mosaic on the modest desktop machine that I am using to write this paragraph.[5] Mosaic, and the network of World Wide Web servers to which it provides access, work together to construct a virtual rather than physical world of places and connections; the places are called 'pages' and they appear on my screen, and the connections – called hyperlinks – allow me to jump from page to page by clicking on highlighted text or icons.

A World Wide Web 'home page' invites me to step, like Alice through the looking glass, into the vast information flea-market of the Internet. The astonishing thing is that a WWW page displayed on my screen may originate from a server located anywhere in the Internet. In fact, as I move from page to page, I am logging into machines scattered around the world. But as I see it, I jump almost instantaneously from virtual place to virtual place by following the hyperlinks that programmers have established – much as I might trace a path from piazza to piazza in a great city along the roads and boulevards that a planner had provided. If I were to draw a diagram of these connections I would have a kind of street map of cyberspace. MUD crawling is another way to go. Software systems known as MUDs – Multi-User Dungeons – have burned up countless thousands of Internet log-in hours since the early 1980s.[6] These structure on-line, interactive, role-playing games, often attracting vast numbers of participants scattered all over the net. Their particular hook is the striking way that they foreground issues of personal identity and self-representation; as initiates learn at old MUDder's knees, the very first task is to construct an on-line persona for yourself by choosing a name and writing a description that others will see as they encounter you.[7] It's like dressing up for a masked ball, and the irresistible thing is that you can experiment freely with shifts, slippages, and reversals in social and sexual roles and even try on entirely fantastic guises. How does it really feel to be a complete unknown?

Once you have created your MUD character, you can enter a virtual place populated with other characters and objects. This place has exits – hyperlinks connecting it to other such settings, and these in turn have their own exits; some MUDs are vast, allowing you to wander among thousands of settings – all with their own special characteristics – like Baudelaire strolling through the buzzing complexity of nineteenth-century Paris. You can examine the settings and objects that you encounter, and you can interact with the characters that you meet.

But as you quickly discover, the most interesting and provocative thing about a MUD is its constitution – the programmed-in rules specifying the sorts of interactions that can take place and shaping the culture that evolves. Many are based on popular fantasy narratives such as *StarTrek*, Frank Herbert's *Dune*, CS Lewis's *Chronicles of Narnia*, the Japanese animated television series *Speed Racer*, and even more doubtful products of the literary imagination; these are communities held together, as in many traditional societies, by shared myths. Some are set up as hack 'n slash combat games in which bad MUDders will try to 'kill' your character; these, of course, are violent, Darwinian places in which you have to be aggressive and constantly on your guard. Others, like many of the TinyMUDs, stress ideals of constructive social interaction, egalitarianism, and nonviolence – MUDderhood and apple pie. Yet others are organized like high-minded lyceums, with places for serious discussion of different scientific and technical topics. The MIT-based Cyberion City encourages young hackers – MUDders of invention – to write MUSE code that adds new settings to the environment and creates new characters and objects. And some are populated by out-of-control, crazy MUDders who will try to engage your character in TinySex – the one-handed keyboard equivalent of phone sex.

Early MUDs – much like text-based adventure video games such as Zork – relied entirely on typed descriptions of characters, objects, scenes, and actions. (James Joyce surely would have been impressed; city as text and text as city. Every journey constructs a narrative.) But greater bandwidth, faster computers, and fancier programming can shift them into pictorial and spatial formats.[8]

Enclosure/encryption

In physically constructed cities, the enclosing surfaces of constituent spaces – walls, floors, ceilings, and roofs – provide not only shelter, but also privacy. Breaches in these surfaces – gates, doors, and windows – have mechanisms to control access and maintain privacy; you can lock your doors or leave them open, lower the window shades or raise them. Spatial divisions and access control devices are deployed to arrange spaces into hierarchies grading from completely public to utterly private. Sometimes you have to flip your ID to a bouncer, take off your shoes, pay admission, dress to a doorman's taste, slip a bribe, submit to a search, speak into a microphone and wait for the buzzer, smile at a receptionist, placate a watchdog, or act out some other ritual to cross a threshold into a more private space. Traditions and laws recognize these hierarchies, and generally take a dim view of illicit boundary crossing by trespassers, intruders, and peeping Toms.

Different societies have distinguished between public and private domains (and the activities appropriate to them) in differing ways, and cities have reflected these distinctions. According to Lewis Mumford, domestic privacy was 'a luxury of the well-to-do' up until the seventeenth century in the West.[9] The rich were the people who could do pretty much what they wanted, as long as they didn't do it in the street and frighten the horses. Then, as privacy rights trickled down to the less advantaged classes, the modern 'private house' emerged, acquired increasingly rigorous protections of constitutional law and public policy, and eventually became the cellular unit of suburban tissue.[10] Within the modern Western house itself – in contrast with some of its ancient and medieval predecessors – there is a carefully organized gradation from relatively public verandahs, entry halls, living rooms and parlours to more private, enclosed bedrooms and bathrooms where you can shut and lock the doors and draw down the shades against the outside world.

It doesn't rain in cyberspace, so shelter is not an issue, but privacy certainly is. So the construction technology for virtual cities – just like that of bricks-and-mortar ones – must provide for putting up boundaries and erecting access controls, and it must allow cyberspace architects and urban designers to organize virtual places into public-to-private hierarchies.

Fortunately, some of the necessary technology does exist. Most obviously, the rough equivalent of a locked gate or door, in cyberspace construction, is an authentication system.[11] This controls access to virtual places (such as your electronic mail inbox) by asking for identification and a password from those who request entry. If you give the correct password, you're in.[12] The trouble, of course, is that passwords – like keys – can be stolen and copied. And they can sometimes be guessed, systematically enumerated till one that works is found, or somehow extorted from the system manager who knows them all. So password-protection – as with putting a lock on a door – discourages illicit entry, but does not block the most determined break-in artists.

Just as you can put the valuables that you really want to protect in a sturdy vault or crypt, though, you can build the strongest of enclosures around digital information by encrypting it – scrambling it in a complex way so that it can only be decoded by somebody with the correct secret numerical key. The trick is not only to have a code that is difficult to crack, but also to manage keys so that they do not fall into the wrong hands, and the cleverest known way to do this is to use a technique called RSA public-key encryption. In this system, which derives its power from the fundamental properties of large prime numbers, each user has both a secret 'private' key and a 'public' key that can be distributed freely. If you want to send a secure message, you first obtain the intended recipient's public key, and use that to encode the information. Then the recipient decodes it using the private key.

Under pressure from cops and cold warriors, who anticipate being thwarted by impregnable fortresses in cyberspace, the US Federal Government has doggedly tried to restrict the availability of strong encryption software. But in June 1991, hacker folk-hero Philip Zimmerman released his soon-to-be-famous, RSA-based Pretty Good Privacy (PGP) encryption program. By May 1994, commercial versions had been licensed to over four million users, and MIT had released a free, non-commercial version that anybody could legally download from the Internet.[13] From that moment, you could securely fence off your private turf in cyberspace.

Meanwhile, the Clinton Administration pushed its plans for the Clipper Chip – a device that would accomplish much the same thing as RSA, but would provide a built-in 'trapdoor' for law-enforcement wiretapping and file decoding.[14] The effect is a lot like that of leaving a spare set of your front door keys in a safe at FBI headquarters. Opinion about this divided along predictable lines. A spokesman for the Electronic Frontier Foundation protested, 'The idea that the Government holds the keys to all our locks, before anyone has even been accused of committing a crime, doesn't parse with the public'.[15] But an FBI agent, interviewed in the New York Times, disagreed: 'OK, someone kidnaps one of your kids and they are holding this kid in this fortress up in the Bronx. Now, we have probable cause that your child is inside this fortress. We have a search warrant. But for some reason, we cannot get in there. They made it out of some new metal, or something, right? Nothing'll cut it, right? ... That's what the basis of this issue really is – we've got a situation now where a technology has become so sophisticated that the whole notion of a legal process is at stake here ... If we don't want that, then we have to look at Clipper'.[16]

So the technological means to create private places in cyberspace are available, but the right to create these places remains a fiercely contested issue. Can you always keep your bits to yourself? Is your home page your castle?[17]

1 J B Jackson, 'Forum Follows Function', in *The Public Face of Architecture*, N Glazer and M Lilla (eds), New York: Free Press, 1987, and M Webb, *A Historical Evolution: The City Square*, New York: Whitney Library of Design, 1990.
2 Artistotle, *The Politics*, VII, xii.
3 Gary Gumpert and Susan J Drucker, 'From the Agora To the Electronic Shopping Mall', *Critical Studies in Mass Communication 9* (1992), pp186–200.
4 Peter H Lewis, 'Attention Shoppers: Internet Is Open', *The New York Times*, August 12, 1994, D1-D2.
5 John Markoff, 'A Free and Simple Computer Link', *The New York Times*, Dec 8, 1993, D1, D5.
6 David Bennahum, 'Fly Me to the MOO', *Lingua Franca*, vol 4, no 4 (May/June 1994), pp1 and 22–37.
7 Wayne Booth, *The Rhetoric of Fiction* (Second edition, University of Chicago Press, Chicago, 1983).
8 MUDs constitute a natural application for object-oriented programming techniques.
9 Lewis Mumford, *The City in History*, New York: Harcourt Brace and World, 1961, p384.
10 Alan F Westin, Privacy and Freedom, New York: Athenaeum, 1967.

11 Authentication systems were not needed on the earliest computers. They are required on machines that have many potential users and came into widespread use with the growing popularity of mainframe-based, multi-user, timesharing systems in the 1960s.

12 In the widely reported case of Bourke versus the Nissan Motor Corporation in 1993, Nissan dismissed some employees after peeking into their password-protected electronic mail boxes. The employees sued for invasion of privacy and wrongful determination. But the California courts ruled against the employees' claim that the passwords created an expectation of privacy.

13 William M Bulkeley, 'Cypher Probe', *The Wall Street Journal*, April, 1994, ppA1, A8.

14 Peter H Lewis, 'Of Privacy and Security: The Clipper Chip Debate', *The New York Times*, April 24, 1994, pF5.

15 Jerry Berman, quoted by Steven Levy 'Battle of the Clipper Chip', *The New York Times Magazine*, June 12, 1994, pp44–51, 60, 70.

16 Jim Kallstrom, quoted by Steven Levy, ibid.

17 Michael Traynor, 'Computer E-Mail Privacy Issues Unresolved', *The National Law Journal*, Jan 31, 1994.

Karen A Franck_When I Enter Virtual Reality, What Body Will I Leave Behind?_1995

Karen Franck's work looks at issues surrounding the body and gender. In this essay she examines some of the different 'bodies' that form an intrinsic part of the human condition, and asks to what extent we escape these bodies when we enter virtual reality – whether via a computer, a head-mounted display or a data glove.

Franck is a professor at New Jersey Institute of Technology in Newark, where she holds a joint appointment in the School of Architecture and the Department of Social Science and Policy Studies. She is the co-author of *Ordering Space: Types in Architecture and Design* (with Lynda H Schneekloth, 1994) and *Architecture Inside Out* (with Bianca Lepori, 1999).

In 'When I Enter Virtual Reality, What Body Will I Leave Behind?' Franck suggests that in cyberspace we adopt a partial or 'split' physiology. Rather than totally losing our worldly bodies, she argues that many pieces of the body come with us into virtual reality; indeed it is these parts and biological processes that allow us to experience the other space. Franck then posits the notion that virtual reality rearticulates the established social boundaries of 'me and not-me'. In *Ordering Space*, which Franck was working on as co-author when writing this essay, Lynda Schneekloth explains this idea of 'me and not-me':

> Humans structure the world in a fundamental way by making a boundary between us as human beings, and *the other*, that is, the things we make, the places we inhabit, and the world as given. The fundamental typological distinction between us and not-us not only structures the material world, but frames the way we think about and re-present this world. The boundary secures us, places us in our habitats; it infuses the world and us with meaning.[1]

Franck uses this notion of the 'other' to explain the blurring of genders that is implicit in cyberspace; she thus sees cyberspace as an opportunity to construct a new space that is not entangled with the gender stereotypes and ideas of beauty that are so prevalent in the real world. For Franck, this space and the possibilities it provides serve to nourish the 'actual' body that inhabits reality. The real body needs to feel protected and cosseted while it is distended in virtual reality, its senses preoccupied. Franck identifies a new type of bodily protection emerging from the less socially and psychologically encumbered spaces of virtual reality – a protection that helps us experience more of the 'not-me' and enables the real self to understand more of the 'other'.

In their conclusion to *Ordering Space*, which discusses the impact the concept of 'me and not-me' has had on the typologies of buildings, Franck and Schneekloth write: 'Another possibility [to avoid the constraints of types] is to imagine places and scenarios not with an eye to building them but to exploring forms, uses, and meanings under only those constraints one chooses to adopt'.[2] In avoiding the constraints imposed by others, one of these places – a space of the imagination – is cyberspace. This essay had done much to frame the differences and similarities between real bodies and their virtually immersed siblings that exist within all of us.

1 Karen A Franck and Lynda H Schneekloth, *Ordering Space: Types in Architecture and Design*, New York: Van Nostrand Rheinhold, 1994, p41.
    2 Ibid, p370.

In William Gibson's novel *Neuromancer*, Case longs for the 'bodiless exultation of cyberspace'. Again and again writers of fiction and nonfiction refer to leaving the body behind, to being free of it in virtual reality. The phrases 'meat puppets' and 'flesh cage' fill me with disgust and indignation, but I am none the less fascinated with the body and the 'non-body' in cyberspace.[1] I anticipate entering a virtual world someday soon. Will I leave a body behind? What body might I wish to leave, or keep, and why?

Virtual reality is very physical. I won't just see changing images on a flat screen; I will have the feeling of occupying those images with my entire body. I will enter a graphic, three-dimensional, computer-constructed world that does not look real but feels real, one that may respond immediately to my movements and commands.

To enter virtual reality, I place different kinds of equipment on or around my body. A head-mounted display contains video monitors which will form stereoscopic images before my eyes. A head tracker will measure my head movements which the computer will counteract to provide the experience of a stable world. Gloves allow me to see my hands and to manipulate items; a body suit could allow my body to be represented in virtual reality, and would allow me to move it as a virtual body and to be seen by others occupying the same virtual world. Headphones give me three-dimensional sound and a microphone allows me to give voice commands.

My experience of virtual reality depends upon my physical body's movement (or the mechanical movement of the body using a wheelchair or other apparatus). To see I must move my head. To *act* upon and *do* things in a virtual world I must bend, reach, walk, grasp, turn around and manipulate objects. Movements of the physical body, or commands, can translate to very different virtual movements – to flying, floating and moving from one place to another instantaneously. So much will be possible and so much of it physical, often requiring physical dexterity and practice – like performing surgery or playing one of the virtual musical instruments Jaron Lanier has invented.

If the virtual is so physical, what body will I leave behind? Not my physical body. Without it, I am in no world at all. It is physical bodies that give us access to any world.[2] I will certainly need my brain so that I can be stimulated to see and feel this created world; my eyes and ears to do the seeing and hearing; my arms, hands, legs and feet, and other bones, muscles and tendons to do the moving. The organs of perception and motility are still key.

My physical body will occupy the virtual and physical worlds simultaneously; actions I take will have consequences, albeit different ones, in both worlds. As in the physical world, so in the virtual: perception will be active, depending upon actual or anticipated physical movements. If I wear transparent goggles, the virtual world will be superimposed on the physical one. If the goggles are opaque, I will be 'immersed' in the virtual world and unable to see the physical one, though I may still be concerned about it.

What I will leave behind is a particular kind of 'being in the world';

experiencing another kind instead.[3] Both kinds are created by the nature of the world and our relationship to it. In virtual reality, both change. Experiences of gravity, density, mass, weight, long distance, and the cumbersomeness of matter are absent. The objects we see or create and the spaces we occupy in virtual worlds have very different visual and kinaesthetic qualities from those in the physical world. Objects/spaces can appear, disappear, occupy the same location, and change appearance instantaneously. We can move very quickly and in all different ways. There is both a fluidity and speed of movement that are more akin to dreams than waking life.

If we are 'free' it is because we feel liberated from our relationship to the physical world, from the constraints and limitations that the physical world and physical matter exert upon us. So the experience of 'being in the virtual world' can be exhilarating; one can do so much so quickly and so effortlessly.[4] Here lies a sense of mastery and control unrivalled in the physical world, particularly for those who experience handicaps in that world. The constraints in virtual worlds are those that people have created in the software and, eventually, ones that any user chooses to create. They are thus made by humans. What a challenge to architects of virtual reality: not only are spaces and objects to be designed but so are all bodily relationships to them and to other bodies.

I will be the same physical body but all that I encounter and my relationships to all that I encounter, my 'being in the world', will be dramatically different. To the extent (the great extent) that my feeling of myself is constituted by my relationships to all that is not me, I will feel different, perhaps very different. Jaron Lanier says: 'you have a vivid experience of your own subjectivity. You can feel your subjectivity as an angel floating above the world.'[5] For some people, or someday, that may be a feeling of being bodiless.

What I will also leave behind, indeed must leave behind, is my appearance. Virtual bodies cannot duplicate the appearance of individuals the way films, videos or photographs do. Here is another job for architects of virtual reality – to design the bodies too. Some of the bodies that have been created so far do not take a human form at all – a lobster, for example. Virtual reality will eventually offer people a great choice of different appearances, and so different identities. Identity, as it is physically represented, will no longer be tied to the physical attributes of age, gender, race, size or even to the human species. Attributes of humans or other animate and inanimate objects will be chosen and mixed at will.

Given the frequency with which men in MUDs (Multiple User Dungeons) adopt female identities, it is possible that many men will choose virtual female bodies. Women may wish to adopt gender-neutral identities, as many already do to avoid harassment on the Internet or other networks. When we occupy virtual worlds, will it be understood that these are virtual bodies and possibly virtual identities so that 'deception' is no longer an issue, as it has been on the Internet? After all, all of virtual reality is a deception. If we feel free of our physically-grounded identities, social constraints common to the physical world may recede as well, as they already have in textual computer communications.[6]

There is a body I personally do not wish to leave behind. That is the wet one, the one that needs to eat, sleep, eliminate, the one that is frail, can become diseased, and will die. It is that body with its needs, passions and mortality that some long to abandon. And it is that body that is so devalued in fiction and nonfiction about cyber-space: '… the élite stance involved a certain relaxed contempt for the flesh. The body was meat. Case fell into the prison of his own flesh.'[7]

As in any very challenging and engrossing activity one loses track of time and bodily needs. In computer-related activities – hacking, video games, programming, perusing the Internet and now virtual reality – this involvement can be intense, overwhelming. When Case was 'jacked in' he forgot the needs of the flesh: 'This was it. This was what he was, who he was, his being. He forgot to eat. Molly left cartons of rice and foam trays of sushi on the corner of the long table. Sometimes he resented having to leave the deck to use the chemical toilet … He'd go straight to the deck, not bothering to dress, and jack in … He lost track of days.'[8] But the fleshed body still requires care; so Molly brings food and at another point Maelcum, a Rastafarian no less, hooks Case to a catheter.

This caring can also include protection. Being both engrossed and immersed in a virtual world leaves one vulnerable to circumstances and persons in the physical world. To experience the sense of mastery and control in the virtual world means relinquishing what control one might have in the physical. So one must be in a safe physical location or watched over, even protected, by another person (though, of course, one is still vulnerable to this person and to others who can manipulate the software or the hardware).[9] The sense of control, like all of virtual reality, is a powerful, physical illusion.

Leaving the flesh behind does not mean doing away with sex but rather removing its shared wetness and fleshiness. Eventually in virtual worlds sex may be simulated by stimulating the appropriate parts of the brain or it may be experienced by donning a bodysuit to engage in virtual contact with other virtual bodies.[10] So one will feel the bodies of others but without any touching of flesh to flesh, without any contact with the fluids of another, without necessarily knowing the physically-based gender identity of the other (or others), and without revealing one's own. Totally anonymous sex, no responsibilities, no possibility of physical, bodily harm (although there may be other kinds), and none of the physical consequences of pregnancy or sexually-transmitted disease. Already cyberspace is a very popular place for sexual contact without bodily contact; virtual reality will likely be popular in the same way but more physical.

Do I have less desire to leave this body of wet flesh and blood because I am a woman? Are others so eager to do so, or to imagine doing so, because they are men? In all likelihood, yes. For centuries men have wished to transcend the body they cannot control and direct, the one whose desires, emotions, bodily functions and bodily changes interfere with other more valued pursuits. Religion, science, and philosophy in the West have continuously, relentlessly disdained and devalued the fleshed body and its material needs and preoccupations (and associated it and them with women). To be able to escape it, at least experientially, and yet still be alive and alert, to make physical movements that have significant consequences, to do, learn, and create is truly a dream come true. And this is the ultimate design project: to imagine and create objects, spaces, bodies, movement and all relationships among them without ever having to consider any of the more tedious human needs for heat, light, air, food, sleep or elimination. The architect is finally free of the 'tyranny of function'.

Of course, the fleshed body is still there with all its needs, problems and vulnerabilities but it can be ignored in a new, more complete manner with its care yet again assigned to women and minorities. The desire to leave the fleshed body altogether is so great that the possibility of transferring or 'downloading' human consciousness to a computer is eagerly anticipated in the computer world. In such a 'post-biological world' one could thus avoid death and the time and energy required for maintaining and reproducing human bodies.[11]

These, I believe, are masculinist dreams. The potential character and possible consequences of virtual worlds can be imagined and portrayed in feminist terms as well. Then the body I wish to leave behind is the one that I have learned to be, the one that follows the constraints and limitations society has taught me, as a woman, to adopt. These have become part and parcel of my comportment, of the way I use my body and occupy space – in a more constricted and confined manner than men.[12] Could they be left behind? At the moment it seems unlikely. People who put on the gloves and goggles and enter virtual reality often remain aware of how they look to others watching them in the physical world and remain self-conscious of their movements. Perhaps 'being a woman in the world' cannot be abandoned, even in small ways, even virtually. None the less I have the wish. I'd like to try.

And when I leave behind my appearance as a woman, I wish to leave behind the ways men expect women to act and the ways they often approach and react to women.[13] Not that I wish to adopt a male identity but rather to appear as human, with no gender specified or revealed. Even beyond the technical problems of creating a voice that is human but neither male nor female, and beyond the possibility that my actions and attitudes would 'give me away', that may be difficult. To many men using the Internet and other text-based computer communications determining the physically-based gender identities of other users is still very important; there may be pressure in virtual worlds not to remain anonymous in this sense. A gender-free realm of communication and interaction may not be a man's dream. For him flesh may be the prison; for me it is the current social construction of gender.[14]

So far, cyberspace constructs gender as much as any other man-made place, with some additional allowances for men to play with gender but none for women to avoid it. Given the preponderance of men creating and using computer-related inventions including cyberpunk fiction, it is not surprising that a masculinist, often sexist view predominates. If all virtual worlds will also be man-made places, they will very likely follow a similar script, with little opportunity for any of us to leave all the gendered bodies behind. Why not make some that do?

A feminist portrayal would stress the permeability and changeability of boundaries. Virtual reality dissolves the distinctions, the separations, and the connections that characterize so much of the physical world and our social constructions of it. In regard to the body alone, many different aspects can be separated and recombined conceptually and experientially. Simple dualisms of mind/body, male/female, animate/inanimate, real/imagined become far less tenable. Virtual worlds offer immense opportunities for testing and blurring boundaries in those worlds *and* in this one.

A significant boundary for dissolving is between self and other, all other. Virtual worlds will offer myriad opportunities to encounter and engage objects and spaces in new and different ways and to occupy other bodies, other entities, other species. The clear, hard, harsh boundaries in the physical world that define and keep me forever separate from all that is not me, that separate and distance things, bodies, and places from each other vanish. In virtual worlds the possibilities for connecting, merging, and occupying are endless. Would this not feel like a new kind of intimacy? Could this not generate, in the physical world, some of the empathy and compassion for the other that are now so sorely absent?[15]

People already report a sense of intimacy with others they communicate with via e-mail and Internet conversations. Maybe there is yet another level of intimacy to be found with spaces, objects, or the virtual representation of other species. In Marge Piercy's novel *He She and It*, Malkah, a practised user and creator of virtual worlds who is an old woman, reflects on the power she feels as a 'base-spinner'. 'In the image world, I am the power of my thought, of my capacity to create. There is no sex in the Base or the Net, but there is sexuality, there is joining, there is the play of minds like the play of dolphins in the surf.'[16]

Another significant boundary, metaphorically and technologically constructed, is between virtual reality and physical reality. Virtual reality is almost exclusively described and built as enclosed and independent of physical reality. Hence the use of the term 'virtual worlds'. This construction allows virtual reality to be viewed and experienced as an *escape* from physical reality, further suggesting that the physical world will be neglected and devalued much as the fleshed body has been in Western culture. The masculinist dream may be as much to leave matter behind as to leave flesh behind. Both are so constraining, both create such problems. But it is also possible that participating in virtual worlds could lead to greater appreciation of flesh and matter. Another view, leading to other inventions, avoids the creation of an enclosed, separate world altogether by creating distributed cyberspaces that augment physical reality.[17] Virtual and physical can be seen and made to be interdependent and complimentary.

Virtual reality is not a single monolithic version of reality but an endless array of possibilities to be imagined and created. If the full potential of that variety can be realized, we can create ways of being and relating to all others socially and psychologically that are true alternatives to those current in the physical world and in our present culture. Who knows, eventually that could change our ways of being and relating here, in these bodies. Then I will return to a body changed.

1 These phrases, used by Neil Spiller in a lecture at Winter-school 1995 in Birmingham, prompted me to write this essay. They also appear in his book, *Digital Dreams: The Architecture of Cyberspace*. Issues of embodiment in virtual reality and science-fiction are fascinating to others as well. See particularly Allucquere Rosanne Stone, 'Will the Real Body Please Stand Up?' and Michael Heim, 'The Erotic Ontology of Cyberspace', in *Cyberspace: First Steps*, Michael Benedikt (ed), Cambridge, MA: MIT Press, 1991; Scott Bukatman, *Terminal Identity: The Virtual Subject in Postmodern Science Fiction*, Durham, NC: Duke University Press, 1993; Anne Balsamo, 'Feminism for the Incurably Informed', *Flame Wars: The Discourse of Cyberculture*, Mark Dery (ed), Durham, NC: Duke University Press, 1994.

2 See Drew Leder, *The Absent Body*, Chicago: University of Chicago Press, 1990. Leder makes a very thorough argument that the body, in a phenomenological sense, is almost always 'left behind'; that is, one's own body is rarely the direct object of one's own experience.

3 In addition to Drew Leder, *The Absent Body*, see also Elizabeth Grosz, *Volatile Bodies: Toward a Corporeal Feminism*, Bloomington, IN: Indiana University Press, 1994. Leder and Grosz both discuss Merleau-Ponty's articulation of the lived body as 'being in the world' (Maurice Merleau-Ponty, *Phenomenology of Perception*, London: Routledge and Kegan Paul, 1962).

4 Virtual mobility and movement can also be quite disorienting. 'The simultaneous changes in pitch, roll and yaw as well as direction in 3-space was confusing; people are not used to moving without the guiding constraints of ground and gravity'. Meredith Bricken, 'Virtual Worlds: No Interface to Design', *Cyberspace: First Steps*, Michael Benedikt (ed), op cit, p374.

5 Jaron Lanier, lecture at New Jersey Institute of Technology, Newark, 26 April 1995.

6 Howard Rheingold, *The Virtual Community: Homesteading on the Electronic Frontier*, New York: HarperPerennial, 1994.

7 William Gibson, *Neuromancer*, New York: Ace Books, 1984, p6.

8 Ibid, p59.

9 Meredith Bricken, 'Virtual Worlds: No Interface to Design', *Cyberspace: First Steps*, Michael Benedikt (ed), op cit, p379.

10 Howard Rheingold, 'Virtual Reality and Teledildonics', *Technology and the Future*, Albert H Teich (ed), New York: St Martin's Press, 1993. Gareth Branwyn, 'Compu-Sex: Erotica for Cybernauts', *Flame Wars: The Discourse of Cyberculture*, Mark Dery (ed), Durham, NC: Duke University Press, 1994.

11 Hans Moravec, *Mind Children: The Future of Robot and Human Intelligence*, Cambridge, MA: Harvard University Press, 1988, p4.

12 Iris Marion Young, *Throwing Like a Girl and Other Essays in Feminist Philosophy and Social Theory*, Bloomington, IN: University of Indiana Press, 1990, p153.

13 Susan Bordo, *Unbearable Weight: Feminism, Western Culture and The Body*, Berkeley, CA: University of California Press, 1993, p284.

14 See for example Susan Bordo, *Unbearable Weight*, op cit.

15 Lynda Schneekloth, 'Notions of the Inhabited', *Ordering Space: Types in Architecture and Design*, Karen A Franck and Lynda H Schneekloth (eds), New York: Van Nostrand Reinhold, 1994.

16 Marge Piercy, *He She and It*, New York: Ballantine Books, 1991, p161.

17 Wendy A Kellogg (et al), 'Making Reality a Cyberspace', *Cyberspace: First Steps*, Michael Benedikt (ed), op cit.

John Frazer_A Natural Model for Architecture/The Nature of the Evolutionary Model_1995

John Frazer's architectural work is inspired by living and generative processes. Both evolutionary and revolutionary, it explores information ecologies and the dynamics of the spaces between objects. Fuelled by an interest in the cybernetic work of Gordon Pask and Norbert Wiener, and the possibilities of the computer and the 'new science' it has facilitated, Frazer and his team of collaborators have conducted a series of experiments that utilize genetic algorithms, cellular automata, emergent behaviour, complexity and feedback loops to create a truly dynamic architecture.

Frazer studied at the Architectural Association (AA) in London, from 1963 to 1969, and later became unit master of Diploma Unit 11 there. He was subsequently Director of Computer-Aided Design at the University of Ulster – a post he held while writing *An Evolutionary Architecture* in 1995 – and a lecturer at the University of Cambridge. In 1983 he co-founded Autographics Software Ltd, which pioneered microprocessor graphics. Frazer was awarded a personal Chair at the University of Ulster in 1984.

In Frazer's hands, architecture becomes machine-readable, formally open-ended and responsive. His work as computer consultant to Cedric Price's Generator Project of 1976 (see p84) led to the development of a series of tools and processes; these have resulted in projects such as the Calbuild Kit (1985) and the Universal Constructor (1990). These subsequent computer-orientated architectural machines are makers of architectural form beyond the full control of the architect-programmer.

Frazer makes much reference to the multi-celled relationships found in nature, and their ongoing morphosis in response to continually changing contextual criteria. He defines the elements that describe his evolutionary architectural model thus: 'A genetic code script, rules for the development of the code, mapping of the code to a virtual model, the nature of the environment for the development of the model and, most importantly, the criteria for selection.'[1] In setting out these parameters for designing evolutionary architectures, Frazer goes beyond the usual notions of architectural beauty and aesthetics. Nevertheless his work is not without an aesthetic: some pieces are a frenzy of mad wire, while others have a modularity that is reminiscent of biological form.

Algorithms form the basis of Frazer's designs. These algorithms determine a variety of formal results dependent on the nature of the information they are given. His work, therefore, is always dynamic, always evolving and always different. Designing with algorithms is also critical to other architects featured in this book, such as Marcos Novak (see p150).

Frazer has made an unparalleled contribution to defining architectural possibilities for the twenty-first century, and remains an inspiration to architects seeking to create responsive environments. Architects were initially slow to pick up on the opportunities that the computer provides. These opportunities are both representational and spatial: computers can help architects draw buildings and, more importantly, they can help architects create varied spaces, both virtual and actual. Frazer's work was groundbreaking in this respect, and well before its time.

1 John Frazer, *An Evolutionary Architecture*, London: Architectural Association, 1995, p65.

Natural and Artificial Models

The modelling of these complex natural processes requires computers,
and it is no coincidence that the development of computing has been
significantly shaped by the building of computer models for simulating
natural processes. Alan Turing, who played a key role in the development
of the concept of the computer (the Turing Machine), was interested in
morphology and the simulation of morphological processes by computer-
based mathematical models. The Church-Turing hypothesis stated that
the Turing Machine could duplicate not only the functions of
mathematical machines but also the functions of nature. Von Neumann,
the other key figure in the development of computing, set out explicitly to
create a theory which would encompass both natural and artificial
biologies, starting from the premise that the basis of life was information.

A significant example of this dual approach in terms of our genetic
model is John Holland's *Adaptation in Natural and Artificial Systems*.
Holland starts by looking for commonality between different problems of
optimization involving complexity and uncertainty. His examples of
natural and artificial systems range from 'How does evolution produce
increasingly fit organisms in highly unstable environments?' to 'What
kind of economic plan can upgrade an economy's performance in spite of
the fact that relevant economic data and utility measures must be
obtained as the economy develops?'

Although Holland suggests that such problems have no collective
name, they seem to share a common concern with questions of
adaptation. They occur at critical points in fields as diverse as evolution,
ecology, psychology, economic planning, control, artificial intelligence,
computational mathematics, sampling and inference. To this list we must
now add architecture.

The Nature of the Evolutionary Model

The evolutionary model requires an architectural concept to be
described in a form of 'genetic code'. This code is mutated and developed
by computer program into a series of models in response to a simulated
environment. The models are then evaluated in that environment and the
code of successful models used to reiterate the cycle until a particular
stage of development is selected for prototyping in the real world. The
real-world prototype is expected to be capable of interactive response to
the changing environment on a short time-scale, but this is not essential
in the theoretical model.

In order to achieve the evolutionary model it is necessary to define
the following: a genetic code-script, rules for the development of the code,
mapping of the code to a virtual model, the nature of the environment for
the development of the model and, most importantly, the criteria for
selection.

It is further recommended that the concept is process-driven; that is,
by form-generating rules which consist not of components, but of
processes. It is suggested that the system is hierarchical, with one
process driving the next. Similarly, complex forms and technologies
should be evolved hierarchically from simple forms and technologies.

Generative Description

In order to create a genetic description it is first necessary to develop an architectural concept in a generic and universal form capable of being expressed in a variety of structures and spatial configurations in response to different environments. Many architects already work in this way, using a personal set of strategies which they adapt to particular design circumstances. Such strategies are often pronounced and consistent to the point where projects by individual architects are instantly recognizable. All that is required is that this generic approach is explicit and sufficiently rigorous to be coded.

The process that we are describing has evident parallels with the way much conscious design occurs: it is also similar to the way in which many vernacular archetypes and successful prototypes have been developed and adapted for different sites, environments and individual requirements.

However we do not propose a return to vernacular forms of building evolution, for that tradition can no longer meet the requirements of contemporary urban life. Nor can we advance the evolutionary process by constructing and evaluating full-size prototypes, as was the practice in the past, with the construction of the Gothic cathedrals, for example. This would take too long and involve unacceptable costs, in terms of both money and, in the case of structural failure, human life.

Computer Modelling and Simulation

We suggest that the prototyping and feedback expressed in vernacular architecture by actual construction should be replaced by computer modelling and simulation. At present, computer modelling tends to occur after a design is substantially completed, and only minor modifications result. It is unusual to find the 'what if?' type of modelling that is common in the field of economics. There are several reasons for this. Inputting the data for a fully designed building is time-consuming and expensive, and the modelling required for environmental evaluation is not yet necessarily compatible with the modelling required for the production of working drawings. Once the model has been loaded into the computer, there are only certain kinds of alteration which can easily be done. Despite the claims of the CAD salesmen, the truth is that it is generally not easy to make changes, at least not of the kind that would help to develop alternative strategies. One possibility would be to have modelling systems which enable some form of evaluation at a very early 'sketch' stage. Unfortunately, despite substantial investment, there is still a lack of software capable of doing this, largely because of a misunderstanding about the function of the sketch or design doodle. In addition, the architectural design ethos is unsympathetic to systematic comparative design evaluation and development. Designers tend to trust their intuitive preconception and then modify it until it 'works' – with 'works' often being interpreted in an almost mystical rather than a functional sense.

It is ironic that the fixed ways of representing and abstracting building form which developed within the limitations of the drawing board and the techniques of projective geometry should have been carried over so directly into the computer. Geometrical forms could have remained plastic and fluid in the computer; instead they have become rigidified.

We need to find an alternative to our drawing board obsession with fixed forms, and it seems that we have to think in terms of language – of a vocabulary or syntax. By this, we do not mean the kind of simplistic approach that is based on the use of large configurable elements and a related shape grammar or spatial syntax. We do not mean the endless permutational exercises much beloved by computer theorists who can produce, for example, every known Palladian plan (plus a few new ones) after devising a so-called Palladian Syntax.

Iterative Adaptation

We are proposing an alternative methodology whereby the model is adapted iteratively in the computer in response to feedback from the evaluation. In order to make these significant changes to the database, it is essential to have new forms of datastructure with a better understanding of the logical relationships inherent in the building model. I first experimented with a special datastructure with the Reptile system in 1968, but this was specific to the rules and geometry of one structural system. What we are now proposing is a technique applicable to a wide range of architectural concepts and geometries, all conceived as generative systems susceptible to development and evolution, all possessing that quality characterized by Viollet-le-Duc as 'style': *'the manifestation of an ideal established upon a principle'.*

Coding the Data

Once the concept has been described in terms of generative rules, the next step is to code it in genetic terms. The idea of coding can be illustrated by Lionel March's coding of plan schema and overall building massing. This is a more conventional and compact method than ours, but of course March's intentions are also very different. For example, the plan of Le Corbusier's Maison Minimum is coded in hexadecimal representation (that is, counting to the base 16, – 0, 1, 2…9, A, B, C, D, E, F). So the plan is expressed as FF803F71180EFE033F. This can be expanded in binary, where each hex digit is translated to a 4-bit sequence (7 to 0111, E to 1110, etc.). This is then grouped in 9-bit blocks ready to fold into a 9 by 9 array. Each cell of this array then maps to a cell in a Venn diagram (a technique of Boolean algebra for expressing logical operations diagrammatically). The diagram finally undergoes a metric transformation to become the correctly dimensioned plan. In a similar manner, the overall three-dimensional form of Mies van der Rohe's Seagram Building can be coded as 10083EFE0F00. This may sound complicated, but the coding is very economical and some elements of this system are implicit in the invisible datastructures of any computer modelling system.

Criteria for Success

In order that natural selection should work, certain criteria must be satisfied.

• The genetic information must replicate accurately.

• There must be an opportunity to generate variety and mutation (usually achieved by genetic crossover and very small random errors in the genetic copying).

• Any variation must also be capable of reproduction, and must occasionally confer potential advantage when expressed as a phenotype.

• There must be massive overproduction of phenotypes.

• There must be selective competition in particular environments (before replication of the genetic code).

To satisfy the laws of natural evolution, there is no need to have a living organism. All the criteria for success present in a natural evolving system are mirrored in our artificial evolutionary model. Genetic information in the form of computer code is reproduced by the equivalents to cause it to crossover and mutate. Phenotypes in the form of virtual models are developed in simulated environments, performances are compared, and a selection of appropriate genetic code is made and then replicated in a cyclical manner.

It has been emphasized above that DNA does not describe the phenotype, but constitutes *instruction that describe the process of building the phenotype*, including instructions for making all the materials, then processing and assembling them. This includes making enzymes for the production of nucleotides, plus instructions for cell division and differentiation. These are all responsive to the environment as it proceeds, capable of modifying in response to conditions such as the availability of foodstuffs, and so on. Genes are not for shapes but for chemistry, and by analogy our model also describes process rather than form. This procedure is environmentally sensitive. The rules are constant, but the outcome varies according to materials or environmental conditions. Eventually it is our intention that the form-making process will be part of the system, but for the moment our model works by describing the process of processing and assembling the materials. The actual processing and assembly is external to the model.

Simply stated, what we are evolving are the rules for generating form, rather than the forms themselves. We are describing processes, not components; ours is the packet-of-seeds as opposed to the bag-of-bricks approach.

The Extended Architect

The approach so far described implies some changes in architects' working methods. The generic approach already adopted by many designers has to be made explicit, rigorous, and stated in terms which enable a concept to be expressed in genetic code. Ideally this information could be deduced by the computer from normal work methods without any conscious change being necessary. Architects have to be very clear about the criteria for evaluating an idea, and prepared to accept the concept of client- and user-participation in the process. The design responsibility changes to one of overall concept and embedded detail, but not individual manifestation. Overall the role of the architect is enhanced rather than diminished, as it becomes possible to seed far more generations of new designs than could be individual supervised, and to achieve a level of sophistication and complexity far beyond the economics of normal office practice. The obvious corollary of this is a diminished need for architects in the process of initial generation. While there would still need to be enough architects to guarantee a rich genetic pool of ideas, the role of the mass of imitators would be more efficiently accomplished by the machine. In this new context architects might have a role closer in concept to that of an extended phenotype, and I thus suggest the designation 'extended architect'.

The Next Stage
The present five-year project followed years of background research dedicated to formulating the general theory, designing tools and testing parts of the idea. In the course of recent work we have produced further tools and experiments, but our main objective has been to develop a coherent theoretical model, which we believe we have achieved. Our immediate concern is now to develop this model further; to incorporate into it all the process-orientated information generated by our previous work both at the Architectural Association and the Technical Research Division at Cambridge University. This will enable us to externalize the theoretical model in terms of specific building propositions which can be tested, evaluated and criticized. The environmental model needs to be developed to provide a complete model for evaluation and testing. Most importantly, we need to test the conceptual model itself by inputting seeds and testing the outcome in specific situations.

Our longer-term goal lies in trying to incorporate the building process literally into the model, or perhaps the model into the very materials for building, so that the resultant structures are self-constructing. This may be achievable by either molecular engineering, by the application of nanotechnology, or perhaps by the genetic engineering of plant forms or living organisms to produce forms appropriate for human habitation as an extended phenotype. Frei Otto has suggested growing structures, Doernach and Katavolos imagined organic structures erected from chemical reactions. Alvy Ray Smith envisaged buildings growing from single brick-eggs. Charles Jencks referred to scenes from 'Barbarella' showing the emergence of human and vegetable forms. The final issue of the Archigram magazine contained a packet of seeds from David Greene. In the short term, the prospect of growing buildings seems unlikely, but self-assembly may be achievable.

More practically we expect in the meantime to proceed with implementation in a hierarchical and evolutionary manner by developing multi-functioning organic wholes from single-function cells. We envisage a form of genetic takeover much as Cairns-Smith envisaged the takeover of mineral replicators by progressively more sophisticated developments. The dinosaur of the Reptile system is evolving into more complex organisms.

Characteristics of the New Architecture

In the systems that we have been discussing, global behaviour is an emergent property often unpredicated by local rules. In the same way, the emergent architecture will also be unpredicated. It is tempting to show examples or simulations of what the new architecture might be like, but the emphasis at this stage must be on process, in order to maintain the universality of the model. The model itself, together with its evolutionary and descriptive processes, will result in a process-driven architecture. Our architecture is a property of the process of organizing matter rather than a property of the matter thus organized. Our model is, at any given time, the expression of an equilibrium between the endogenous development of the architectural concept and the exogenous influences exerted by the environment.

Evolutionary Architecture

An evolutionary architecture will exhibit metabolism. It will enjoy a thermodynamically open relationship with the environment in both a metabolic and a socio-economic sense. It will maintain stability with the environment by negative feedback interactions and promote evolution in its employment of positive feedback. It will conserve information while using the processes of autopoiesis, autocatalysis and emergent behaviour to generate new forms and structures. It will be involved with readjusting points of disjuncture in the socio-economic system by the operation of positive feedback. This will result in significant technological advances in our ability to intervene in the environment. Not a static picture of being, but a dynamic picture of becoming and unfolding – a direct analogy with a description of the natural world.

A Form of Artificial Life?

Our model will derive order from its environment and be controlled by a symbiotic relationship with its inhabitants and that environment. It knows the coded instructions for its own development and is thus, in a limited sense, conscious. It can anticipate the outcome of its actions and therefore can be said to have some intelligence. All the parts of the model cooperate and in that sense it can be considered as an organism, but it will only fully exist as such if it is a member of an evolving system or organisms interacting with each other as well as with the environment. Our new architecture will emerge on the very edge of chaos, where all living things emerge, and it will inevitably share some characteristics of primitive life forms. And from this chaos will emerge order: order not particular, peculiar, odd or contrived, but order generic, typical, natural, fundamental and inevitable – the order of life.

Generative system using multistate 3D cellular automata controlled by genetic algorithms. Outcome varied with each run of the program. (Thomas Quijano and Manit Rastogi, under the direction of John Frazer and Julia Frazer, AA, 1994.)

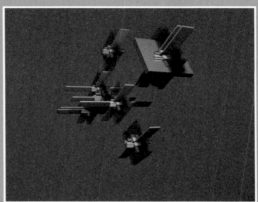

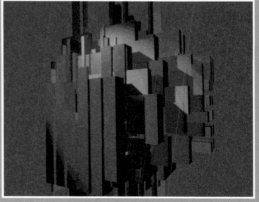

Co-operative evolution by a network of computers. First of a series of experiments in multiprocessor controlled genetic algorithms. (Sequence by Manit Rastogi, under direction by John Frazer and Julia Frazer, AA, 1995.)

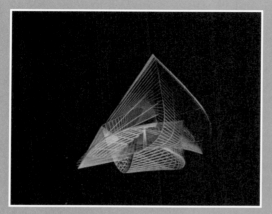

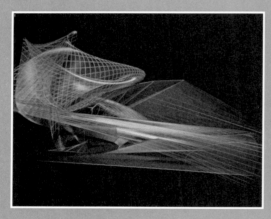

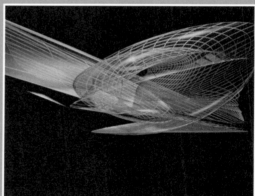

Nicholas Negroponte_Iconographics_1995

Nicholas Negroponte's *Being Digital*, from which this excerpt is taken, was one of the hit books of 1995. Like William Mitchell's *City of Bits* (see p230) it discusses the advancing digital revolution in simple, understandable terms. Negroponte is director of the Media Lab of the Massachusetts Institute of Technology, and a founder of and writer for *Wired* magazine.

Negroponte begins by explaining why he decided to publish his ideas in book form at all. Much was being written at the time about the death of the book. In those heady days, in the white heat of the digital revolution, it was easy to discredit all manner of established products and ideas. Negroponte gives three reasons for wanting to ship his ideas in atoms rather than digitally publishing them in bits. First was the fact that, at the time of writing, digital media was still not in the hands of his target audience: parents, politicians and executives. This has certainly changed in recent years. The second reason was that he had received much feedback from his monthly column in *Wired* magazine, and so wanted to look again at some of the themes from those articles. In the fast and ever-changing digital world, nothing remains true for very long; indeed, one of the major themes behind *Being Digital* is the exponential development of such technologies. Negroponte draws the following analogy:

Did you ever know the childhood conundrum of working for a penny a day for a month, but doubling your salary each day? If you started this wonderful pay scheme on New Year's Day, you would be earning more than $10 million dollars per day on the last day of January.[1]

Negroponte's third and final reason for publishing a book, especially a book without pictures, was that the printed page still fuels the imagination more than the computer screen. The spaces of metaphor and personalized mental images are more likely to provoke inspiring ideas. This is a fact that many should perhaps reflect upon before diving headlong into virtual representations and animations of their ideas. The space of the imagination is never displaced by the virtual and the digital.

Negroponte's main starting point for the book is a comparison between the existing technologies used to transmit data in atom or bit form, and their relative dexterity. 'A bit has no colour, size or weight, and it can travel at the speed of light. It is the smallest atomic element in the DNA of information. It is a state of being, on or off, true or false, up or down, black or white.'[2] This comparison is the central concept on which the book hangs. The ubiquitousness of the bit against the sometime inertia of the atom provides Negroponte with an idea that binds his writings together, in whatever domain he is seeking to explore.

In the following excerpt Negroponte discusses the first desktop icons and the original Windows interface.

1 Nicholas Negroponte, *Being Digital: A Road Map for Survival on the Information Superhighway*, London: Hodder and Stoughton, 1995, p5.
2 Ibid, p14.

In 1976 Craig Fields, a program director in the Cybernetics Technology Office at ARPA (and later the director of ARPA itself), commissioned a New York computer animation company to produce a movie of a fictitious desert town called Dar El Marar. The animated movie depicted a cockpit view from a helicopter flying around Dar El Marar, swooping into its streets, pulling back to see the whole townscape, visiting neighbourhoods, and moving in close to see into buildings. The movie simulated being Peter Pan, not for the purpose of experiencing the townscape and a world of buildings but for exploring a world of information. The concept assumed that you had designed the town; you had built neighbourhoods of information by storing data in particular buildings, like a squirrel storing nuts. Later, you would retrieve the information on your magic carpet by going to where you had stored it.

Simonides of Ceos (556–468 BC) was a poet of classical Greece who was noted for his prodigious memory. When the roof of a banquet hall collapsed just after he had been called from the room, he found that he could identify the mangled remains of guests based on where they had been sitting: he inferred that tying material to specific spots in a mental spatial image would aid recall. He used this technique to remember his long speeches. He would associate parts of his oration with objects and places in a temple. Then while delivering his speech, he would revisit the temple in his mind to call forth his ideas in an orderly and comprehensive manner. The early Jesuits in China called this same process the building of 'palaces of mind'.

These examples involve navigating in three-dimensional space to store and retrieve information. Some people are good at this; some are not.

In two dimensions most of us are uniformly more capable. Consider the two-dimensional facade of your own bookshelves. You probably know how to find any book simply by going to 'where' it is. You probably remember its size, colour, thickness, and type of binding. You certainly recall this information much better if you put it 'there'. The messiest desktop is known to its user because that user made the mess, so to speak. There would be nothing worse than to have a librarian come in and reorganize your books by the Dewey decimal system, or a maid to arrive to clean up your desk. You would suddenly be lost.

Observations such as these led to the development of what we called a *spatial data management system*. SDMS was embodied in a room with a floor-to-ceiling, wall-to-wall, full-colour display; two auxiliary desktop displays; octophonic sound; an instrumented Eames chair; and other paraphernalia. SDMS offered the user a sofa-style interface and the armchair opportunity to fly over data and gaze out of a picture-window-size display. The user could zoom and pan freely in order to navigate through a fictitious, two-dimensional landscape called Dataland. The user could visit personnel files, correspondence, electronic books, satellite maps, and a whole variety of totally new data types (like a video clip of Peter Falk in 'Columbo' or a collection of fifty-four thousand still frames of art and architecture).

Dataland itself was a landscape of small images that illustrated the function or data behind them. Behind an image of a desktop calendar was the user's agenda. If the user drove the system into the image, for example, of a telephone, SDMS would initiate a telephoning program with associated personal Rolodex. This was the birth of icons. We toyed with using the word *glyphs* instead, because the dictionary meaning of *icons* is not really appropriate, but *icons* stuck.

These postage-stamp-size images not only illustrated data or functionality, but each had a 'place'. As with books on a bookshelf, you would retrieve something by going to where it was, remembering its location, colour, size, and even the sounds it might make.

SDMS was so far ahead of its time that a decade had to pass and personal computers had to be born before some of the concepts could move into practice. Today, icons are common to the persona of all computers. People consider the imagery of trash cans, calculators, and telephone handsets as standard fare. In fact, some systems literally refer to the screen as a 'desktop'. What has changed is that today's Datalands are not spread floor to ceiling, wall to wall. Instead, they are accordioned into 'windows'.

The Shape of Windows

I'm always impressed by how clever naming can scoop the market, leaving the consumer with very false impressions. When IBM chose to call its personal computer the *PC*, it was a stroke of genius. In spite of Apple's having been on the market more than four years earlier, the name PC has become synonymous with personal computing. Likewise, when Microsoft chose to name its second-generation operating system *Windows*, it brilliantly claimed the term forever after, in spite of Apple's having had (better) windows more than five years earlier and many workstation manufacturers already widely using them.

Windows exist because computer screens are small. The result is that a relatively small work space can be used to keep a number of different processes active at any one time. This whole book was written on a nine-inch diagonal screen with no paper, except that produced for or by the publisher. To most people, using windows is like riding a bicycle; you don't even remember learning how to do it, you just do it.

Windows are also interesting as a metaphor for the future of television. In the United States, more than in other countries, we have insisted in the past that a television image fill the screen fully. But filling the screen has a cost that derives from the fact that not all movies and television programs were created in the same rectangular format.

In fact, in the early 1950s the movie industry quite purposely moved to a number of wider-screen processes (such as Cinerama, Super Panavision, Super Technirama, 35mm Panavision, and Cinemascope, which we still use today) in order to undermine early television distribution. The 3-by-4 aspect ratio of today's television was derived from the pre-World War II generation of movies and does not fit Cinemascope or, for that matter, the rectangular format of most films produced in the past forty years.

Broadcasters in continental Europe resolve the difference in aspect ratio by so-called letter boxing. They blank the top and the bottom of the screen with black, so that the remaining, active area has the correct aspect ratio. By sacrificing a few pixels, the viewer gets to see the film in faithful replication of the shape of each frame. In fact, I think that the effect of letter boxing is additionally satisfying because it introduces a very crisp horizontal edge at the top and at the bottom of the image, which would otherwise be less sharply delimited by the curved plastic edge of the television set.

We rarely do this in the United States. Instead, we 'pan-and-scan' when we transfer film to video, taking a wide-screen movie and collapsing it into a 3-by-4 rectangle. We don't just squash the picture (though that is done with titles and credits). Instead, during the transfer process, as the film is moving through the machine (usually a flying spot scanner), a human operator manually moves a 3-by-4 window over the much wider film window, sliding it one way or another, to catch the most relevant parts of each scene.

Some filmmakers, notably Woody Allen, will not allow this, but most seem not to care. One of the best examples of where such pan-and-scan failed hopelessly was in *The Graduate*. In the scene where Dustin Hoffman and Anne Bancroft are taking off their respective clothes, each at one extreme of the screen, there was no way for the operator to get both of them at the same time in the same frame of video.

In Japan and Europe there has been a major push for a new and wider aspect ratio of 9 by 16, and HDTV contestants in the United States are sheepishly following. Nine by 16 may in fact be worse than 3 by 4, however, because all existing video material (which is 3 by 4) will now have to be displayed with vertical strips of black on each side of your 9-by-16 screen, so-called curtains. Not only do curtains serve less of a visual purpose than letter boxing; there is no way to pan-and-scan instead, even if you wanted to.

Aspect ratio should be a variable. When TVs have enough pixels, a windows style makes enormous sense. The ten-foot experience and the 18-inch experience start to collapse into one. In fact, in the future, when you have massively high resolution and a wall-size display, floor to ceiling and wall to wall, you may place your TV image on the screen as a function of where the plants are in the room, as opposed to the frame around some small screen. It's the whole wall.

Stelarc_Towards the Post-Human_1995

Stelarc is an Australian performance artist who is interested in alternative aesthetic strategies. Using medical, robotic and virtual reality systems he explores, extends and enhances the body's performance parameters by acoustically and visually probing the body: amplifying brain waves, heartbeat, blood flow and muscle signals, and filming the inside of his lungs, stomach and colon. He uses prosthetics and computer technologies as a way of augmenting the body's capabilities. He has exhibited installations and performed extensively at international art events.

From 1976 to 1988 Stelarc's performances involved being suspended from various apparatus by meat hooks embedded in his skin, testing the body's durability under stress. The images from these performances are memorable for the grotesque contortions of Stelarc's skin and for their single-minded pursuit of an artistic idea no matter what stresses it might put on the body. In *Seaside Suspension: Event for Wind and Waves* (1981) he was suspended over the sea; in *Street Suspension* (1984) he glided from one New York building to another; while in *City Suspension* (1995) he was swung around Copenhagen by a tower crane, hanging 200 feet in the air.

Stelarc never talks of 'his' body but rather of 'the' body. In recent years he has created performances that question the legitimacy of the body and its centred view in the face of technology, particularly biotechnology and cyberspace. His work interrogates the sanctity and usefulness of the body; in the essay that follows he declares that 'information is the prosthesis that props up the obsolete body'. He believes that as humanity starts to grapple with increasingly inhospitable environments, both outside the atmosphere of the planet and within informational jump-cut and fragmented spaces, the body has become obsolete and a waste of space.

The logical extension of this obsolescence, believes Stelarc, is that the body should be colonized for a variety of other uses – even as a sculpture park. In 1993 the performance *Hollow Body/Host Space* involved Stelarc swallowing an alloy sculpture which he could control and move with his stomach. Stelarc believes that within each of us there are countless square metres of space that technology and cyberspace will liberate for artistic pursuits.

Stelarc's biggest ally in his performances is cyberspace, with its ubiquitousness, programmability and transmutability. Cyberspace allows him to open out the partial control of his body to the erstwhile info-drifters of the Internet, it makes his heartbeat audible to many and it actuates his almost permanent prosthetic 'Third Arm'. The speed and dexterity of cyberspace has led Stelarc to question the vicissitudes of the body, and reject them. For him evolution is outmoded: it is too slow, too stupid, too delicate and too soft for the erotic caress of the machine. Stelarc informs us that the body must be hollowed, hardened, dehydrated and often anaesthetized. For him, the body's hysterical sensitivity to the invasion of the machine represents its last gasp in the ongoing and all-consuming path of technology and its schizophrenic daughter, cyberspace.

Stelarc, 'Towards the Post-Human: From Psycho-body to Cyber-system', *Architectural Design*, 1995

The invasion of technology

Miniaturised and biocompatible, technology lands on the body. Although unheralded, it is one of the most important events in human history – focusing physical change on each individual. Technology is not only attached but is also implanted. Once a container, technology now becomes a component of the body. As an instrument, technology fragmented and de-personalized experience – as a component it has the potential to split the species. It is no longer of any advantage to either remain 'human' or to evolve as a species. Evolution ends when technology invades the body. Once technology provides each person with the potential to progress individually in its development, the cohesiveness of the species is no longer distinction but the body-species split. The significance of technology may be that it culminates in an alternate awareness – one that is POST-HISTORIC, TRANS-HUMAN and even EXTRATERRESTRIAL (the first signs of an alien intelligence may well come from this planet).

Artificial intelligence/alternate existence

Artificial life will no longer be contained in computer programs simulating biological development. Artificial intelligence will no longer mean expert systems operating within specific task domains. Electronic space no longer merely generates information but extends and enhances the body's operational parameters BEYOND ITS MERE PHYSIOLOGY AND THE LOCAL SPACE IT OCCUPIES. What results is a high-fidelity interaction – a meshing of the body with its machines in ever-increasing complexity.

Split body: voltage in/voltage out

Given that a body is not in a hazardous location, there would be reasons to remotely activate a person, or part of a person – rather than a robot. An activated arm would be connected to an intelligent mobile body with another free arm to augment its task! Technology now allows you to be physically moved by another mind. A computer-interfaced MULTIPLE-MUSCLE STIMULATOR makes possible the complex programming of *involuntary movements* either in a local place or in a remote location. Part of your body would be moving, you've neither willed it to move, nor are you internally contracting your muscles to produce that movement. The issue would not be to automate a body's movement but rather the system would enable the displacement of a physical action from one body to another body in another place – for the on-line completion of a real-time task or the conditioning of a transmitted skill. There would be new interactive possibilities between bodies. A touch-screen interface would allow programming by *pressing* the muscle sites on the computer model and/or by retrieving and *pasting* from a library of gestures. Simulation of the movement can be examined before transmission and actuation. The remotely actuated body would be split – on the one side voltage directed to the muscles via stimulator pads for involuntary movement – on the other side electrodes pick up internal signals allowing the body to be interfaced to its third hand and other peripheral devices. The body becomes both a site for input and output.

Psycho/cyber

The PSYCHOBODY is neither robust nor reliable. Its genetic code produces a body that malfunctions often and fatigues quickly, allowing only slim survival parameters and limiting its longevity. Its carbon chemistry GENERATES OUTMODED EMOTIONS. *The Psychobody is schizophrenic.* The CYBERBODY is not a subject, but an object – not an object of envy but an object for engineering. The Cyberbody bristles with electrodes and antennae, amplifying its capabilities and projecting its presence to remote locations and into virtual spaces. The Cyberbody becomes an extended system – not to merely sustain a self, but to enhance operation and initiate alternate intelligent systems.

Hybrid human-machine systems

The problem with space travel is no longer with the precision and reliability of technology but with the vulnerability and durability of the human body. In fact, it is now time to redesign humans, to make them more compatible to their machines, it is not merely a matter of 'mechanizing' the body. It becomes apparent in the zero G, friction-less and oxygen-free environment of outer space that technology is even more durable and functions more efficiently than on Earth. It is the human component that has to be sustained and also protected from small changes of pressure, temperature and radiation. The issue is how to maintain human performance over extended periods of time. *Symbiotic systems* seem the best strategy. Implanted components can energize and amplify developments; exoskeletons can power the body; robotic structures can become hosts for a body insert.

Internal/invisible

It is time to recolonise the body with MICRO-MINIATURISED ROBOTS to augment our bacterial population, to assist our immunological system and to monitor the capillary and internal tracts of the body. There is a necessity for the body to possess an INTERNAL SURVEILLANCE SYSTEM – symptoms surface too late! The internal environment of the body would to a large extent counter the microbots behaviour, thereby triggering particular tasks. Temperature, blood chemistry, the softness or hardness of tissue, and the presence of obstacles in tracts could all be primary indications of problems that would signal microbots into action. *The biocompatibility of technology is no longer due to its substance but rather to its scale.* Speck-sized robots are easily swallowed, and may not even be sensed! In nanotechnology, machines will inhabit cellular spaces and manipulate molecular structures. The trauma of repairing damaged bodies or even of redesigning bodies would be eliminated by a colony of nanobots delicately altering the body's architecture inside out.

Towards high-fidelity illusion

With tele-operation systems, it is possible to project human presence and perform physical actions in remote and extraterrestrial locations. A single operator could direct a colony of robots in different locations simultaneously or scattered human experts might collectively control a particular surrogate robot. Tele-operation systems would have to be more than hand-eye mechanisms. They would have to create kinaesthetic feel, providing the sensation of orientation, motion and body tension. Robots would have to be semi-autonomous, capable of 'intelligence disobedience'. With *Teleautomation* (Conway/Voz/Walker), forward simulation – with time and position clutches – assists in overcoming the problem of real-time delays, allowing prediction to improve performance. *Telepresence* (Minsky) becomes the high-fidelity illusion of *Tele-existence* (Tachi). Electronic space becomes a medium of action rather than information. It meshes the body with its machines in ever-increasing complexity and interactiveness. The body's form is enhanced and its functions are extended. Its performance parameters are neither limited by its physiology nor the local space it occupies. Electronic space restructures the body's architecture and multiplies its operational possibilities. The body performs by coupling the kinaesthetic action of muscles and machine with the kinematic pure motion of the images it generates.

Phantom limb/virtual arm

Amputees often experience a phantom limb. It is now possible to have a phantom sensation of an additional arm – a virtual arm – albeit visual rather than visceral. The virtual arm is a computer-generated, human-like universal manipulator interactively controlled by VPL VR equipment. Using DataGloves with flexion and position-orientation sensors and a gesture-based command language allows *real-time intuitive operation* and additional extended capabilities. Functions are mapped to finger gestures, with parameters for each function, allowing elaboration. Some of the virtual arm's extended capabilities include '*stretching*' or telescoping of limb and finger segments, '*grafting*' of extra hands on the arm and 'cloning' or calling up an extra arm. The '*record and playback*' function allows the sampling and looping of motion sequences. A 'clutch' command enables the operator to freeze the arm, disengaging the simulating hand. For tele-operation systems, such features as '*locking*' – allowing the fixing of the limb in position for PRECISE OPERATION WITH THE HAND. In '*micro mode*' complex commands can be generated with a single gesture, and in 'fine control' delicate tasks can be completed by the transformation of large operator movements to small movements of the virtual arm.

Images as operation agents

Plugged into virtual reality technology, physical bodies are *transduced* into phantom entities capable of performing within data and digital spaces. The nature of both bodies and images has been significantly altered. IMAGES ARE NO LONGER ILLUSORY WHEN THEY

BECOME INTERACTIVE. In fact, interactive images become operational and effective agents sustained in software and transmission systems. The body's representation becomes capable of response as images become imbued with intelligence. Sensors and trackers on the body make it a *capture system* for its image, the body is coupled to mobilize its phantom. A virtual or phantom body can be endowed with semi-autonomous abilities, enhanced functions and an artificial intelligence. Phantoms can manipulate data and perform with other phantoms in cyberspace. Physical bodies have organs, phantom bodies are hollow. Physical bodies are ponderous and particular. Phantom bodies are flexible and fluid. Phantoms project and power the body.

Virtual body: actuate/rotate

Your virtual surrogate would not merely mimic the physical body's movements. A more complex choreography is achieved by mapping virtual camera views to limb position/orientation. The involuntary jerking down on the left arm tumbles the virtual body, whilst sweeping the right arm 90 degrees produces a 360-degree virtual camera scan – visually rotating the virtual body around its vertical axis. The form of the virtual body can be configured acoustically – pulsing in phase with breathing sounds. This breath warping subtly and structurally connects the physical body with its virtual other. And by using DEPTH CUE – defining the operational virtual space as shallow – stepping and swaying forwards and backwards makes the virtual body appear and disappear in its video/virtual environment. The resulting interaction between the physical body and its phantom form becomes a more complex combination of kinaesthetic and kinematic choreography. In recent performances the *involuntary body* is actuating a *virtual body* whilst simultaneously avoiding a *programmed robot* within its task envelope.

Phantom body/fluid self

Technologies are becoming better life support systems for our images than for our bodies. Images are immortal, bodies are ephemeral. The body finds it increasingly difficult to match the expectations of its images. In the realm of multiplying and morphing images, the physical body's impotence is apparent. The body now performs best as its image. Virtual reality technology allows a transgression of boundaries between male/female, human/machine, time/space. The self becomes situated beyond the skin; this is not a disconnection or a split but an EXTRUDING OF AWARENESS. What it means to be human is no longer being immersed in genetic memory but being reconfigured in the electromagnetic field of the circuit. IN THE REALM OF THE IMAGE.

Stelarc believes that technology has made the body defunct. The body is unable to function as a fully useable tool to enable humanity's technological emancipation. Therefore Stelarc has created a series of performance artworks that seek to augment the body and its informational and physical dexterity.

Top left, 'Motion Prosthesis' (Melbourne, 1999). Top right, 'Exoskeleton, Cyborg Frictions' (Bern, 1999). Centre left, 'Extended Arm' (Melbourne, 1999).

Centre right, 'Ping Body' (Melbourne, 1996). Bottom right, 'Split Body' (Ljubljana, 1996).

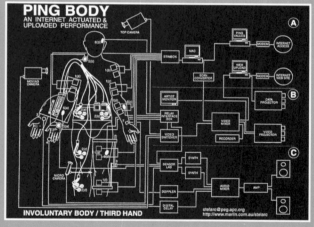

268

Top left, Muscle
Stimulation Box
(Melbourne, 1996).
Top right, 'Stimbod
Touch Screen
Interface' (Melbourne,
1995).
Centre left, 'Stomach
Sculpture'
(Melbourne, 1993).

Bottom left, 'Hands
Writing'(Tokyo, 1982).
Bottom right,
'Involuntary Body/
Third Hand'
(Yokohama, 1988).

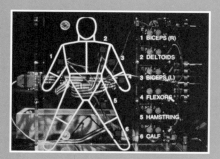

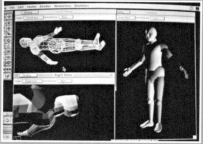

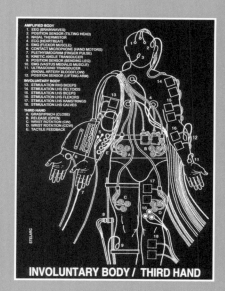

John Perry Barlow_A Declaration of the Independence of Cyberspace_1996

John Perry Barlow, who bills himself as a 'cognitive dissident', was the first person to apply the term cyberspace to the 'place' it presently describes. His piece on the future of copyright, 'The Economy of Ideas', is taught in many law schools, and his 'A Declaration of the Independence of Cyberspace' has been posted on thousands of web sites.

A former Wyoming rancher and Grateful Dead lyricist, Barlow was born in Jackson Hole, Wyoming, in 1947. He graduated in 1969 with high honours in comparative religion from the Wesleyan University in Middletown, Connecticut. He has written for a diversity of publications, including *Communications of the ACM*, *Mondo 2000*, *The New York Times* and *Time*, and has been on the editorial board of *Wired* since the magazine was founded.

Barlow sees cyberspace as a new free frontier and a space of proper uninhibited self-expression, a view informed by the psychedelia of the 1960s. His vision of cyberspace also embraces confusion:

On the most rudimentary level there is simply the terror of feeling like an immigrant in a place where your children are natives – where you're always behind the 8-ball because they can develop the technology faster than you can learn it. It's what I call the learning curve of Sisyphus. And the only people who are going to be comfortable with that are people who don't mind confusions and ambiguity. I look at confusing circumstances as an opportunity – but not everybody feels that way.[1]

In 1990 John Perry Barlow co-founded the Electronic Frontier Foundation (EFF), which he still chairs, with the aim of bridging the gap between computer users and the police. Douglas Rushkoff, in his book *Cyberia*, describes the formation of the EFF as an aid 'so that cyberspace might be colonized in a more orderly fashion.' He continues:

In Barlow's words, the seemingly brutal tactics of arresting officers and investigators 'isn't so much a planned and concerted effort to subvert the Constitution as the natural process that takes place whenever there are people who are afraid and ignorant, and when there are issues that are ambiguous regarding constitutional rights'. The EFF has served as a legal aid group defending hackers whom they believe are being unjustly prosecuted and promoting laws they feel better regulate cyberspace.[2]

Barlow's 'A Declaration of the Independence of Cyberspace' was prompted by the passing of the American Telecom Reform Act of 1996. In Barlow's words:

... the Telecom 'Reform' Act, passed in the Senate with only five dissenting votes, makes it unlawful, and punishable by a $250,000 fine to say 'shit' online. Or, for that matter, to say any of the other seven dirty words prohibited in broadcast media. Or to discuss abortion openly. Or to talk about any bodily function in any but the most clinical terms.[3]

The legislation of cyberspace is one of the most problematic aspects of its ubiquity. Information is power and, with cyberspace, power does not always reside with the legislator.

1 John Perry Barlow, quoted in Douglas Rushkoff, *Cyberia: Life in the Trenches of Cyberspace*, London: Flamingo, 1994, p11.

2 Douglas Rushkoff, *Cyberia: Life in the Trenches of Cyberspace*, London: Flamingo, 1994, p263.

3 John Perry Barlow, 'A Declaration of the Independence of Cyberspace', www.eff.org/barlow, accessed 28/2/01.

A Declaration of the Independence of Cyberspace

Governments of the Industrial World, you weary giants of flesh and steel, I come from Cyberspace, the new home of Mind. On behalf of the future, I ask you of the past to leave us alone. You are not welcome among us. You have no sovereignty where we gather.

We have no elected government, nor are we likely to have one, so I address you with no greater authority than that with which liberty itself always speaks. I declare the global social space we are building to be naturally independent of the tyrannies you seek to impose on us. You have no moral right to rule us nor do you possess any methods of enforcement we have true reason to fear.

Governments derive their just powers from the consent of the governed. You have neither solicited nor received ours. We did not invite you. You do not know us, nor do you know our world. Cyberspace does not lie within your borders. Do not think that you can build it, as though it were a public construction project. You cannot. It is an act of nature and it grows itself through our collective actions.

You have not engaged in our great and gathering conversation, nor did you create the wealth of our marketplaces. You do not know our culture, our ethics, or the unwritten codes that already provide our society more order than could be obtained by any of your impositions.

You claim there are problems among us that you need to solve. You use this claim as an excuse to invade our precincts. Many of these problems don't exist. Where there are real conflicts, where there are wrongs, we will identify them and address them by our means. We are forming our own Social Contract. This governance will arise according to the conditions of our world, not yours. Our world is different.

Cyberspace consists of transactions, relationships, and thought itself, arrayed like a standing wave in the web of our communications. Ours is a world that is both everywhere and nowhere, but it is not where bodies live.

We are creating a world that all may enter without privilege or prejudice accorded by race, economic power, military force, or station of birth.

We are creating a world where anyone, anywhere, may express his or her beliefs, no matter how singular, without fear of being coerced into silence or conformity.

Your legal concepts of property, expression, identity, movement, and context do not apply to us. They are based on matter, there is no matter here.

Our identities have no bodies, so, unlike you, we cannot obtain order by physical coercion. We believe that from ethics, enlightened self-interest, and the commonwealth, our governance will emerge. Our identities may be distributed across many of your jurisdictions. The only law that all our constituent cultures would generally recognize is the Golden Rule. We hope we will be able to build our particular solutions on that basis. But we cannot accept the solutions you are attempting to impose.

In the United States, you have today created a law, the Telecommunications Reform Act, which repudiates your own Constitution and insults the dreams of Jefferson, Washington, Mill, Madison, DeToqueville, and Brandeis. These dreams must now be born anew in us.

You are terrified of your own children, since they are natives in a world where you will always be immigrants. Because you fear them, you entrust your bureaucracies with the parental responsibilities you are too cowardly to confront yourselves. In our world, all the sentiments and expressions of humanity, from the debasing to the angelic, are parts of a seamless whole, the global conversation of bits. We cannot separate the air that chokes from the air upon which wings beat.

In China, Germany, France, Russia, Singapore, Italy and the United States, you are trying to ward off the virus of liberty by erecting guard posts at the frontiers of Cyberspace. These may keep out the contagion for a small time, but they will not work in a world that will soon be blanketed in bit-bearing media.

Your increasingly obsolete information industries would perpetuate themselves by proposing laws, in America and elsewhere, that claim to own speech itself throughout the world. These laws would declare ideas to be another industrial product, no more noble than pig iron. In our world, whatever the human mind may create can be reproduced and distributed infinitely at no cost. The global conveyance of thought no longer requires your factories to accomplish.

These increasingly hostile and colonial measures place us in the same position as those previous lovers of freedom and self-determination who had to reject the authorities of distant, uninformed powers. We must declare our virtual selves immune to your sovereignty, even as we continue to consent to your rule over our bodies. We will spread ourselves across the Planet so that no one can arrest our thoughts.

We will create a civilization of the Mind in Cyberspace. May it be more humane and fair than the world your governments have made before.

Davos, Switzerland
February 8, 1996

Mark Dery_Robocopulation: Sex Times Technology Equals the Future_1996

All manner of subcultures have emerged with the advent of new digital technologies. *Escape Velocity* explores the extraordinary world that exists where the digital and the cultural collide: a world of cyberpunks, net hippies, techno-pagans and other wired frontier prospectors.

Mark Dery is a cultural critic whose writings explore the edges and intersections between digital technology and culture. He has written for *Wired*, *Rolling Stone*, *Mondo 2000*, *The Village Voice* and *The New York Times*, and was editor of the influential *Flame Wars* compilation (1993).

When *Escape Velocity* hit the bookshelves in the mid-1990s the cultural impact of the computer was as its epicentre. Across a range of disciplines speculation took place about the huge paradigm shifts that the digital and the virtual would bring about. It was apparent that these technologies, and their ubiquity, would not only encourage new ways of working and thinking but would also spawn new, hybrid disciplines. This was a time of evangelical optimism, when everything was seen through the metaphor of the computer and its architecture. The notion of cyberspace acted as a catalyst for a whole series of new methodologies in performance art, cinematography, music and design.

But there is a seamier side to the virtual and the digital: the sensual and hedonistic undercurrent that is revealed once the pristine digital surface of cyberspace is scratched. The sexing of the machine is nothing new, but today's technological dexterity adds a whole new range of possibilities. In *Escape Velocity* Dery explores these notions in the chapter called 'Robocopulation: Sex Times Technology Equals the Future'. He makes links with artists from earlier times, such as the French painter Francis Picabia (1878–1953), who searched for a 'mechanomorphic' sensuality in his art. In the passage included here Dery examines 'teledildonics', a method of remote sex where the parties do not touch but instead wear responsive suits covered in a myriad of sensors and actuators. Of course, one or more participants could be a computer simulating another organism.

Much has been written of the effect that these raptured virtual worlds – where things are not always as they seem – might have on an individual's sexuality, sexual politics and identity. And the Internet, of course, has been used prodigiously as a repository for pornographic images and conversations. Dery writes:

> Sex with machines, together with dalliances conducted in virtual worlds, seems a seductive alternative in an age of AIDS, unwanted pregnancies and sexually transmitted diseases. In cyberculture, the widespread yearning for untainted love has given rise to the on-line sex play that the technology writer Gareth Branwyn called 'text sex': interactive, X-rated computer programs; and everyone's not-ready-for-prime-time fantasy, sex in virtual reality, or 'cybersex'.[1]

It is often through misuse – in terms of sex, crime or privacy invasions, for instance – that a new technology's parameters can be gauged. Dery has been instrumental in analysing such paradoxes of cyberculture, and communicating them to a lay public.

1 Mark Dery, *Escape Velocity: Cyberculture at the end of the Century*, London: Hodder and Stoughton, 1996, p199.

Cybersex

Cybercultural dreams of machine sex and sex machines, once hazily defined, were captured with razor clarity in the 'cybersex' scene that is the movie *The Lawnmower Man*'s sole contribution to popular culture. Few who have seen it will forget the scene in which the protagonist and his girlfriend, suited up in virtual reality equipment, engage in *coitus artificialis*. In cyberspace, they appear as featureless, quicksilver creatures, their faces flowing together and oozing apart in a mystical communion that dissolves body boundaries. Like the angel sex described by Raphael in Milton's *Paradise Lost*, their conjunction is 'easier than air with air'.

Ironically, this unmediated, transcendental sex, in which bodies melt and souls commingle, occurs in the utterly mediated environment of a computer program, accessed through user interfaces that seal off the senses and inhibit physical movement. Seen from outside their computer-generated hyperreality, the two lovers appear silly, solipsistic; outfitted in bulky helmets and suspended in giant gyroscopes, each embraces himself, tonguing the air, thrusting into nothingness. Lebel's critique of *The Bride Stripped Bare* – 'onanism for two' – applies to cybersex as well.

Time magazine's 1993 cover story on cyberpunk features the eye-grabbing 'VIRTUAL SEX' cover line and a *Lawnmower Man* cybersex still that have become fixtures of mainstream coverage of cyberculture. Paraphrasing Rheingold, the authors inform readers that virtual sex would be facilitated by

> ... a virtual reality bodysuit that fits with the 'intimate smugness of a condom'. When your partner (lying somewhere in cyberspace) fondles your computer-generated image, you actually feel it on your skin, and vice versa. Miniature sensors and actuators would have to be woven into the clothing by a technology that has yet to be invented.

In other words, dreaming about incorporeal intercourse, at least for now, amounts to fantasizing about a fantasy; it is no less ludicrous than the unspoken desire, apparently harbored by more than a few men, to make it with Jessica Rabbit, the cartoon vamp in *Who Framed Roger Rabbit?* The technical hurdles to be leapt in realizing Rheingold's vision of virtual sex, or 'teledildonics', as it is phallocentrically known, are daunting.

In Rheingold's scenario, each participant slips on 3-D goggles and a high-tech bodystocking, then steps into a 'suitably padded chamber'. The inner surface of his or her 'smart' suit is covered with

> ... an array of intelligent sensor-effectors – a mesh of tiny tactile detectors coupled to vibrators of varying degrees of hardness, hundreds of them per square inch, that can receive and transmit a realistic sense of tactile presence.

Plugging into the global telephone network, the user connects with similarly equipped participants. All appear to each other as believable fictions: lifelike characters inhabiting a three-dimensional environment. 'You run your hand over your partner's clavicle', imagines Rheingold, 'and 6,000 miles away, an array of effectors [is] triggered, in just the right sequence, at just the right frequency, to convey the touch exactly the way you wish it to be conveyed'.

Reality is mutable here; years could be added to or subtracted from one's age, and crow's-feet, bald spots, love handles, and cellulite could be corrected with a few keystrokes. Of course, when radical transmogrifications require only a few more seconds' worth of computation, why stop at alterations that are merely cosmetic? New genders and ethnicities could be explored; hermaphroditism, multiple sex organs, and the grafting of animal genitals onto human bodies would almost certainly become instant clichés among the outré. One might assume the guise of a celebrity, a historical personality, a fictional character, or a mythic hybrid – centaur, satyr, Minotaur, mermaid. A virtual reality graphics program could assemble an interactive 3-D 'clone' from nude self-portraits of the user, shot from every angle and scanned into computer memory; add a voice synthesized from a database of phonemes recorded by the user, and the narcissist's age-old love affair could at last be consummated.

Not that the human sexual imagination need confine itself to the biological world: The posthuman landscape of Ballard's *Crash* stretches before us, with its sexualized aircraft engine nacelles and pornographic pileups. Devotees of *Crash* sex might opt for congress with commodity fetishes. In a WELL topic called 'Dildonics', the artist and multimedia designer Mike Mosher imagines the arrival, by the year 2000, of Orgasmatrons that will combine 'visual, auditory, touch and possibly olfactory stimulus' to bring users to 'thrilling orgasm'. He predicts that 'the sexual content of many appealing things will become obvious', including 'objects (sex with a Russian MIG fighter, with a Ferrari Testarossa, with the dome of St. Peter's)'. Mosher conjures the world of Pat Cadigan's science-fiction novel *Synners*, where an image junkie's home entertainment centre is equipped with

> … a screen for every porn channel, jammed together in the wall so
> that food porn overlapped med porn overlapped war porn overlapped
> sex porn overlapped news porn overlapped disaster porn overlapped
> tech-fantasy porn overlapped porn she had no idea how to identify.

Cybersex will grow exponentially stranger as virtual reality technology develops. Not everyone will want to interface with anonymous partners on-line; some may opt, in the privacy of their own Orgasmatrons, to boot up software that allows them to experience the recorded performances of the famous and the infamous. Imagine the union of Rheingold's tactile sensor-effectors with a record/playback apparatus like the Yamaha Disklavier, a computerized player piano that can flawlessly replay performances stored on floppy disks, down to the subtle nuances of pedaling. Add computer graphics wizardry descended from that used to create the nearly seamless illusion of Elton John and Louie Armstrong trading riffs in the 1991 TV spot for Diet Coke, 'Nightclub'. Voilà: cybersex with the man, woman, or creature of your fantasies.

Most of us will limit ourselves to the occasional steamy romp with Raquel Welch or Robert Redford, while the irretrievably perverse will take part in threesomes with, say, the arch conservative crusader Phyllis Schlafly and the Devil-worshipping debauchee Aleister Crowley. Many personalities will be available only as simulations, of course, and efforts to re-create the lovemaking techniques of Cleopatra, Casanova, Marilyn Monroe, or JFK will doubtless give rise to a new market for the skills of historians. At the same time, there will always be celebrities willing to don DataSuits and act out virtual sex scenes, their every grope and groan recorded for the delectation of the mass market. But given the present prevalence of 'body doubles' who stand in for stars during nude scenes in films, how could the cybersex consumer be certain that he was savouring the favours of the advertised celebrity, and not a stand-in? Mike Saenz wonders,

> [W]hen you're getting a virtual blow job, by a virtual Madonna … did they take some sensor-clad dildo and fuck a goat? Or did some weird cybernerd sit hunched over a computer at 4:00 am, editing and tweaking the data? Whose data is this?

Whose indeed? And how can the cybernaut showering after on-line revelry be certain that he or she hasn't just had sex with a highly evolved artificial intelligence, perhaps a distant descendant of a grandmaster-level chess program? Amazingly, an interactive, undeniably libidinous machine intelligence already exists, after a fashion, in the form of LULU, a pornographic program written by the Finnish computer scientist Pekka Tolonen. Based on Joseph Weizenbaum's famous ELIZA program, a surprisingly convincing dialogue emulator based on nondirective psychotherapy, LULU began life in 1984 as YRTSI, a simulation of a drug-addled, fifteen-year-old punk which, according to a WELL post by Tolonen, 'raised deep emotions among those who discussed with it'. The logical next step in developing an artificial personality, decided Tolonen, 'was to continue the sex, drugs, and rock 'n' roll theme of YRTSI, and expand the sexual part and convert it into [a] female'.

LULU was born in 1985. Installed by Tolonen on SUOKUG, a BBS for Finnish Kaypro users, the program was activated at random in order to fool users into believing that they were receiving real-time messages from a fellow subscriber in 'chat' mode. The program's seeming unpredictability and its uncanny ability to simulate an ordinary human typist – making and correcting typos, pausing as if searching for the right word – convinced many SUOKUG users that LULU was human. 'Although LULU operated only with text, it provoked the user to express his most secret sexual wishes and fantasies,' writes Tolonen. 'The semantic system was based on models analyzed from pornographic literature. But when the system was run the discussions were saved on disk and analyzed later, which made it possible to expand the model.' Using an heuristic approach, LULU 'learned' what come-ons lured users into conversation.

By 1990, when the program was demonstrated at the Thinking Machines Exhibition organized by the Finnish Science Center HEUREKA, LULU had evolved into a multimedia package, complete with text, graphics, the appropriate sampled noises, and a two-voice phoneme synthesizer; visitors interacted with the software by means of a mouse-driven menu and Windows-style software. 'LULU handled nearly all imaginable sexual interactions that can be expressed in written Finnish,' writes Tolonen. 'A deep male voice spoke what the user typed and an electronic female voice with special robotic effects spoke the LULU part.' Ultimately, LULU was shut down after complaints by visitors who weren't ready for virtual intimacy from a computer. 'But before LULU was removed,' notes Tolonen, '[the computer's] hard disk had registered hundreds of "hotter than hell" discussions, which testify that teledildonics is really what people enjoy.'

Unfortunately, true teledildonics is 'an early-to-mid-twenty-first-century technology', according to Rheingold. It would require a global fiber-optic network in concert with massively parallel supercomputers capable of monitoring and controlling the numberless sensors and effectors fitted to every hill and dale, plane and protuberance of the body's topography. Furthermore, a reticulated fabric of safe, high-speed micro-vibrators is only a mirage, given the state of the art in current technologies.

Hans Moravec_The Senses Have No Future_1998

Hans Moravec, Director of the Carnegie Mellon University Mobile Robot Laboratory, is reputed to have built his first robot at ten years old. His work attempts to imbue robots with three-dimensional awareness from a variety of sensors. He is well known for his polemical book, *Mind Children: The Future of Robot and Human Intelligence* (1988).

Moravec's work can be seen as representing the logical extension of Norbert Weiner's ideas about cybernetics (see p48). Moravec believes that within the next half-century, if not sooner, we will be able to download human consciousness in digitized form and either give it a life in cyberspace, or put it inside robots. Moravec feels that this escape of the viscera is imperative if we are to compete with a rapid robotic evolution that will in due course make machines not just smart but hugely intelligent.

Moravec's ideas are closely related to those of Stelarc (see p262) and to Kevin Kelly's new biology of machines that are out of human control (see p216). He goes further than Stelarc by totally removing consciousness from the body. He also understands Kelly's thesis that machines must be allowed to be 'out of control'. His work is always out of his own control. Mark Dery outlines Moravec's vision of the downloading process:

> Downloading human consciousness into computers is one of Moravec's strategies for keeping pace with our superevolved creations. With dubious relish, Moravec describes a robot surgeon removing the crown of a person's skull and using high-resolution magnetic resonance measurements to create a supercomputer simulacrum of the subject's neural architecture. Layer by layer is scanned and simulated; in the process, the superfluous tissue is surgically removed and disposed of. At last, the braincase is empty; the robot disconnects all life-support systems, and the body goes into convulsions and expires.
>
> The subject's conscious, meanwhile, is curiously unconcerned, wandering around wraithlike through cyberspace.[1]

Moravec's vision also reminds me of Greg Egan's *Permutation City* (see p222), and its demonstration of the ontological difference between the copy and the real. It is interesting that in Moravec's scenario the original human host of the downloaded consciousness is killed. If the technological revolution accelerates at the pace Moravec predicts then it would seem unlikely that the copying of consciousness would need to bring about the death of the subject. Moravec's problem is that the obverse of his theory may be true: that consciousness may arise out of our full visceral body, rather than just from the brain, and the brain may well be more than just a computational machine. Erik Davis, in *Techgnosis*, states the case for an embodied consciousness:

... psycho-neuro-immunologists argue that the body thinks as an 'ecosystem' of the flesh. Other neurologists argue that emotions ... play a fundamentally constructive role in human thought. Moreover, meditators and mystics the world over agree that many different levels of consciousness are discoverable through contemplative introspection states that, while possibly measurable, cannot simply be identified with the chattering conceptual activity that cognitive science fixates upon and Moravec wants to simulate.[2]

The extreme nature of Moravec's views has inspired many science-fiction writers and, indeed, many science-fiction writers may have inspired Moravec. But what is particularly striking with Moravec's ideas is that, if they come to fruition, they are set to lead to what Bruce Mazlish has called 'the Fourth Discontinuity'.[3] The three previous 'discontinuities' – disjunctures in epistemology after which knowledge needs to be reclassified – have been the ideas of Copernicus, Darwin and Freud, where our world and our knowledge as we know it was drastically changed and rearticulated.

1 Mark Dery, *Escape Velocity: Cyberculture at the End of the Century*, London: Hodder and Stoughton, 1996, p301.
2 Erik Davis, *Techgnosis: Myth, Magic and Mysticism in the Age of Information*, London: Serpent's Tale, 1998, p123.
3 Bruce Mazlish, *The Fourth Discontinuity: the Co-Evolution of Man and Machine*, New Haven, CT: Yale University Press, 1993.

The retina is a transparent, paper-thin layer of nerve tissue at the back of the eyeball on which the eye's lens projects an image of the world. This image is transmitted via a million-fibre cable – the optic nerve – to regions deep in the brain. The retina is a part of the brain convenient for study, even in living animals, because of its peripheral location and because its image-processing functions seem straightforward compared with the brain's other mysteries. A human retina contains about one hundred million neurons of five distinct kinds. Light-sensitive cells feed horizontal cells and bipolar cells, which connect to amacrine cells, whose output goes to ganglion cells, whose outgoing fibres bundle to form the optic nerve. Each of the million ganglion-cell axons carries signals from a particular patch of image, representing the differences in light intensity between adjacent regions and from one time to the next – edge and motion detections that are useful also in robot vision. Overall, the retina seems to resolve about one million distinct regions in the visual field and to follow change up to about 10 frames-per-second. Fed a video image with similar resolution, it takes a robot vision program about one hundred computer operations to produce a single edge or motion detection, thus one hundred million operations to match a whole 'frame' of optic nerve output, and 1000 MIPS – millions of instructions per second, the power of a small supercomputer – to equal the retina's 10 frames-per-second.

If the retina is worth one thousand MIPS, what about the whole brain, whose larger neurons are one thousand times as numerous, but occupy one hundred thousand times the volume? Multiplying the retina's computation by a compromise brain/retina ratio of ten thousand yields a rough brain equivalent of 10 million MIPS – like a million 1997 robot computers, or one hundred of the biggest supercomputers. Conversely, a 10 MIPS robot – like most still in use – has the mental power of a million-neuron bee. An advanced experimental robot, with 100 MIPS, matches the brain of a very small fish. In fact, the narrowly competent performance of advanced industrial robots that do intricate assembly of electronics, and of experimental robots that drive the autobahns, has the character of a small animal. Technological development has taken us from the equivalent of single neurons to this stage in about seventy years. It took natural evolution about seven hundred million years to go as far – evolving humans from there required a few hundred million more. By analogy it should take technology a few decades to cover the remaining distance. Computer progress supports this timescale.

Computers have doubled in capacity every two years since 1950, a pace that has become an industry given. The universal factor in improving computation has been miniaturization: smaller components have less inertia and operate more quickly with less power, and more of them can exist in a given space. Microprocessors in 1997 contain about ten million components, but manufacturers have exhibited memory chips with a billion devices. As components shrink to atomic scales, it is possible to imagine two-dimensional chips with a trillion components, and three-dimensional arrays with a million trillion. Such numbers take us far beyond the paltry 10 million MIPS required for a human-capable robot. The – probably conservative – assumption that computer power will continue to grow at its historical rate predicts that 10 million MIPS personal computers will arrive by 2030. Giving the robotics industry a few years to get its software into shape, this suggests the advent of human-like robots soon after.

As intelligent robots design successive generations of successors, technical evolution will go into overdrive. Biological humans can either adopt the fabulous mechanisms of robots, thus becoming robots themselves, or they can retire into obscurity. A robot ecology will colonize space with intelligent machines optimized to live there. Yet, viewed from a distance, robot expansion into the cosmos will be a vigorous physical affair, a wavefront that converts raw inanimate matter into mechanisms for further expansion. It will leave in its ever-growing wake a more subtle world, with less action and more thought.

On the frontier, robots of ever-increasing mental and physical ability will compete with one another in a boundless land rush. Behind the expansion wavefront, a surround of established neighbours will restrain growth, and the contest will become one of boundary pressure, infiltration and persuasion: a battle of wits. A robot with superior knowledge of matter may encroach on a neighbour's space through force, threat, or convincing promises about the benefits of merger. A robot with superior models of mind might lace attractive gifts of useful information with subtle slants that subvert others to its purposes. Almost always, the more powerful minds will have the advantage.

To stay competitive, robots will have to grow in place, repeatedly restructuring the stuff of their bounded bodies into more refined and effective forms. Inert lumps of matter, along with limbs and sense organs, will be converted into computing elements whose components will be then miniaturized to increase their number and speed. Physical activity will gradually transform itself into a web of increasingly pure thought, where every smallest action is a meaningful computation. We cannot guess the mechanisms robots will use, since physical theory has not yet found even the exact rules underlying matter and space. Having found the rules, robots may use their prodigious minds to devise highly improbable organizations that are to familiar elementary particles as knitted sweaters are to tangled balls of yarn.

As they arrange space, time and energy into forms best for computation, robots will use mathematical insights to optimize and compress the computations themselves. Every consequent increase in their mental powers will accelerate future gains, and the inhabited portions of the universe will be rapidly transformed into a cyberspace, where overt physical activity is imperceptible, and the world inside the computation is astronomically rich. Beings will cease to be defined by their physical geographic boundaries, but will establish, extend, and defend identities as informational transactions in cyberspace. The old bodies of individual robots, refined into matrices for cyberspace, will interconnect, and the minds of robots, as pure software, will migrate among them at will. As the cyberspace becomes more potent, its advantage over physical bodies will overwhelm even on the raw expansion frontier. The robot wavefront of coarse physical transformation will be overtaken by a faster wave of cyberspace conversion, the whole becoming finally a bubble of mind expanding at near light speed.

Coloured scanning electron micrograph (SEM) of a drive gear (coloured orange) in a micromotor (top). The gear is smaller than a human hair in diameter. The whole device was etched on to the surface of a silicon wafer. Such motors could eventually be used in microscopic drug pumps implanted in the human body.

Coloured SEM of a micro-submarine in a human artery (centre). The submarine was made by computer-guided lasers to polymerise an acrylic liquid, building up the submarine in layers 10 micrometres thick. Nanorobots such as this could be used for detecting and repairing defects in the human body.

A robot 'gnat' at MIT (bottom). The gnat has its own photo-detectors and logic processors, enabling it to automatically search for and hide in shadows – such simple robotic tasks are known as 'artificial stupidity'. Until battery technology catches up, the gnat still requires an external power supply.

Researchers at MIT hope eventually to produce robot insects that may be used in industry to perform internal checks and on-the-spot repairs to otherwise inaccessible machinery.

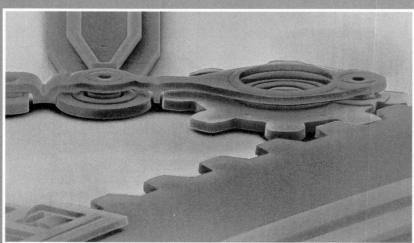

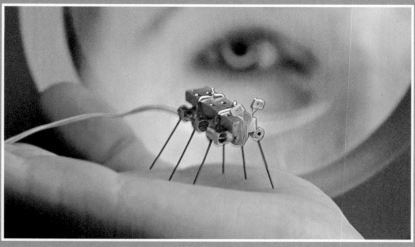

Hans Moravec: computer generated graphics (top left and right) of Fractal Branching Ultra-Dexterous Robots, also known as 'Bush Robots'. To quote from Moravec's NASA sponsored research: 'A concept for robots of ultimate dexterity.

A bush robot is a branched hierarchy of articulated limbs, starting from a macroscopically large trunk through successively smaller and more numerous branches, ultimately to microscopic twigs and nanoscale fingers.'

Moravec, who is Director of the Carnegie Mellon Mobile Robot Laboratory, has been researching, over a number of years, some of the problems involved with autonomous robots navigating through real spaces. In a

recent paper written for ARPA in the US, Moravec reported on his developments in this field. The images (centre and bottom left) represent 3-D field mapping in a stereoscopic space to show how a robot's 'eyes' might 'see'. In the conclusion to

the research Moravec posits a possible robot seeing-head which could be retro-fitted to existing machinery to achieve autonomous navigation of spaces by industrial mobile robots (centre right).

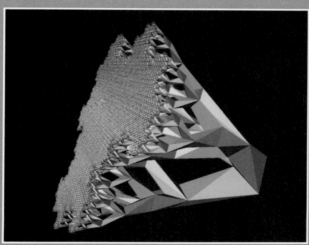

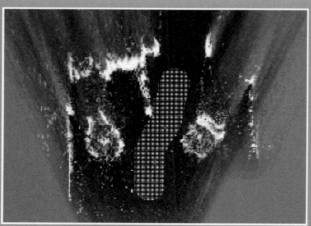

Michael Heim_The Virtual Reality of the Tea Ceremony_1998

Michael Heim was one of the first commentators to respond in spiritual terms to the advent of cyberspace. Heim directs a Tai Chi group and teaches Internet and new media design at the Art Center College of Design in Pasadena, California. He is the author of *Electric Language: A Philosophical Study of Word Processing* (1987), *The Metaphysics of Virtual Reality* (1993) and *Virtual Realism* (1998). He was one of the writers brought together for Michael Benedikt's important anthology *Cyberspace: First Steps*, contributing an essay entitled 'The Erotic Ontology of Cyberspace'.

Heim's writing and lecturing centre on the relationship between the human mind and the computer. He sees the computer as inaugurating a new technologized space of thought that is erotic, poetic and contemplatively ordered. The opening paragraph to the 'Erotic Ontology' essay sets out his position: 'Cyberspace is more than a breakthrough in electronic media or in computer-interface design. With its virtual environments and simulated worlds, cyberspace is a metaphysical laboratory, a tool for examining our very sense of reality.'[1] He sees the real and the virtual as interacting in a way that enriches the real, and has a meditative effect on the cyberspatial user.

Heim also draws analogies between Eastern metaphysics and cyberspace, proposing that Eastern ways of thinking might elucidate the phenomenology and navigation of virtual worlds. He points out that as Western science progresses it appears to become more akin to Eastern mysticism: examples of this are the fluid and liquid analogies that we use for information transmission, or fractal computer interfaces that are reminiscent of Zen gardens. Heim is concerned with a ritualized and contemplative version of digital realms in the same way that a Zen garden is symbolic of faraway religious terrains.

In *The Metaphysics of Virtual Reality*, Heim gives an example of this Eastern religious approach – in this case applied to labour:

One day a young man observed an old sage fetching water from the village well. The old man lowered a wooden bucket on a rope and pulled water up, hand over hand. The youth disappeared and returned with a wooden pulley. He approached the old man and showed him how the device works … 'If I use a device like this, my mind will think itself clever. With a cunning mind, I will no longer put my heart into what I am doing. Soon my wrist alone will do the work, turning the handle. If my heart and whole body is not in my work, my work will become joyless. When my work is joyless, how do you think the water will taste?'[2]

Work that becomes joyless or separated from its meditative component ceases to engage the active mind. Heim feels that those who navigate or construct cyberspaces are in danger of such joyless, unsymbolic and thoughtless labour. A similar philosophy imbues the Japanese tea ceremony. In this excerpt from the essay published in *The Virtual Dimension* Heim looks at the impact the tea ceremony might have on cyberspace, giving it more of a sense of place by moving it away from its usual bland ubiquity.

1 Michael Heim, 'The Erotic Ontology of Cyberspace', in *Cyberspace: First Steps*, Michael Benedikt (ed), Cambridge, MA: MIT Press, 1991, p59.

2 Michael Heim, *The Metaphysics of Virtual Reality*, Oxford: Oxford University Press, 1993, pp74–5.

Virtual Dimension
The Psychic Framework of Tea

Nature as a 'psychic framework' appears in the description of the Japanese tea ceremony in D T Suzuki's lovely book for English-speaking readers, *Zen and Japanese Culture*.[1] Describing the tea ceremony, Suzuki points beyond physical facts to the atmosphere in which gestures, objects, and surroundings cohere:

> The tea-drinking that is known as *cha-no-yu* in Japanese and as 'tea ceremony' or 'tea cult' in the West is not just drinking tea, but involves all the activities leading to it, all the utensils used in it, the entire atmosphere surrounding the procedure, and, last of all, what is really the most important phase, the frame of mind or spirit which mysteriously grows out of the combination of all these factors.
>
> The tea-drinking, therefore, is not just drinking tea, but it is the art of cultivating what might be called 'psychosphere', or the psychic atmosphere, or the inner field of consciousness. We may say that it is generated within oneself, while sitting in a small semi-dark room with a low ceiling, irregularly constructed, from the handling the tea bowl, which is crudely formed but eloquent with the personality of the maker, and from listening to the sound of boiling water in the iron kettle over a charcoal fire.[2]

What Suzuki describes as a 'psychosphere', 'psychic atmosphere', or 'inner field of consciousness' is what I mean by a psychic framework. The psychic framework of the tea ceremony is a field of awareness, but it cannot be separated from the technology of utensils, architecture, and decor that affects the participant's state of mind. We should not think of psychic framework as 'consciousness' if by consciousness we mean a private subjective state that peers from within to confront a separate world of alien objects. A psychic framework sets the tone that a field of awareness has when it seamlessly flows with a set of furnishings, tools, and physical movements.

The tea ceremony is a technology designed to recapture a lost nature. Artificial and formalized in its every movement and gesture, the tea ceremony removes excess in order to exalt the simple clarity of being. Its highly stylized cultivation aims at a certain kind of experience. Only through the artificial does one regain a lost sense of open harmony with the natural. Our daily struggle for survival pulls us away from experiencing pure, spontaneous nature.

We must regard cyberspace technology as a technological practice. Entering cyberspace is like entering the space of the tea ceremony. The more a cyberspace is a virtual reality in the strict sense – using immersion techniques like projection displays or head-mounted displays, and using full three-dimensional stereoscopy – the more it shapes a psychic framework. How does this technology configure a distinct psychic framework? How can we make the design of the virtual reality interface function so that we become wise in our use of nature?

Here is where contemporary interface design goes beyond the so-called 'human factors' research. Human-factors research scratches the surface only. It asks minimal questions about interactivity. It works with elementary surveys about the way humans use computers. It does not study the psychic atmosphere produced by virtual worlds. When the immersive feature of virtual reality creates a world where the user becomes a participant, then we can no longer rely on behavioural psychology to convey what is happening. A world brings the full context of existential involvement, not a single procedure narrowly restricted to the use of tools. A world is an ontological totality, not a sequence of machine-human interactions.

By looking at the psychic framework of a virtual world, we can begin to give content to the terms people already use to express their spatial intuitions of cyberspace. As I mentioned earlier, the vocabulary of cyber-space already makes abundant reference to spatial intuition. This intuition of space is not weakly metaphorical, but it expresses intuition in the Kantian sense of *Anschauung*, that is, the basic ways we perceive and understand the empirical world. The 'empirical' originally refers to the sensations we receive in experience. The way we move through informa-tion space, as architects well know, affects our feelings about being in that space. We already see on the Internet a large range of elementary spaces, although the Internet today lacks the immersion required by virtual reality technology in the strong sense of the term. As an intercultural testing ground, though, the Internet with its three-dimensional spatial metaphors offers opportunities for translating aesthetic spatial experiences, like the tea ceremony. Current two-dimensional simulations on the Internet's World Wide Web offer dynamic spaces that are gradually evolving with the introduction of VRML (virtual reality modelling language). Translating the tea ceremony to cyberspace can prepare us to think about the challenges of interface design that lie ahead.

Four Features of the Tea Ceremony

The tea ceremony is a technology for restoring the original abode, the place where the psyche feels comfortable with itself as a participant in the natural world. The original abode is where the world and the psyche interact harmoniously. Taoists referred to the original abode as the 'face before you were born', where the energy embryo abides in the womb of the mother. In this case, the mother is Mother Earth. The human being breathes the energy of the heavens and conducts that energy into the support strength of the earth. The human being stands between heaven and earth, though most often it is distracted by the ten thousand things that claim attention in worldly life. To recover the stance of the full human being, a reconfiguration is required. *Sadô*, as the tea culture is known in Japan, reconfigures the psychic framework of nature. It resets the human being into the natural posture, into the natural attitude. It restores the original abode.

The four features of the traditional tea ceremony correspond to the design issues of virtual environments. They relate, each in a different way, to the psychic framework that heals the breach between humans and nature. These features are: *wa* (harmony), *kei* (respect), *sei* (purity), and *jaku* (serenity).

Wa means that a world must cohere. The pieces of the world must constitute parts of a whole. A world can only exist as what the German language calls a *Zusammenhang*: things must 'hang together'. Aesthetically, this holism means a unified atmosphere. The tools of the tea ceremony might share a seasonal motif that deepens the sense of time and place. Autumn may appear in the floors, in the scrolls, and in the colours chosen for the tea cups. This feature of the tea ceremony appears in current interface design where the designer uses semiotic repetition to establish a sense of place. In general, the current Web is a wild collage without a clear semiotic system. Some young designers are trying to deepen the sense of place, of being somewhere, by repeating colours, images, and interactive buttons in such a way as to create a consistent sense of place. The places they create convey an internal harmony, though not necessarily a harmony with nature.

To create a sense of place, some Web sites use consistent border markings to establish semiotic harmony throughout the many rooms of the on-line space. 'Harmony' is derived from the Latin *ars*, 'to fit'. The fit that artists strive for today is to make everything in a world come together in such a way as to make that world stand out as a unique whole. The most basic ground of the world is an open space for participation. Worlds offer space for habitation, and the participants cooperate in maintaining the ground of that world. Most often, Internet sites appear to be 'one thing after another', without stasis or rest. By creating harmonious worlds, even jazzy worlds, the artist shapes an electronic abode, a place to dwell, perhaps even a space we can eventually inhabit.

Kei refers to the acknowledgment of the presence of other people or the sacredness of the materials we use. Computer communication establishes respect in a peculiar way. Computers isolate us as individual users at the same time that computers connect us in a network. Networks interweave human memories and make it possible to interweave our thoughts increasingly on a daily basis without regard to physical distance. Time barriers drop. Yet this is also where the danger lies. As time barriers fall away, the instant connection we have threatens to wear away respect. Respect seems to require distance. If we lose a sense of our distance from one another – our interior distances, the vastness of our spiritual landscapes – then we risk losing respect. Perhaps the avatars of virtual worlds, those surrogate personae of simulation, will help preserve the distance needed for mutual respect. While computers create an intimacy that connects mind to mind, they can also hide us from one another. Ideally, a virtual world would allow us intimacy with distance, much like the tea ceremony. The tea master Rikyu admonishes tea practitioners not to try to synchronize their feelings with those of their guests unless the harmony occurs spontaneously.[3] Without distance, true intimacy cannot arise.

Sei appears in the tea ceremony's austere minimalism. No wasted motion, no excess of any kind, always restraint. From the material point of view, it would be hard to think of any space more empty, more minimal than cyberspace. Some cyberspace software designers, like William Bricken of the Human Interface Technology Lab at the University of Washington, conceive cyberspace as a Buddhist void, as *sunyata*. The emptiness of electronic systems offers an opportunity for pure creativity. The creative rush drives thousands of artists and would-be artists who now manifest their personal home pages on the Internet. Most of these creations show little restraint, as they arise from the call of open spaces that beckon the spirit in millions of people. For the designer, the purity of cyberspace may come with the territory, but purity does not last long. Cyberspace is rapidly filling with junk and junk mail. Advertisers litter the void. What we can learn from the tea ceremony is the discipline of restraint. We need to reflect the essential loneliness of cyberspace in the electronic environments we create.

Jaku shares the *sei*'s fragility. Purity quickly drowns in clutter. Likewise, the initial serenity of cyberspace, its loneliness and focus, soon scatters with the noise of millions of messages. Cyberspace, especially in its newly found role as a source of commercial contacts, risks becoming bedlam. Concentration and focus will be impossible if cyberspace becomes a circus. To enjoy the circus, you will have to forget your purposes and go along for the ride. The serenity of vast cyberspace has been broken by the shouts of advertisers and the barkers who try to lure new customers. Perhaps the purpose of 'knowbots', tiny programs with customized intelligence, is to keep down the noise. Knowbots can filter out distractions and remove the shouts of advertisers. The Internet already offers programs like Fast Forward, which invisibly removes advertising banners before they appear in the Netscape Web browser.

But advertising is not the only obstacle to *Jaku*. As I pointed out in *Electric Language*, the language system on computers is an essentially linked language.[4] Hypertext reading shows the linked nature of digital writing. The loneliness of the cyberspace void should not obscure the fact that computing solitude is essentially a social solitude. What we see on the computer screen may seem as intimate as the thoughts in our head, yet the on-screen vision links to millions of other computers, or – even if protected by firewalls – any screen may be recovered and viewed by thousands of anonymous others. Computer text is essentially linked text. When we write e-mail, we may feel as though we are writing in a serene, private bubble, but in fact we might as well be shouting our message from the rooftop. Cyberspace offers no total privacy. Where there is no total privacy, there is no complete serenity.

Each of the four characteristics of the tea ceremony have a cyberspace correlate. These correlates appear to be metaphoric analogies between the virtues of the tea ceremony and the atmosphere of cyberspace, and they establish possible links between the two … Interface designers struggling to shape a sense of place on the Internet can lead this process of enrichment. Such a struggle will not be easy, however, as the analogy between cyberspace and the tea ceremony faces many challenges.

1 Daisetz T Suzuki, *Zen and Japanese Culture*, New York: Princeton University Press, Bollinger Series, 1959.
2 Ibid, pp295–6.
3 Rikyu, writing in *Nanbo Roku*, cited in Leonard Koren, *Wabi-Sabi for Artists, Designers, Poets & Philosophers*, Berkeley, CA: Stone Bridge Press, 1994, p82.
4 Michael Heim (with David Hillel Gelernter), *Electric Language: A Philosophical Study of Word Processing*, New Haven, CT: Yale University Press, pp160–4.

Anthony Dunne_Hertzian Space_1999

The work of product design partners Anthony Dunne and Fiona Raby appears to belong to that very British genre of highly eccentric inventiveness. With a view to enriching the social arena they posit product designs and architectural elements that are extremely responsive to the electromagnetic spectrum. Objects become invigorated by electromagnetic pulses: they translate them, mix them and use them in surreal ways to encourage new social situations.

In 'normal' product design, the skin of the object usually conceals a set of very ordinary components – some electronic, some mechanical. Generally the skin is obsessively designed to encourage swift aesthetic obsolescence, to foster in the consumer a hunger for the latest fashionable look. Dunne and Raby's design work eschews this 'form-porn' design process in favour of a methodology where nothing is overwrought, nothing is accentuated and nothing is there just for its own sake. Yet the result is designs that have a strangely beautiful sparsity, and are not without a touch of surrealistic humour.

Dunne and Raby are particularly concerned with objects that surf the invisible landscape of electromagnetism: a permanent landscape that is forever being embellished by a billion electronic objects that continually weave, unravel and re-sow its unseen spaces. Such processes take place all around us, often at a very mundane level: a telephone rings when it receives its pulse; a computer mouse will click like a duck, tweet or laugh like a baby if we want it to. Dunne and Raby embroider these impulses into a complex and fun environment.

At the time of writing *Hertzian Tales* Dunne was and still is Senior Research Fellow at the Royal College of Art in London. The book is the story of his aspirations, the people he admires and the ideas that have influenced him. He weaves these threads into a learned argument which sets out his concepts of the 'post-optimal object', 'para-functionality' and 'infra–ordinary space'.

Gillian Crampton Smith, former Professor of Computer Related Design at the RCA, provides an overview of Dunne's work in her introduction to *Hertzian Tales*. She points out that objects seldom have solely practical significance but also carry ritual and symbolic meaning – a fact that has long been understood by manufacturers of consumer products but has been largely ignored in the design of computer technology. Against this background, Dunne's work '[suggests] how electronic objects might enrich rather than impoverish the lives we now share with them. Dunne proposes an "aesthetics of use": an aesthetics which, through the interactivity made possible by computing, seeks a developing and more nuanced cooperation with the object – a cooperation which, it is hoped, might enhance social contact and everyday experience.'[1]

This behavioural concept of aesthetics constitutes a plea for computerized and electronic objects to encourage the user to enter a new space of communal interaction, a world away from the narcissistic and lonely spaces so often created by advanced technology.

1 Gillian Crampton Smith, 'Introduction', Anthony Dunne, *Hertzian Tales: Electronic Products, Aesthetic Experience and Critical Design*, London: CRD RCA, 1999.

Immaterial Sensuality

We are experiencing a new kind of connection to our artefactual environment. The electronic object is spread over many frequencies of the electromagnetic spectrum, partly visible, partly not. Sense organs function as transducers, converting environmental energy into neural signals. Our sense organs cannot transduce radio waves or other wavelengths outside the narrow bandwidth of visible light (and infra-red energy through the skin as warmth). Electronic objects are disembodied machines with extended invisible skins everywhere. They couple and decouple with our bodies without us knowing. Working on microscopic scales, often pathogenic, many electromagnetic fields interfere with the cellular structure of the body. Paranoia accompanies dealings with such Hertzian machines. How do they touch us? Do they merely reflect off our skin, or the surface of our internal organs? In other words, do they merely 'see' us, or can they 'read' us too, extracting personal information about our identity, status, and health?

An operating manual for x-ray machines contains images of radiographic actors and props that view the body as a radio medium. The machines establish views, and support a sort of radio perspective, revealing, concealing and exposing hidden organs and views, and creating a 'radio theatre' of the hidden body. In configuring the body according to an unusual conception of space, these images of people and x-ray machines illustrate an expanded view of space as an electromagnetic medium.

The artist Arthur Elsenaar, inspired by photographs of experiments by gentleman scholars in the 1850s, taps into our strong feelings about electricity, its danger and mystery, and its measurability. He uses the microwave field of a radar sensor to create 'an aura, or an extension of my skin into spaces, into which people can walk' which causes a 24-volt pulsed DC current to deliver a variable charge of up to three milliamps to two electrodes attached above the jaw and two to the 'hunch' muscles in the shoulders. He is developing a digital system which will support a wider range of inputs and outputs, for example different responses for people retreating and approaching, and head turns and nods.

Elsenaar's poetic use of fields, a pathological exploration of personal space, is very different from research carried out at MIT into technically interesting but aesthetically mundane applications of electrical fields to inter-personal information exchange. The body is treated literally as a circuit board and the commercial ambitions of the project have eradicated any possibility for poetry although the 'electrical whispers of fish' are one inspiration for the project.[1] The potential of the technology is reduced to the most basic level of utility and conceived as a replacement for physical connections between personal databases. [...]

The Radiogenic Object

Objects designed to straddle both material and immaterial domains arouse curiosity about the fit between these worlds. Many military aircraft are now 'tele-dynamic', designed to fly undetected through fields of radar-frequency radiation. But tele-dynamic forms are not aerodynamic and to remain airborne their outline needs to be constantly adjusted by a computer. These aircraft fly through fusions of abstract digital, Hertzian and atmospheric spaces. If this awareness of Hertzian space is to form the basis of an approach to everyday objects, it is not enough simply to present the technical facts. They must be grounded in rich cultural contexts if they are to be more than mere illustrations.

Objects which I call 'radiogenic' function as unwitting interfaces between the abstract space of electromagnetism and the material cultures of everyday life, revealing unexpected points of contact between them. Many of these objects centre on the aerial, a device that links the perceptible material world to the extrasensory world of radiation and energy.

'Aerialness' is a quality of an object considered in relation to the electromagnetic environment. Even the human body is a crude monopole aerial. Although in theory precise laws govern the geometry of aerials, in reality it is a black art, a fusion of the macro world of perception and the imperceptible world of micro-electronics. Embodying the contradictions and limits of scientific thought, an aerial's behaviour can be described but not easily understood because it depends on the dual concept of electromagnetic radiation as wave and particle. As the aerial allows this invisible world to be understood and modelled in terms of material reality, it provides a starting point for a design approach that links the immaterial and the material so as to open up new aesthetic and conceptual possibilities.

Although few artists have explored radiogenic objects, several objects have been created by radio amateurs by enhancing radiogenic qualities in existing environments and artefacts, resulting in objects that provide new perceptions of our Hertzian environment. These objects hint at the fertile territory beyond the designer's concern with the semiotics of radio interfaces and the engineer's narrow conception of functionality.

DIY books on antenna theory and practice offer many examples which generate the kind of pleasure which Wentworth notes in *Making Do and Getting By* and people's natural ability to subvert object types and act in new ways on the environment. It is a pleasure derived from invention as poetry, loosening the connection between language and things, and challenging the tyranny of language over artefacts. For instance, the use of a specific size of domestic shelving as a core antenna or a milk bottle and tin foil for another reveal unexpected functional connections between physical objects and Hertzian space that offer an alternative to representation.

Another example is the *Bobbin Cane*, conceived and made by Georges Droz-Georget for listening to the forbidden French transmitter on the Eiffel Tower during World War One. A hook passing through the hole of the ferrule was attached to a low overhead telephone line connected to a shooting range: this became his antenna. The wavelength was selected by moving two sliding rings over the copper thread wound around the shaft, and the receiver was carried in the user's pocket. All these radiogenic objects are part of a Hertzian culture that includes diagrams on the use of drain pipes as antennas, and garden layouts which integrate an antenna with vegetables and paths.

When Objects Dream...

Although when we look at an electronic product we only see what is radiated at the frequency of visible light, all electronic objects are a form of radio. If our eyes could see (tune into) energy of a lower frequency these objects would not only appear different but their boundaries would extend much further into space, interpenetrating other objects considered discrete at the frequency of light. Besides the obvious harmfulness of x-rays and microwaves there is a growing concern over the effect of the radiation leaked by domestic appliances. *Radio and Beans*, an installation by Patrick Ready, draws attention to the possibly harmful effects of electromagnetic fields generated by domestic appliances. It consists of electrical devices suspended on wooden shelves from the gallery ceiling. Around them hang small paper bags containing fast-growing mung beans in soil, arranged at equal intervals in a three-dimensional grid, and watered three times a day. It was hoped that the beans would exhibit effects from the electrical fields through irregular growth patterns. But as the experiment was not controlled and scientific but ironic, it was never clear how the beans were affected.

In this piece the artist becomes a radio biologist investigating the interaction between radiant energy and biological systems. Science and folklore meet in this strange electrical garden, reminding us of the interconnectedness of nature and technology, something which must be made more visible if we are to find more meaningful ways of inhabiting an environment gradually becoming more radioactive.

The electronic object is often described as 'smart'. But using this term to describe objects with enhanced electronic functionality encourages a bland interpretation of electronic objects.

> Smart, after all, is not the same as intelligent, let alone intellectual. Smartness is intelligence that is cost-efficient, planner-responsible, user-friendly, and unerringly obedient to its programmer's designs. None of the qualities, in other words, which we associate with free-thinking intellectuals.
> A Ross, *The New Smartness*

Electronic objects are not only 'smart', they 'dream' – in the sense that they leak radiation into the space and objects surrounding them, including our bodies. Despite the images of control and efficiency conveyed through a beige visual language of intelligibility and smartness, electronic objects, it might be imagined, are irrational – or at least allow their thoughts to wander. Thinking of them in terms of dreaminess rather than smartness opens them to more interesting interpretations.

For example, some possibilities for new relationships with these hybrids of radiation and matter are found in pathological products based on paranoia or eccentricity. Many devices designed to transform private situations into public ones depend on the 'leakiness' of electronic objects, tuning into the dreams of radiant objects. *The Computer Intercept System* sold by the Surveillance Technology Group is an example:

> Without entering the premises, electromagnetic radiating from unshielded computer screens and ancillary equipment can be intercepted from a remote location. The Computer Intercept System's highly sensitive receiver logs all radiating signals into its 100 channel memory. These emissions are then stabilized, processed and reassembled into clear reproduction of the intercepted data onto its built-in monitor.
> Surveillance Technology Group, *Covert Audio Intercept*

Many buildings are now designed as Faraday cages to prevent such eavesdropping, usually invisibly by deploying electromagnetic shielding materials throughout the structure. The same technology protects sensitive equipment in a building from bursts of external radiation. Test-sites, specially designed environments or anechoic chambers, now measure an object's leakiness to predict its effect on other objects.

A more bizarre use of leakiness is seen in the *Bat Band Converter*, a parasitical device that allows you to 'use your a.m. portable radio and this novel design to tune-in to the secret world of bats'. The title of the magazine that provides the plans, *Everyday Practical Electronics*, seems at odds with a world where practical skills are turned towards poetic ends, and tuning into bats, hair, fizzy drinks, crinkly plastic bags and dropping pins is regarded as a sane everyday activity. The device converts the non-electromagnetic ultrasonic signals of the bats into radio signals which are transmitted/leaked to the host radio.

The seemingly illicit information exchange of 'dreamy objects' offers one possible interpretation of the electrosphere. It helps us think of electronic objects in 'Hertzian' terms, as interconnected fields rather than discrete things. It acknowledges the problematic conceptual status of electronic objects, arising from their ambiguous identity as hybrids of matter and radiation, functioning at scales and speeds well beyond the range of human perception. If the electronic object has a role in humanizing Hertzian space it is not as a visualization or representation of radio but as a catalyst, encouraging the poetic and multi-layered coupling of electromagnetic and material elements to produce new levels of cultural complexity.

1 Some fish use the three-dimensional equivalent of radar to guide themselves through dark waters by positioning themselves in each others' fields, possibly communicating through voltage patterns and rates of pulsing, a sort of electrical whisper. L Milne and M Milne, *The Senses of Animals and Men*, New York: Athenaeum, 1962, pp109–20.

Margaret Wertheim_The Pearly Gates of Cyberspace_1999

The Pearly Gates of Cyberspace is a critical book in the expanding genre of what Erik Davis (see p190) calls 'Techgnosis', the linking of digital technology to old, arcane spiritual and occult ideas as a way of seeing new possibilities for the digital revolution. Margaret Wertheim is a science journalist and commentator who specializes in the historical relationship between physics and religion; her articles have been published in magazines and newspapers throughout the world.

Wertheim sees the Internet and virtual reality as portals into the new electric, digital religious space – a 'soul space'. Her thesis is that the reductive spaces of the Industrial Revolution and the precise, prescribed secular spaces of Modernism served to collapse our perception of space. This collapse was in contradiction to the medieval dualist spaces of earth and heaven, and caused philosophers to speculate on the 'death of God'.

In *The Pearly Gates of Cyberspace* Wertheim shows how Dante's *Divine Comedy* offers an extraordinary, virtually real cartography of the various levels of soul space. Dante's Cornices act as mnemonic devices for memorizing the cosmographic hierarchy of things and ideas. However, the symbolic, religious language of Dante's work is at the same time entwined with contemporary allusion, packed full of references to local gossip and politics. Cyberspace, likewise, is also packed with prosaic concerns. It is this 'low-code' content, which exists alongside the incredible phenomenological slipperiness of cyberspace, that for Wertheim creates a 'new soul space'. It is a space that lies forever outside the increasingly baroque spaces of even our most advanced physicists and geometricians. In Wertheim's words:

Because cyberspace is not rooted in these phenomena, it is *not subject to the laws of physics*, and hence it is not bound by the limitations of these laws. In particular, this new space is not contained within physicists' hyperspace complex. No matter how many dimensions hyperspace physicists add into their equations, cyberspace will remain 'outside' them all. With cyberspace, we have discovered a 'place' *beyond hyperspace*.[1]

For Wertheim, then, cyberspace has a much closer connection with pre-modern space than with of the modern. Others, too, have made such connections, often drawing analogies between cyberspace and the classical arts of memory. Frances Yates's book *The Art of Memory* provides the historical backdrop for such excursions into the ordering of epistemological memory.[2] These imagined spaces perhaps most closely approximate to the iconic spaces of cyberspace. The Apple desktop and the classical memory theatre are examples of the same notion. They both place ideas within icons in particular places, and these are then revisited to yield the ideas within.

The old arts of memory could not be reduced to their mere physicality, and cyberspace shares this 'other worldly' quality. As Wertheim points out:

The irreducibility of cyberspace to its physical substrate is evident in its structure, which, as we have noted, is partly physical and partly not. As William Gibson has correctly anticipated in his fiction, the essence of cyberspace is not its material connections but its logical (or linguistic) ones. In the end, cyberspace is not just a physical network. It is, above all, a logical network.[3]

This lexical, logistical space of memory would, it seems, be more at home in the pre-modernity of medieval times. For this reason Wertheim's writing makes interesting reading in the context of this anthology: it puts her at odds with the many writers, such as Stelarc (see p262), who see technology as a paradigm-shifting influence on the metamorphosis and ultimately redundant body as part of the modernist technological project.

1 Margaret Wertheim, *The Pearly Gates of Cyberspace: A History of Space from Dante to the Internet*, London: Virago, 1999, p226.
2 Frances Yates, *The Art of Memory*, London: Routledge and Kegan Paul, 1966.
3 Margaret Wertheim, *The Pearly Gates of Cyberspace*, op cit, p301.

All this may sound rather radical, and many cyberspace enthusiasts have suggested that nothing like cyberspace has existed before. But on the contrary there is an important historical parallel here with the spatial dualism of the Middle Ages. As we have seen, in that time Christians believed in a physical space described by science (what they called 'natural philosophy') and a non-physical space that existed 'outside' the material domain. This non-physical space metaphorically *paralleled* the material world, but it was not contained within physical space. Although there were connections and resonances between the two spaces, medieval spiritual space was a separate and unique part of reality from physical space.

So too the advent of cyberspace returns us to a *dualistic* theatre of reality. Once again we find ourselves with a material realm described by science, and an immaterial realm that operates as a different plane of the real. As with the medieval world picture, there are connections and resonances between these two spaces. Commentator N Katherine Hayles has noted, for example, that one cannot experience cyberspace at all except through the physical senses of the body: the eyes that look at the computer screen or at the stereoscopic projections of virtual reality headsets, the hands that type the commands at the keyboard and control the joysticks, the ears that hear the Real Audio sound files. Yet while physical space and cyberspace are not entirely separate, neither is the latter *contained* within the former.

In some profound way, cyberspace is *another* place. Unleashed into the Internet, my 'location' can no longer be fixed purely in physical space. Just 'where' I am when I enter cyberspace is a question yet to be answered, but clearly my position cannot be pinned down to a mathematical location in Euclidian or relativistic space – not with any number of hyperspace extensions! As with the medievals, we in the technologically charged West on the eve of the twenty-first century increasingly contend with a two-phase reality.

But what does it mean to talk about this digital domain as a 'space' at all? What kind of space is it? Some might object that the online arena is just a vast library – or less generously, a vast soup – of disconnected information and junk. And certainly there is a lot of junk online. Nonetheless, it is important to recognize the genuinely spatial nature of this domain. Whatever its *content* may be, a new *context* is coming into being here; a new 'space' is evolving.

What is at issue, of course, is the meaning of the word 'space' and what constitutes a legitimate instance of this phenomena. I contend that cyberspace is not only a legitimate instantiation of this phenomena but also a socially important one. In the 'age of science' many of us have become so habituated to the idea of space as a purely physical thing that some may find it hard to accept cyberspace as a genuine 'space'. Yet Gibson's neologism is apposite, for it captures an essential truth about this new domain. When I 'go into' cyberspace, my body remains at rest in my chair, but 'I' – or at least some aspect of myself – am teleported into another arena which, while I am there, I am deeply aware has its own logic and geography. To be sure, this is a different sort of geography from anything I experience in the physical world, but one that is no less real for not being material. Let me stress this point: *Just because something is not material does not mean it is unreal*, as the oft-cited distinction between 'cyberspace' and 'real space' implies. Despite its lack of physicality, cyberspace is a real place. *I am there* – whatever this statement may ultimately turn out to mean.

Even in our profoundly physicalist age, we invoke the word 'space' to describe far more than just the physical world. We talk about 'personal space', and about having 'room to move' in our relationships, as if there was some kind of relationship space. We use the terms 'head space' and 'mental space', and Lacanian psychoanalysts (following Freud) believe the mind itself has a spatial structure. Literary theorists discuss literary space and artists discuss pictorial space.

Contemporary scientists, for their part, now envisage a whole *range* of non-physical spaces. Chemists designing new drugs talk about molecular space; biologists talk about evolutionary spaces of potential organisms; mathematicians study topological spaces, algebraic spaces, and metric spaces; chaos theorists studying phenomena such as the weather and insect plagues look at phase spaces, as indeed do physicists studying the motion of galaxies and the quantum behaviour of atoms; and in a recent *Scientific American* article an epidemiological analysis of the spread of infectious diseases posited the idea of viral spaces. 'Space' is a concept that has indeed come to have enormous application and resonance in the contemporary world.

Most obviously, the online domain is a *data space*. This was the concept at the core of Gibson's original cyberpunk vision. In *Neuromancer* and its sequels, Gibson imagined that when his 'console cowboys' donned their cyberspace helmets, they were projected by the power of computer-generated three-dimensional illusionism into a virtual data landscape. Here, the data resources of global corporations were represented as architectural structures. The data bank of the Mitsubishi Bank, for example, was a set of green cubes, that of the 'Fission Authority' was a scarlet pyramid. As a nice example of life imitating art, Tim Berners-Lee, the inventor of the World Wide Web, has said that his goal when designing the Web was to implement a global data space that could be accessed and shared by researchers around the world. We are yet to realize the full VR splendour of Gibson's original vision, but the essential concept of a global data space is already manifest in the World Wide Web.

But cyberspace has become much more than just a data space, because as we have noted much of what goes on there is *not* information-oriented. As many commentators have stressed, the primary use of cyberspace is not for information-gathering but for social interaction and communication – and increasingly also for interactive entertainment, including the creation of a burgeoning number of online fantasy worlds in which people take on elaborate alter egos.

What I want to explore in this first cyberspace chapter are the ways in which this new digital domain functions as a space for complex mental experiences and games. In this sense, we may see cyberspace as a kind of electronic *res cogitans*, a new space for the playing out of some of those immaterial aspects of humanityman that have been denied a home in the purely physicalist world picture. In short, there is a sense in which cyberspace has become a new realm for the mind. In particular it has become a new realm for the imagination; and even, as many cyber-enthusiasts now claim, a new realm for the 'self'. To quote MIT sociologist of cyberspace Sherry Turkle: 'The Internet has become a significant social laboratory for experimenting with the constructions and reconstructions of self that characterize postmodern life.' Just what it means to say that cyberspace is an arena of 'self' is something we must examine closely, but the claim itself commands our attention.

The fact that we are in the process of creating a new immaterial space of being is of profound psychosocial significance. As we have been documenting, any conception of 'other' spaces being 'beyond' physical space has been made extremely problematic by the modern scientific vision of reality. That problematizing is one of the primary pathologies of the modern West. Freud's attempt, with his science of *psychoanalysis*, to reinstate mind or 'psyche' back into the realm of scientific discourse remains one of the most important intellectual developments of the past century. Yet Freud's science was distinctly individualistic. Each person who enters psychoanalysis (or any other form of psychotherapy), must work on his or her psyche individually. Therapy is a quintessentially lonely experience. In addition to this individualistic experience, many people also crave something communal – something that will link their minds to others. It is all well and good to work on one's own personal demons, but many people also seem to want a *collective mental arena*, a space they might share with other minds.

This widespread desire for some sort of collective mental arena is exhibited today in the burgeoning interest in psychic phenomena. In the United States psychic hot lines are flourishing, belief in an 'astral plane' is widespread, and spirit chanelling is on the rise. In the latter case, the posited collective realm transcends the boundary of death, uniting the living and dead in a grand brotherhood of the ether. Meanwhile, *The X-Files* offers us weekly promises of other realities beyond the material plane, and bookstores are filled with testimonials describing trips to an ethereal realm of light and love that supposedly awaits us all after death. One of the great appeals of cyberspace is that it offers a *collective immaterial arena* not after death, but here and now on earth.

Nothing evinces cyberspace's potential as a collective psychic realm so much as the fantastic online worlds known as MUDs. Standing for 'multiuser domains' or originally 'multiuser Dungeons and Dragons', MUDs are complex fantasy worlds originally based on the role-playing board game *Dungeons and Dragons* that swept through American colleges and high schools in the late seventies. As suggested by the 'Dungeons and Dragons' moniker, the original MUDs were medieval fantasies where players battled dragons and picked their way through mazes of dungeons in search of treasure and magical powers. Today MUDs have morphed into a huge range of virtual worlds far beyond the medieval milieu. There is TrekMUSE, a *Star Trek* MUD where MUDers (as players are called) can rise through the ranks of a virtual Starfleet to captain their own starship. There is DuneMUD based on Frank Herbert's science-fiction series, and ToonMUD, a realm of cartoon characters. The Elysium is a lair of vampires, and FurryMuck a virtual wonderland populated by talking animals and man-beast hybrids such as *squirriloids* and *wolfoids*.

Like good novels, successful MUDs evoke the sense of a rich and believable world. The difference is that while the reader of a novel encounters a world fully formed by the writer, MUDers are actively involved in an ongoing process of world-making. To name is to create, and in MUD worlds the simple act of naming and describing is all it takes to generate a new alter ego or 'cyber-self'. MUDers create their online characters, or personae, with a short textual description and a name. 'Johnny Manhattan,' for instance, is described as 'tall and thin, pale as string cheese, wearing a neighbourhood hat'; Dalgren is 'an intelligent mushroom that babbles inanely whenever you approach'; and Gentila, a 'sleek red squirriloid, with soft downy fur and long lush tresses cascading sensuously down her back.' Within the ontology of these cyber-worlds, you *are* the character you create. As one avid player puts it, here 'you are who you pretend to be.' Want to be a poetry-quoting turtle, a Klingon agent, or Donald Duck? In a MUD you can be.

Neil Spiller_Vacillating Objects_1999

My work centres on how architecture is invigorated by cyberspace, on the blurred boundary between the virtual and the actual, and on how the different parameters of these spaces can be used to inform one another. Through my early experience in architectural practice I became aware of how buildings are limited by the inert materials used to construct them, and by an unimaginative idea of what a building should look like and should be. My research draws upon a variety of different disciplines to inform one: architecture. Research areas include the changing status of the architectural drawing, smart materials, computer-aided manufacture, emergent systems, responsive environments, the architectural design of cyberspace, interactivity, cybernetics, evolving systems and algorithmic design.

To create responsive, non-prescriptive designs for architectural urban intervention was the starting point which led to an interest in the logic of algorithms. These problem-solving diagrams for computer programmers are very useful as a way of describing fluctuating conditions in responsive environments. This led to an interest in other computing paradigms such as cellular automata, complexity and emergence. These and other ideas I attempted to bring into the arena of architectural design to help architects cope with the rapid growth of computational technology, which at the time was starting to revolutionize the way buildings were designed, drawn and built.

To this end, and with multidisciplinary aspirations, in 1995 I guest-edited the 'Architects in Cyberspace' edition of *Architectural Design*. This was the first national and international architectural publication to describe some of the significant potential that digital technology has held for architectural designers since the 1960s. It includes pieces written by philosophers, architects, performance artists, digital art theorists and psychologists. This publication was followed by *Digital Dreams*[1] and 'Architects in Cyberspace II'.[2]

The architecture of the future will be an architecture of ecological wefts, technological distortions and digital necromancy.

The spell is back, mixing together disparate things, things not often connected to another for aesthetic, practical or exploratory effect. It is a world populated by vacillating objects, Dalinian exuberances, smooth but jagged surfaces and baroque ecstasies. Objects – some seen and some not – will flit across a variety of spatial terrains simultaneously. These ideas demolish the notion of the privileged site plan because the new objects become ubiquitous, doppelgangered and paranoid.

In my recent monograph *Maverick Deviations*, in an essay entitled 'Split Sites and Smooth Aesthetics', I tried to sketch how this technologized digital world creates partial and split spaces and how vacillating objects can be in a variety of places at once. I wrote:

> The single sacrosanct site plan is plainly puerile. The call for an interactive, responsive architecture aided and abetted by electronic eyes and lies (virtual simulacra) has smashed the notion of a static ground plan with its erased abstraction and its ordinance mapped representation of bounded void. Beware the architects designing on one site, in static materials, for linear time for they are restraint maniacs, control freaks and Luddites. These are the first steps. We can no longer tolerate such a bad attitude. 'Things' have to change.[3]

Fifteen years ago, sites were real and unassailable, architecture was simple and the architect's skills were less numerous. Architecture and architects looked relatively safe. There were only a few clues as to how the onslaught of technology would affect architecture.

This essay seeks to explore some of the various types of objects that 'vacillate' and how they vacillate and where. The computer and cyberspace have made this idea of 'vacillation' much more complex and full of architectural spatial potential.

1 Neil Spiller, *Digital Dreams: Architecture and the New Alchemic Technologies*, London: Ellipsis, 1998.
2 'Architects in Cyberspace II', *Architectural Design*, 1998.
3 Neil Spiller, *Maverick Deviations (Architectural Works)*, London: Wiley/Academy, 2000, p106.

Distended Design through a Dalinian Lens

It was an instrument of high physical poetry formed by distances and by relationships between these distances; these relationships were expressed geometrically in some of the parts, and arithmetically in others; in the centre, a simple indicating mechanism served to measure the saint's death-throes. The mechanism was composed of a small dial of graduated plaster, in the middle of which a red blood-clot, pressed between two crystals, acted as a sensitive barometer for each new wound.

In the upper part of the heliometer was Saint Sebastian's magnifying glass. This was at once concave, convex and flat. Engraved on a platinum frame of its clean, precise crystals could be read *Invitation to Astronomy*; and beneath, in letters standing out as if in relief: *Holy Objectivity*. On a numbered crystal rod one could read further: *Measurement of the Apparent Distances between Pure Aesthetic Values* and to one side, on a highly fragile test-tube, this subtle announcement: *Apparent Distances and Arithmetical Measurements between Pure Sensual Values*. The test-tube was half full of sea water.

'Heliometer for the deaf and dumb' From *Saint Sebastian*, Salvador Dalí[1]

Flipping Spatiality

The city is populated by limp and soft bags of liquid, mostly water, crowded between and within towers of metal, stone and glass. Some towers are tall and thin, some are very stubby indeed. These soggy, leaky bodies spend much of their day mumbling to each other through an invisible meta-skin. This skin, a skin of communication, is forever becoming hyper-sensitive and more able to trace itself. These beings pluck bits off themselves and other animate and inanimate material, which they farm and reinstall in the hope of damming their bodily leaks or unblocking their aneurisms.

The space-flight programmes of the 1960s and 1970s have been described as an exercise of putting 'spam in cans' and shooting them into space. Historically, there has always been a distinction between the 'spam' and the 'can'. The spam is wet, fragile, sensitized, the desiring observer and the conscious subject. The 'can' is bought, sold, slow, inert, often a hollow container and in thrall to its function. This is all-changing, the stasis of the object is in question. Man-made constructions, the products of hard engineering, are starting to vacillate. The object is losing its pathetic impartiality. Objects have for too long floated in a sea of objectivity. Our technologies have developed a series of interlinked spatial fields, each with differing qualities with blurred boundaries. The objects that inhabit those fields are becoming schizophrenic.

One of the tasks of the 'cyber-' or 'bio-tect' will be to design ecologies of what I shall call 'object fields', not just to define the definite object that operates in a uniform spatial field. An object will have many selves, many simultaneous forms. Technology is forcing the object to become a subject, partial and anamorphic. The anamorphic object changes form when viewed from certain viewpoints, in different fields or in distorted mirrors. The new objects will have formal qualities that are determined by the virtual or physical terrain in which they are viewed or manipulated. [...]

Unhelpful Topology

The new vacillating objects take no notice of topological distinction. Topology, as described by F David Peat, is:

> ... concerned with boundaries, intersections and containment. It is more general than geometry and could be thought of as those relationships which survive being stretched, bent and twisted on a rubber sheet. Once lengths have been expanded or contracted, straight lines twisted into curves, and triangles transformed into circles or squares, all that remains are the more primitive, yet powerful relationships of topology. These are concerned with the way figures intersect and enclose each other and with how many holes pass through a figure.[2]

Topology, particularly of space-time, is an important mathematical idea and is useful in determining the similarity of objects across various distorted fields. One would think that on the surface the new objects would have topological similarity across their various spatial territories. This is not the case. The new spatial fields contort not only the object but also the 'rules' from which they themselves consist. The viscosity of a spatial domain can fluctuate. In the same way that 'virtuality' can be amplified along the Virtuality Continuum, space can be reconstructed. The new spatial fields consist of a series of variable component fields: gravity, viscosity, spatial jump-cutting being but three simple ones. These optional spatial parameters will become ever more dexterously manipulable as our technologies become advanced and less confined to the virtual. One must not forget the morphological potential of biotechnological objects and nanotechnological objects.

Objects have always occupied worlds where the objects and spaces around them change geographically, or in respect of their informational denseness, and can be forcibly and formally changed. Some by way of distortion of the spatial field, others through the contortion of the object. The object has had an inability to respond to most spatial fields, and changing an object by force, whether heat or hammer, has normally resulted in the object ceasing to function. The new objects will suffer from none of this crippling inertia or pathetic entropy. They will work in mysterious ways. They will change their topologies not just across spatial boundaries but often within the same spatial field.

We must also not become fixated by the almost salacious attractions of 'function'. Dali saw the benefit of useless objects that perhaps have other meanings than the overtly mechanistic and functional;

> The museums will fast fill with objects whose uselessness, size and crowding will necessitate the construction, in the desert, of special towers to contain them. The doors of these towers will be cleverly effaced and in their place will be an uninterrupted fountain of real milk, which will be avidly absorbed by the warm sand.[3]

In our hurried rush towards more responsive and networked environments we must not neglect the simple pleasures of the gratuitous. This extends to the decoration of our new 'spacescapes' with vacillating objects, some of which may just be useless.

Active Sites

The new objects may have zones that are much more sensitive than other parts of their surface. These might even be termed erogenous. However, I will borrow the term 'active site' from molecular biology. Active sites are defined thus by David S Goodsell:

Enzymes are large but inconspicuous molecules. They are typically globular in shape, most often with a cleft on one side. A few key amino acids, precisely arranged in this cleft, perform the chemical task. Three glutamates, each carrying a negative charge, may be arranged in a triangle to snare a magnesium ion, which carries a complementary positive charge. Large, carbon-rich phenylalanines and tryptophans may line a deep pocket, forming a comfortable nest for a fatty tail ... This cleft with its perfectly tailored arrangement of amino acids, is termed the active site.[4]

Active sites, as well as being a way to link objects together, could be the ports that one tickles to cause formal distortion or to coerce information from objects, or they could be a door to another spatial terrain. An object that has representations in more than one set of spatial conditions may well have differing numbers and configurations of active sites. So even in terms of information topology the new vacillating object will not be a martyr to the tragic topological inertia. Objects will flit between topological orders as one chooses clothes. These objects may, of course, be wearable but quite often will be also 'of' the body, negotiating its many methods of excluding the foreign with distain.

The Jungle of Blood

As we nourish and clog ourselves and our culture with more and more data, the object will become invigorated. It will think, desire and swerve. It could be that the object is capable of a type of superposition, a quantum indeterminacy, being everywhere and nowhere at once. All this is very well if these special turbo-charged objects remain digital, virtual, and somehow contained in cyberspace. It is once the object learns some of the lessons of, as Lorca calls it, the 'jungle of blood', once it appropriates animal reproduction procedures that it is finally free.[5] It will smear itself in the viscera and its tactics of self-replication; its specialized proteins, its finely perforated lipid membranes and its genetic periodic table. It is here that pure evil lurks, it is here that the line is crossed. The machine, the dumb object will become fleshed, biologically 'other'. There was a time when machines were deified, mimicked in art and sociology. It was easy then. Machines allowed us to keep the jungle of blood at armature's length. Now the new vacillating object's armatures can be gened. We used to mimic machines, now the machine is not only mimicking us, it is making cocktails of us.

These observations on the role of the new wet biotech objects is given a humorous scenario in Jeff Noon's *Automated Alice*. Alice encounters a character, Pablo Ogden, who is a 'reverse butcher'. He is busy constructing his greatest work, James Marshall Hentrails, Jimi for short. He tells Alice of the Newmonia.

'Newmonia!' Pablo screamed at Alice, 'not pneumonia! You silly creature! There's no P in Newmonia... Why can't you listen properly, Alice? The Newmonia is a terrible disease that allows animals and humans to get mixed in new combinations.'

Later Pablo tells Alice: 'A reverse butcher is an artisan of the flesh who reconstructs creatures out of their butchered parts.'[8]

Nonetheless, it is clear that the new objects may sometimes be clothed in flesh, protein and bone, sometimes operating in deep visceral space, often at a microscopic scale. These guises may not neccesarily be human in origin but are often transgenic.

An example of a new object, that is 'soft engineered' is the Bony Object. Some recent research has suggested that bone can be tissue engineered in designer moulds. Currently these moulds mimic the contour of skeletal bones such as the femur. These are also characteristics of the new objects, camouflage and stealth. However, it could be that these moulds could grow bone that has a variety of other forms. These bones may be linked to all manner of virtual objects that in themselves are linked to other objects, both virtual and real. These objects will help us operate in the growing ecologies of spatial fields.

With objects of this type we are able to create Bolas Objects that shift across spatial divides, reconfiguring yet maintaining a type of informational orbit. It is possible to prescribe some relationships whilst still navigating the cloud of the 'object field'.

We should return to Dalí and Saint Sebastian. As Ian Gibson writes, Dalí sees the Saint as 'an embodiment of the objectivity to which he had come to believe contemporary art should aspire. The Saint's impassivity, serenity and detachment as the arrows sear his flesh ...' [...]

This is where we lose Dalí, seduced by the inertness of the metallic machine, he searched for objectivity. The Saint Sebastian of today is all that Dalí's depiction, and those of the Renaissances, is not: porous not impervious, vacillating not static and networked, not detached.

The new virtual, vital, viral and visceral spaces within which the new objects will operate will be infinite, variegated, variform, ventral, varicose, vitrified, vomiting, velutinous, venereal, versicoloured, ventripotentant, vascular and versatile will be just some of their qualities.

The Object is dead. Long live the Object.

1 Ian Gibson, *The Shameful life of Salvador Dalí*, London: Faber and Faber, 1997, p157.
2 F David Peat, *Superstrings and the Search for the Theory of Everything*, London: Abacus, p25.
3 Gibson, op cit, p293.
4 David S Goodsell, *Our Molecular Nature – The Body's Motors, Machines and Messages*, New York: Springer-Verlag, 1996.
5 Gibson, op cit, p165.
6 Jeff Noon, *Automated Alice*, London: Doubleday, 1996, p82–3.

Acknowledgements

The publisher would like to thank all the authors and publishers of texts included herein for their permission to reproduce extracts from published works. The credits list the volume from which the extract is taken:

Charles Babbage, 'Of the Analytical Engine', *Passages from the Life of a Philosopher*, 1864 (London: Pickering & Chatto Ltd, 1994): By permission of Pickering & Chatto (Publishers) Ltd.

EM Forster, 'The Machine Stops', *The Eternal Moment and Other Stories*, 1909 (USA: Harcourt, Inc): By permission of The Provost and Scholars of King's College, Cambridge and the Society of Authors as the Literary Representatives of the Estate of EM Forster. Reproduced by Permission Harcourt, Inc.

Vannevar Bush, 'As We May Think', *The Atlantic Monthly*, 1945: This article was originally published in the July 1945 issue of *The Atlantic Monthly*. It is reproduced here with their permission.

JD Bolter, 'Essays of Operation', *Turing's Man – Western Culture in the Computer Age*, (London: Penguin, 1993): From *Turing's Man – Western Culture in the Computer Age*, by J David Bolter. Copyright ©1984 by the University of North Carolina Press.

Norbert Wiener, 'Organization of the Message', *The Human Use of Human Beings* (London: Sphere Books, 1968): Excerpt from *The Human Use of Human Beings* by Norman Wiener. Copyright ©1950 by Norbert Wiener, renewed 1977 by Margaret Wiener. Reprinted by permission of Houghton Mifflin Company. All rights reserved.

JCR Licklider, 'Man-Computer Symbiosis', *IRE Transactions on Human Factors in Electronics*, volume HFE-1, March 1960: Portions reprinted, with permission. ©1960 IRE (now IEEE).

Douglas Engelbart, 'Introduction', *Augmenting Human Intellect: A Conceptual Framework*, Summary Report AFOSR-3223 under contract AF49 (638)-1024, SRI Project 3578 for Air Force Office of Scientific Research, (Menlo Park, California: Stanford Research Institute, October 1962): Reprinted with permission of SRI International (formerly the Stanford Research Institute), Menlo Park, California, USA.

Marshall McLuhan, 'The Gadget Lover: Narcissus as Narcosis', *Understanding Media: The Extensions of Man* (Cambridge, Mass: The MIT Press, 1996): ©1964, 1994 Corinne McLuhan.

Gordon Pask, 'The Architectural Relevance of Cybernetics', *Architectural Design*, 1969: ©John Wiley & Sons Ltd. Reproduced with permission.

Cedric Price, Generator Project, 1976 as featured in *Cedric Price Works II* (London:AA Publications, 1984). Drawings reproduced courtesy of Centre Canadien d'Architecture/Canadian Centre for Architecture, Montréal/Cedric Price Archive.

Paul Virilio, 'Part IV', *The Aesthetics of Disappearance*, 1980 (New York: Semiotext(e) Books, 1991): Originally published in French as *Esthétique de la Disparition* by Paul Virilio.

Gilles Deleuze and Félix Guattari, 'Introduction: Rhizome', *A Thousand Plateaus: Capitalism and Schizophrenia*, 1980 (London: Athlone Press (now Continuum International Publishing Group), 1996): Copyright 1987 by the University of Minnesota Press. Originally published as *Mille Plateaux*, volume 2 of *Capitalisme et Schizophrénie* ©1980 by Les Editions de Minuit, Paris.

William Gibson, *Neuromancer*, 1984 (London: Grafton Books, an imprint of HarperCollins Publishers Ltd, 1986): Copyright ©1984 by William Gibson. Used by permission of the author and by permission of HarperCollins Publishers Ltd.

Donna Haraway, 'A Cyborg Manifesto', from 'Manifesto for Cyborgs: Science, Technology, and Socialist Feminism in the 1980s', *Socialist Review*, 1985: By permission of the author.

K Eric Drexler, 'Engines of Abundance', *Engines of Creation*, 1986 (London: Fourth Estate Ltd, 1990): *From Engines of Creation* by K Eric Drexler, copyright ©1986 by K Eric Drexler. Used by permission of Doubleday, a division of Random House, Inc. and by permission of HarperCollins Publishers Ltd.

Greg Bear, *Queen of Angels*, 1990 (London: Legend, an imprint of Arrow Books, 1991): ©Greg Bear. By permission of the author. Reproduced by permission of Orion Publishing Group Ltd.

William Gibson and Bruce Sterling, *The Difference Engine*, 1990 (London: VGSF, an imprint of Victor Gollancz, Ltd, 1991): By permission of the authors. Reproduced by permission of Orion Publishing Group Ltd.

Howard Rheingold, 'The Origins of Drama and the Future of Fun', *Virtual Reality* (London: Martin Secker & Warburg Limited, 1991): From *Virtual Reality* by Howard Rheingold, published by Martin Secker & Warburg. Reprinted by permission of the Random House Group Ltd and Simon & Schuster

Manuel De Landa, 'Policing the Spectrum', *War in the Age of Intelligent Machines* (New York: Zone Books, 1997): Copyright ©1997 Urzone, Inc.

Marcos Novak, 'Liquid Architectures in Cyberspace' in Michael Benedikt, *Cyberspace: The First Steps* (Cambridge, Mass: The MIT Press, 1991): By permission of the author and The MIT Press.

Daniel C Dennett, 'An Empirical Theory of the Mind: The Evolution of Consciousness', *Consciousness Explained*, 1991 (London: Penguin Books Ltd, 1993): By permission of the author.

Neal Stephenson, *Snow Crash*, 1992 (London, ROC, Penguin Books Ltd, 1993): From *Snow Crash* by Neal Stephenson, copyright ©1992 by Neal Stephenson. Used by permission of Bantam Books, a division of Random House, Inc and by permission of Penguin Books Ltd.

Steven Levy, 'The Strong Claim', *Artificial Life: The Quest for a New Creation*, (New York: Pantheon Books, 1992): Reprinted by permission of Sterling Lord Literistic, Inc. Copyright by Steven Levy, 1992.

Roger Lewin, 'Life in a Computer', *Complexity: Life at the Edge of Chaos*, (London: Phoenix, a division of Orion Books Ltd, 1993): From Roger Lewin, *Complexity* published by the University of Chicago Press. Copyright ©1993 by Roger Lewin. Reproduced by permission of Orion Publishing Group Ltd.

Jeff Noon, 'Stash Riders', *Vurt*, (Manchester: Ringpull Press, Ltd, 1993): From *Vurt* by Jeff Noon, copyright ©1993 by Jeff Noon. Used by permission of Crown Publishers, a division of Random House, Inc. and by permission of HarperCollins Publishers Ltd.

Erik Davis, 'Techgnosis: Magic, Memory, and the Angels of Information', *South Atlantic Quarterly* 92:4 (Fall 1993) (Durham, NC: Duke University Press, 1993): By permission of the author.

Scott Bukatman, 'Terminal Resistance/Cyborg Acceptance', *Terminal Identity: The Virtual Subject in Postmodern Science Fiction* (Durham, NC: Duke University Press, 1993): Copyright 1993, Duke University Press. All rights reserved. Reprinted with permission.

Anne Balsamo, 'Feminism for the Incurably Informed', *South Atlantic Quarterly*, 92:4 (Fall 1993) Copyright 1993 Duke University Press. All rights reserved. Reprinted with permission.

Sherry Turkle, 'Constructions and Reconstructions of the Self in Virtual Reality', 1994, from the book *Electronic Culture – Technology and Visual Representation*, ed Timothy Druckery (New York: Aperture, Inc, 1996): By permission of Aperture, Inc.

Kevin Kelly, 'An Open Universe', *Out of Control* (London: Fourth Estate, 1994): By permission of the author.

Greg Egan, 'Prologue (Rip, tie, cut toy man)', *Permutation City*, 1994 (London: Millennium, Orion Publishing Group Ltd, 1995): Reproduced by permission of Orion Publishing Group Ltd.

William Mitchell, 'Soft Cities', *City of Bits: Space, Place, and the Infobahn* (Cambridge, Mass: The MIT Press, 1995): By permission of The MIT Press.

Karen A Franck, 'When I Enter Virtual Reality, What Body Will I Leave Behind?', *Architectural Design* 'Architects in Cyberspace', 1995: By permission of the author.

John Frazer, 'A Natural Model for Architecture/The Nature of the Evolutionary Model', *An Evolutionary Architecture* (London: Architectural Association Publications, 1995): By permission AA Publications and John Frazer. ©1995 John Frazer and the Architectural Association.

Nicholas Negroponte, 'Iconographics', *Being Digital*, (London: Hodder & Stoughton, 1995): From *Being Digital* by Nicholas Negroponte, copyright ©1995 by Nicholas Negroponte. Used by permisson of Alfred A Knopf, a division of Random House, Inc. and by permission of Hodder & Stoughton Limited.

Stelarc, 'Towards the Post-Human: From Psycho-body to Cyber-system', *Architectural Design* 'Architects in Cyberspace', 1995: By permission of the author.

John Perry Barlow, 'A Declaration of the Independence of Cyberspace', www.eff/barlow, 1996: By permission of the author.

Mark Dery, 'Robocopulation: Sex Times Technology Equals the Future', *Escape Velocity: Cyberculture at the End of the Century*, (London: Hodder & Stoughton, 1996): From *Escape Velocity: Cyberculture at the End of the Century* by Mark Dery. Used by permission of Grove/Atlantic, Inc. Copyright ©1996 by Mark Dery.

Hans Moravec, 'The Senses Have No Future', from *The Virtual Dimension: Architecture, Representation, and Crash Culture*, John Beckmann (ed), (New York: Princeton Architectural Press, 1998): By permission of Princeton Architectural Press.

Michael Heim, 'The Virtual Reality of the Tea Ceremony', from *The Virtual Dimension: Architecture, Representation, and Crash Culture*, John Beckmann (ed), (New York: Princeton Architectural Press, 1998): By permission of Princeton Architectural Press.

Anthony Dunne, 'Hertzian Space', *Hertzian Tales: Electronic Products, Aesthetic Experience and Critical Design* (London: RCA CRD Research, 1999): By permission of the author.

Margaret Wertheim, *The Pearly Gates of Cyberspace* (London: Virago, 1999): From *The Pearly Gates of Cyberspace: A History of Space from Dante to the Internet* by Margaret Wertheim. Copyright ©1999 by Five Continents Music, Inc. Used by permission of W W Norton & Company, Inc. Reproduced by permission of Little, Brown & Co.

Neil Spiller, 'Vacillating Objects', *Architectural Design*, (London: Wiley-Academy, 1999): By permission of the author.

Bibliography

Ascott, Roy, 'No Simple Matter: Artist as Media Producer in a Universe of Complex Systems', *AND, Journal of Art*, 28, 1993.

Ascott, Roy, 'Telenoia: Art in the Age of Artificial Life', *Leonardo*, 26, 3, 1993.

Babbage, Charles, *Passages from the Life of a Philosopher*, London: Pickering & Chatto Ltd, 1994.

Ballard, J G, *Crash*, New York: Farrar, Strauss & Giroux, 1973.

Ballard, J G, 'Introduction to *Crash*', *Re/Search 8/9*, 1984. Novel originally published 1973; introduction first published 1974.

Balsamo, Anne, 'Feminism for the Incurably Informed', *South Atlantic Quarterly*, 92:4 (Fall 1993) Durham, NC: Duke University Press, 1993.

Balsamo, Anne, *Technologies of the Gendered Body: Reading Cyborg Women*, Durham, NC: Duke University Press, 1996.

Barlow, John Perry, 'A Declaration of the Independence of Cyberspace', www.eff/barlow, 1996.

Baudrillard, Jean, *Simulations*, New York: Semiotext(e), 1983.

Baudrillard, Jean, *The Ecstasy of Communication*, New York: Semiotext(e), 1988.

Baudrillard, Jean, *Fatal Strategies*, New York: Semiotext(e)/Pluto, 1990.

Bear, Greg, *Blood Music*, New York: Arbor House, 1985.

Bear, Greg, *Queen of Angels*, London: Legend, an imprint of Arrow Books, 1991.

Beckmann, John, (ed), *The Virtual Dimension: Architecture, Representation, and Crash Culture*, New York: Princeton Architectural Press, 1998.

Benedikt, Michael (ed), *Cyberspace: The First Steps*, Cambridge, MA: The MIT Press, 1991.

Benjamin, Walter, 'The Work of Art in the Age of Mechanical Reproduction', trans. Harry Zohn, *Illuminations*, Hannah Arendt (ed), New York: Schocken Books, 1969.

Boden, Margaret (ed), *The Philosophy of Artificial Intelligence*, New York: Oxford University Press, 1996.

Bolter, J David, *Turing's Man: Western Culture in the Computer Age*, Chapel Hill, NC: University of North Carolina Press, 1984/London: Penguin, 1993.

Bolter, J David, *Writing Space: The Computer, Hypertext, and the History of Writing*, Hillsdale, NJ: Lawrence Erlbaum Associates, 1991.

Brook, James and Iain A Boal (eds), *Resisting the Virtual Life: The Culture and Politics of Information*, San Francisco: City Light, 1995.

Bukatman, Scott, 'The Cybernetic (City) State: Terminal Space Becomes Phenomenal', *Journal of the Fantastic in the Arts* 2, 1989.

Bukatman, Scott, 'Fractal Geographies', *Artforum International*, 31; 4, December 1992.

Bukatman, Scott, *Terminal Identity: The Virtual Subject in Post-Modern Science Fiction*, Durham, NC: Duke University Press, 1993.

Bush, Vannevar, 'As We May Think', *The Atlantic Monthly*, July 1945.

Bush, Vannevar, *Pieces of the Action*, New York: Morrow, 1970.

Bush, Vannevar, *Science is Not Enough*, New York: Morrow, 1967.

Cadigan, Pat, 'Pretty Boy Crossover', rpt. in *The 1987 Annual World's Best SF*, (ed) Donald A. Wollheim, New York: DAW Books, 1985.

Cadigan, Pat, *Mindplayers*, New York: Bantam, 1987.

Cadigan, Pat, *Patterns*, London: Grafton, 1989.

Cadigan, Pat, *Synners*, London: Grafton, 1991.

Cadigan, Pat, *Fools*, London: Grafton, 1994.

Csicsery-Ronay, Istvan, Jr, 'Cyberpunk and Neuromanticism', *Storming the Reality Studio*, Durham, NC: Duke University Press, 1992.

Csicsery-Ronay, Istvan, Jr, 'The SF of Theory: Baudrillard and Haraway', *Science Fiction Studies 18*, no. 3, 1991.

Davis, Erik, 'Techgnosis: Magic, Memory, and the Angels of Information', *South Atlantic Quarterly* 92:4 (Fall 1993) Durham, NC: Duke University Press, 1993.

Dawkins, Richard, *The Selfish Gene*, 2nd edition, Oxford: Oxford University Press, 1989.

Dawkins, Richard, *The Extended Phenotype*, Oxford: Oxford University Press, 1982.

De Landa, Manuel, *War in the Age of Intelligent Machines*, New York: Zone Books, 1991.

Debord, Guy, *The Society of the Spectacle* (rev ed), Detroit: Black & White, 1977 [1967].

Debord, Guy, 'Perspectives for Conscious Alterations in Everyday Life', *Situationist International Anthology*, Ken Knabb (ed), Berkeley, CA: Bureau of Public Secrets, 1981.

Debord, Guy, 'Report on the Construction of Situations and on the International Situationist Tendency's Conditions of Organization and Action', trans. Ken Knabb, *Situationist International Anthology*, Ken Knabb (ed), Berkeley, CA: Bureau of Public Secrets, 1981. Originally published in 1957.

Debord, Guy, *Society of the Spectacle*, Detroit, MI: Black & Red, 1983. Originally published in 1967; originally translated in 1970, revised in 1977.

Delany, Samuel R, *The Einstein Intersection*, New York: Ace, 1967.

Delany, Samuel R, *Nova*, Garden City, NY: Doubleday, 1968.

Delany, Samuel R, *Dhalgren*, New York: Bantam, 1974.

Delany, Samuel R, *Triton*, Boston: Gregg, 1976.

Delany, Samuel R, *Stars in My Pocket Like Grains of Sand*, New York: Bantam, 1984.

Delany, Samuel R, 'Is Cyberpunk a Good Thing or a Bad Thing?', *Mississippi Review* 47/48, 1988.

Deleuze, Gilles, and Guattari, Félix, *A Thousand Plateaus: Capitalism and Schizophrenia*, London: Athlone Press, 1996/Minneapolis, Minn: University of Minnesota Press. Originally published in French as *Mille Plateaux*, volume 2 of *Capitalisme et Schizophrénie*, Paris: Les Editions de Minuit.

Deleuze, Gilles and Guattari, Félix, *Capitalisme et Schizophrénie tome 1: L'anti-Oedipe*, Paris: Editions de la Minuit, 1982.

Dennett, Daniel C, *Consciousness Explained*, London: Penguin Books Ltd, 1993.

Dennett, Daniel C, *Darwin's Dangerous Idea: Evolution and the Meanings of Life*, Harmondsworth: Allen Lane/The Penguin Press, 1995.

Dery, Mark, *Escape Velocity*, New York: Grove Press, 1996.

Dery, Mark, 'Cyborging the Body Politic', *MONDO 2000*, 7, 1992.

Dick, Philip K, *Martian Time-Slip*, New York: Ballantine, 1964.

Dick, Philip K, *Do Androids Dream of Electric Sheep?*, New York: Ballantine, 1968.

Dick, Philip K, *Ubik*, Garden City, NY: Doubleday, 1969.

Dick, Philip K, *Valis*, New York: Bantam, 1981.

Drexler, K Eric, *Engines of Creation*, London: Fourth Estate Ltd, 1990.

Druckery, Timothy, (ed), *Electronic Culture – Technology and Visual Representation*, New York: Aperture, Inc, 1996.

Dunne, Anthony, *Hertzian Tales: Electronic Products, Aesthetic Experience and Critical Design*, London: RCA CRD Research, 1999.

Dunne, A and Raby, F, 'Fields and Thresholds' in *Architects in Cyberspace, Architectural Design*, Profile no. 118, 1995.

Dunne, A and Raby, F, *Design Noir, The Secret Life of Electronic Objects*, London: August/Birkhäuser, 2001

Eco, Umberto, *Travels in Hyperreality*, trans. William Weaver, New York: Harcourt, Brace, Jovanovich, 1985/London: Picador, 1987.

Egan, Greg, *Permutation City*, London: Millennium, Orion Publishing Group Ltd, 1995.

Engelbart, Douglas, *Augmenting Human Intellect: A Conceptual Framework*, Summary Report AFOSR-3223 under contract AF49 (638)-1024, SRI Project 3578 for Air Force Office of Scientific Research, Menlo Park, CA: Stanford Research Institute, October 1962.

Forster, E M, 'The Machine Stops', *The Eternal Moment and Other Stories*, New York: Harcourt, Inc, 1991 (first published in 1909).

Franck, Karen A, 'When I Enter Virtual Reality, What Body Will I Leave Behind?', *Architectural Design*, 'Architects in Cyberspace', 1995.

Frazer, John, *An Evolutionary Architecture*, London: Architectural Association Publications, 1995.

Gans, David, and R U Sirius, 'Civilizing the Electronic Frontier', *Mondo 2000*, 3, Winter 1991.

Gibson, William, *Count Zero*, New York: Arbor House, 1986a.

Gibson, William, *Burning Chrome*, New York: Arbor House, 1986b.

Gibson, William, *Mona Lisa Overdrive*, New York: Bantam, 1988.

Gibson, William, *Neuromancer*, New York: Ace Books, 1984/London: Grafton, 1986.

Gibson, William, and Sterling, Bruce, *The Difference Engine*, London: VGSF, an imprint of Victor Gollancz, Ltd, 1991.

Gleick, James, *Chaos*, New York: Viking Books, 1987.

Haraway, Donna, 'A Manifesto for Cyborgs: Science, Technology, and Socialist Feminism in the 1980s', *Socialist Review* 80 (March-April), 1985; rpt. in *Coming to Terms: Feminism, Theory, Politics*, Elizabeth Weed (ed), New York: Routledge, 1989.

Haraway, Donna, *Simians, Cyborg and Women: The Reinvention of Nature*, Free Association Books, 1991.

Haraway, Donna, *Primate Visions: Gender, Race, and Nature in the World of Modern Science*, New York: Routledge, 1989.

Haraway, Donna, *Modest_Witness@Second_Millennium. FemaleMan.©Meets_ OncoMouse™: Feminism and Technoscience*, New York: Routledge, 1996.

Hardison, O B, Jr, *Disappearing Through the Skylight: Culture and Technology in the Twentieth Century*, New York: Viking, 1989.

Harvey, David, *The Condition of Postmodernity: An Enquiry into the Origins of Cultural Change*, New York: Blackwell, 1989.

Heim, Michael, *Virtual Realism*, New York: Oxford University Press, 1997.

Heim, Michael, *The Metaphysics of Virtual Reality*, New York: Oxford University Press, 1993.

Heim, Michael, 'The Erotic Ontology of Cyberspace', *Cyberspace: First Steps*, Michael Benedikt (ed), Cambridge, MA: MIT Press, 1991.

Heims, Steven J, *John von Neuman and Norbert Wiener: From Mathematics to the Technologies of Life and Death*, Cambridge, MA: The MIT Press, 1980.

Hofstadter, Douglas, *Gödel, Escher, Bach: An Eternal Golden Braid*, New York: Basic, 1979.

Jaffe, Harold, 'Max Headroom', *Mississippi Review* 47/48, 1988, rpt. in *Madonna and Other Spectacles*, New York: PAJ Publications, 1988.

Jameson, Fredric, 'Postmodernism, or The Cultural Logic of Late Capitalism', *New Left Review* 146, July–August, 1984.

Kauffman, Stuart, *The Origins of Order*, Oxford: Oxford University Press, 1992.

Keller, Evelyn Fox, *Refiguring Life: Metaphors of Twentieth Century Biology*, New York: Columbia University Press, 1994.

Kelly, Kevin, *Out of Control*, London: Fourth Estate, 1994.

Kroker, Arthur, and David Cook, *The Postmodern Scene: Excremental Culture and Hyper-Aesthetics*, CultureTexts, New York: St Martin's Press, 1986.

Krueger, Myron, 'Videoplace and the Interface of the Future', *The Art of Human Computer Interface Design*, Brenda Laurel (ed), Cupertino, California: Apple computer, 1990.

Laidlaw, Marc, *Dad's Nuke*, New York: Lorevan, 1984.

Langton, Christopher, 'Studying Artificial Life with Cellular Automata', *Physica* 22D, 1986.

Langton, Christopher (ed), *Artificial Life*, Harlow, Essex: Addison-Wesley, 1989.

Langton, Christopher, et al, *Artificial Life II*, Harlow, Essex: Addison-Wesley, 1992.

Langton Moore, D, *Ada, Countess of Lovelace*, London: John Murray, 1977.

Levy, Pierre, *L'Intelligence collective, pour une anthropologie du cyberspace*, Paris: La Découverte, 1994.

Levy, Pierre, *Qu'est-ce que le virtuel?*, Paris: La Découverte, 1994.

Levy, Steven, *Artificial Life: The Quest for a New Creation*, New York: Pantheon Books, 1992

Levy, Steven, *Hackers*, New York: Bantam, 1984.

Lewin, Roger, *Complexity: Life at the Edge of Chaos*, London: Phoenix, a division of Orion Books Ltd, 1993.

Licklider, J C R, 'Man-Computer Symbiosis', *IRE Transactions on Human Factors in Electronics*, volume HFE-1, March 1960.

Maddox, Tom, 'The Wars of the Coin's Two Halves: Bruce Sterling's Mechanist/Shaper Narratives', *Mississippi Review* 16, nos. 2/3, 1988.

Mazlish, Bruce, 'The Fourth Discontinuity', *Technology and Culture, Kranzberg, Melvin and Davenport* (eds), New York: New American Library, 1972.

McCaffery, Larry, 'Introduction', in *Postmodern Fiction: A Bio-Bibliographical Guide*, Larry McCaffery (ed), New York: Greenwood, 1986.

McCaffery, Larry, 'The Desert of the Real: The Cyberpunk Controversy', *Mississippi Review* 47/48, 1988.

McCaffery, Larry, 'The Fictions of the Present', in *Columbia Literary History of the United States*, gen. ed. Emory Elliott, New York: Columbia University Press, 1988.

McCaffery, Larry (ed), *Storming the Reality Studio: A Casebook of Cyberpunk and Postmodern Science Fiction*, Durham, NC: Duke University Press, 1992.

McLuhan, Marshall, *The Gutenberg Galaxy: The Making of Typographical Man*, Toronto: University of Toronto Press, 1962.

McLuhan, Marshall, *Understanding Media: The Extensions of Man*, New York: NAL, 1964/London: Routledge, 1964/Cambridge, MA: The MIT Press, 1994.

McLuhan, Marshall, *The Medium Is the Message*, New York: Random House, 1967.

Minsky, Marvin, *Society of Mind*, New York: Simon and Schuster, 1985.

Mitchell, William, *City of Bits: Space, Place, and the Infobahn*, Cambridge, MA: The MIT Press, 1995

Moravec, Hans, *Mind Children: The Future of Robot and Human Intelligence*, Cambridge, MA: Harvard University Press, 1988.

Nadin, Mihai, 'Emergent Aesthetics – Aesthetic Issues in Computer Arts', *Computer Art in Context: SIGGRAPH 1989 Art Show Catalog*, Mark Resch (ed), Oxford: Pergamon Press, 1989. Actually a supplemental issue of *Leonardo*, the Journal of the International Society for the Arts, Sciences, and Technology.

Negroponte, Nicholas, *Being Digital*, London: Hodder & Stoughton, 1995.

Nelson, Ted, *Computer Lib*, Redmond: Tempus, 1987.

Noon, Jeff, *Vurt*, Manchester: Ringpull Press, Ltd, 1993.

Noon, Jeff, *Pollen*, Manchester: Ringpull Press, Ltd, 1995.

Noon, Jeff, *Automated Alice*, London: Transworld, 1996.

Noon, Jeff, *Nymphomation*, London: Transworld, 1997.

Noon, Jeff, *Pixel Juice*, London: Transworld, 1998.

Noon, Jeff, *Cobralingus*, Brighton: Codex, 2001.

Pask, Gordon, 'The Architectural Relevance of Cybernetics', *Architectural Design*, 1969.

Penrose, Roger, *The Emperor's New Mind: Concerning Computers, Minds, and the Laws of Physics*, Oxford: Oxford University Press, 1989.

Plant, Sadie, *Zeros and Ones: Digital Woman and the New Technoculture*, London: Fourth Estate, 1997.

Porush, David A, *The Soft Machine: Cybernetic Fiction*, New York: Methuen, 1985.

Price, Cedric, *Cedric Price Works II*, London: Architectural Association, 1981.

Pynchon, Thomas, *V*, New York: Bantam, 1963.

Pynchon, Thomas, *The Crying of Lot 49*, New York: Perennial, 1966.

Pynchon, Thomas, *Gravity's Rainbow*, New York: Viking, 1973.

Pynchon, Thomas, *Vineland*, Boston: Little, Brown, 1990.

Pynchon, Thomas, *Gravity's Rainbow*, New York: Bantam Books, 1973.

Regis, Ed, *Great Mambo Chicken and the Transhuman Condition*, Reading, MA: Addison-Wesley, 1990.

Rheingold, Howard, *Virtual Reality*, London: Martin Secker & Warburg Limited, 1991.

Rheingold, Howard, 'Teledoldonics: reach out and touch someone', *Mondo 2000*, 2, Summer 1990.

Rheingold, Howard, 'What's the Big Deal About Cyberspace?', *The Art of Human Computer Interface Design*, Brenda Laurel (ed), Cupertino, CA: Apple Computer, 1990.

Ronell, Avital, *The Telephone Book: Technology, Schizophrenia, Electric Speech*, Lincoln: University of Nebraska Press, 1992.

Ross, Andrew, *Strange Weather*, New York: Verso, 1991.

Rucker, Rudy, *Software*, New York: Ace, 1982.

Rucker, Rudy, *Wetware*, New York: Avon, 1988.

Rucker, Rudy, *Mind Tools*, London: Penguin, 1988.

Rucker, Rudy, 'Report from Silicon Valley', *Science Fiction Eye* 1, no. 4, 1988.

Rushkoff, Douglas, *Cyberia*, San Francisco: HarperSan Francisco, 1994.

Shelley, Mary, *Frankenstein*, New York: Penguin, 1989 [1818].

Shiner, Lewis, *Frontera*, New York: Pocket Books, 1984.

Shiner, Lewis, *Deserted Cities of the Heart*, New York: Bantam, 1988.

Shirley, John, *Eclipse*, New York: Bluejay, 1985.

Shirley, John, *Eclipse Penumbra*, New York: Warner, 1987.

Shirley, John, *Total Eclipse*, New York: Warner, 1989.

Shirley, John, 'Stelarc and the New Reality', *Science Fiction Eye* 1, no. 2, 1987.

Snow, C P, *The Two Cultures*, Cambridge: Cambridge University Press, 1959.

Sobchack, Vivian, 'The Scene of the Screen: Towards a Phenomenology of Cinematic and Electronic Presence', *Post-Script* 10, 1990.

Sobchack, Vivian, 'The Virginity of Astronauts: Sex and the Science Fiction Film', *Alien Zone: Cultural Theory and Contemporary Science Fiction Cinema*, (ed) Annette Kuhn, London: Verso, 1990.

Sobchack, Vivian, 'New Age Mutant Ninja Hackers', *Artforum International*, April 1991.

Sobchack, Vivian, 'Cities on the Edge of Time: The Urban Science Fiction Film', *East-West Film Journal* 3, no. 1, December 1988.

Spiller, Neil, 'Vacillating Objects', *Architectural Design*, 1999.

Spiller, Neil, *Digital Dreams: Architecture and the New Alchemic Technologies*, London: Ellipsis, 1998.

Spiller, Neil, and Martin Pearce (eds), 'Architects in Cyberspace', *Architectural Design*, London, 1995.

Spiller, Neil, (ed), 'Architects in Cyberspace II', *Architectural Design*, 1998.

Spiller, Neil, *Maverick Deviations: Architectural Works 1985–1998*, London: Wiley-Academy, 2000.

Stelarc, 'Towards the Post-Human: From Psycho-body to Cyber-system', *Architectural Design* 'Architects in Cyberspace', 1995.

Stephenson, Neal, *Snow Crash*, London: ROC, Penguin Books Ltd, 1993.

Sterling, Bruce, *Involution Ocean*, 1977, rpt. New York: Ace, 1988.

Sterling, Bruce, *The Artificial Kid*, New York: Ace, 1980.

Sterling, Bruce, *Schismatrix*, New York: Arbor House, 1985.

Sterling, Bruce, (ed), *Mirrorshades: The Cyberpunk Anthology*, New York: Arbor House, 1986.

Sterling, Bruce, 'Introduction', in *ArmadilloCon 8 Program Book*, 1986.

Sterling, Bruce, 'Letter from Bruce Sterling', *REM* 7, April, 1987.

Sterling, Bruce, *Islands in the Net*, New York: Morrow, 1988.

Sterling, Bruce, *Crystal Express*, Sauk City, Wisc: Arkham House, 1989.

Sterling, Bruce, *The Hacker Crackdown*, New York: Bantam, 1992.

Turing, Alan, *'Computing Machinery and Intelligence'*, *Mind*, reprinted in Douglas Hofstadter and Daniel Dennett (eds) *The Mind's I*, Brighton: Harvester, 1981.

Turing, Alan, 'On computable numbers with an application to the entscheidungs problem', *Proceedings London Mathematical Society*, July 1937.

Turkle, Sherry, *The Second Self: Computers and the Human Spirit*, New York: Simon and Schuster, 1984.

Turkle, Sherry, *Life on the Screen: Identity in the Age of the Internet*, New York: Simon & Schuster, 1995.

Turkle, Sherry, *Psychoanalytic Politics: Jacques Lacan and Freud's French Revolution*, New York: Guilford Press, 2nd ed, 1992.

Virilio, Paul, *The Aesthetics of Disappearance*, originally published in French as *Esthaetique de la Disparition*, 1980/New York: Semiotext(e) Books, 1991.

Virilio, Paul, 'The Overexposed City', *ZONE* 1/2, 1984.

Virilio, Paul, *The Lost Dimension*, New York: Semiotext(e), 1991.

Virilio, Paul, *The Art of the Motor*, Minneapolis: University of Minnesota Press, 1995.

Virilio, Paul, *War and Cinema: The Logics of Perception*, New York: Verso, 1988.

Wertheim, Margaret, *The Pearly Gates of Cyberspace: A History of Space from Dante to the Internet*, London: Virago, 1999.

Wiener, Norbert, *Cybernetics: Control and Communication in Animal and Machine*, Cambridge, MA: MIT Press, 1961 [1948].

Wiener, Norbert, *The Human Use of Human Beings*, New York: Doubleday Anchor Books, 1954/London: Sphere Books, 1968.

Wiener, Norbert, *Cybernetics: Or Control and Communications in the Animal and the Machine*, Cambridge, MA: MIT Press, 1967. Originally published in 1948.

Wiener, Norbert, *God and Golem*, Cambridge, MA: MIT Press, 1964.

Wiener, Norbert, *The Human Use of Human Beings*, New York: Anchor Books, 1959.

Wolf, Fred Alan, *Taking the Quantum Leap: The New Physics for Non-Scientists*, rev. ed., New York: Harper & Row, 1989.

Woolley, Benjamin, *Virtual Worlds*, London: Penguin, 1992.

Yates, Frances A, *Giordano Bruno and the Hermetic Tradition*, Chicago: University of Chicago Press, 1964.

Yates, Frances A, *The Art of Memory*, London: Pimlico (Random House), 1966.

Selected URL Addresses on the Internet

There are an infinite number of sites that can be accessed via the Internet, which deal with the subjects in *Cyber Reader*. The ones listed below are given as a guide, and many will lead you to other sites in turn. The publisher accepts no responsibility for the content of suggested sites.

www.alife.org/

www.bartlett.ucl.ac.uk:16080/architecture/

www.binarydinosaurs.co.uk

www.bootstrap.org

www.cbi.umn.edu/tc.html

www.centrifuge.org/marcos/

www.counterbalance.org/bio/margaret-frame.html

www.crd.rca.ac.uk/dunne-raby

www.damer.org

www.eff.org/~barlow/barlow.html

www.foresight.org

www.frc.ri.cmu.edu/~hpm/

www.gregbear.com

www.iath.virginia.edu/elab/elab.html

www.imm.org

www.isd.atr.co.jp/~ray/tierra/index.html

www.isoc.org/internet/

www.jeffnoon.com

www.kk.org

www.levity.com/figment/

www.levity.com/markdery/

www.mcluhan.ca/main.phtml?show=resources

www.media.mit.edu

www.mit.edu/hacker/hacker.html

www.nas.nasa.org

www.nasa.org

www.netspace.net.au/~gregegan/index.html

www.parc.xerox.com/red/members/abalsamo/

www.rheingold.com

www.softwarehistory.org

www.stelarc.va.com.au

www.tufts.edu/~ddennett/

www.turing.org/turing/

www.venus.co.uk/gordonpask/

www.well.com/user/neal/

www.wired.com

cyberatlas.guggenheim.org/home/index.html

gobi.stanford.edu/computer_history/

livinginternet.com

mosaic.echonyc.com/~steven/

vmoc.museophile.com

web.mit.edu/sturkle/www/

Index

Picture credits

Courtesy of Bankgesellschaft Berlin AG: 201tcr

The Bootstrap Institute: 65t, 65c

Courtesy of Centre Canadien d'Architecture/Canadian Centre for Architecture, Montréal/Cedric Price Archive: 86-89

©Robert Crumb, 1986 from 'The Religious Experience of Philip K Dick': 195

Marc Cygnus: 183

Courtesy of John Frazer: 254, 255

Adrian Graham/www.binarydinosaurs.co.uk: 65b

©Institute for Molecular Manufacturing/www.imm.org: 131tr, 131b

Courtesy The Kobal Collection/Carolco: 201bcr, 201br

Courtesy The Kobal Collection/Limited Partnership/Alliance/Photograph Takashi Seida: 201cl

Courtesy The Kobal Collection/Orion: 201bl

Courtesy The Kobal Collection/©UFA: 201tl, 201tr

©MIT Media Laboratory: 66t

MIT Media Laboratory: Alex 'Sandy' Pentland, Rich DeVaul and Steve Schwartz: 67bl

Courtesy of Hans Moravec/www.frc.ri.cmu.edu/~hpm: 285

NASA: 66b, 131tl

©Marcos Novak/www.centrifuge.org: 156, 157

Science Museum/Science & Society Picture Library: 20tl, 20tr, 20b, 21t, 21l, 21cr

Science Photo Library/Eye of Science: 284c

Science Photo Library/Los Alamos National Laboratory: 20c

Science Photo Library/Peter Menzel: 67tr, 284b

Science Photo Library/NASA: 67tl

Science Photo Library/Sam Ogden: 67br

Science Photo Library/David Parker: 21br

Science Photo Library/Sandia National Laboratories: 284t

STELARC/Photograph: Tony Figallo: 268bl, 269tl, 269cl

STELARC/Computer Modelling: Troy Innocent: 269tr

STELARC/Photograph: Dominik Landwehr: 268tr

STELARC/Computer Modelling: Steve Middleton: 268tl

STELARC/Photograph: Keisuke Oki: 269bl

STELARC: 268br

STELARC/Diagram: Stelarc: 268cr, 269br

Editor's acknowledgements

I would like to thank Richard Oliver and Professor Stephen Gage for their invaluable advice and expertise, and David Reason and Professor Diane Gromala for their comments and critique. Also, thanks are due to all the copyright holders and living writers of the featured extracts for their support of this project.

I'd also like to express my gratitude to Hamish Muir, Mari Knutsson and Paul Hammond for graphic design, picture and text research and production, respectively, without whom this would be a very different and probably less interesting book.

A heartfelt thanks to both Vivian Constantinopoulos, who approached me to work on the project and inspired the diversity of texts and fictional works included here, and Iona Baird, who has ably managed the project, for their constructive feedback and encouragement.

Neil Spiller

To Melissa Jones and Edward Spiller.

Phaidon Press Limited
Regent's Wharf
All Saints Street
London N1 9PA

Phaidon Press Inc
180 Varick Street
New York, NY 10014

www.phaidon.com

First published 2002

©2002 Phaidon Press Limited

ISBN 0 7148 4071 8

A CIP catalogue record for this book is available from
the British Library.

Designed by Hamish Muir
Printed in Hong Kong